Apology, Forgiveness, and Reconciliation

For Good Attorneys and Other Peacemakers

Peter Rufo Robinson

Book Cover Design by Kathryn Olsen

Table of Contents

Acknowledgements

The thinking in this book is substantially the product of over ten years of teaching a course titled Apology, Forgiveness, and Reconciliation at the Straus Institute for Dispute Resolution at Pepperdine University School of Law. Pepperdine is a somewhat unique law school because my courses are populated by Juris Doctor candidates preparing to become lawyers, mid-career lawyers preparing to become mediators, international LLM (advanced law degree) students, and non-law professionals interested in studying dispute resolution and becoming mediators. First, I need to express my appreciation to the School of Law faculty and administration for allowing me to teach such a unique course.

Second, I am in debt to numerous student comments and class discussions that have contributed greatly to my understanding. This book contains excerpts from journals submitted by students in the class who have generously given permission for their thoughts and experiences to be a part of this book. Please know that students wrote their journals as ungraded assignments to be read only by the professor. When I asked for their permission to include their journals in the book, they expressed concern about the quality of their writing. Please read the student journals in that light. For these invaluable contributions I am grateful to, in alphabetical order: Pashtana Abedi, Jenieva Abner, Hussain Alkazemi, Jonathan Allen, Rashed AlMousoori, Yesay An, Jonathan Andrews, Caroline Austerman, Alyssa Ayotle, Ricardo Barcellos, Audrey Beeson, Casey Caton, Beverly Cawyer, Alistair Chong, Danielle Claypool, Melanie Cockram, Richard Copeland, Adriel Darvish, Majlie de Pug Kamp, Kaliegh Du Vermet, Andrew Duncan, Fabio Franco, Henry Gereis, Jamie Goldman, Isabel Grabowski, Lauren Guccione, Alexis Harris, Carole Helfert, Rachel Hews, Fernando Hoffman, Jeffrey Husserl, Martha Jacobs, Catherine Jung, Andrew Kahng, Maura Kingseed Giesl, Karen Kogan Barash, Stacy Lee, Danielle Lewis, Mahru Madjidi, Dr. Amora Rachelle Magna, Bhavya Mahajan, Marisa Martin, Chelsea McGrath, Mallory Miller, Lauren Montana, Doroteia Mota, Brian Murphy, Alan Nager, Nancy Nager, Andy Nguyen, Sean Olk, Kyle Pang, Beatriz Pelayo-Garcia, Arianna Perfecto, Adrianna Perfecto, Caitlyn Peskind, Cory Ray, Benjamin Reccius, Gabriella Robinson, Luke Robinson, Stacy Rouse, Monica Ryan, Ricardo Sadicoff, Elise Sanchez, Amanda Saunders, Nina Sprenger, Hunter Stanfield, John Stanley, Clay Strickland, Hilary Stump, Abdullah Sulaiman Alluhaydan, Helen Supanich, Heidi Swarvsky, Emily Tanaka, Kristine Toma, Frank Toti, Rahel Ueltschi, Jaime Verducci, Ainsley Waller, Kaylee Walsh, Shelby Warwar, Lauren Wilkins, Emma Williams, Brittany Wiser, Colleen Yorke, Rachel Yoshimura, and Z Zeller.

I am grateful to Casey Caton, my Research Assistant, who provided essential feedback on the content and presentation of this material. The clients who retain him as an attorney will be blessed by his competence, generosity, and faithful counsel.

I also need to express my appreciation to the extended network of professors, visiting professors, and adjunct professors at the Straus Institute who have joined together to form a community committed to providing as good a preparation as possible for future dispute resolvers, mediators, and peacemakers. Members of this community who reviewed early drafts and provided important feedback include Lee Taft, Lisle Baker, and Robert J. Mauer. I have been especially blessed by the friendship and leadership of Randy Lowry as Straus's Founding Director and Thomas Stipanowich as Straus's Co-Director. I have become a better teacher and person because of their friendship and support. The entire Straus team, consisting of Straus Professors Sukhsimran Singh, Stephanie Blondell, and Sarah Park and administrators Shellee Warnes, Randi Redman, Marcelo Rosadilla, Jeannie Ruse, Lori Rushford, Joanna Reese, Deborah Jasmin, Seth Hackett, Aparna Gupta, and Sammy Liu have been nothing short of inspirational in their encouragement and competence.

Finally, I need to recognize the host of people in my life from whom I learned, sometimes the hard way, how to love others and God. This collection includes my wife, children, parents, siblings, preachers, Sunday school teachers, church youth leaders, Boy Scout leaders, roommates, and professional colleagues. Those closest to me will know that I can discuss many of the mistakes described in this book from personal experience. I pray for grace when they learn that I have dared to write on these topics considering their many experiences when I have been less than I should have been.

Introduction

This book focuses on the heart of dispute resolution. After teaching mediation and other dispute resolution courses at Pepperdine Law School's Straus Institute for Dispute Resolution for twenty years, I realized that there was a gap in our curriculum for future lawyers and peacemakers. We taught how to reach a settlement and resolve a dispute from a variety of angles. The 300 mediations I conducted provided ample evidence that it is possible to settle a dispute without helping the participants heal from the conflict. This book is the result of a journey to explore how can we help people heal from conflict.

I began focusing on apology, forgiveness, and reconciliation and started teaching a course with the same title. For more than a decade I expanded my exposure to authors knowledgeable in these areas. Ecclesiastes declares that there is nothing new under the sun and that all we know and has been known before. I don't believe the contents of this book reveals new truth. My goal is to capture existing truths and present it in a way to equip good lawyers and other peacemakers to assist in these building blocks of healing.

Some may be amused by the title's target audiences of Good Lawyers and Other Peacemakers. I am suggesting that Good Lawyers are peacemakers. I am a lawyer, a law professor, and a mediator. I have observed some lawyers who have not been peacemakers but have also observed many who are. My bias is that the lawyers who are peacemakers are Good Lawyers. The obvious question is what I mean by "Good Lawyers." Am I using the word "good" to describe effectiveness or to describe admirable character? Abraham Lincoln's famous admonition to lawyers seems to refer to admirable character.

> Discourage litigation. Persuade your neighbors to compromise whenever you can. As peacemaker the lawyer has a superior opportunity of being a good man (person). There will still be business enough.

Lincoln is so revered that I hate to take a different path ... but the content of the book will argue that mastery of apology, forgiveness, and reconciliation is necessary for both the effectiveness and the character of a good lawyer.

But what is the intended meaning of "Other Peacemakers?" I consider "other peacemakers" to include professional and volunteer mediators, other helping professions like therapists, clergy, accountants, people working in crisis communication and public relations, and health care workers, as well as anyone who cares when they see their clients, family, or friends suffering because of conflict.

The book dedicates a chapter to how lawyers can encourage apology and another chapter on how lawyers can encourage forgiveness. Likewise, there are dedicated chapters on how peacemakers can encourage apology and encourage forgiveness. I believe there is value in cross-pollination, so readers will benefit from reading the chapter that is not directly focused on their role. It is also understandable that the hurried reader may skip the chapters that are not directed at them.

Understanding apology, forgiveness, and reconciliation is essential because we live in relationships with imperfect people. We all have parents and many of us have been parents. All parents are imperfect. Many of us have siblings. All siblings are imperfect. We have all loved and been loved in romantic relationships, many of which have culminated in marriage. Every romantic partner is imperfect. We have all had supervisors and many of us have had subordinates in the workplace. All supervisors are imperfect. Most of us belong to organizations or associations with leaders. All leaders are imperfect. Some of us lead those organizations or associations. All followers are imperfect.

Sometimes we injure others and need to handle that situation appropriately and maybe rehabilitate that relationship. Sometimes we are the victim of another person's wrong treatment and need to know how to recover individually and maybe relationally. Mastering apology, forgiveness, and reconciliation will enrich our personal and professional lives because we will have healthy relationships. Hopefully we will experience personal peace and rich community and be a resource to coach others towards those goals.

Jesus is famously quoted as challenging a group of accusers by suggesting that "He who is without sin should cast the first stone." In the same vein, this book is unnecessary for people who have never injured or suffered injuries in relationships. I believe all of us fit into both categories and need to study how to appropriate handle both sides of the transaction.

From the reference above, you might have correctly surmised that I am a Christian. This is an important part of my life and I see the world through this filter. Pepperdine is a Christian university and my guess is that about half of the law students at Pepperdine share a Christian perspective. That means that about half of the law students at Pepperdine DO NOT share a Christian perspective. We have students from all religious traditions and some without any organized religious convictions. When I studied these topics and created the content for this class and book, I went out of my way to NOT allow this investigation to be from a Christian or religious perspective.

Periodically, and especially in the forgiveness material, the topics are enriched by including a religious perspective, but those sections are clearly labeled. I have also invited my students to share their religious or philosophical approaches to the topics in class and in their journals. I have included many of those journals from a variety of religious traditions, including a "No Sacred Text" category. The reader can decide if she wants to be exposed to some of these thoughts or skip those sections.

How to read this book! This book invites you into the Pepperdine Law School classroom. A unique aspect of this book are the extensive quotes from student journals expressing how they have experienced the relevant concept in their personal lives. (Every journal was used with the student's permission, but some of them include material that is embarrassing to the author or others; thus, some of journals are listed as written by an anonymous student.) Many of these real-life vignettes illustrate the concept's truth, but some of them use their experience to disavow the concept or add an entirely new perspective. I reviewed seven years of student journals and only included the ones I thought added value. The student quotes are all indented, so the hurried reader can choose to skip those sections and only follow my narrative. I have also underlined the key comments in a sentence or two out of every student journal. This will empower the semi-hurried reader to catch the highlight of a student journal without reading every word.

Mastering apology, forgiveness, and reconciliation will dramatically increase the reader's healing. Competence with these concepts not only empowers a person to govern their own relationships well, but they can advise others to do the same. This is true for all of us but is especially important for professionals who support clients in conflict. My goal is that this book can be a resource for people who train and mentor those future professionals.

The approach I am taking is to maximize the understanding of various types of apologies and forgiveness. I tried to avoid static declarations about best practices because if the parties are well educated on these topics, they can exercise their own informed judgements when deciding to offer or accept an apology, forgive, and reconcile. Individuals uneducated about these topics are subject to potential abuse and manipulation. The goal of this book is to equip people to handle themselves and their relationships in ways that are healthy, and to equip people to encourage their circle of influence likewise.

Part I
Apology

Chapter One

Meanings, Motives, and Quality[1]

"Listen, I just want to say this right up front so there are no hurt feelings later on. ... I'm very, very sorry for what I'm about to do to you."

1.1 Introduction

This chapter explains the types and purposes of apologies. The types of apologies that will be discussed are a remorse, regret, empathy, social harmony, and externally motivated. The basis for distinctions between these apologies is the message the speaker seeks to convey. This chapter also seeks to look at the heart of the matter by examining a variety of motives for apology. My focus is on equipping the reader to accurately deliver or interpret an apology. I am not inclined to recommend a certain approach to apology as better than the others, but instead believe that each can be used to accurately communicate the speaker's reality. This chapter should assist a speaker in delivering the apology that honestly reflects her perspective on a situation. Also, it should assist the recipient of an apology to understand exactly what is being communicated.

1.2 Meanings of an Apology

What does it mean to you when a person says, "I'm sorry?" What do you intend to communicate when you apologize? The potential confusion surrounding the meaning of an apology is illustrated by the experience one of my students described in her class journal.

The Disapproving Parent Case Study

I recently began a relationship with a very close friend of mine, but unfortunately, this relationship has been a point of contention between my mother and I because of differing cultural viewpoints as well as a culmination of previous bad experiences and hurt feelings. In short, my boyfriend is of African-American descent, and my mother, being very conservative (Ethnic Ethnicity), was disappointed and angry that I chose not to pursue a man from the same cultural and ethnic background as mine. In our initial exchange after he and I decided to pursue a relationship, she expressed her frustrations about the situation to me in a verbally abusive manner that hurt my feelings, and I cut off communication with her for about three weeks. Suffice to say, it has been an emotionally fraught summer trying to balance the joy of new beginnings with the drama of a family member conflict.

On the Sunday before our first class, my mother drove up from home to drop off some furniture and apologized to me. I was caught off guard by this because I can honestly count on one hand the number of times I feel that she has attempted to offer me a sincere and legitimate apology. I know that she would feel differently about this, but I do not feel that the way she apologizes fulfills my needs for healing. Growing up, I have heard many variations of the "apologies" we discussed in class: "I'm sorry *but*..." and "*If* you were hurt, I'm sorry..." as well as "I'm sorry for anything I might have done," which is frustrating to me because her version of apologizing is a dismissal of my emotions and also a blanket statement that does not take responsibility for actions.

I asked her what she was sorry for, and she said she was sorry for the hurtful statements she made towards me, but when I wanted to delve into the conversation deeper and ask why she made those types of comments towards me and if she planned on repeating her behavior, she began getting defensive and justifying why she blew up at me. I do understand the cultural differences at play that come from conservative families from (this ethnicity.) People of "elder" status like my mother should be respected to the point where he/she does not have to apologize because the younger person (me) should be submissive and accepting of all decisions made by the elders. I am also expected to date and marry people from the same ethnicity.

I see now that she was offering me a mix of a social harmony apology and a justification apology motivated by the external circumstances of culture; being from a collectivistic mindset, she feared the backlash from the rest of my family if my extended family found out that we were in conflict. Much like the example taught in class about smoothing over tensions at Thanksgiving dinner, I need to recognize that my mother "took one for the team" and for her cultural pride to try to smooth things over with me, but what made it less significant for me was that she began making excuses for her behavior, could not promise me that the behavior would not happen again.

Her justifications became fervent to the point that I questioned if she even felt remorseful, and according to the criteria for a legitimate apology discussed in class, she could not ensure that this behavior would not be repeated and therefore it was hard for me to feel like my needs were met as the victim. Thank you for the opportunity to process this because I am still figuring out how I feel about all of this.

Many of us have left an apology conversation trying to figure out how we "feel about all of this." What did the other person mean by his apology and how does that affect my reaction to his statement? The variety of meanings creates confusion and possibly makes an apology conversation one of the most complex interactions.

The apology message is complex because there are two essential variables that determine the meaning of an apology. The first is the degree the apologizer acknowledges that his behavior injured someone. It may be surprising, but we will see that some apologies do not accept that they injured someone. The other variable is the degree that the apologizer believes that the hurtful behavior was wrong. Believe it or not, sometimes the person apologizing does not believe her behavior was wrong. A visual for these two factors creates the following "types of apology diagram."

Acknowledges

their behavior

injured another

Believes the hurtful
behavior was wrong

For many of us, the classic apology occurs when both of these factors are present to a high degree. The apologizer realizes her behavior hurt someone and she believes her actions were morally or ethically wrong. The apology condemns her own behavior and she repents! For example, a driver caused a car accident when he was texting while driving; he knows his behavior was negligent and feels terrible for injuring others. His apology includes statements of self-condemnation for texting while driving. In this type of situation, the apology is the result of and an expression of remorse. This is the "remorse apology." Its place on the Types of Apology Diagram is:

Remorse Apology

Acknowledges

their behavior

injured another

Believes the hurtful
behavior was wrong

The Remorse Apology is the default meaning for many people. This is the meaning they attribute when they hear the words, "I'm sorry" unless context or an explanation dictate otherwise. For many of us, life is moving at such a quick pace that we don't take the time to thoroughly discuss the intended meaning of an apology. At most, we look to see if the other person means what they say, but a deeper and meaningful analysis of the entire context of the apology, which includes motivations for making the apology are not discussed. The listener believes she knows what the speaker is trying to communicate and adopts that meaning. In the case of an apology, the meaning could reasonably be interpreted to include a confession of wrongful behavior that injured another.

While an expression of remorse is often an accurate meaning of an apology, there are other possible meanings. There is a dramatic shift in the meaning of "I'm sorry" when the apologizer believes that his behavior injured someone, but believes the behavior was appropriate and/or necessary. This apology is based on the apologizer's empathy for the injury caused by her behavior. She recognizes that someone has been hurt by her behavior and feels bad about hurting others. This apology is distinct from the Remorse Apology because the apologizer denies moral culpability for her behavior. In fact, she affirms that her behavior was appropriate and/or necessary. If she is faced with the same situation in the future, she will repeat the behavior.

An example is when city workers apologize for closing a road to repair the sewer. The sewer repair workers feel bad for the people who will be inconvenienced and thus post a sign apologizing. With the Regret Apology the offender accepts that his behavior created a harm, but he believes the harmful behavior was necessary and justified. The sewer repair workers believe they didn't do anything "wrong" and would do it again under the same circumstances. The workers don't have guilt or remorse about their behavior. After all, no one wants raw sewage floating down the street. Here, the meaning of the apology is a recognition that my behavior is negatively affecting you and I feel bad about this. But the behavior is the right thing to do or necessary.

Another example is the parent or healthcare worker who gives a shot to a toddler. Whoever administers the shot feels bad about hurting the child but knows that it is necessary for the child's long term health. The "Regret Apology" is represented on the Types of Apology Diagram as:

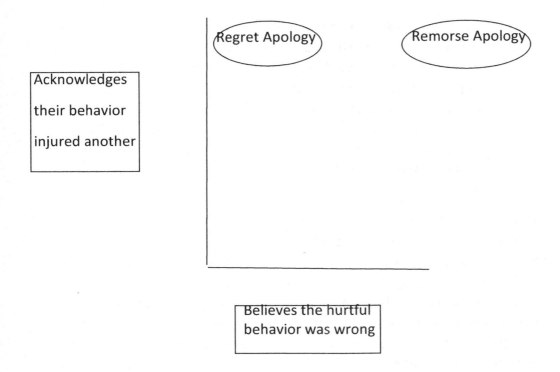

The Regret Apology allows someone to express both compassion and empathy without accepting moral responsibility for the injury. It empowers the speaker in complex nuanced situations. One example is President Truman's interviews about his decision to use nuclear weapons to end World War II.[2] Most Americans agree that it saved hundreds of thousands of American and Japanese lives and was a justifiable decision. In defending the decision, President Truman could have affirmed both the legitimacy of the decision and the harm suffered by the citizens of Hiroshima and Nagasaki by using the regret apology. Instead he was so committed to defending the decision that he stated he had no regrets. The Regret Apology allows the apologizer to both affirm the correctness of the behavior and recognize the injury and suffering it inflicted.

Another modern-day example is when a police officer justifiably uses her weapon to protect herself and kills a citizen. The law clearly allows an officer to defend herself if her safety is at risk. If a citizen points a gun at the officer, the officer is justified in shooting the citizen. Most police departments do not feel obliged to apologize under those circumstances. The Regret Apology enables the police department to recognize the grief of the deceased's family and friends while simultaneously affirming that the police officer's behavior was appropriate. Imagine the impact of a statement that the police department strives to "protect and serve" and to do everything it can to de-escalate these kinds of situations; the police department regrets whenever this outcome is necessary and expresses its condolences to the deceased's family, friends, and community. The Los Angeles Police Department (LAPD) started a program in 2016 to assign a community relations officer to every family who has had a member killed by LAPD to serve as a liaison and bridge builder to those affected by the tragedy.[3]

It is important to distinguish between the Regret Apology (where the apologizer recognizes that his behavior injured someone) and the Empathy Apology. The Empathy Apology is used to express compassion and caring for a person's situation. The Empathy Apology is used when the apologizer was not involved in creating the situation. An example is, "I am sorry you lost your job." The person apologizing did not have anything to do with the other person's job loss, but such statements are often given to show kindness. The Empathy Apology's place on the Type of Apology Diagram is:

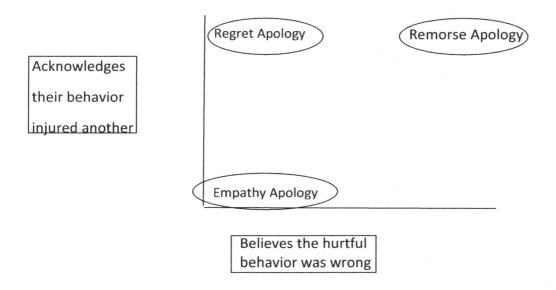

The apologizer does not believe that their behavior injured another and does not believe their behavior was wrong. This is different from the Regret Apology, where the apologizer at least admits that his behavior hurt someone. The Empathy Apology expresses caring and compassion. While this is appropriate usage of the English language, our exploration of the Empathy Apology will be limited. We will spend more time considering apologies where the perpetrator is at least accused of a wrongful act that injured another.

The Type of Apology Diagram includes another category. The lower right quadrant of the diagram reveals the Harmless Error Apology. The Harmless Error Apology describes when a person believes his behavior was wrong, but it didn't hurt the other person. An example is when a driver of a car runs a red light with a passenger in car. The driver was negligent and perpetrated a wrong. Fortunately, there wasn't a collision and the passenger did not suffer physical harm. The driver may decide to apologize for running the light because it was wrong, even though the passenger was not physically injured. For the sake of the illustration, assume the passenger was not emotionally traumatized, so the apology is in the context of no harm to the victim. This describes a Harmless Error Apology.

The Harmless Error Apology has the following place on the Type of Apology Diagram.

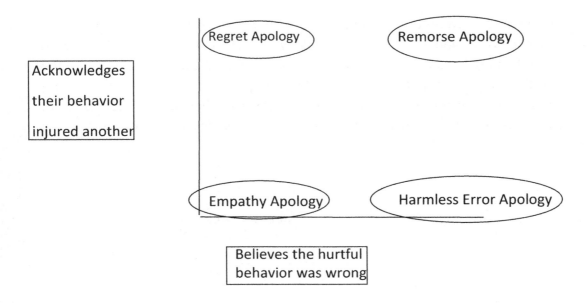

The Harmless Error Apology is described in the following student journal.

My boyfriend constantly tells me to stop apologizing so often. I've heard from several sources that apologizing is a sign of weakness. And especially because I am a woman and already prone to being viewed as less assertive or powerful that I should avoid such belittling language. …

Before our first class, I honestly had not thought in depth about the different types of apologies. In the back of my mind I knew that there were different kinds of "I'm sorry." The sorry I said sassily to my sister because my mom told me to apologize is not the same as the offering a condolence to a friend whose brother recently passed and not the same as apologizing for something I feel truly guilty about. Reading and hearing about the distinct types of apologies gave me the resources and vocabulary in which to identify and analyze apology.

Returning back to what my boyfriend and other sources have told me about apologizing, I now see that they condemn only certain types of apology. <u>My boyfriend saw that my excessive use of sorry was in large a result of feeling guilty for things he believes I shouldn't feel guilty for.</u> … <u>He saw that I was offering "remorse apologies" in which I condemned by my own behavior and felt guilty when it was a situation he saw as a minuscule incident or a behavior I should not condemn.</u> Submitted by Rachel Yoshimura, emphasis added.

The Harmless Error Apology happens, so it needs to be recognized in our discussion of types of apology. Like the Empathy Apology, it will not be the focus of further analysis.

The final type of apology discussed in this section is when a person is obliged to apologize, but she does not understand or accept that her behavior hurt another and denies that her behavior was wrong. Instead of empathy for injured person, the apologizer believes the injured person's complaint is unfounded. Why would a person apologize in such a scenario? Because he wants to keep the peace in the relationship. An apology is such a healing experience for a person who is offended, that sometimes an apology is given just to accomplish the healing. The apologizer determines that the best way to get through the difficult situation is to apologize, regardless of whether he believes his behavior injured another or that his behavior was wrong. This maintains the relationship and thus is the Social Harmony apology.

An example of a social harmony apology is when there is a public incident at a holiday celebration with extended family. To entertain, one family member shares a mildly provocative joke or political editorial. Another family member takes offense to the comment and publicly confronts the entertainer. The family members who are conflict averse get nervous. Everyone feels the tension in room and wonders if this is going to escalate into an even more uncomfortable scene. The person who offered the joke or editorial believes the values represented by his comment and believes his comment was appropriate. Yet, from prior experience he knows that the family member confronting him will make a scene that will chill the celebratory event for the extended family unless he receives an apology. The jokester apologizes so that the extended family can enjoy the event, even though he doesn't think he did anything wrong; in fact, he believes that challenging the beliefs of extended family members was not an injury, but an uncomfortable gift.

The Social Harmony apology's place on the Types of Apology Diagram is:

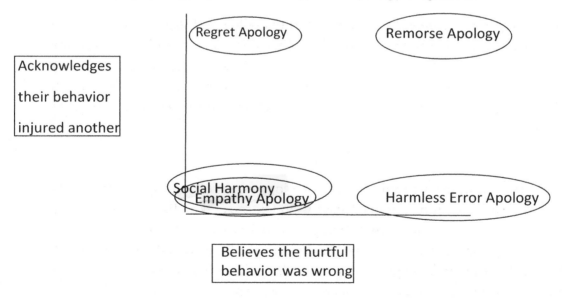

Notice that the Social Harmony Apology has the same characteristics as the Empathy Apology: the apologizer does not recognize either injuring another or wrongful behavior. The difference is the reason the person is apologizing. To express kindness and compassion to another or to keep the peace.

Excerpts from two student journals illustrate the Social Harmony apology.

> Whenever I tell people that I am taking a class on apology and forgiveness, they immediately respond with, "There's a class for that?" The first class has illuminated the valid reasons for studying these concepts in a formal classroom context. I think many people, like me, are not completely honest about the potential for manipulation that an apology can possess. I discovered myself engaging in an important process of self-reflection regarding my own experiences with apology, and I am convicted by the many forms that an apology can take. In particular, I discovered that my "people-pleasing" tendencies substantially affect my approach to conflict resolution and apology. A question that was posed during class that I will continue to consider is, should apology be the end of the conversation or should it be the beginning? I can point to several moments in my life when I have offered an apology in an effort to avert conflict or solely for relationship maintenance purposes. Submitted by Danielle Claypool, emphasis added.

> I have also noticed about myself that I can convince myself quickly that I am right in how I perceive certain actions by others and by myself; however, getting married in August tore the veil from my eyes. I have started to realize that I miss so much especially when it comes to understanding other people. When I apologize, most of the time I only do so to make the situation better in the short term, rather than focusing on the long-term health of the relationship. The social harmony apology is always tempting for me because I want everyone to be happy with one another, and I like it when everyone is at peace and comfortable.

> But when there is a serious issue at hand, and I need to apologize, I should reflect on how my actions caused the situation, why it hurt the other person, why I did it, how I feel about it, and how I can apologize in such a way as to make sure the other person knows that I have remorse over my actions, and that I will no longer do the action that caused the harm. Then I must back up my words through my actions. Submitted by Casey Caton, emphasis added.

Casey's comments question whether a social harmony apology maintains the relationship. The concern is that the relationship is built on a foundation of sand because the offended person may have been tricked into releasing their grievance. If that person ever realizes that the apology was given only to placate him, his perception of the relationship might be justifiably diminished. In some situations, the social harmony apology will maintain the relationship in the short term and damage it in the long run because of a lack of honest communication.

A similar analysis of the social harmony apology explains why some people declare that they will only apologize when they believe they are wrong. Such a person's apology philosophy is concerned about a lack of personal integrity in the social harmony apology. These people believe that the inherent message in an apology is at least a recognition of injury (the Regret Apology) and usually also the admission that the behavior was wrong (the Remorse Apology). When an apology is given without the presence of at least one of these elements, the concern is that the apology is a manipulative lie. Thus, some condemn the social harmony apology as a fraud.

Another student's journal is instructive.

> I found the first lecture of our course to be particularly intriguing. I had no idea what studying apology, forgiveness, and reconciliation would actually look like, but after going over the syllabus, looking forward to future content, and the topic of this week's lecture I have a better grasp at what the study of these disciplines means and am excited to learn more. I believe this course will be particularly helpful to my personal life. In fact, I have already realized some very interesting things about my own form of apologies after just a brief introspection.

> The various different forms of apology are of a particular interest to me. I have never thought of the roots of an apology before and how that could change the actual meaning of the apology. To me an apology was simply just an apology, but now I am beginning to question both my own motives of apologizing and others. The empathy apology and the social harmony apology were the two forms I most related to. In my personal life I apologize so often and using these new categories for apology I think I most often use empathy and social harmony apologies to ensure my relationships will be maintained. Sometimes, I enact these apologies even when I do not actually feel regret and will not actively try to change my behavior.

> I had never thought of these apologies being deceptive or deceitful, but after learning about these different categories I can see how the people I am apologizing to could feel hurt by my apology if they learned of these different categories. I think the main root of deception is the loss of personal integrity associated with apologizing for something you do not regret or feel remorse for. Submitted by Mallory Miller, emphasis added

The indictment of the social harmony apology as lacking personal integrity could be more balanced. The advocates for social harmony apologies explain that the foundation for such a gesture could be a concern for the well-being of the group. The virtue of group well-being could be more important than the virtue of individual integrity. The social harmony apologizer generously sacrifices his individual integrity as a gift to the community of people who would be negatively affected by an imminent breach in relationship. The description of the holiday celebration with extended family is a good example. The jokester who apologizes for the good of the extended family is acting virtuously, even though his act lacks personal integrity.

The group well-being justification for the social harmony apology makes sense when the conflict would create collateral damage for innocent bystanders. Supporters for this approach to apology explain that it also has legitimacy when only the two combatants are involved. Their interpretation of the social harmony apology is, "I care more about this relationship than I do about being right." Again, the virtue of relationship/harmony trumps the virtue of critical analysis/truth. It doesn't matter who is right in this conflict; often neither of the participants will care about the substance of the conflict the next morning, week, year, or decade. Maybe it is a wise perspective to remove yourself from the front line of hand-to-hand verbal battle to remember that relationships are what matters most in the long run.

Another student journal explores this perspective.

> However, I feel conflicted about the 'loss of integrity' because at the same time you could be apologizing for the other person's good. Unless the apology is externally motivated and used simply to ensure that the apologizer will continue to get something out of the relationship, a social harmony apology could be seen as not purposely deceptive. The idea of caring so deeply for the relationship in jeopardy that you are willing to take the blame on yourself and sacrifice your personal integrity to save the relationship could be seen as not deceptive or bad, but actually self-sacrificing. Maybe I want this idea to be true simply for my own self-interest and self-preservation, but I see the distinction as internal motivation. If you are using a social harmony apology to continue to further your own interests within the relationship, then that lapse of personal integrity should be seen as deceptive, however, if you sacrifice your integrity to protect the relationship or the other person's feelings this sacrifice should not be seen as deceptive. Submitted by Mallory Miller

I have experienced this wisdom in my marriage. In the early stages of our marriage my wife would sometimes tell me that she disagreed with me about an issue, but after experiencing her father's death at a young age, she realizes that the issue that could become an argument isn't worth it. She went on record that she thought I was wrong but refused to argue about it and let me do it my way. This is the sentiment in the popular series of books about, "Don't Sweat the Small Stuff …. And it is All Small Stuff."

The debate about the legitimacy of social harmony apologies is rooted in the tension between the virtue of personal integrity and the virtue of group well-being. Reactions to this tension are often significantly influenced by cultural orientations. Scholars who study cultures have identified a contrast between individualistic and collectivist cultures.[4] Individualistic cultures encourage members to view situations from the individual's perspective and to make decisions based on the best interests of the individual. Collectivist cultures encourage members to view situations from the group's perspective and to make decisions based on the best interests of the group.

A friend experienced this contrast when she taught elementary school on the Navajo reservation. She had a few years teaching experience in the greater Phoenix area with largely Caucasian students. Her teaching methods were traditional and often included asking for volunteers to answer questions in a class discussion. When she asked for volunteers to answer questions in a class discussion on the Navajo reservation, she was surprised. No one would volunteer. She would ask an easier question that she was certain many of the students could answer, and still no one would raise their hand to participate.

She adjusted and after gaining the trust of some of the students over time, she asked them about this situation. The Navajo students confirmed that they frequently knew the answer to the teacher's question and explained that it would be rude to share it in front of the other students in case some of them did not know the answer. They were concerned about asserting themselves in a way that might humiliate a classmate. It was more important to be concerned about everyone in the class than just about themselves. This was a stark contrast to the values and norms in the suburban Phoenix classroom.

The culture identity scholars identify the United States as highly individualistic.[5] The rugged individualism that is part of our way of approaching life might favor personal integrity over group well-being. This can contribute to the conclusion that the social harmony apology is a lie or fraud. Before becoming too attached to this interpretation, remember that the customs in many other parts of the world value group harmony much more than personal integrity. There are strengths and weaknesses to either emphasis. The point is that there are times and places where social harmony apologies are legitimate, honorable, virtuous, and appropriate.

A student journal is illustrative.

> Thus, it is clearly evident that individualist and collectivist cultures hold the ability to shape the meaning, motivation, and criteria for an apology. This part of class stood out to me as I thought about my upbringing as an Asian American. My parents did emphasize apologizing, especially to my elders. Even if I feel that I did not do anything wrong, I should apologize to GIVE face.
>
> Therefore, I feel that the spectrum of apologies presented in class is specific to individualistic cultures. In a collectivistic culture, I believe the social harmony apology would be respected as much as the remorseful apology. This is because it involves lowering one's pride for the good of the collective group. Submitted by Kyle Pang, emphasis added.

Organizing the various meanings of apology on a continuum based on the amount of culpability in the apology creates the following graph:

Empathy Apology

Social Harmony   Regret   Remorse

/_____/_____/

Low Culpability   High Culpability

Understanding the meaning of apology begins with examining the extent that the apology is acknowledging behavior that injured another and the extent that the apology is condemning the behavior. The four categories of apologies have various strengths and deficiencies in these elements. The next stage of our journey to understanding apology is to explore an apology's underlying motivations.

1.3 Motivations for an Apology

Considering a menu of motives for an apology enriches the understanding of an apology's purpose and meaning. Apology scholar and psychiatrist Aaron Lazare describes motives for apologies in two categories: internal and external.[6] A person receiving an apology may have different reactions depending on her assessment of "Why are they apologizing?" and "Do they really mean it?" The motive behind an apology can make a difference.

One of the internal motives for an apology is guilt. A person's conscience accuses him of bad behavior. Lazare's emphasizes the importance of resolving guilt from a mental health perspective. A healthy motivation for an apology is to attend to the sense of guilt for someone who agrees that his behavior was inappropriate.

There is an important gap between the sense of guilt and the person agreeing that his behavior was inappropriate. People have conscious and unconscious responses to guilt. When our conscience accuses us, we have a variety of responses.

First, we need to decide if we agree with our conscience. Sometimes people debate their conscience with rationalizations. Common rationalizations are, "It's not that bad" and "Everybody does it." These are defense mechanisms reacting to the internal accusation. They defend the image and identity of the person. His conscience questions the virtue of certain behavior. If the person views himself as virtuous, that voice will try to refute the internal accusation. If the defensive voice prevails, the person has resolved his guilt and does not apologize. This person doesn't apologize because admitting to himself that he committed this bad act is too threatening to his self-image.[7]

A student journal offers a description.

> Most of the time I feel like I am walking on eggshells. I grew up in a family full of conflict and what felt like continuous fighting. Everyone in my family loved each other without a doubt, but there were only a couple days out of the week that everyone was at peace with each other. I think this is large part of what make me so hypersensitive to not wanting to make anyone upset.

In contrast though, there have been times that I definitely should have apologized but did not. In today's class, we covered the difficulties surrounding apologies. One that rang especially true in my life, for both those close to me and to me myself at times, is that it is difficult to apologize because we are prideful. I can be a rather stubborn person. I have inherited this trait from both sides of my family. Once I truly make my mind up about something, particularly an action I have done, it is hard to change my perspective about it. I have no problem offering social harmony apologies. They were a way I kept peace in my family for short periods of time. <u>But sometimes my stubbornness acts as a barrier for me to offer a true remorse apology. I think the most difficult aspect of offering a remorse apology is admitting that you have done something wrong. I fully support and agree with the notion that a majority of the human population has a positive self-image and any threats to that cause us to have miniature identity crises. That is why I think apologizing requires courage.</u> Submitted by an anonymous student, emphasis added.

Generally, lawyers are especially skilled at constructing arguments to defend their behavior. It is an occupational hazard. Having been trained to present a situation in the best possible light for our clients, those same abilities can be marshaled to defend our self-view from our conscience. The result is that we deceive ourselves as to our true selves. Many examples are available from my wife.

Another strategy when admitting the mistake is too damaging to one's self-image is to pretend that it never happened. Admitting the mistake to the other person may be too humiliating. The response to the indictment of the conscience is to ignore that voice and act as if the incident never occurred. You never talk to the other person about it. You may go out of your way to create more positive experiences with this person to cover over the negative experience. The plan, conscious or unconscious, is that if the perpetrator pretends it didn't happen long enough, and maybe creates enough more recent positive experiences, the victim will forget about it.

A danger is that the perpetrator may not only be pretending to the victim, but also to herself. Like the rationalization response, integrating this deficient behavior into the person's self-image may be too difficult so the perpetrator is not honest with herself. Self-pretending could be an example of the more common concern that someone is "in denial." If rationalizing and pretending are unhealthy responses to guilt, apologizing is the healthy choice. Telling the truth to ourselves and others about failures is often difficult, but there are costs to the other responses.

Lazare gives a wonderful description of this internal debate I will refer to as the, "Tell the truth and take responsibility" approach to apology.

> Interesting duality in most of us: we can simultaneously feel that we should acknowledge the offense and yet we avoid doing so at all costs. To apologize effectively would require an accurate and complete acknowledgement of actions that hurt others. Instead, we sometimes offer apologies in which the so-called acknowledgment was actually a denial or minimization of the offense. Rather than accepting responsibility and telling the truth–behaviors that could have restored relationships with offended parties–the offenders choose to preserve their view of themselves and to avoid punishment. [8]

For those whose strong self-image make it difficult to apologize, the concept of "complicating one's self-image" may be a helpful tool. The book <u>Difficult Conversations</u> describes three levels of conversations when discussing a conflict. [9] First, the facts of what happened. Second, how parties feel about those facts. Third, what do these facts mean about a person's identity, who I am. In this third section, the authors Douglas Stone, Bruce Patton, and Sheila Heen discuss the same phenomenon of people resisting admitting certain facts because to do so would destroy their positive self-image. Their suggestion is to develop a more complex self-image. A simple self-image might be that a person tells the truth and has integrity. A more complicated self-image might be that a person usually tells the truth and has integrity, but that sometimes he does not live up to that standard. Having a more complicated self-image allows a person to admit negative behaviors and maintain their view of themselves.

This is illustrated by another student's journal.

> Additionally, I find myself continually reflecting on the concept of complicating one's identity. As was mentioned in the reading and in the class discussion, many people struggle to embrace responsibility in that to do so would be a threat to his or her carefully maintained sense of self. In the interest of honesty, I am fully aware that this motive influences my willingness to apologize frequently. I often find that, if I were to admit externally that I've done something decidedly wrong, that I would also be required to dismantle how I perceive my identity. In general, I am a very self-aware person and I suffer from what many people identify as an unnecessary "guilty conscience."
>
> I frequently feel sorry for any sort of negative impact that I may have made. However, I've found that I still struggle to apologize out loud and I think that it has something to do with the fragility of my own self-perception. While I am very honest with myself internally, my pride still occasionally prevents me from offering an apology. Even as I am writing this, I am finding comfort in the knowledge that we are all very complex beings. <u>Thus, I think it can be confirmed that our internal state of being and our sense of identity is not always consistent with reality. I included all of this to say that I think it is healthy and good to accept that our identities are complex, that imperfections are not evidence of a completely spoiled character, and that there is room for repentance and growth if humility is allowed to exist.</u> Submitted by Danielle Claypool, emphasis added.

Apology as a tool to relieve guilt is a powerful realization. When a person agrees that his behavior was inappropriate, apologizing to the person affected by the wrongful behavior attends to the guilt. Such an apology will include an offer of reparations if it is authentic. Once a person has admitted her failing to the injured party and offered reparations, she knows she has done all that can be done. Her conscience condemns the bad behavior, but the person accepts the indictment by her conscience and makes the effort to acknowledge and take responsibility for the wrong. Now her conscience condemns the person's original wrongful behavior and applauds the person's honorable reaction to the guilt. Even if the injured person does not accept the apology, the perpetrator knows she did everything possible to make things right.

Understanding apology as a tool to relieve guilt expands the interpretation and meaning. Instead of apology as a gift to restore an injured person, apology can be viewed as a gift to relieve the guilt of the perpetrator. Considering this perspective, apology can be viewed as a very selfish act. An example is the man who's dying spouse is unaware of an extra-marital affair that ended twenty years earlier; the man considers apologizing, but family members counsel that to do so would relieve his guilt at the cost of unfairly burdening his wife's final hours.

The recognition that an apology can be a selfish act is reflected in the Twelve Step Program utilized by Alcoholic Anonymous. Step Nine instructs participants, "Make direct amends to such people wherever possible, except when to do so would injure them or others."[10] The Twelve Step Program recognizes that there are times when making amends would injure the other person and counsels adherents to forgo amends in such situations. The cleansing of guilt can be a positive aspect of apology and sometimes it can be exploitive.

A second category of internal motivation for an apology is empathy. Guilt is the essence of a remorse apology, but it is absent from a regret, or social harmony apology. The regret apology believes the behavior was hurtful and necessary; the person doing the act did not do anything wrong and would do it again. Likewise, the person delivering a social harmony apology does not believe they have done anything wrong. Thus, these apologies are not founded on guilt.

Empathy is one explanation for the motivation behind these apologies. Merriam-Webster's definition for empathy is "the ability to identify with or understand another's situation or feeling." The apology is not motivated by a sense of guilt but is a response to suffering. It is empathy for the people inconvenienced by the road closure that motivates the sewer repair workers to apologize. It might be empathy for the awkwardness of others witnessing a conflict at the dinner table that leads to a social harmony apology. It might be empathy for others who need a group to be at peace that leads to a social harmony apology. Empathy sometimes explains apologies lacking guilt or remorse.

The contrast to the internal motivations for apologies is the external motivations. In this situation, the impetus for the apology is external to the person apologizing. Neither guilt nor empathy are present. The primary motivation to apologize comes from external forces.

A classic example of an externally motivated apology is when a parent requires her child to apologize to a sibling. Sometimes people apologize because of awareness of imminent harm if they remain silent. The harm might be physical (the offended person or authority figure might resort to violence), emotional (the offended might abandon or seek to demean or humiliate the offender), or social (the offender might be shunned or ridiculed by a group.) Contrition often avoids retaliation or mitigates the amount of punishment.

Even coerced contrition serves a purpose in clarifying the norms of acceptable behavior. Thus, the parent who requires a child to apologize to a sibling is establishing that certain behavior will not be permitted in that family. The child apologizing may not have guilt or remorse, but the parent is sending a message to both children.

An excerpt from a student journal is instructive.

From a German family that believes in "fixing problems" rather than leaving them, my sister and I have been raised to offer apologies when warranted and even when unwarranted. ...Here in the U.S., it seems as if coerced or forced apologies are frowned upon. Some do not accept coerced apologies, because they are not voluntary, and thus not "meant." The offender shows no remorse for the action. Had the offender not be forced to apologize, they argue, he or she would have come up with all kinds of excuses, justifications and denials. There may be some truth to this argument. However, <u>I also think a forced apology mandated by a figure of authority may help overcome hurdles we may experience in apologizing on our own terms. We may not be able to work up the courage to apologize, or we may not want to shatter that image we have of ourselves as a virtuous person and choose to opt out of apologizing altogether. Like deeply held fears of public speaking, coerced apologies actually can be quite useful.</u> Submitted by Colleen Yorke, emphasis added.

Notice that the externally motivated apologizer may or may not recognize that their behavior hurt someone and that such behavior was wrong. These elements are irrelevant to this apologizer. The calculus of their apology decision matrix is driven by a pragmatic assessment of the consequences if they neglect to apologize.

The social harmony apology could be externally motivated if the apologizer is acting out of a fear of exclusion from the group. The distinction could be whether the apologizer is seeking to maintain the relationship for selfish reasons (externally motivated) or out of concern for the best interest of others (social harmony.) Repeating a section of Mallory Miller's journal is illustrative.

> If you are using a social harmony apology to continue to further your own interests within the relationship, then that lapse of personal integrity should be seen as deceptive, however, if you sacrifice your integrity to protect the relationship or the other person's feelings this sacrifice should not be seen as deceptive.

The externally motivated apology is distinct from the other types of apologies. The meaning is different enough to earn its own a place on the Continuum of Apology Meanings. Because its purpose is self-preservation that minimizes consequences, it accepts even less culpability than the Empathy or Social Harmony Apologies. It is to the left of the social harmony apology because that apology at least seeks the well-being of a group. The externally motivated apology only seeks the well-being of the person apologizing.

The menu of apology meanings now consists of the following.

Externally	Empathy		
Motivated	Social Harmony	Regret	Remorse

/_____/_____/_____/

Low Culpability   High Culpability

A summary of meanings would be:

Remorse: I wrongfully hurt you and am sorry.

Regret: My actions were justified, but they hurt you and I am sorry I hurt you.

Social Harmony: I disagree with your accusation that my actions wrongfully hurt you but will apologize to keep the peace.

Empathy: I had nothing to do with your injury but am sorry you are hurting.

Externally Motivated: My beliefs about whether I wrongfully hurt you are irrelevant; I will apologize to avoid negative consequences of not apologizing.

The above list not only confirms that there are a variety of potential meanings behind an apology but creates a specific menu of categories to help the sender and recipient of an apology to use in attempting to construct or decipher the message.

The following student journal gives perspective.

> My sister says it is important not to say "I'm sorry" when you are not at fault, but to say something else instead like "excuse me" or "that is awful" or " how can I help" or "I never meant to make you feel that way, what could I have done differently." In her experience, when she says "I'm sorry" for anything other than a remorse apology (especially for social harmony and empathy apologies) she finds that she takes on guilt and shame as if she had done something wrong and was taking full responsibility for that. Even when she would apologize for little things by saying "I'm sorry," her feelings of shame and blameworthiness would build and build. So now she only says "I'm sorry" when she really does mean she believes she has done something wrong.

> No offense to my sister, but sometimes it is more expedient to say, "I'm sorry." It is easier to control myself than to control others. On a team, if something has gone wrong, it is easier for me to find some fault in what I have done, say, "I'm sorry," and attempt to fix the problem. If the other people did something wrong and do not realize it, are they likely to change? Probably not, unless I am their boss and I can make them change. No, on a team I can try to fix whatever I did wrong and /or try to find ways to make up for whatever they did (and will continue doing) wrong, or I can blame the other people, they will resent me, there will be a fight, and, most importantly, they will not change and we will continue to have negative outcomes.

> So, I apologize, a lot, and I overwork myself. Is that fair to the team? No, it does not help them grow, it shows I have no faith in them, and it is not fair to me either since a team is supposed to work as a team and not one person doing the work while everyone else watches or bumbles around. But projects get done, and they get well, and that is what I prefer. This does not just avoid conflict- it avoids frustrations. I am not correcting those on my team, so I do not look like more of a know-it-all than I already to normally, that is

an added bonus for me.

I am not sure if this falls under an "externally motivated" or "social harmony" apology. Maybe it is a blend of both; maybe it is a kind of "utilitarian" apology. Submitted by a student who will remain anonymous, emphasis added.

The following Apology Decision Tree might be another way to try to understand the different reasons for offering different apologies and might assist a person considering offering an apology.

Apology Decision Tree

1. Do you believe your behavior hurt someone and was wrong?

   Yes, Remorse Apology

   No, continue

2. Do you acknowledge your behavior hurt someone, but believe your actions were justified or necessary?

   Yes, Regret Apology
   No, continue

3. Do you have compassion for the circumstances of your accuser, even though those circumstances are not your fault?

   Yes, Empathy Apology

   No, continue

4. Is it important to maintain harmony in the relationships affected by this potential conflict between you and the accuser or the extended community of people who could be affected by the conflict?

   Yes, Social Harmony Apology

   No, continue

5. Do you want to avoid potential retaliation by the accuser or being ostracized because of the appearance of your conduct to others?

   Yes, Externally Motivated Apology

   No, don't Apologize

6. Are you willing to have conflict over this issue?

   Yes, Don't Apologize

   No, reconsider above options

A student applied the flow chart in a journal.

Two days after our class, I was able to test out the apology "flow chart" method. Every opportunity I get now, I find myself trying out some of these new theories from class. On this particular day, I was called by my old law firm, for whom I have been doing contract work. I recently left the firm on good terms to start my own practice and to pursue my masters through the Straus program. As is customary, I was asked not to tell clients that I was leaving the firm, as my former employers were fearful that the clients would leave them, and that was one particular conflict I wished to avoid. My former employers were asking me to come into the office and ease the fears of a client who was threatening to leave them because I was no longer at the firm. They wanted me to assure her that the new attorney handling her case is competent.

When I met my former client at my old office, I was met with a cold stare. We walked in silence to the conference room where we met her new attorney. After introducing the new attorney, I said, "Sharon I understand that you are probably upset that I left the firm and did not tell you. For that I am very sorry. We had a good relationship and I would like it to continue that way. I would have felt the same way if I were in your shoes." "You're right, I am very upset with you," she said. "I felt you should have said something to me." "Well," I explained," the reason that I didn't is simple. The firm was afraid that if I told you I was leaving, that you'd leave too. A lot of times when this actually happens, where the client leaves, the associate ends up getting sued by their former firm." "I understand that," she said. "Actually, I probably owe you an apology. I think I over-reacted when I found out you left, but now that I know why you left, I feel much better." With that, I was able to transition her to the new attorney and everything ended on good terms.

During my apology, I found myself mentally going through the flow chart. "Do I think my behavior was wrong?" Well, no, like every other law firm I left, I was asked not to tell the clients because my former employers were afraid that the clients would leave to go with me. "Was I willing to have conflict over the issue?" No, I wanted her to be comfortable with why I left and didn't tell her and wanted her to remain with the firm. "Did I have compassion for her even though I believed the circumstances were not my fault (but maybe that of my former firm)?" Yes. I felt badly, understood her situation, and wanted her to understand that. Accordingly, I showed empathy to her situation, offered a reasoned justification for my conduct, and ultimately, it ended with her apologizing to me. While I don't agree with all of (Robinson's) positions, I think the method is effective, and can make me a better apologizer, able to smooth over even the most difficult of situations. Submitted by an anonymous student, emphasis added.

1.4 Criteria for Quality Apologies

When should you trust an apology? When should you reject one? What criteria do you consciously or unconsciously apply when making this decision?

Many people suggest that an apology is trustworthy if it is "sincere" or "heartfelt." The menu of potential meanings reveals why these criteria are suspect. The concern is that the recipient of an apology is confusing sincerity with remorse. They may be willing to accept a sincere remorse apology, but would they feel the same way about a sincere externally motivated apology? A sincere externally motivated apology means that the person apologizing truly wants to avoid the external consequences of their behavior: retaliation, abandonment, or humiliation. The sincere social harmony apology means the person truly wants relational peace while believing he has not done anything wrong. These sincere or heartfelt apologies may not satisfy the victim if she knew the motives and meanings behind these apologies.

Lazare identified three different criteria to measure the quality of an apology. [11] They are different, and he doesn't reconcile them. He is satisfied if any of the three are present. The first is whether remorse is present. Under this criterion, only the remorse apology has legitimacy. The other types of apologies are imposters seeking a benefit that accompanies a remorse apology, the potential to re-establishment trust.

Another criterion for a person receiving an apology is whether the behavior will be repeated. This is different from the remorse apology because a person can commit to not repeat the behavior without believing that the behavior was wrong. A friend took great exception to calling a person "stupid." She was raised to believe that word was an inappropriate insult. The author adjusted and learned to replace stupid with dumb, but only in that friend's company. The author did not agree with this distinction and had no remorse but modified his behavior in that person's presence because of the importance of the relationship.

On one occasion, I refused to apologize to my wife because I knew I would repeat the behavior. She was driving and I realized that she was turning the wrong direction. I tried to help by saying the word "right." My wife did not respond and continued turning left. I assumed that she must not have heard him, so I said "right" again louder. As she was completing the left turn, I said "right" again, yet louder. My wife became frustrated as she was making a U-turn and said that she was entitled to an apology. I reflected on whether the behavior was likely to be repeated and concluded that it would. I then explained to my wife that if I apologized, that might falsely lead her to believe that the behavior was not likely to be repeated, and that I respected her too much to give such an apology. My wife rolled her eyes at my pathetic intellectual gymnastics to protect my pride and said she would forgive me anyway!

Lazare's third criterion is whether the apology meets the needs of the victim. In this case the rehabilitation of an injured innocent party is paramount. The mental state or future intentions of the person apologizing are irrelevant. If the apology mitigates the injury and/or advances the healing of the offended party, a social good has been accomplished and it should be celebrated.

This standard allows a manipulative social harmony or externally motivated apology to placate a naïve injured party. The injured party is naïve because he is allowing a questionable apology to meet his needs. This standard is custom made to support a social harmony apology. The recipient of the apology may wrongfully perceive that the offender has remorse and therefore feels better after the apology. It doesn't matter that the victim has misinterpreted the situation. The objective of helping the victim feel better has been accomplished so the apology should not be subject to further scrutiny.

An interesting issue is whether this criterion of meeting the needs of the victim should be applied subjectively or objectively. A subjective application can create two extreme results. A very sloppy apology that is fully accepted by a naïve victim. It meets the victim's needs and thus is legitimate despite its shortcomings.

The second extreme result is when the victim does not accept a comprehensive apology. The application of this criterion is important because it determines if an offender must continue punishing himself or being in debt to a victim who will not forgive. The subjective application of this criterion could be understood to require the offender to continue seeking forgiveness until it is granted by the victim. If so, the offender is dependent on and held hostage by the victim until the victim accepts the apology.

The objective standard would allow the offender to release himself from any duty to the victim if "the reasonable person" would have forgiven after the apology. There are advantages and power that come from being a victim; does an offender have a right to forgive themselves when the victim is refusing to forgive? Can an offender be trusted to make the determination that she has adequately apologized, and that the victim is being unreasonable when they refuse to accept the apology? The victim can choose to continue living in the pain of the offense forever, but that does not require the offender to do the same. Under the objective application of the "meet the needs of the victim" standard, the offender can conclude that his efforts to make things right have been adequate and that he can release himself from the burden of his bad behavior.

Conclusion

Why is it important to understand meanings, motives, and criteria for assessing the quality of apologies? When to accept and reject an apology requires wisdom. The opportunities for miscommunication are rampant. How important is it to clarify the meaning and motives of an apology? When giving an apology, is it necessary to clarify when an apology is mistakenly interpreted as an expression of remorse? When receiving an apology, how important is it for the recipient to explore the intended meaning ... and motives?

The depth of the relationship might impact the effort parties are willing to make to clarify the apology conversation. Casual relationships might not justify the work of clearly communicating about apologies. The investment of effort may be more appropriate in more intimate relationships. Clarifying whether there is agreement about the impropriety of certain behavior might be more important in a marriage as compared to a distant relative you see once a year.

Again, a student journal is instructive.

> I loved the stories you (Professor Robinson) shared about your own life and the way apologies work in your marriage relationship. I got married this summer, and even though I have only been married a month and a half, I felt that I could appreciate your stories all the more. Every type of relationship provides a new dynamic for how apologies work and are communicated (or not communicated), and the marriage relationship is particularly interesting. Some relationships are more distant or temporal, so the lack of an apology has less effect, but it is also easier to give an apology because the humility it takes is far less.
>
> Something I noticed from the beginning of my marriage relationship was that little things made us way more upset than they normally would. After discussing it, my husband and I realized the reason for this is most likely because there is a level of fear that whatever we just let go now will be that way for the rest of our lives together. Sure, getting distracted during a conversation in which I'm sharing about my day is not a big deal and could happen to anyone, particularly when the person is tired or going through a lot themselves. Ordinarily I would be overly forgiving if someone did that, and my husband would be overly apologetic. However, now the apologies err on the side of justification, and forgiveness is harder to offer because while it isn't a big deal once, if it happened for the rest of our lives, obviously that would be an issue. (I could have easily offered an example in the opposite direction, by the way - my husband is awesome.) Seems over dramatic, and it is, but the dynamic of the relationship has a huge effect on how readily apologies are offered. I appreciated that we talked about that in class.
>
> I also appreciated your initial comment about your wife when you said, "If she says I owe her an apology, I usually do. I trust her." It is amazing how trust in relationships can have a huge impact on the apology. Knowing that the relationship is a safe place to admit mistakes, accept responsibility, and move forward can increase willingness to apologize readily. Submitted by Hillary Stump, emphasis added.

One way to frame the question is to ask, "Is an apology supposed to be the end of the conversation or is it supposed to be the beginning?" On multiple occasions, a woman student taking the Apology, Forgiveness, and Reconciliation class will share that her boyfriend hates that she is taking this class. She explains that prior to the class, her boyfriend would do something hurtful, she would be mad or hurt, he would apologize, and she would forgive him. After studying apology, he would apologize, and she would ask questions to explore the meaning of the apology. (One student asked what her boyfriend was apologizing for and he replied that he didn't know, but he was sorry.) Sometimes the boyfriend would get frustrated because he apologized hoping to be done with this topic, but the apology simply became the platform to further explore their relationship.

A student's description addresses much of the material in this chapter.

When I was a little girl my parents taught me the concept of an apology. I was expected to apologize to the victim when I did something wrong, and in return I learned to expect an apology when someone did something wrong to me. The lesson of apologizing is one of the first lessons I learned, and I thought I was a master of apologies. In fact, my family has told me multiple times to stop apologizing for everything.

Then the first day of class was an eye-opening experience. The concept I thought I had mastered was more complicated than I could have imagined. Yet as I learned about the different meanings to "I'm sorry," the criteria for a good apology, and the motivations for apologizing, I realized that these concepts were things I had a vague familiarity with but had never actually acknowledged.

Before this class, I knew that apologies could have different meanings behind them. For instance, I knew that apologizing for offending someone was different than apologizing to someone out of gratitude and feeling bad for asking them a favour. However, I did not realize that there were so many different meanings of an apology.

For me, the two most confusing types of apologies are the social harmony apology and the externally motivated apology. I understand that the social harmony apology is for the group's well-being. The main purpose for that kind of apology is to fix the relationship because the apologizer cares more about the relationship than the satisfaction of knowing that the apologizer was right. However, I was confused because I thought that particular motivation could also be the motivation behind an externally motivated apology.

Learning about the three criteria for a good apology made me realize how much work and emotion goes into an apology. It also made me think about how unfortunate it is that today an apology is not given the respect it deserves. Outside of the people who have studied this topic, people do not understand the deeper meanings and implications of an apology.

It is astonishing to think about how one word, "sorry," can have so many different meanings behind it. For instance, people who have taken this class or educated themselves about this topic will understand that an apology should not be taken lightly. Apologizing for something should be heartfelt and thought about beforehand. However, people who have not taken this class may just throw around apologies as if they mean nothing.

Does that mean from now on people should inquire what it means when they receive an apology? The next time someone apologizes to me should I ask them if they really thought about what they did wrong and realized the error of their ways before apologizing to me? Should I not forgive someone if they apologize to me while not understanding how to properly approach an apology? Or should I chalk up their lack of education on the topic as excusable and forgive them anyways? Submitted by Catherine Jung.

1.5 Spiritual Growth Applications

For readers whose religious beliefs include the practice of confessing their deficits to a Creator, it might be insightful to consider the quality of our confession. The premise is that a confession to God is like an apology and that many of the concepts discussed in this chapter apply. This possibly gives the reader new filters to evaluate his confession.

Some confessions/apologies consist of subtle and not so subtle justifications. Jesus gave an example of such situations when he compared the confessions of the self-righteous religious leader to the despondent sinner.[12] The religious leader prayed, "God, I thank you that I am not like other men –robbers, evildoers, adulterers – or even like this tax collector…." The despondent sinner prayed, "God, have mercy on me, a sinner." Jesus declared the despondent sinner went home justified before God because he humbled himself.

As we towards accepting more culpability, we might ask what percentage of the people who regularly participate in your religious community do so out of external motivations. Some attempts to recruit religious adherents rely on the fear of going to hell. Such a convert will follow the instruction to confess/apologize to the Creator, but it will be an externally motivated confession based on avoiding punishment. This confession is like the toddler repeatedly apologizing as they anticipate an imminent punishment.

The empathy confession might center on how difficult it must be for God. The prayer contrasts God's infinite love with mankind's petty selfishness. How difficult it must be for God to put up with us. I will humble myself and apologize because I understand God's frustrations with humanity.

Further to the right we need to consider the social harmony confession. This might take the form of essentially asking God if we can just get along. My religious tradition or leader require a confession/apology to you God, so I will give one to make my peace with you. But I am not sure if I have done anything wrong and am only giving this confession/apology because you or my religious mentor demand it. I will comply with this tradition or ritual so we can be at peace.

The regret confession acknowledges our misdeeds but sees them as inevitable and unavoidable. The world we live in is complicated and mean. It does not allow people to be kind and loving all the time. I understand that I have not met the highest standards of my religious tradition like loving my enemies, turning the other cheek, and lending to those in need without expecting repayment but these ideals are not possible in my context.[13] I regret not meeting these standards, but also believe my behavior was necessary to protect myself and my loved ones.

The remorse confession communicates to God that you have reflected on your sins of commission and omission. That you realize that you are hopelessly inadequate when judged by a holy and righteous God. That you hate your petty self-centered nature and need forgiveness and, in some religious teachings like Christianity, a savior. Your reparations are a surrender of your selfish will and request for God to transform you into a loving, generous, kind person. You recognize that you can only live up to the highest standards of your religion's teachings when you are in this state of submission to God, allowing Him to transform you.

Again, one student integrated the spiritual dimension in his journal comments.

> This class discussion made me think about my own life and my own attitude toward apology. As Prof. Robinson stated, my entire framework for dealing with apology stems from my Christian faith and the teachings of Jesus, who told me to forgive not just seven times, but essentially infinity times for the same offense committed against me by the same person. This leads me to believe that while maybe an apology isn't necessary for forgiveness, it provides an important window of opportunity for forgiveness to take place. This of course, all stems out of the love that I should have for both my neighbors and my enemies. <u>For me it is crystal clear that if there is even a chance that I acted wrongly toward another individual, I should not think twice about offering a remorse based apology rather than letting my pride get in the way of making myself into a better person that places the needs of others equal to or maybe even higher than my own.</u> Even Jesus on the cross, essentially apologized for those who tortured him and crucified him. It is this example that we as Christians are supposed to follow. The bar is set extremely high and this class is teaching me that not all apologies are equal. Submitted by Casey Caton, emphasis added.

1.6 Crazy Making Roommate Questionnaire

(Whether, Type of Apology, and Importance of Clarity)

You arrived home from a long day at school and work to a note on the kitchen table from your roommate. The note expressed anger at you because an important assignment s/he needed to turn in today was in your car. S/he borrowed your car yesterday and left a backpack in the back seat. You saw the backpack when you were leaving this morning, but didn't take it back to the apartment for the following reasons:

1. you were right on time and didn't want to be late to your first class;
2. your roommate borrows your car (and everything else) often and leaves stuff in it all the time;
3. your roommate is always unorganized and on the edge of chaos--- it isn't your job to take care of him/her.

You know this was an important assignment because s/he has been stressing over it for a few weeks. S/he worked hard on it and now will receive a significant reduction in the grade because it is late.

Your reaction to the note is ambivalent:

On one hand you feel bad that s/he will receive a reduced grade on an important assignment.

On the other hand, you aren't sure you did anything wrong.

1. S/he will be home in about five minutes . . . . You need to decide quickly if you should apologize and what kind of apology to offer.

Choose one type of apology below and circle it:

No Apology... Externally Motivated... Empathy... Social Harmony... Regret... Remorse

How important is it to clarify the intended meaning of your apology?   1   3   5   7   10

                                                                        Not very   Very

2. Same situation, but this time s/he told you that the assignment was completed and was in his/her backpack in your car. S/he said s/he would get it in the morning.

Choose one type of apology below and circle it:

No Apology... Externally Motivated... Empathy... Social Harmony... Regret... Remorse

How important is it to clarify the intended meaning of your apology?   1   3   5   7   10

                                                        Not very   Very

3. Same situation, but this time s/he told you that the assignment was completed and was in his/her backpack in your car. S/he said s/he would get it in the morning and made you promise to not leave with it. You don't know why, but your commitment to not leave with it completely slipped your mind until you saw the note when you returned home.

Choose one type of apology below and circle it:

No Apology... Externally Motivated... Empathy... Social Harmony... Regret... Remorse

How important is it to clarify the intended meaning of your apology?   1   3   5   7   10

                                                        Not very   Very

Endnotes

1. The material in this chapter is heavily dependent and influenced by Aaron Lazare's writings, especially his book *On Apology*. Some of this material is paraphrased. In other places, this material reacts to and adapts some of Dr. Lazare's concepts. These endnotes notes include acknowledgements of specific instances of Dr. Lazare' material, but I wish to generally recognize how Dr. Lazare's writings have contributed to my understanding.

2. Correspondence between Irv Kupcinet and Harry S. Truman, including draft copies of Truman's letter, July 30 and August 5, 1963, responding to Mr. Kupcinet's column in the Chicago Sun-Times about the dropping of the atomic bomb on Japan. Papers of Harry S. Truman: Post-Presidential Files. https://www.trumanlibrary.org/flip_books/index.php?tldate=1963-07-30&groupid=3707&titleid=&pagenumber=1&collectionid=ihow.

3. Kate Mather, "Their loved ones were killed by police. Now the LAPD wants to help them out," *Los Angeles Times*, August 24, 2016.

4. Gorodnichenko, Y., & Roland, G. (2011). Understanding the individualism-collectivism cleavage and its effects: Lessons from cultural psychology, Proceedings of XVIth Congress of the International Economic Association, Beijing, China.

5. *See id*. at 4.

6. Lazare,*On Apology*, 134-58

7. For a more technical description of this see the explanation and citations for "intrapsychic denial" in Jonathan R. Cohen, *The Immorality of Denial*, 79 TUL. L. REV. 903, 910 (2005). This discussion includes the recognition that modern psychiatric practice accepts that denial can sometimes be a 'healthy coping mechanism.' Citations omitted.

8. Lazare, *On Apology*, 106.

9. Douglas Stone, Bruce Patton, and Sheila Heen, *Difficult Conversations*, (New York: Penguin Books, 2010).

10. Editorial, "Alcoholics Anonymous Step 9: Apologize to People You've Harmed," RECOVERY.ORG, November 22, 2015, http://www.recovery.org/topics/step-9-aa/.

11. Lazare, *On Apology*, 23, 26, and 31.

12. *See* Luke 18:9-14.

13. *See* Luke 6:27-36.

Chapter Two

Psychological Needs and How to Apologize

2.1 Introduction

2.2 Psychological Needs Met by an Apology

2.3 How to Apologize

2.4 The Spilt Water Exercise

2.1 Introduction

In this chapter, I hope to equip the reader with an understanding of the psychological needs surrounding an apology and offer suggestions for how to apologize. Understanding the psychological needs is especially important because one of the criteria for a successful apology is meeting the needs of the victim. Again, the writings of those professionally trained in psychology are important sources for those of us who are not psychologically trained.[1] The discussion of how an apology might satisfy various psychological needs of the victim helps the offender craft the apology; also, it is a good way to study the interpersonal dynamics between offenders and victims. The suggested templates for constructing various types of apologies enable readers to understand their options and accurately express their intended message. The importance of the material in this chapter is highlighted by the following student journal.

The Generational Disconnect Case Study

Submitted by a Student

Last class we talked about conditional, passive, and minimizing apologies. The class wasn't illuminating so much as validating. I have been on the receiving end of *so* many of these "apologies" and left feeling unsatisfied and then vaguely at fault for not being more forgiving. It makes me wonder if teaching children *how* to apologize has changed generationally. My father was a big believer in the "silent gesture" or implied apology. He would lose his temper, yell, and stop for ice cream on the way home. He would get frustrated helping with homework (definitely all my fault in retrospect), but then offer to figure it out and teach me his way. However, I never heard my dad say, "I'm sorry" to anyone except my mom (and then more a defeated sort of empathy reflex: "I'm sorry, honey.") He was from a stoic, "men don't cry," big Catholic family upbringing. Apologies meant admitting fault, and admitting fault was admitting weakness.

My mother is the person who thrives on the "fake apology." I have been on the receiving end of many "I'm sorry you feel that way," "I'm sorry you're so sensitive," or "I'm sorry you can't see my side." She thrives on the passive guilt and forcing her way to preserve social harmony and the instinctual elder respect ("Is that how you're going to talk to your mother?") At *most* she'll give an explanation; "I was tired," or "It wasn't anyone's fault." Like my father, I've never heard my mother say, "I'm sorry," with anything but sarcasm or a hope to edge the unpleasantness back into mother-daughter harmony.

Perhaps my parents were just singularly bad at apologizing, but something in me wonders if preschool/primary school has changed the way society approaches one another. In the 1960s, children were primarily left to raise themselves (or be raised "by hand" with the emphasis "hands on"). My father, third in eight children, would be gone by nine in the morning and not get home until dark. My mother, raised by a single mother, would often spend days without seeing her if her mother was working nights or on dates. School was much the same: disciplinarian, strict, and teachers interacted personally with students only when they were acting out. Fights between students, bullying, and situations now deemed "in need of apology" were carried out by students alone, with minimal to no teacher involvement.

In contrast, in preschool children in time out were asked to talk and explain their feelings to one another. "Helicopter parenting" became in vogue. My parents enforced their laws upon us: If I tried to tease my sisters, I would have to apologize. If I tried to hit/fight with them, I would go to my room. If I talked back to my parents, my teachers, or authority figures, I would be forced to say sorry. In fact, apologizing became more nuanced as I got older: "Say you're sorry." "Sorry." "No, say it like you mean it." "*Sorry*." "Why are you sorry?" And so on.

However, while I got older and better at discerning when to apologize, my mother seemed to stagnate in how and when to apologize. If she embarrassed me in front of her peers for an amusing story and I reprimanded her, she would only explain: "Oh honey, it didn't hurt *you*. You won't see them," much less promise forbearance in the future. (I shudder to think how much strangers have heard about my childhood secrets). Especially as I became an adult, her apologies grew thinner and less satisfying. She became more defensive, frustrated that I wouldn't just "take the apology and move on." I tried to challenge her behavior, motivating her through shame to change it. However, like most children, I discovered my mother has no shame (or at least not when it comes to her daughter's feelings – where obviously she knows best).

I know my father—since passed—would probably regard the new culture of apology to be distasteful. But I can't help wonder how the children of today will interact in this "softened" culture. In a society that teaches apology and shamelessness in unequal portions, I am not sure if apology is coming forward as more relevant or fading into the media impudence of less.   Submitted by an anonymous student.

2.2 Psychological Needs Met by an Apology

Dr. Lazare describes a variety of psychological needs that could be met by an apology.[2] This summary of Lazare's observations will be comparatively brief so students interested in a deeper exploration will need to expand their study of this topic.

The most obvious psychological need that could be satisfied by an apology is the **restoration of the victim's dignity.**[3] Many offenses are offensive because they are disrespectful and/or humiliating. This behavior elevates the offender to a position that is superior to the victim. The offender is important, and the victim is not. Examples include arriving late to appointments, losing composure and directing loud and crude language at the victim, and being insensitive or inconsiderate of the victim's feelings. This assertion of superiority communicates the inferiority of the victim. This inferiority diminishes the victim's dignity.

If no apology is given, the offender is signaling his perception of this relationship. The offender is important, and the victim is subservient. The offender feels entitled to treat the victim this way. The victim can decide if he wants to accept this definition of the relationship or if he wants to seek some form of power to redefine the relationship. There could be a variety of reasons why the offender may be willing to apologize for the oppressive behavior (see chapter one). Whatever the reason, the offender empowers the victim and restores the victim's dignity by apologizing.

A visual picture of this could be the offender and victim standing in side by side elevators on the first floor of a hotel. Both parties are equals when both elevators are at the first floor. When the offender is inconsiderate to the victim, his elevator goes up to the second floor and the victim's elevator drops to the basement parking level. If the offender apologizes, his elevator drops to the basement and the victim's elevator rises to the second floor. Notice that the apology raises the victim's elevator higher than the offender, signifying that the victim has power over the offender.

How does an apology give a victim power over an offender? What power does the victim have? The power to decide whether to accept the apology and/or forgive. When the offender apologizes, she humbles herself and admits her behavior was not appropriate. She expresses her own fallibility by admitting that she acted wrongly. She is inadequate and in need of rehabilitation. Therefore, some people find it so hard to apologize. It is an act of self-humiliation and requires one to sacrifice his pride. The apology voluntarily subjects the offender to the victim's choice to either be gracious and accept the apology and/or forgive, or to withhold acceptance of the apology and/or forgiveness and try to keep the offender in a subservient position. Thus, the apology transforms the dominant offender into the subservient party vulnerable to the reaction of the now empowered victim.

If the victim accepts the apology and/or forgives, the elevators return to ground floor where both parties have dignity and respect. If the victim does not accept the apology and/or forgives, the offender's elevator remains in the basement.

An example where an apology was not provided because of the refusal of the alleged offender to humble themselves is an incident between Israel and Turkey. Israeli soldiers killed nine Turkish activists on board a pro-Palestinian protest flotilla that was attempting to break Israel's blockade of the Gaza strip. Turkey recalled its ambassador and nearly broke off relations with Israel in protest of the May 2010 incident. Turkey's Prime Minister refused to restore relations unless Israel publicly accepted responsibility and paid compensation to the families of the victims. Israel offered to pay compensation so long as its soldiers were protected from lawsuits but resisted a formal apology. Israeli leaders who opposed calls for an apology said it would hurt the country's image, saying that an apology would be interpreted as a sign of weakness. A former Israeli ambassador to Turkey said "Leaders on both sides are having this fistfight over the honor of their countries but they're overlooking their interests. It's completely crazy to not find a diplomatic solution."[4]

A student provides a personal example from a journal.

> I really like the elevator imagery of offenses/apologies. When the offender does an act against the victim, the offender is on a higher level than the victim. However, when the offender apologies to the victim, the offender puts themselves on a lower level than the victim. I really liked this imagery because I had never realized that apologizing to someone means you are essentially placing yourself at their mercy depending on whether they want to forgive you or not. This imagery made me realize why a situation in my past made me so angry.

> I lost a friendship two years ago when a friend thought that I had insulted/offended his girlfriend. They had misconstrued what I was saying and had thought I had attacked her by offending her family. Those were not my intentions at all, and I was actually surprised to hear that they construed my words so differently from what I was intending. He and I got into a fight, and he wanted me to apologize. I am not good with apologies nor awkward situations, but, at his insistence, I decided to text his girlfriend with an apology. The apology was heartfelt and explained how I did not mean my words to be interpreted the way she understood them. I explained that I would never offend her family because I believe that offending someone's family is off limits. I sincerely meant the apology; although I probably <u>should</u> have apologized through a better way instead of through text.

> <u>She never responded. It made me furious to think that I had thought out a sincere apology because I genuinely did not want my words to have the effect they did. I knew I was angry, but I didn't know how to put it into words. But after learning about this elevator imagery of apologies, I realize why I was mad. Although I had placed myself in a lower position than her by apologizing, she didn't feel the need to accept, or at least acknowledge my apology.</u> Because of my pride, I hated being on the lower level. Submitted by Catherine Jung, emphasis added.

Another student's experience describes how apologizing to restore another person's dignity may have a surprisingly healing outcome. The 29-year-old student described that she worked as a newly admitted attorney in a law office for three years and had earned the respect of the other nine lawyers in the office. A 50-year-old woman attorney with decades of experience joined the office and quickly began belittling the young attorney. After ignoring her private and occasionally public put-downs for about a year the younger attorney decided to initiate a conversation about their relationship. Her description of the conversation is:

> "I went in and said I had gotten the sense that I had frustrated her on a couple of different projects recently, so I wanted to apologize and clear the air for anything I had done that was out of line or disrespectful. She 180'd the conversation and ended up apologizing to me. She said she wanted to initiate the same conversation but was too proud. She said she is a really insecure person in general and seeing someone the age of her kid being very highly regarded by the entire office and potentially being promoted above her made her 'feel like shit' (her words.) So, it isn't personal, but situational.

> I explained that I personally don't view it that way and have a lot of respect for her and her position and don't want there to be a wedge between us. She was grateful and apologized 'for being a bitch' (her words.)   Submitted by an anonymous student.

Another possible psychological need met by an apology is the **assurance of shared values**. The victim judges and condemns the offensive behavior; that is how he comes to the conclusion that he has been victimized. When the offender apologizes, he agrees with the victim in judging and condemning the behavior. The victim's assessment of the injustice is confirmed by the offender. The victim senses the agreement and shared values about the incident. This is certainly the case with a remorse apology. The regret, social harmony or externally motivated apology might affirm social norms, but since the offender does not believe she has done anything wrong, the parties to not have shared values. The issue of whether the apology demonstrates shared values may be a reason the victim will want to explore the apology's intended meaning.

When there are shared values condemning the behavior, the victim's possible psychological need of **assurance that the incident was not their fault** is met. An example is when my family felt a giant sense of relief when the other driver in a car accident admitted he didn't see a stop sign and took full responsibility for the accident. A victim might wonder if they are being too sensitive or may have contributed to the incident in some way. When the offender takes responsibility for the incident by an apology, he is affirming that the behavior was wrong and that it was his fault. The victim is relieved of her doubts and concerns about whether she should have taken offense.

When an apology includes the assurance of shared values, it also meets a possible psychological need of providing **assurance of safety in the future relationship**. When the offender apologizes, she may be communicating that the victim can assume the behavior will not be repeated.[5] This can be true for all types of apologies, but is another area to explore when discussing the intended meaning of the apology. It is also possible that an offender is truly remorseful, but that the behavior is a pattern or habit that will be hard to break; it may be wise to expect in some situations that even if the offender despises the behavior, it may be repeated, hopefully on a decreasing frequency.

Finally, sometimes an apology meets the victim's potential psychological desire to **see the offender suffer.** The self-humiliation aspect of an apology satisfies the victim's desire to see the arrogant offender humbled. This may be a reason why an apology is not immediately accepted. Now that the apologizer has become subservient and humbled, the victim wants him to linger in that state before restoring the offender's dignity by accepting the apology. It is possible that the victim never accepts the apology because the offense was so egregious and/or the victim has such a strong desire to see the offender suffer. If you object to and do not understand this psychological desire, consider an especially grievous injury and an especially arrogant offender.

An understanding of some of the possible psychological needs met by an apology can assist the offender in crafting the apology. When the apology is not accepted, assessing which of the potential psychological needs may not have been satisfied can inform the offender about how to possibly reconstruct the apology so that it will be accepted.

The following student journal provides a personal assessment of her psychological needs.

> My boyfriend of over two years told me he will not be able to follow me when I graduate. This was particularly difficult because we had a social contract that he would follow me; the reasoning was that he is a rhetoric major and can find work in most places. I am an international studies major and need to follow the fellowships (mostly in Washington DC and state capitals) and then attend graduate school somewhere else. He graduated before me and decided to stay in the area to be with me, but I had been quite upfront with my intentions to move from the beginning; I told him I only wanted to continue in our relationship if he thought we could be together. He knew I was serious about moving because I left twice before—once for a semester in Argentina and then another semester in an internship in Washington DC. My moving was something he could see coming. Still, he assured me that he would be able to follow me because he was working a job he did not love with hopes of getting a new job where I go.

He quit the job he did not love and found an incredible opportunity with a company in the growth phase that wants him to expand them into New York and London. Now he wants to stay with that company for the next few years. The problem is that I have spent the last few months applying to incredibly competitive fellowships that I may actually have a shot at. If I get one, I would have to leave everything I have worked for behind. I am happy for him, but at the same time I am so mad because I thought he was really serious about following me. His explanation was that it would be very difficult to be successful at a company if he has to move every few years, which is true. But I thought he thought that out before he decided to stay with me.

He has tried to apologize to me, but it just doesn't feel like enough, and I can't figure out what I want from an apology. I do not feel like he can restore my dignity. This is something we both invested two years in and his explanation basically means he really didn't think things through, which is humiliating. I don't know if we can assure shared values because those values have become blurred. For so long I thought we both valued staying together because we have already done a year of long distance, but now he is valuing success over us being together. I don't blame him because I also value pursuing my calling, but I have been very up front as to what that is and what it requires. I am in a dilemma because I can't condemn him for something I value as well. I do want assurance that the incident is not my fault as he changed all of his values on me and is thus putting our relationship at stake. I also would like to know there is assurance of safety in the future relationship, but I am not sure how much more long-distance I want to do. I gave up applying to the Peace Corps for that value we both agreed on. The last option is to see the offender suffer. I feel like a terrible person, but I kind of do want to see him suffer – at least to the extent I am.

He has now put the future of our relationship in my hands, stating that he wants us to be together and would be willing to do long distance, but if that was the case I wish he would have told me when I was considering doing the Peace Corps. The only thing that would make me happy is if he told me he wants to stick with the original plan and find work where I go. I understand he wants to be successful and I am happy for him, but I did tell him from the beginning that I would be moving and the only way we could work is if he could follow me. I feel like he broke our contract and am thus stuck in a situation where I have to find a creative solution or let my relationship go, neither of which I want to do. Submitted by an anonymous student, emphasis added.

2.3 How to Apologize

An analysis of how to apologize starts with two variables. First, what type of apology will be delivered? The offender sends dramatically different messages depending on the type of apology offered. Each type has a different primary purpose. A remorse apology communicates self-condemnation of the behavior. A regret apology communicates empathy for a negative impact but denies any moral culpability. A social harmony apology communicates a desire to smooth things over and get along. An externally motivated apology communicates the offender's desire to mitigate his punishments for the behavior. This discussion will address the offender's choice between remorse, regret, socially harmony, and externally motivated apologies.

The second aspect of this analysis is how clear the offender will be about the true meaning of the apology. The offender will need to choose whether to be transparent or intentionally ambiguous about the meaning of the apology. There may be times when the offender is externally motivated, but he knows that the victim will find the apology offensive if he realizes the reason for the apology; thus, the offender may choose to deliver an apology that camouflages the reason behind the apology. In other situations, the offender may conclude that the victim is not offended by an externally motivated apology; so, the offender can be transparent about why she is apologizing. Decisions about how to apologize should be thoughtful about both the type of apology and the amount of clarity in the meaning of the apology.

The type of apology to deliver

The straightforward response to this issue is to deliver the type of apology that is true for the offender. The apology educated offender understands the different meanings of apology, reflects on what she feels/believes about the situation and should deliver the type of apology that most closely reflects those feelings/beliefs. This conforms to the **"Tell the Truth and Take Responsibility"** approach to apology.

The first step is for the offender to take the time to objectively determine her feelings and beliefs about the situation. For many of us our initial feelings and beliefs will be influenced by our defense mechanisms encouraging denial and rationalization. Thus, the effort to determine our "objective" version of truth includes confronting and circumnavigating our defense mechanisms.

I have this reaction when my wife identifies one of my behaviors or attitudes that she believes is inconsiderate. My first instinct is defensive; I don't know if my abilities and instinct for rationalization and denial are typical or if I am especially gifted in these areas. After fifteen years of marriage, I learned to ask my wife for 24 hours to reflect on the criticism. I regularly wake up at 5:30 and take a 30-minute walk to think and pray. I am frequently willing to acknowledge and accept the criticism after a good night's sleep and a 30-minute reflecting walk. Prayerfully examining my life (and my wife's criticism) from an eternal perspective usually helps me see more of my shortcomings and brings out the need for humility.

Even if the offender can be objective, sometimes determining the truth can be difficult because situations can be complex. So far, this analysis about apologies has assumed that there are a clear offender and victim. While that may be in some situations, there are also many situations where the incident is more complicated. Our previous binary black and white approach to offenses sometimes needs to be modified to acknowledge shades of grey.

Sometimes the offender is also a victim. Sometimes both parties contributed to creating the offense. Sometimes despite an honest, objective effort to reflect on the situation, the offender is not sure of how much responsibility to assume.

A medical malpractice lawyer described such a situation. The unresolved issue in a lawsuit was whether the doctor and hospital followed appropriate procedures to diagnose a patient. They ran a series of tests in a sequence that took 24 hours to determine the source of the symptoms. The patient suffered permanent injuries that might have been avoided had the doctor/hospital been able to diagnose the cause quicker. Both the plaintiff and defending lawyers had professors at medical schools offer conflicting testimony under oath about whether the doctor/hospital had administered the right tests in the right sequence. The family was angry because the doctor and hospital never apologized, even over ten years of litigation. As the doctor/hospital considered offering an apology at a settlement conference a few weeks before trial, they wrestled with the challenge of telling the truth, when the truth was not clear; in fact, it will never be clear, even if the case goes to trial and the jury has to decide which of these medical school professors is more believable.

Clarity of the Meaning of the Apology

My usual advice is that it is best to communicate as clearly as possible. This is generally accepted as the best approach to creating healthy long-term relationships. In the apology context, there can be a conflict sometimes between communicating what the offender truly feels/believes and the outcome they are attempting to accomplish with the apology.

Assume that the offender's goal is for the apology to be accepted and to be forgiven. If the offender's objective truth results in one of the apologies other than the Remorse Apology, there is a good chance the apology will be rejected by the victim. Only the remorse apology provides the victim with the assurances of shared values. Only the self-condemnation in the remorse apology reduces some victims' desire to punish the offender. Clearly communicating one of the types of apology when the "offender" doesn't accept full responsibility might insult the victim.

Jennifer Robbennolt's research includes an empirical study where she compares victims' responses to apologies that "merely express sympathy" to apologies that "both express sympathy and accepts responsibility." She documented that the apologies expressing sympathy and accepting responsibility were twice as likely to cause a person to accept a settlement offer than an apology that only expresses sympathy. [6] Her study confirms that a Remorse Apology is more likely to be accepted, if a willingness to accept a settlement offer is an appropriate proxy for accepting the offender's apology and forgiveness. Her study confirms that being honest is challenging when the offender is not truthfully remorseful because the apology that can be truthfully delivered often does not satisfy the victim's needs.

Thus, the offender must not only assess his objective truth about how he feels about the situation but needs to also anticipate the victim's response to such an apology. In some instances, an honest apology that does not accept responsibility will lead to a constructive and very meaningful conversation about the parties' relationship. In other instances, not so much!!!

The offender needs to weigh the importance of being transparent and authentically known in the affected relationship(s) against the need to:

 -contain/resolve the conflict and avoid negative consequences (Externally Motivated Apology);

 -maintain the relationship (I care more about you than being right-Social Harmony Apology); and

 - compassionately respond to the victim's pain (Regret or Empathy Apology).

Sometimes the offender will veil the meaning of the apology and hope they will not be asked to explain or clarify. Sometimes an offender will purposely mislead the victim. The intentional ambiguity can be based on expediency or kindness.

Usually the degree of the clarity should increase the more honorable the motives behind the apology. While the victim's preference would be a clearly communicated remorse apology, they would probably be more responsive to an explanation that the offender "feels terrible about the impact of his behavior, but denies doing anything wrong" (Regret Apology) compared to an explanation that "My behavior didn't hurt you and wasn't wrong, but I care more about you than I do about being right" (Social Harmony Apology). Likewise, either of the above apologies might be better received than an explanation that "I want to avoid retaliation and other punishments" (Externally Motivated Apology). A visual for this proposed relationship between the likely type and clarity of an apology is provided below:

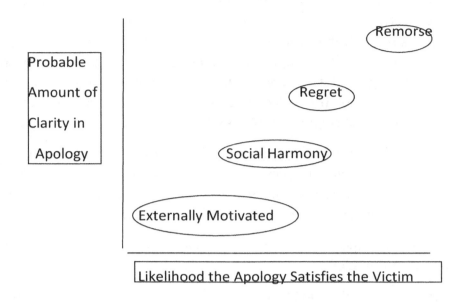

The chart above describes general trends. Every situation is unique, and offenders should assess how the clarity and type of apology are likely to be received by the affected people.

The suggestion that the offender may consider shielding the true meaning of his apology is offensive to some. Good friend and respected apology scholar Lee Taft has pleaded with apology associated professionals like mediators and attorneys to respect the inherent moral nature of an apology. He argues against seeing apology "simply as a strategic device to expedite the resolution of a dispute."[7] In contrast he writes,

> Apology is moral because it acknowledges the existence of right and wrong and confirms that a norm of right behavior has been broken. It is moral, too, because the person who apologizes also exposes himself to the consequences of his wrongful act.[8]

According to Taft's standards, only an apology that captures the elements of "repentance" satisfies the moral necessities to qualify as an appropriate apology. He recognizes the needs for empathetic expressions, but requests that they not be delivered in the form of an "apology." His appropriate concern is that the victim might be confused or misled. He correctly challenges offenders and professions advising them, like lawyers and mediators, to remember that the apology discourse is a "sacred space" and to avoid using strategic apologies in a manipulative way that might cause the victim "later to realize that he has been victimized again."[9]

The discussion below will consider the elements of various types of apologies, not because Taft is wrong, but because such an examination deepens the understanding of the variety of ways apologies are used. Every offender will need to be responsible for the moral ramifications of how they apply and use this understanding. We will start and spend the most space on the Remorse Apology because it is widely recognized as having the most legitimacy.

A student's journal describes three of her apologies in a single day.

> The work of this class has had a creeping and subtle effect on me. I find myself using the techniques almost every day. Just last night, my mother and I started in on a pattern of dialogue that invariably leads to a fight. I give her information about my life and she starts questioning or playing devil's advocate and asking me questions like I am on the witness stand. It is her way of helping me. It feels like second-guessing to me. Our whole family understands that this is just her style, but I can still find myself falling into the trap of escalating a fight by taking her questions as criticism and unsolicited advice rather than taking them in the spirit that she intends. As the fight started to escalate, I took a breath, slowed down and said, "Mom, I just don't want you to be disappointed if it doesn't work out the way you want." She softened. She said, "Oh, I won't be disappointed." And then we moved on. This felt like a semi-apology on my part. My statement required me to be vulnerable and to speak to the interests rather than the issues (mediation theory.)

> Hours later I found the opportunity to use the methods learned in the class again! My mother texted me to ask if I had "seen the lid to her beverage dispenser." Damnit, I thought. I had borrowed her dispenser and then broke the lid when I was trying to transfer it back to her house. Instead of starting with an excuse I just met it head on. I replied, "I broke it taking it out of the car. I'm sorry. I should have told you." She wasn't mad and we moved on.

> Third apology of the day. I was annoyed with some errand that I had to do for my family, which was going to add more trouble to an already hectic day. I called my brother (who was playing golf at the time, the dilettante!) to see if he could do the errand instead. He was clearly eating and told me it was inconvenient for him. I was so annoyed! I started shouting at him and hung up on him. It was definitely an over-reaction. And I dreaded talking to my brother about it because he holds grudges and I knew I might not get the vindication I sought. I bit the bullet. I left him a message: "I'm sorry. I lost my temper. I'm not mad at you. I just got frustrated because I am trying to do a lot of things today." He wrote back, "All good. My feelings were not hurt." Ha-ha, forgiveness triumph triumvirate. Submitted by an anonymous student, emphasis added.

2.31 How to Offer a Remorse Apology

The Remorse Apology might be viewed as the gold standard for apology because it satisfies the requirements of most of the apology literature. Consider how the Remorse Apology conforms to the following definitions of respected apology scholars, which were used as reference points by Jennifer Robbennolt.[10]

Nicholas Tavruchis—at a minimum, an apology must incorporate "acknowledgement of legitimacy of the violated rule, admission of fault and responsibility for its violation, and the expression of genuine regret and remorse for the harm done."[11]

Erving Goffman—"In its fullest form, the apology has several elements: expression of embarrassment and chagrin; clarification that one knows what conduct had been expected and sympathizes with the application of negative sanction; verbal rejection, repudiation, and disavowal of the wrong way of behaving along with vilification of the self that so behaved; espousal of the right way and an avowal henceforth to pursue that course; performance of penance and the volunteering of restitution."[12]

Hiroshi Wagatsuma and Arthur Rosett—the elements of a meaningful apology must include the offender acknowledging the following: "1. the hurtful act happened, caused injury, and was wrongful; 2. the apologizer was at fault and regrets participating in the act; 3. the apologizer will compensate the injured party; 4. the act will not happen again; and 5. the apologizer intends to work for good relations in the future.[13]

While most observers include some version of remorse, its necessity is described on a spectrum. Notice that for Tavruchis it is necessary to meet minimum standards. For Wagatsuma and Rosett, it is part of a meaningful apology. For Goffman it is part of achieving an apology in the "fullest form."

Lazare takes about a third of his book, *On Apology* to describe how to offer a Remorse Apology.[14] The following description of how to deliver a Remorse Apology is largely based on Lazare's model and suggestions. Readers interested in a more detailed description should consult *On Apology*.

Step One: Acknowledge the Offense

The starting point of a Remorse Apology is a clear identification of the offensive behavior. Because this is a remorse apology, the offender is willing to label his behavior as offensive (Step Two). But before condemning the behavior, it must be articulated and recognized that it happened. Admitting that he did the offensive behavior requires the offender to overcome the temptation to rationalize or pretend it didn't happen. Admitting it happened stipulates that the behavior is now an agreed chapter in the history of this relationship.

As simple as this stage sounds, this is where the offender's defense mechanisms may undermine the execution. Lazare identifies common techniques offenders use to sabotage this stage. The offender has decided to apologize, but her execution is maddeningly inadequate because she hedges the statement acknowledging the offense. Lazare uses the phase, "a verbal sleight of hand"[15] to describe how these techniques may cause an unsuspecting victim to falsely perceive that he has been the beneficiary of a legitimate apology.

Vagueness is first technique employed to avoid acknowledging the offense. "Sorry for whatever I did" or "Sorry for that thing yesterday." The task is to name the inappropriate behavior. One female student described confronting her boyfriend who just apologized, but when asked, could not explain what he was apologizing for; he knows she was hurt and angry and apologized to try to make things better, but he did not have a clue how he hurt her. Naming the offense in specific detail assures the victim that the offender understands what behavior should not be repeated.

An example of the vague apology is the baseball player Paul Lo Duca's apology for using performance enhancing drugs. Two months after his name was listed as violator in Senator George Mitchell's report for Major League Baseball, Lo Duca issued the following statement through his team. "In regard to Senator Mitchell's Report, I apologize … for mistakes in judgment I made in the past." When he arrived at training camp, he offered the following comments. "You do something wrong in your life and you get away with it, you still have something inside you that burns. And, um, it's been a big relief for me to know that I've come to grips with it. That I made a mistake." Asked whether the Mitchell Report was accurate about him, Lo Duca said, "I'm not going to comment on that." When another reporter asked what he was apologizing for, Lo Duca replied, "Come on, bro. Next question."[16]

A second defensive technique is the conditional apology. "If I offended anyone, then I am sorry" or "Sorry if I offended anyone." The concept in the remorse apology is that I condemn my behavior. It doesn't matter if other people took offense. The offender's conscience is convicting him by telling him that he should not have behaved that way. By making the acknowledgement of the offense dependent on the victim, the offender is raising the question of whether the victim is being too sensitive. The offender is even creating the scenario where they are the generous one who offers an apology when it usually wouldn't be necessary, to meet the needs of the pathetically thin-skinned victim. The conditional apology is as much of an indictment of the victim as it is an admission of wrongdoing.

This dynamic is illustrated by Pope Benedict XVI's expression of regret to Muslims. Early in his papacy he included a quote in a speech saying, "Show me just what Muhammad brought that was new, and there you find things only evil and inhuman." Observers suggest that Pope Benedict's antagonistic speech is consistent with his 25 years prior to becoming Pope as an academic theologian defending the Christian faith. The Muslim community's reaction to the speech created a crisis. A scheduled trip to Turkey was in jeopardy, a predominantly Muslim country withdrew their ambassador to the Vatican as a protest, and four churches were bombed in Palestine's West Bank. Numerous Muslim leaders condemned the statement and called for a retraction.

In response the secretary of State for the Vatican issued a statement that included the following explanations.

> "In reiterating his respect and esteem for those who profess Islam, he hopes they will be helped to understand the correct meaning of his words . . . . The Holy Father thus sincerely regrets that certain passages of his address could have sounded offensive to the sensitivities of the Muslim faithful and should have been interpreted in a manner that in no way corresponds to his intentions." [17]

This is an example of a statement that avoids acknowledging an offense and, instead, accuses the victim of misunderstanding the "correct meaning of his words." The Vatican doesn't say that parts of the speech were offensive; instead the Pope regrets that they "could have sounded offensive." The statement insinuates that the offended either misunderstood the meaning of the Pope's words or that they are overly sensitive. The statement tries to smooth things over without acknowledging an offense.

A third defensive technique to avoid acknowledging the offense is attempting to minimize the behavior. "It isn't really a big deal, but I am sorry." The offender is sending a mixed message. On one hand, I shouldn't need to apologize. On the other hand, I am apologizing. This fails to clearly identify the behavior/belief/attitude that the offender believes is wrong. The offender appears to have mixed feelings about whether the behavior is wrong. One-way offenders minimize the offense is when they cite statistics to prove that it is unusual for them to make this mistake. They are seeking to divert attention away from the offensive behavior to their normally good behavior. As much as it pains the offender, the Remorse Apology requires a laser-like focus highlighting the bad behavior.

The final defensive technique to minimize acknowledging the offense is the use of the passive voice. "Mistakes were made" instead of "I made a mistake." Using the passive voice acknowledges the incident, but suggests it is the fault of the universe and forces beyond my control. Acknowledging the offense requires the offender to own the behavior or take responsibility for the incident. It not only happened, but I am responsible for it.

For many of us, the root of these defensive techniques is the desire to protect our pride. It is difficult to admit that we were wrong and behaved badly. This is true even after we have decided to "tell the truth to ourselves and others and take responsibility." As we commence with telling the truth, we might unintentionally compromise our confession with something like the techniques described above to maintain some of our dignity. This undermines the self-humiliation aspect of the apology and sometimes is the reason an apology is not accepted.

A student journal provides an explanation.

> So far, I have really enjoyed studying the theory of apology. I really think this class will be practically beneficial for me in any career I pursue in dispute resolution, my own personal life, and any alternative career paths I may encounter. Previously I had given little thought to how to formulate an apology and what all the intricacies could actually mean. I simply went through my life both giving and accepting any apology given to me without looking further into the structure, delivery, or underlying meaning of the apology. Specifically, this reading section and class lecture has sparked a fire to reflect on both the apologies I give and the apologies I receive.

The apologies I give are an easier starting point for revolutionizing the information regarding underlying meaning with apologies. For me, it is easier to point out the flaws in my own life than to potentially recognize that people who I hold so dearly could have not been honest with me. I know that I am a flawed human. I see it constantly throughout my day, but it's harder for me to think people who I have looked up to, modeled my life after, or divulged my deepest secrets to could not be the people I have made them out to be in my head.

When delivering my own apologies I realized that I tend to talk passively, stating things like "I am so sorry for the things that happened." Building on this, I realize I use the hypothetical a lot when I am giving apologies like, "I am so sorry if I hurt you," making the action I have done be up for debate that I actually did anything wrong. Looking deeper, I realize I tend to shift blame back onto the person I am apologizing to, stating apologies like, "I am really sorry I overreacted. I thought you were mad at me, so I reacted poorly." This statement may seem like it is innocent, but really I have communicated to them that it was your fault I overreacted.

When contemplating why I apologize in this way I realized it is because I apologize for things I am not actually sorry for. When giving an insincere apology it is inevitable that the apology will come out with some sort of deflection, like I have previously mentioned, because I am not actually sorry. My subconscious will find a way to deliver the apology so that it reflects my actual feelings that I have done nothing wrong. It makes sense to think why my apologies usually feel so empty when I say them because deep down they are just social tools to maintain my relationships.

There are a lot of sensitive people in my life and I have a known problem of being a people pleaser. I spend so much of my time and effort catering to the needs of the many people in my life, making sure our relationship is perfectly kept. I am not sure where this uncontrollable need to have every relationship be in perfect order comes from, but I do know that it leads me to do things I regret very often. People tend to walk all over me and I submit in fear of rocking the boat of our relationship. In the context of apologies, this means I offer countless apologies that I do not actually mean simply to ensure the relationship will have no damage.

I have known for a long time I have a lot of unhealthy relationships and a skewed perception of what friendship should look like, but up until this class I had never thought about how deceptive I have been to them. I apologize for things I am not even remotely sorry for just to keep up the other person's expectations of me. In doing this, I am actively and consistently deceiving them, making them think whatever behavior I have done is wrong and giving them a false security that both this behavior will never happen again, and the relationship is in a secure place.

I know I make my friends sound like these horrible people, but this characterization is mostly false. I need to work on being more honest in the way I handle conflict and really consider the weight of an apology before I throw it around carelessly. Submitted by an anonymous student, emphasis added.

Step Two: Express Remorse

Once the offender has identified the inappropriate behavior/attitude, she needs to condemn it. She needs to explain that she disagrees with the behavior and is angry at herself for doing it. She creates two personas: one that committed the unkind act and another that condemns the one who committed the unkind act. Expressing remorse is an attempt to persuade the victim that the persona who is condemning the unkind act is dominant and should be the one remembered as the true character of the person who was unkind.

Sharing remorse is the offender's opportunity to reveal that the offender has been punishing himself for the behavior. This is the time to share that he has been very upset about what he did; he couldn't eat and didn't sleep last night because he was so angry and disappointed with himself. He knows that he would be livid if someone did the same thing to him. This description of an offender punishing himself might help attend to some victims' instincts to retaliate in some way to teach the offender a lesson. Expressing remorse communicates that the offender is punishing himself and has learned his lesson.

Condemning one's own behavior is an act of humility. To admit to yourself and others that sometimes you are not the person you aspire to be requires the offender to acknowledge a more complex identity. The offender needs to admit that he committed the offense and that this is one aspect of himself that he does not admire. The expression of remorse requires the offender to condemn the parts of her personality that, in excess, injures others.

Step Three: Offer an Explanation

The offender must be careful that the explanation is not perceived as an excuse. The offender might emphasize condemning the offense, and then offer an explanation. A example is:

> There is no excuse for my behavior yesterday. It was unequivocally wrong. I was raised in an environment where that behavior was acceptable, and I am trying very hard to change this thinking and behavior. When I see how I have hurt you, I see how much more work I must do.

Be very careful to not allow the explanation to become a justification! The purpose of your message is to condemn the behavior. Explaining why or how it happened should always be done in the context of that the behavior was wrong and inexcusable! If the listener asks if you are excusing the behavior, assure them of your shared values that the behavior is not okay and suggest that the explanation for how it happened is not important. To be safe, the offender should ask the victim for permission to explain why and how this wrong happened. Only proceed with the explanation with the victim's permission.

Step Four: Offer Reparations

The offer of reparations shows that the offender is taking responsibility for the injury. If the offender is taking responsibility for the offense, he must offer to reimburse the victim for any financial loss caused by the offense. The injuries could be intangible, like a humiliation or lack of respect for the victim's time. Financial reparation may not be possible or adequate, so the offender might need to offer symbolic reparations. Examples might include offering to buy lunch to show the victim that the offender really recognizes the injury and feels bad about it.

If the injury is a humiliation that occurs in public, part of the symbolic reparations might be restoring the dignity of the victim in front of the same public audience. If the other people witness the insult, the offender needs to do her best to make sure they witness or are made aware of the apology. Their awareness of the apology hopefully reinstates the victim as a valuable and respected member of the community. Public apologies also establish that the behavior is inappropriate and should not be repeated by the offender or anyone else.

Symbolic reparations could be creative and designed to punish the offender. For example, if someone arrives 15 minutes late for a lunch appointment, the offender can inform the victim that he condemns this inconsiderate act and has decided to stay at the restaurant for 15 minutes after the victim leaves. If the victim says such a gesture is not necessary, the offender might insist that it is important to the offender.

Offering a Remorse Apology that does not include an offer of reparations sends a confusing message. The offender condemns the behavior and hates that he did it. Such a declaration without an offer of reparations can be criticized by the maxim, "talk is cheap." Neglecting to offer reparations signals that the offender may be telling the truth, but he is not taking responsibility for his actions.

While recognizing general elements is helpful, a student comment shows how each of us can have different standards.

> It is tricky to exhaustively define the aspects of apology as was attempted in class. Each apology situation is unique in circumstances and in regard to the personalities of the people involved. However, considering the difficulty of defining apology, I feel that the above categories do a good job. I see more issue with the way that "failures" are defined.

Perhaps it is <u>just my personal inclination, but I might actually accept an apology that is</u> <u>vague or conditional, depending upon the situation. For me, the apology doesn't</u> <u>necessarily fail altogether if it has these qualities. Then again, this might be due to the</u> <u>fact that I am very lenient and laid-back when it comes to others apologizing to me.</u> In fact, I feel that it's usually exhausting to hold onto past transgressions, and if I see that someone made a good-hearted attempt to apologize and I feel that I can let go, then I genuinely do. In my experience an explanation can help as long as it's not seen as someone simply justifying his/her actions and not actually apologizing at all.

In addition, I don't see reparations (when they are available) as necessary every time. For me—most of the time—all that is necessary for the apology to go over well is an offer to replace/repair the damage caused. I will often insist that the reparation is not necessary— but it is the fact that an attempt was made that is key. If the damage/mess is very slight, I might not even be upset if the offender doesn't offer to help/repair it.

<u>A lot of it depends on the general attitude/tone of the offender. It's not so much about</u> <u>what is said—it's how it is said. If I can hear the genuine remorse/sincerity in the</u> <u>offender's voice, I instantly soften. Again, this might be a reflection of my own</u> <u>tendencies, which many do not share. It's possible that my tendencies aren't in my own</u> <u>best interest—perhaps I get less respect as a result. Maybe it's "not right" for me to</u> <u>accept apologies so willingly. But then again, who's to say that I shouldn't feel the way I</u> <u>feel?</u> Submitted by Helen Supanich, emphasis added.

2.32 How to Offer a Regret Apology

The regret apology acknowledges their behavior injured another, but believes their actions were appropriate. A purely empathetic apology is appropriate when there is no question that the apologizer is innocent of contributing to injury. The regret apology is reserved for instances where actions injure another, but the actor does not believe he did anything wrong.

As discussed above, there are times when the responsibility for the injury is complicated. The accused cannot honestly accept responsibility because they are reasonably uncertain of her role. The injury is clear and maybe significant. The regret apology is the humane acknowledgement of sadness over the victim's suffering, but clearly expressed, includes an honest reservation about their level of responsibility. The apology can include regret for not being able to prevent the harm.

A sample statement by the hospital and doctors in the medical malpractice example described above might be as follows.

We are very sorry that the patient will suffer serious and permanent injuries because we could not diagnose the cause of the symptoms sooner. We are in the medical profession because we want to help patients heal and, in this instance, we failed. We hate the fact that we failed. The patient is a good person and now has terrible permanent injuries. We assure you that we did our best and followed established medical protocols in seeking a diagnosis. We are so sorry for this outcome!

This apology only offers partial satisfaction to the victim. Remember Robbennolt's research showing that apologies are twice as likely to be accepted if they include acceptance of responsibility in addition to expressions of sympathy. Her research demonstrated that only expressing sympathy reduces the likelihood of accepting a settlement offer compared to not giving any apology.[18] The apologizer must be aware of this danger when deciding to offer a regret apology. This knowledge may influence the clarity of such an apology.

A current event example of a regret apology is provided by Northwestern University Psychology Professor J. Michael Bailey.[19] Bailey arranged an optional, after class demonstration for his Human Sexuality class which consisted of a live sex act. After the president of the university called for an investigation and said he was "troubled and disappointed by what occurred," Bailey issued an apology statement.

The statement defended the demonstration as relevant to a topic in his course and noted that the observers were students older than 18 who were "legally capable of voting, enlisting in the military, and consuming pornography." He also complained that his critics condemned the demonstration but did not illuminate their reasoning. The statement also expressed regret for "the effect that this has had on Northwestern University's reputation. I regret upsetting so many people in this particular manner. I apologize." He also assured that nothing like this has occurred before and that he will not allow anything like it to happen again. His message is a good example of a person who believes their behavior was not wrong but apologizes for the injuries it created.

2.33 How to Offer a Social Harmony Apology

A clearly delivered Social Harmony apology explains that the offender does not believe he has done anything wrong but will apologize for the sake of the relationship. Returning to the example of the extended family holiday gathering, a distant relative is creating a scene by demanding an apology for a comment about politics. The offender's honest and clearly delivered social harmony apology might consist of the following.

You (the victim) should know that I don't believe I did anything wrong. I think I should be allowed to be open and honest about my political views with my family, even though most people in this room are supporting the other party. Since this is a family gathering, I think we should all accept each other, despite our differences, even over something as important as politics. However, I also think it is important for me to show my love for everyone in this room. I care more about the unity of this family and the joy of being together for this celebration than I do about being right. I love you Uncle John and am sorry for offending you with my comment. I hope you will forgive me and that we can all return to enjoying being together today.

The force behind the social harmony apology is the shared importance of the relationship but does not communicate shared values about the behavior that the victim found offensive. Uncle John in the above example wants the relative to have shared values about politics or about not discussing politics at family gatherings. The sample apology makes it clear that the "offender" does not share either of those values.

So, acknowledging the offense in the social harmony apology is difficult because the offender does not agree that she has been offensive. Likewise, honestly communicating remorse is complicated. The "offender" cannot honestly express remorse for her behavior; she can honestly express remorse for hurting others. (So now we understand the, "Sorry I hurt your feelings" apology as a social harmony apology.) Assuming the goal is a social harmony apology that hopes to meet the needs of the victim, the "offender" can approximate the remorse apology by clearly stating the behavior that victim is objecting to and promising forbearance.

Forbearance promises to not repeat the behavior. The "offender" may be willing to make this commitment universally or it may be limited to when the victim is present. If the offender is going to refrain only when the victim is present, the offender will need to decide whether it is necessary or helpful to communicate the limited scope of this commitment. Not disclosing the limited scope of the commitment may be planting seeds of misunderstanding. Promising to not repeat the behavior might give the victim the perception that the offender is admitting that the behavior is inappropriate.

This version of the social harmony at the family gathering might consist of the following.

I have clearly upset you, Uncle John, by bringing disagreement about politics into our family gathering. I promise to not do this in the future (when you are in the room?). I hope you will forgive me and that we can all return to enjoying this day.

Substituting forbearance for remorse with an intention to mislead the victim fulfills Professor Taft's worst nightmares regarding ethical uses of apology. It isn't much better, but the other option for delivering a social harmony apology is to simply say you are sorry without explanation or clarity about the meaning. In this instance, the offender has offered a vague apology that can mean different things to different people. This intentional ambiguity might "meet the needs of the victim" because they did not probe the actual meaning. Crisis averted, conflict resolved! As mentioned earlier, there are legitimate concerns about the foundation for this resolution. But a student comment reminds us of its place.

> This week's class on how to apologize really convicted me to many of the conflicts and situations I am currently dealing with in my life. When we covered what constituted a "proper" (Remorse) apology, and what constituted a shallow apology, I found that most of the time my apologies were indeed very shallow by the definitions highlighted in class. This may once again go back to my cultural experiences growing up in Singapore, where the collective good of the group is prioritized over the integrity of the individual.
>
> This raised a question for me: what is the actual intention behind an apology? I believe for the most part the "ideal" apology here in America is made with the intention of "coming clean" with the other party and having personal clarity and absolution of guilt. In contract, back where I am from I found that most apologies are made from the perspective that seeks to restore peace in the relationship. Ultimately, the emotional needs of the individual for integrity and clarity must be cast aside to produce an apology that would minimize conflict. In a sense, I feel that I come from a culture that treats apology in a far more pragmatic manner.
>
> This led me to wonder if I was being unethical in my perspective of apology. Though Dr. Robinson at multiple points did highlight that every apology has its function and the hierarchy that it is placed under is usually fluid in nature and subject to the situation, I could not shake the intuition that I personally had an unethical view of the purpose behind saying sorry—that being that it is meant for practical purposes. I hope that subsequent classes help offer some clarity on this matter. I feel that it very directly applies to many experiences that I have had up to this point and would add a great deal of meaning to them. Submitted by Alistair Chong, emphasis added.

Apple's apology to Chinese consumers could be viewed as a social harmony apology in a commercial context. Government controlled media led a two-week campaign severely criticizing Apple's repair policy. They accused Apple of arrogance, greed and "throwing its weight around." The government-controlled People's Daily ran an editorial with the headline, "Strike down Apple's incomparable arrogance."

In response Apple CEO Tim Cook posted a statement in Chinese on its website confessing that the complaints had prompted "deep reflection" and persuaded the company of the need to revamp its repair policies and boost its communication with Chinese consumers. His statement continued,

"We've come to understand through this process that because of our poor communication, some have come to feel that Apple's attitude is arrogant and that we don't care about or value feedback from the consumer. For the concerns and misunderstandings passed on to the consumer, we express our sincere apologies."

I use this an example of a social harmony apology because Apple was accused of being arrogant. It didn't admit to that accusation but needed to offer some kind of apology to make peace with the Chinese media. Its sincere apologies are offered for "the concerns and misunderstandings." The only acknowledged wrong is not communicating better. The LA Times offers another analysis of Apple's apology.

"Although Apple enjoys strong support from Chinese consumers, the vehemence of the attacks and the importance of the Chinese market appeared to have persuaded the Cupertino, California, company to smooth its relations with Chinese consumers and authorities."[20]

2.34 How to Offer an Externally Motivated Apology

A clearly delivered Externally Motivated apology explains that the offender is apologizing to avoid some type of punishment. (The offender may or may not believe they have done anything wrong.) The offender has a choice whether to name the potential punishment. Sometimes the punishment may be social, like retaliation or abandonment, which results in a blurring between social harmony and externally motivated apologies. There is a subtle difference between an offender recognizing that we need each other (social harmony) compared to I need you (externally motivated). Some punishments are not social, like paying fine or penalty, which clearly differentiates the externally motivated and social harmony apology.

It will be the exception when clearly explaining non-social externally motivated reasons for an apology will meet the needs of the victim. There are no shared values, no assurance of future safety, and no restoration of the victim's dignity. It is more likely that the victim will respond that the offensive behavior showed the offender's true character and that this character deserves to be condemned and punished.

At least the social harmony apology had some virtuous value: to affirm the hopefully shared value of the importance of the relationship. The fully exposed externally motivated apology reveals an entirely selfish agenda. There may be some instances where the victim will appreciate the honesty in the explanation. Usually, the externally motivated apology will need to be delivered with limited clarity.

An LA Times Editorial affirmed the value of an externally motivated apology involving the massacre at Srebrenica. In 2010, the Serbian Government offered an apology for the 1995 massacre of 8000 Muslim men and boys in the region of Srebrenica, Bosnia. The resolution passed by the Serbian legislature "strongly condemns the crime committed against the Bosnian Muslim population of Srebrenica," and offers condolences and an apology to families of the victims. The LA Times described that "Critics decried the resolution as a cynical gesture driven by economics and calculated to satisfy the European Union, which demands that Serbs come clean on war crimes before it can join. ... Some Bosnian Muslim leaders and relatives of the victims say the declaration is too little, too late..." The Editorial Board embraces that sometimes externally motivated apologies have value with the following statement.

> "Still, we consider this a huge step forward, one that hopefully advances the process of reconciliation. In politics, the right thing often is done for the wrong reasons. More important is that the right thing gets done. It is never too late to address crimes of the past. This is a good and welcome start."[21]

2.35 Essential Terms of an Apology

Recent research investigated which elements of an apology were most important when trust had been violated. Apology in this study was defined as consisting of the following six components: expression of regret, explanation of the violation, acknowledgement of responsibility for the violation, declaration of repentance, offer of repair, and request for forgiveness. One of the conclusions was that the acknowledgement of responsibility and an offer of repair were more important than the other elements.[22] One way to interpret these findings is, when all is said and done, the victim wants to know if the offender is taking responsibility for the behavior and going to make it right. Explanations, repentance/forbearance, and even remorse are nice, but in the end does the offender own the bad behavior and offer reparations?

While this was the general result of apology research, a student journal comment reminds us that each person will have her personal perspective on essential terms and elements.

> I have been really wrestling with the content of this class for the last couple weeks because I have been in the midst of a conflict. In this conflict, I was the one hurt, and the person who hurt me is someone who I have to serve in my job, but someone I also have a position of authority over. Additionally, it is also someone my husband and I had considered a friend and had welcomed into our home. This week I have been processing the need to forgive without an apology, and have done so, though there is still some soreness to the relationship because of the incident. Because of the nature of our relationship, I have also been wondering what emotions this person may be thinking and why an apology is not likely.

There are two reasons I don't think an apology is likely. The first relates to part of our text that we read and talked about in class. On page 106 it said: "Rather than accept responsibility and telling the truth, behaviors that could have restored the relationship, the offender chooses to preserve their view of themselves and avoid punishment." I think that because I am in a position of authority over him, despite the fact that he probably knows what to do to restore the relationship, he probably does not want to lower the view of himself and his behavior, which could lead to punishment now or in the future. This fear is not rational or based in how I treat him, but I wonder if this dynamic plays a part in why he wouldn't apologize.

The second reason, which we also talked about in class, is that sometimes in the course of an apology it becomes apparent that there is a need to offer reparations. In this particular case, the reparations are obvious and something he is adamant not to do. I wonder if the fear of having to make reparations makes people not offer any kind of apology.

I thought it was interesting that one quality of an apology is whether it meets the needs of the victim. I know for me any type of apology would be enough. I want reparations, but don't necessarily need it. However, I would still like an apology or at least recognition that what he did was hurtful. I suppose the two aspects I am looking for are acknowledging the offense and remorse, if not for the actions, for the way the actions hurt me. It makes me wonder about apologies in general - is there a set apology that is best in all situations, or is it highly situation dependent? The focus in class on the needs of the "victim" was interesting, and I think apologies would be far more effective if people recognize those needs.

One of the largest obstacles for apologies is pride. The ability to recognize the needs of the victim takes humility, and it takes humility to approach the other person to apologize. I have been realizing that not receiving an apology can also take humility. Knowing that I was the one who needed to forgive rather than apologize made it that much harder to humble myself, but that was crucial in my ability to forgive. I am planning to address the conflict with the other person and express forgiveness, but in preparation for that moment I have had to recognize my need to approach it with a lot of humility. Perhaps it is my desire for social harmony, (that is one of my apologies of choice), but forgiveness is something that can be offered without an apology, but those needs may need to be met by an outside source. For me, that is related to my faith, and recognition of how I have been forgiven by God. Submitted by Hilary Stump, emphasis added.

2.4 Spilt Water Exercise

<u>**Spilt Water Exercise**</u>
<u>**Under which of the following circumstances will you apologize and why?**</u>
<u>**What kind of apology will you give and how clear will it be in each circumstance?**</u>
<u>**Practice delivering your apologies!**</u>

You are the last to sit down at a round dinner table at a social function. The other guests have left you the seat in front of a table leg, so you accidentally bump the table when you scoot your seat in. Someone at the table has their glass/cup near the edge of the table so the bump causes it to spill on them.

1. A small amount of water spills on someone across the table who you have never met; he/she over reacts and is really nasty to you because of it.
2. Same as 1. above, but he/she is being really gracious about it.
3. Same as 1. above, but he/she is sitting next to you.
4. Same as 1. above, but he/she is a very close friend.
5. Same as 1. above, but it is coffee instead of water.

Notice whether the following variables affected your approach to apology.

The victim is gracious or nasty.
The amount of future contact you will have with the victim.
The degree of positive or negative history with the victim.
The extent of damages suffered by the victim.

While these variables may affect our approach to apology for some of us, why do they matter if an apology is "Telling the truth to ourselves and others and taking responsibility for our mistakes."

ENDNOTES

1. *See generally* Lazare, *On Apology*; *see also* Jennifer K. Robbennolt, *Apologies and Legal Settlement: An Empirical Examination*, 102 MICH. L. REV. 460, 485-86 (2003).

2. *See* Lazare, *On Apology*, 44-74.

3. Robbennolt, *Apologies and Legal Settlement*, 477-78 (describing similar dynamics when summarizing "equity theory" and referencing descriptions by Jean Hampton and sociologist Tavuchis).

4. Edmund Sanders, "Israel refuses to apologize to Turkey for flotilla deaths," *Los Angeles Times*, August 18, 2011.

5. Robbennolt, *Apologies and Legal Settlement*, 478-79 (describing a number of articles supporting this point).

6. *Id.*

7. *See* Lee Taft, *Apology Subverted: The Commodification of Apology*, 109 YALE L.J. 1135, 1138 (2000).

8. *Id.* at 1142.

9. *Id.* at 1158.

10. Robbennolt, *Apologies and Legal Settlement*, 469

11. Nicholas Tavuchis, *Mea Culpa: A Sociology of Apology and Reconciliation* (Stanford: Stanford University Press, 1991), 3.

12. Erving Goffman, *Relations in Public: Microstudies of the Public Order*, (New York: Basic Books, 1971), 113.

13. Hiroshi Wagatsuma and Arthur Rosett, "The Implications of Apology: Law and Culture in Japan and the United States," *Law & Society Review* 20, no. 4 (1986): 469-70.

14. Lazare, *On Apology*, 107-33.

15. *Id.* at 102.

16. Bill Shaikin and Dylan Hernandez, "Lo Duca offers apology of sorts," *Los Angeles Times*, February 17, 2008.

17. Tracy Wilkinson, "Pope Is Regretful That His Speech Angered Muslims," *Los Angeles Times*, September 17, 2006.

18. Robbennolt, *Apologies and Legal Settlement*, 485-86.

19. Jodi S. Cohen and Liam Ford, "Professor apologizes for live sex demo," *Los Angeles Times*, March 6, 2011.

20. David Barboza and Nick Wingfield, "Pressured by China, Apple Apologizes for Warranty Policies," *The New York Times*, April 1, 2013.

21. Editorial, "An apology for Srebrenica," *Los Angeles Times*, April 2, 2010.

22. Roy Lewicki, Beth Polin, and Robert. B Lount, Jr., "An Exploration of the Structure of Effective Apologies," *Negotiation and Conflict Management Research* 9(2):177-196 (May 2016).

Chapter Three

Advising Others (and Yourself) to Apologize

3.1 Introduction

3.2 General Concepts

3.3 A Pragmatic Evaluation of the Risks of Apologizing and Not Apologizing

3.4 Risks of Moral and Psychological Consequences of Not Apologizing

3.5 Advising Apology for NYPD Detaining Wrong Person

"It's just their little way of saying, 'Sorry we wrecked the planet.'"

3.1 Introduction

Advising others about apologizing depends on the relationship between the advisor and the person who might want to consider giving an apology. The intensity of delivery of any advice about giving an apology is different when the advisor is a parent, teacher, clergy, mental health counselor, attorney, spouse, or friend. In addition to considering the various roles of the advisor, we need to examine the amount of trust and rapport. For example, a parent might command a toddler to give an apology (external motivation) that would be inappropriate for most other relationships. The relationship dictates if advice can be given and how it should be delivered.

Blind Leader Case Study

Submitted by an anonymous student

My sophomore year I studied abroad with fifty of my peers in Florence, Italy. Two of our peers were chosen to be our in-house Resident Advisors, and we looked to Bob and Sue to be our leaders and enforcers of community standards in the house. As the year progressed, it became very clear to us as a population that our male RA Bob had been blatantly breaking the community standards he was supposed to be upholding - i.e. coming in past curfew, intoxication in the house, etc. The worst part about this was that he was documenting our peers for breaking the same community standards that he was breaking; the only difference was that he was his abusing his power because in short, who was watching the watcher?

One of my classmates began a grassroots vigilante campaign against Bob, and she confronted him with a list of incidences where he had broken the same rules that he was writing others up for, and she told him point-blank that if he did not issue a public apology to the program at house meeting and alter his hypocritical behavior that she would go to our program director.

Bob obliged, and his apology was flippant, something along the lines of, "People have been talking about things that I may or may not have done to hurt them. If I have done anything to hurt you or to hurt this program, please accept this public apology." It was incredibly vague, possessed not an inkling of transparency nor remorse, and of course, my classmate who had confronted him was furious. She - and the rest of us - saw his refusal to acknowledge and spell out exactly what he had done wrong as disrespect towards our feelings and our community. Those who had been written up by Bob went to our program director and told her the truth, and he ended up being removed from our program via suspension.

If I had been Bob's apology consultant, I would have taken him through the thought process we discussed in class and asked him, "Are people going to find out? Who is directly impacted by your confession? Who is directly impacted by your omission?" The answer to the first hypothetical question would have been yes, as Bob knew that our classmate knew the extent of his wrongdoing. I would have encouraged him to apologize fully by outlining why others were upset in order to nip it in the bud.

By coming forward quickly, completely, and transparently, I believe Bob could have been spared his suspension because all we really wanted to hear as a house was an acknowledgment of his actions. By omitting and refusing to admit exactly what he was at fault for, he incited the opposite response he expected. This is a perfect instance of when an apology is not enough to mend because it is a dirty one.

The purpose of this journal is not to shame Bob. Thanks to this class, I am just now able to put words to exactly why his apology fell short, four years after my time in Florence. I cannot count the times I have offered dirty apologies without verbalizing exactly what it is I have done wrong. Apology is confession, and it is difficult, and I cannot hold anyone else in contempt for failing at something that I fail at every day. I was convicted by our conversation in class, and I want to be the type of person that coaches others to take responsibility for their actions, the type of person that creates an environment of integrity over secrecy, the type of person that sways others towards moral and ethical considerations.
1

3.2 General Concepts

Many factors contribute to the complexity of advising others to apologize. The first is the potential moral ramifications of giving an apology.[2] The remorse apology is a confession that at the least, social norms have been violated and at the most, a fundamental human right to dignity has been transgressed.[3] The apologizer is admitting wrongdoing, which inevitably involves morals. Social harmony and externally motivated apologies lack this moral foundation. The potential moral dimension of an apology is what makes misunderstanding about the true intent of the apologizer so dangerous because it is easy to misread another person's moral compass.

A second factor that contributes to the complexity of advising others to apologize is the need to respect the autonomy of the person potentially giving the apology. The "advisor" gives advice, but the response and decision to execute an apology belongs to the person receiving the advice. Especially because the decision to give an apology has a potential moral dimension, the injurer retains the responsibility for his response to the injury. The advisor should be cautious not to project their moral values on the other person.

When respecting another's autonomy, another factor to consider is whether the advice has been requested. Some older friends shared their approach to advising their adult children, and they told me "don't share your opinion unless they ask!" So, respecting another person's autonomy is different when they ask for your advice. They have exercised their autonomy by inviting your input.

A student's journal is illustrative.

> As the class discussed situations in which it may be appropriate to offer advice, I was faced with my own weaknesses in this area. In general, I would say that I am often hasty in my offering of advice. Perhaps it is the solution-oriented part of me or perhaps it is my own arrogance that fuels this tendency. I don't know.

I am still engaged in a process of self-discovery and I sense that it will continue for the remainder of my life. However, I do acknowledge that my tendency to offer advice that may have not been requested is problematic. I can point to several situations in which I prioritized my diagnosis of a conflict over that person's actual experience within the situation. As I consider these past situations, I fear that my eagerness to fix the conflict had the unfortunate result of neglecting that person's emotional and psychological needs.

Recently I was in a situation in which a close friend of mine was explaining a stressful situation in her life. Because she initiated the conversation with me, I think that I subconsciously accepted that as an invitation to apply my own analysis to her problem. In reality, I suspect that she just wanted me to listen. I garnered this conclusion for the general silence and lack of response demonstrated by her after I had delivered (what I thought was) a thorough interpretation of her situation. I misinterpreted her needs and prioritized my own egotistical need to be the one to provide the solution. I regret my contribution to that conversation and, if given the opportunity, I would certainly approach it differently.[4]

The respect for the moral aspect of an apology and consideration of the autonomy of the person who might consider apologizing explain why the parent of a toddler is in a unique position to command an apology. The parent is responsible for the moral development of the toddler. Hopefully, as the child matures the conversation about apology between parent and child evolves to encourage and assist the child in developing empathy. If the parent can enable the child to realize that his behavior hurt others, the child can learn and use a remorse apology. In the early stages, the child may not be capable of empathy, so most parents settle for simply educating the child about what behaviors are unacceptable. The toddler's externally motivated apology accomplishes the task. As the child becomes an adult, the parent recognizes that the child needs to exercise greater autonomy and take responsibility for how he responds when he injures others.

This also explains why the amount of trust and rapport between the advisor and potential apologizer affects the kind of advice provided when the advisor is not a parent. It is possible for a teacher, clergy, therapist, lawyer, spouse, or friend to have a decade's long relationship where they have developed absolute trust by always demonstrating a commitment to the best interests of the other person. The rapport and trust between the people allow the advisor to be more transparent and direct.

If someone asks for assistance from a very trusted advisor regarding an apology, the advisor might strongly recommend an apology without violating the autonomy of the person who asked her opinion. In contrast, when our advice about apologizing has not been requested, it is important that we share our perspective in a non-threatening and non-judgmental way. It is wise to begin by asking permission to share your thoughts about a sensitive situation.

The combination of some of the above factors is presented in the following chart.

	Advice Requested	Advice Not Requested
High Rapport	Advise Freely	Ask Permission
Low Rapport	Advise Cautiously	Don't Advise

The next section will focus on the role of friend and mentor. The professional roles for clergy, therapist, and lawyer will not be addressed here because they need to be addressed considering the expectations and professional ethics for those professions. People considering apologizing sometimes ask for guidance from non-professional mentors and friends. The next section hopes to equip the reader when he is giving non-professional advice about apology. The following discussion will also lay a foundation for the discussion of professional roles and will assist the reader's internal deliberations when he is serving as his own advisor.

3.3 A Pragmatic Evaluation of the Risks of Apologizing and Not Apologizing

Assume a situation where advice from the friend or mentor is requested. Also assume that the requestor is clearly responsible for doing something wrong. Jonathan Cohen shares a similar scenario in his article *Advising Clients to Apologize*. A friend tells the advisor that he was texting while driving and rear-ended the car in front of him. The friend asks the advisor if he should call the driver of the other car with any of the following statements:

1. ask the driver of the other car if they are okay;
2. apologize for hitting their car; and/or
3. offer to pay for the damage to the other person's car?

We will analyze this situation from a pragmatic perspective first and then from a moral perspective. I have observed that pragmatic considerations cause Pepperdine law and dispute resolution students to be hesitant to recommend asking if the driver is okay, much less apologizing or offering to fix the car. The students explain that they fear the costs of admitting wrongdoing. Their concern is that if they encourage their friend to apologize, or even ask if the other driver is okay, they are exposing their friend to a big risk. Their reaction is the same even when the scenario assumes stop and go traffic and thus a minor impact. Loyalty to their friend results in recommending a "wait and see" strategy.

The main risk is that an apology will be interpreted as accepting legal liability. Courts frequently allow evidence of statements made by drivers to help prove negligence. If an apology explicitly or implicitly accepts responsibility for the consequences of the act, the advisor is concerned that her friend may be exploited. Even if the damage to the other car is minor, the driver may claim exaggerated whiplash injuries and demand substantially more compensation for the alleged injuries to his body. The advisor might be willing to recommend volunteering to pay reasonable reparations (especially if they appear to be minor?), but what if the injured person is unreasonable? The advisor does not want to advise her friend to apologize and then see her friend held hostage in an extended legal battle because her friend has accepted legal liability, and the victim is seeking exorbitant compensation.

An anonymous student journal provides an example.

> One experience that immediately came to mind during this class was one that I had back when I was in the Singaporean Armed Forces serving time as an officer. For most of my time as an officer I served as a Platoon Commander for basic military training, basically the "boot camp" aspect of the military. Understandably, most of the interactions between commanders and recruits involved yelling derogatory terms and dishing out punishment in order to train them. As commanders we were given a specific set of guidelines to what was acceptable and unacceptable (or "too far") when it came to handling recruits. Most of the time, when commanders breached these guidelines —which they often did- it would be swept under the rug; most recruits were not familiar enough with the guidelines to report on their commanders.
>
> However, there was one instance where one of my peers (a fellow officer) came into physical contact with a recruit while punishing him. This recruit complained to his parents, who in turn reported on the officer to the school commandant. I remember how the situation escalated into a massive mess. But I also remember how the officer was told by his superiors to not under any circumstance apologize for what he did, as such would result in his immediate prosecution due to admission of guilt. I remember being very uncomfortable with that, as I personally felt that he had indeed overstepped his boundaries and an apology would give the parents and recruit closure.[5]

In addition to fearing getting sued, a second pragmatic risk is that an apology might violate the friend's duties in the contract for insurance. An insurance policy commits the insurance company to pay for the consequences of certain occurrences, like if a car driver's negligence causes a collision. The person buying the insurance agrees to assist the insurance company in defending any claim that the insurance company might be expected to pay. If the person buying insurance violates his duty to assist the insurance company in defending a claim, the insurance company may be relieved of its duty to pay the claim. Thus, if an insured driver gets out of the car at an accident scene, or makes a subsequent phone call, and apologizes with a full acceptance of responsibility, he may have voided his rights under his insurance policy. Some advisors are reluctant to advise apologizing because they fear risking the friend's protections under an insurance policy.

So, the pragmatic advisor might consider the certainty of liability when determining whether to recommend an apology. What is the likelihood that the other side will be able to prove my friend is responsible for the injury without an apology? If liability is clear, then my friend hasn't "given away anything" by apologizing. If liability is unclear, then an apology is premature, and an investigation is needed to establish relative percentages of responsibility for causing the injury. The more complicated situation that will be discussed later is if responsibility clearly belongs to my friend, but the other side will have a difficult time proving it.

Another consideration for the pragmatic advisor is the ability to assess the consequences of the injury. Before an advisor recommends accepting responsibility for an injury, he will probably want to determine the scope of those responsibilities. The advisor may assist the friend in quantifying the amount of likely damages so the friend makes an informed decision including the likely cost of choosing to give an apology that would include an offer of reparations. This analysis should include the likelihood that the injured person may be opportunistic and try to exaggerate their damages. If the injured person is known, then the injurer has a chance to predict the likelihood he will be reasonable or exploitive. If the injured person is a random stranger, the injurer's (or his advisor's) assumption about what percentage of the general public is exploitive may impact the pragmatic decision to apologize. This analysis should also consider whether any insurance is available to cover the cost of the injury and how an apology might affect the friend's rights under the insurance contract.

While the pragmatist's analysis of the risks of apologizing might be helpful, it is incomplete. The pragmatist should also consider the **risks of not apologizing.** If the pragmatic analysis only considers the risks of apologizing, the result will be biased towards a decision to not apologize. The objective pragmatic analysis needs to consider both the ramifications of choosing to not apologize and choosing to apologize.

The discussion about the risks of not apologizing begins with the concept of "the second injury."[6] The first injury is whatever violation of social norms or basic human dignity occurred. Stuff happens and everyone makes mistakes of commission and omission. The human condition is unavoidably imperfect. We will all perpetrate the first injury to others, often reserving the most hurtful for the inner circle to whom we are closest. The second injury is the failure to apologize.

When a person recognizes that he has been the victim of an offense, his dignity looks for acknowledgement and recognition that he has been treated inappropriately. An apology provides this recognition and helps the victim recover from the first injury and avoid the second injury. The failure to apologize signals to the victim that the perpetrator believes he is entitled to the offensive behavior. The lack of apology ratifies the offensive behavior. The ratification is the second injury.

The second injury incites the victim to act because it tends to be a second source of anger and outrage. Not only did the perpetrator injure the victim, but he has ratified his behavior as acceptable. The victim is likely to question the abilities of the perpetrator's parents and conclude that someone needs to teach this person a lesson. The offender needs to learn that he shouldn't treat people like this. Some victims begin to explore if there are ways for them to punish the offender.

This is illustrated by a letter written by a Beverly Hills personal injury attorney.[7] The letter states:

> My clients are extremely upset at you and your mother's incredible lack of concern and common decency at the accident scene by failing to make any inquiry whatsoever as to their injuries. Both my clients are long-time well-respected members of the community, and if not made 100% whole as to their property damage, medical bills, and pain and suffering, they will use their very deep pockets to prosecute their claims against you to the fullest extent possible. Perhaps next time you will behave like human beings, not incredibly rude jerks.

Remember, if the offender humbles herself by apologizing, the victim often does not feel the need to punish or humble the offender. The apology demonstrates that the offenders understand that their behavior was unacceptable and that they are punishing themselves. But if the offenders refuse to humble themselves, some victims take on the task of teaching them a lesson.

A student journal insightfully describes these dynamics.

> The most sound pragmatic evaluation of risks in apologizing revolves around the idea of liability. When I first did the reading this idea seemed like the most valid risk associated with apologizing. The example given was about someone who was obviously at fault in a car accident not apologizing because they did not want to be held culpable for the damages . . .. When we discussed this in class it became clear to me that by not apologizing and taking responsibility in a situation that was so completely one person's fault, the offender begins to lose his social credibility.
>
> As a society, we seem to operate on some kind of invisible social stock that determines if we are a good person and further determines if this person deserves grace, understanding, or special consideration. When someone in the previously mentioned situation does not apologize for something they are clearly responsible for, their stock loses serious value and decreases the chance of the victim having any kind of mercy on or love for them. We discussed in class, and in the reading, that the victim's response is sometimes determined by the offender's response, or lack of response.

A victim is likely to demand whatever reparations they are entitled to, especially if the offender fails to take responsibility. Sometimes the victim will even demand more reparations than actually fits the original offense because now they have experienced a second injury in the offender's act of not apologizing. Furthermore, a victim is very likely to give the offender grace and forgiveness if the offender takes responsibility for his actions.[8]

This leads to a second concept of a tragic cycle that is easily described in the context of the physician-patient relationship.[9] Assume a physician makes an error that injures the patient. The physician is embarrassed and afraid of being sued. Instead of apologizing to the patient, his fear and embarrassment cause him to withdraw and avoid the patient. Proximity to a person he injured without an apology to is awkward. The patient perceives the doctor's withdrawal as a sign that the doctor either doesn't know about the injury or doesn't care. Worst yet, the patient may interpret the doctor's lack of apology as a second injury and may take it upon himself to teach the doctor a lesson. These perceptions make the patient mad at the doctor and increase the likelihood that the patient will seek out a lawyer and sue the doctor. The tragic cycle occurs when the doctor decides to withdraw instead of to lean in and apologize. Withdrawing contributes to the very outcome the doctor was trying to avoid.

This is well documented in the medical field. Both the Lexington Veterans Hospital and the University of Michigan Health Systems have documented significant reductions in number of medical malpractice cases going to court and the amounts of time and money needed to resolve those complaints after adopting full disclosure and candor policies. Thirteen years after Lexington Veterans Hospital adopted an "honesty program," it has settled with patients and families 170 times and gone to court three times. The average payout was $16,000 compared with $98,000 at other Veterans hospitals.[10] Five years after adopting a disclosure and candor policy, the University of Michigan Health System accomplished the following results:

1. pending claims and lawsuits dropped from 262 to 104;
2. the average legal expense per claim dropped from $48,000 to $21,000; and
3. the length of time it takes to process a case dropped from 20 months to 10 months.[11]

The effectiveness of reducing lawsuits by admitting to fault and apologizing has been proven beyond the healthcare arena. The healing and money saving power of an apology is evident in the mediation program initiated by the law care products producer Toro Company in 1995. Toro was tired of the time and fees associated with the "litigate everything" attitude that was prevalent in the corporate defense world, which would cost Toro $60,000-$100,000 before they even reached the courthouse steps. Toro sought to put a human face to their company by putting their best foot forward and sending a qualified and knowledgeable company representative directly to the would-be plaintiff to listen and learn about the harm done to that individual. Most times, the person injured wants to tell their story so that they can be heard, and if Toro believes that it was Toro's fault, it will offer a reasonable settlement or non-binding mediation.[12]

The healing and money saving power of an apology is evident in the mediation program initiated by the law care products producer Toro Company in 1995. Toro was tired of the time and fees associated with the "litigate everything" attitude that was prevalent in the corporate defense world, which would cost Toro $60,000-$100,000 before they even reached the courthouse steps. Toro sought to put a human face to their company by putting their best foot forward and sending a qualified and knowledgeable company representative directly to the would-be plaintiff to listen and learn about the harm done to that individual. Most times, the person injured wants to tell their story so that they can be heard, and if Toro believes that it was Toro's fault, it will offer a reasonable settlement or non-binding mediation.

The second injury concern might best be remembered by the saying, "Many people can forgive a mistake, but not a cover up!"

Besides the victim, the adviser should consider how others might view the injurer. An injurer who chooses to not apologize may not make a good impression on an ultimate adjudicator: jury, judge, arbitrator or supervisor. Not inquiring into the wellbeing of the other driver will be portrayed by the injured or his representatives as heartless and uncaring. If liability is clear, the failure to accept responsibility may be viewed as a character flaw that potentially affects the injurer's credibility on other issues and likability. Ultimate adjudicators tend not to look fondly on people who choose to not accept responsibility when they make mistakes.

This phenomenon is recognized by the Federal Sentencing Standards when they authorize a judge to consider the defendant's contrition in determining the length of the sentence.[13] The positive impact of an apology on an ultimate adjudicator was also documented in a study of labor arbitrators.[14] After comparing labor arbitrator rulings when employees did and did not apologize, the authors found that an apology enhances the likelihood of a favorable ruling. The conclusion suggests, "a union representative has a strong incentive to advise the grievant to apologize or show remorse for his or her conduct or wrongdoing …. If the grievant has offered a sincere apology, management should be aware that labor arbitrators tend to treat this offer favorably when weighing mitigating factors for punishment of the grievant."[15]

Considering other audiences' reactions to the second injury could extend beyond an ultimate adjudicator. If the perpetrator has a public following or the incident attracts media attention, the crisis communication experts often advise full and rapid disclosure. An article in the LA Times questioning the transparency of the Obama administration provides this explanation:

> Lanny Davis, who handled scandals for the Clinton White House, has been critical of the Obama administration. 'The non-transparency instinct of the Obama White House is more about not understanding effective, proactive crisis management' said Davis, who remains an Obama supporter. The idea is to inoculate by being transparent …. "You help write bad stories," Davis said. "That's counterintuitive. But you know this stuff is coming out, so it's to your advantage to get it all out quickly, all completely and make sure it's over and done."[16]

So, the pragmatic advisor must factor in the risks of apologizing and the risks of not apologizing.

3.4 Moral and Psychological Consequences of Not Apologizing

Some emphasize the importance of the moral aspect of the decision to make an apology.[17] Remember that the soundbite definition of an apology is telling the truth to yourself and others and taking responsibility for the consequences. Morals must be involved when telling the truth means acknowledging "wrongful" behavior.

The moral element of an apology is evident when an injury was clearly caused by a perpetrator, but the injured would have a difficult time proving it. An example might be a teenager telling her parent that she dented the neighbor's car but is certain that nobody saw or can otherwise prove it. A pragmatic apology analysis might result in a decision not to apologize. However, because the parent is responsible for the moral development of the teenager, there is usually a consensus that the parent should require the teenage to inform the neighbor that the teenager is responsible for the dent and will pay for the repairs.

This situation describes how not telling the truth and taking responsibility can be viewed as immoral. To damage another person and not apologize can be viewed as morally wrong. Most apology advisors are reluctant to encourage behavior they consider morally wrong.

Jonathan Cohen suggests that the morally wrong act of not apologizing for a known wrongful injury can result in psychological risks.[18] Hopefully, a person who is aware that he has wrongfully injured another is burdened with guilt. This guilt consists of self-condemnation about a distinct action. He could attend to this guilt by apology. If he chooses to not apologize, there is a risk that the guilt might evolve into a sense of shame. Instead of guilt's focus on a distinct action, shame describes a negative identity. The transformation is from "what I did" to "who I am." For example, "I told a lie" becomes "I am a liar." The ratification of the behavior implicit in the decision not to apologize translates to character attribute. The culmination of the psychological risk is a diminished self-esteem. The perpetrator also experiences a second injury by the decision to not apologize. They injure their own self-esteem.

A student expressed this concern in a journal.

> We then broke off into groups of two where we did an exercise together that had one person playing the role of someone who did something that potentially warranted an apology and the other person played the role of their attorney and thus, the role of their advisor. It was pretty interesting because of the complexity that was framed for us by the professor. The exercise tested our own personal resolve with regards to our character, but we also had to weigh the context and the law as it pertained to our plight.
>
> And what happens if a person doesn't apologize? Can he or she wind up being able to look themselves in the mirror after it's all said and done? Would they be able to manage the psychological effects of not owning up to their part in the situation?

The choice between taking responsibility versus denial and avoidance could have tremendous extrinsic and intrinsic effects on the offender if they were to choose the latter as their course of action. The mental wear and tear from avoiding responsibility in a given conflict that could simply be remedied with a remorse apology, could actually be damaging to a person's health if you think about it. That type of stress could lead to internal health problems not to mention the discord in the relationship. Taking ownership and having the courage to apologize can also add to a person's credibility and enhance their character.[19]

Going further into the moral element, there are degrees of "telling the truth." There is a difference between answering a question truthfully and voluntarily confessing. The teenager who dented the neighbor's car would be lying if she was asked and then denied knowing anything about the dent. Hopefully, this lie would be a second source of guilt, a second injury to her view of herself as an honest person. However, she would not be lying if she chose not to inform the neighbor. Here, the sin is not taking responsibility for an injury she inflicted, so the damage to her self-image is that she is sneaky, not a liar. Both are hopefully negative impacts on her view of herself as a virtuous person, but they are different.

Hopefully, a positive self-image includes that a person takes responsibility for their actions. They are transparent, a straight shooter. They tell the truth, even to the point of volunteering incriminating information. Jonathan Cohen summarized Jean Piaget's finding that, "a pivotal step in children's moral development is the internalization of moral norms, namely, learning to do what is right because it is right rather than from the fear of external punishment."[20]

Good parents teach teenagers to voluntarily admit hitting a neighbor's car and paying for the damages because it is the right thing to do. They want their child to feel the satisfaction of doing the right thing, even when they could have gotten away without being caught. They want their child to be virtuous and towards that end, to see themselves as virtuous. The same goes for apology mentors working alongside friends and mentees.

I experienced this with an alumna who had become a friend. She was about ten years younger than me and I had been her advisor when she earned one of Pepperdine's advanced law degrees. We had stayed in touch over the years after she graduated, and we had become friends. She called and said she was in a crisis and needed my advice. If I was available the next day, she would drive a few hours so we could talk.

When we met for breakfast, she told me she was being blackmailed. She confessed that she had paid a friend to write one of the papers she had submitted to earn her Pepperdine degree; she and her friend had become estranged, and her "friend" was threatening to reveal the terms of the bought paper to Pepperdine and the alumna's current employer, where she was in a position of leadership. The "friend" demanded a $5,000 payment to keep this quiet. The alumna concluded that the demands for payments would never stop.

The alumna was in full panic mode, reporting that she hadn't eaten or slept since the "friend" threatened to report this three days earlier. The alumna predicted that she would be fired, have her degree revoked, and would not be able to get another job if her inappropriate behavior was revealed. She was too young and not financially prepared to retire. She envisioned her financial ruin with no way to support herself.

As we brainstormed options, I asked her what she thought would happen if she revealed to Pepperdine and her current employer that she had paid a person to write her paper. Before our breakfast she had assumed the harshest possible reactions and consequences. I suggested that the reaction may not be as harsh if she confesses and apologizes, including an understanding that there will be ramifications. As we began to develop this option, we agreed that full disclosure would require explaining that the confession was under duress because of the threat of blackmail. We rehearsed the confession, and I advised against including some mitigating circumstances I knew to be true. We agreed that the best chance at a sympathetic response was an unequivocal admission of a moral failing.

The alumna had the benefit of a friend advisor who had many experiences with the authority figure at Pepperdine who would receive the confession. While I couldn't guarantee the Dean's reaction, I assured the alumna that the Dean was mature and had the wisdom that comes from working in lots of situations involving human frailties. I trusted the Dean to appropriately balance justice and mercy.

We also thought together about who she could confess to at her employer and how it would be received. Eventually she agreed to this plan and asked me to call the Dean to see if he would agree to an emergency meeting. He did, and we started to leave the restaurant, when the alumna said she couldn't do it. I called the Dean and cancelled the meeting. We sat back down and explored the options other than confessing. When the alumna realized that her best option was confessing, at her request I called the Dean and set up the meeting again.

The Dean's reaction included elements of justice and mercy. The alumna agreed to the Dean's terms to cure the dishonesty in the academic work and the Dean's rehabilitative requirements, including attending counseling for a year to explore why the alumna had such a serious lapse in moral judgement. I was in the meeting and could see the alumna's relief when she realized that the harshest possible consequences that she had imagined would not be imposed. The next day the alumna called to report a similar outcome when she confessed to her employer. There would be ramifications, but she would not lose her job! She even decided to voluntarily share her mistake with many of the senior managers (her peers) at her company.

The alumna informed the blackmailer that she had confessed to both Pepperdine and her employer. About a week later the Dean received a packet from the blackmailer documenting that the alumna had paid the friend to write the paper and requesting a meeting. The Dean wrote back to the blackmailer that Pepperdine was fully informed about the situation and had already taken action; there was no reason to meet.

There were no guarantees that the Dean and employer would not impose the harshest possible punishments. The risks of apologizing and the decision to apologize belonged to the alumna. The friend advisor assisted the alumna to consider all her options, including admitting the truth and apologizing.

Jonathan Cohen summarized the moral and psychological aspects of apology when he described the situation as the apologizer being able to look himself and the injured person in the eye. If he doesn't apologize, both relationships suffer. The choice is between responsibility and respect versus denial and avoidance.[21]

A student journal describing her role as an apology adviser summarizes many of this chapter's concepts.

> I played the role of the peacekeeper in my family throughout both my childhood and adulthood. My two oldest siblings frequently fought, and once I was in my teen years my parents began to ask me advice about their conflicts. It seemed like I was always the neutral third-party people would come to for a shoulder to cry on and advice upon occasion.
>
> Whenever people fought in my family, it seemed like they were on two different planets speaking entirely different languages. My sibling could not understand where my mom was coming from and mom could not understand why my father behaved the way he did. It may sound self-righteous, but I was able to read and understand the people around me from a very young age. This probably was a result of having to keep the peace in my house. I also developed skills to carefully craft my words due to the pressure I felt to never be upset or cause any problems. My ability to empathize and understand members of my family and communication skills made me a source that all members of my immediate family have come to for help.
>
> It's hard to tell people something they don't want to hear, especially when you are close to those people. It's still something I struggle with till this day. But advising others on apologizing often encompasses that. One thing that is involved in the process of apologizing is exploring one's own fault in a given situation. When I advise members of my family within the area of apology, I usually don't start with this step. Emotions tend to flow hot and intensely, and I have found that asking someone if they did something wrong in the situation when they are in an emotionally heightened state is not wise. In my experience, people can become very defensive when asked a direct question like that.
>
> In advising others, I usually try to listen to their side of the story and validate their emotions first. Once that psychological need is met, I slowly try to get that person to see from the other person's or people's perspective. If they are able to see from that other person's perspective, I have found that they are much more likely to be able to see where they are responsible in the incident or at least why the other person is upset.

In my experience, I find it easier to advise people with whom I have close relationships. As we discussed in class, the type and strength of a relationship is an important variable to consider when advisor others on apology. In fact, when I advise members of my family on apologizing, I often use their relationship with the other person as a way to get them to consider apologizing. Sometimes this strategy only ends with a social harmony apology because they live together, but other times it can cause them to truly reflect on their role in the conflict and to offer a remorse apology.[22]

3.5 Advising Apology for NYPD Detaining Wrong Person

A September 10, 2015 New York Times article describes the mistaken detainment of James Blake.[23] A team of plainclothes NYPD officers were investigating a credit card fraud ring who had made 16 purchases totaling $18,000. The police were staking out the delivery of another purchase at the Grand Hyatt Hotel concierge desk. The man who picked up the package was arrested, but then the delivery courier identified Mr. Blake from eight feet away as someone who had also bought items using the false credit card information.

One of the officers immediately tackled Mr. Blake and handcuffed his hands behind his back. Mr. Blake declared there was a mistake but complied. He was detained until a retired police officer working security at the Hyatt told the officers Blake was a retired tennis star. Mr. Blake was leaving the hotel to make an appearance for a corporate sponsor at the United States Open Tennis Tournament. Many questioned the degree of force used by the officer who tackled him and suggested the harsh treatment may have been because Mr. Blake is biracial. Security video tapes and eyewitnesses confirmed that Mr. Blake had been compliant and was roughed up by the police.

The officers made matters worse by not completing a "void arrest" form as they are required to do in such situations. The Chief of Police learned about the incident from the media. The New York Times reported one police officer's reaction that, "A mistake is a mistake. Part of the art of making a mistake like this is how you leave that mistake." He concluded that it did not appear that the officer ever explained things to Mr. Blake or apologized.

Assume you work for the NYPD's Public Affairs Department and have been tasked with advising the Chief whether and how to apologize for this incident. Remember that in the Fall of 2015, there were some very public incidents in the national news in which a police officer killed a member of a minority group.

Endnotes

1. Submitted by a student who will remain anonymous, emphasis added.
2. *See* Jonathan R. Cohen, *The Immorality of Denial*, 79 Tul. L. Rev. 903, 903 (2005), http://scholarship.law.ufl.edu/facultypub/41; *see also* Lee Taft, *Apology Subverted: The Commodification of Apology*, 109 Yale L.J., 1135 (2000).
3. *See* Lazare, *On Apology*, 118.
4. Submitted by a student who will remain anonymous, emphasis added.
5. Submitted by a student who will remain anonymous, emphasis added.
6. Submitted by a student who will remain anonymous, emphasis added.
7. *See* Jonathan Cohen, *Advising Clients to Apologize*, 72 S. Cal. L. Rev. 1009 (1999).
8. Submitted by Mallory Miller, emphasis added
9. Copy of letter from Marvin Louis Wolf in the author's files.
10. *See* Cohen, *Advising Clients to Apologize*, 1011 (describing it as the vicious cycle).
11. Deroy Murdock, "'Sorry' Works," National Review (August 29, 2005) http://www.nationalreview.com/article/215270/sorry-works-deroy-murdock.
12. J. Stratton Shartel, "Toro's Mediation Program Challenges Wisdom of Traditional Litigation Model," 9 Inside Litigation 6, (June 1995), http://www.adrprocess.com/images/20071107094925439.pdf.
13. *See* Groppi v. Leslie, 404 U.S. 496, 506 n.11 (1972) ("Modification of contempt penalties is common where the contemnor apologizes or presents matters in mitigation.")
14. *See* Daniel J. Kaspar and Lamont E. Stallworth's, *The Impact of a Grievant's Offer of Apology*, 17 Harv. Negot. L. Rev. 1 (2012).
15. Christi Parsons and Kathleen Hennessey, "Transparency a challenge for Obama," *Los Angeles Times*, May 26, 2013.
16. Cohen, *The Immorality of Denial*, 79 Tul. L. Rev. 903, 903 (2005), http://scholarship.law.ufl.edu/facultypub/41.
17. *See id.; see also* Cohen, *Advising Clients to Apologize*.
18. Submitted by Clay Strickland, emphasis added.
19. *See* Cohen, *The Immorality of Denial*, 79 Tul. L. Rev. 903, 925 (2005), http://scholarship.law.ufl.edu/facultypub/41.
20. *See* Cohen, *Advising Clients to Apologize*, 1021.
21. Submitted by a student who will remain anonymous, emphasis added.
22. Benjamin Mueller, Al Baker and Liz Robbins, "James Blake's Arrest Brings Swift Apologies From New York Officials," *The New York Times*, September 10, 2015.

Chapter Four

Attorneys and Apologies

4.1 Introduction

4.2 Apology Strategies: The Dynamics Between Attorneys and Clients

    4.21 The Lawyer's Pragmatic Analysis

    4.22 The Lawyer's Analysis of Moral Ramifications

    4.23 Combining Client and Lawyer Attorney Preferences

4.3 The Execution of Attorney Assisted Apologies

    4.31 Apologies Delivered by the Client

    4.32 Clients Apologizing Through their Attorney

    4.33 Attorneys Apologizing for their Client

4.4 Attorneys Negotiating the Terms of the Apology

4.5 Claremont College Crisis Exercise

"Something that says I'm sorry without admitting liability."

4.1 Introduction

The information presented in the last chapter about Advising Others to Apologize aptly applies to the attorney-client relationship. Many clients retain the services of an attorney after they have been accused of wrongdoing. Lawyers are in a special position to help clients make informed decisions about offering apologies. Last chapter's methodology of both pragmatic and moral considerations will be applied in a lawyer-client context. This chapter will also suggest a range of involvement for attorneys assisting their clients with apologies.

This topic will remind many of Chief Justice Warren E. Burger's famous speech at a meeting of the American Bar Association in February 1984 when he said,

> The entire legal profession- lawyers, judges, law teachers- has become so mesmerized with the stimulation of the courtroom contest that we tend to forget that we ought to be healers – healers of conflict.

An experienced lawyer's journal provides some thoughts about attorneys advising apologies.

> I have struggled to articulate this, but to me the power of an apology lies in the willingness to acknowledge an event that has caused some inconvenience (whether intentional or negligent) to another party. It calls for some degree of self-awareness and it suggests a willingness to accept responsibility (but not necessarily fault.)

> As we went through class, a recurring thought I had was, "why do lawyers struggle so much with the concept of apology?" When I looked at my definition from above, it hit me: Lawyers often struggle to recognize the needs of others and –as Professor Robinson pointed out—lawyers learn at an early age the value of deflecting blame. I don't mean to suggest that all lawyers are jerks. Indeed, I believe there are many good-natured, well-intentioned lawyers who still fit my description of being self-absorbed. They are worried about their hours- having had their lives reduced to six-minute intervals; they are worried about their egos-having been told repeatedly that good lawyers are pit bulls; they are worried about failure – having been told that in law school and summer clerkships, only the strong survive.

> <u>Somewhere along the way, too many good people have forgotten that the mission of a lawyer is to be a counselor, trusted advisor, and sometimes friend. In doing so, they need to be open to concepts like integrity, accountability, contrition, and reparation. Both for themselves and their client. The practice of law is not a game – although it can be played like one. Rather, it is an opportunity -- an opportunity to help someone, and in some instances, as Professor Robinson described in the story about his mother-in-law, heal.</u>

I am particularly drawn to this notion of healing. As a litigator, we focus on "breaking cases down" to the core elements. We prepare to win or create the best leverage to achieve our objective. But what about simply trying to do the right thing – whatever that may entail? What about incorporating into a conversation with clients the notion that there can be both legal and practical approaches toward kindness (reconciliation recognition- perhaps an apology) that are not mutually exclusive.

Of course, this is all dependent on lawyers willing to participate in the process and set aside their ego. It depends on whether lawyers are willing to do the right thing. Submitted by a student who will remain anonymous, emphasis added.

4.2 Apology Strategies: The Dynamics Between Attorneys and Clients

The interaction between lawyers and clients depends on the nature of the relationship and the amount of trust and rapport. Some attorneys are part of an ongoing inner circle of advisors and decision makers for an individual or organization. Their long-term involvement is likely to allow them to advise an apology more aggressively than the attorney in a one transaction relationship, such as a trial attorney who is retained only when an individual or organization is served with a lawsuit. Usually, the attorney's advice is being solicited; if so, there is little risk of violating the client's autonomy if she advises the client to apologize. A student comment helps.

Today I was taught something that is so obvious and important, but I have never really considered it by itself before. It was the specialness of being in a position to advise someone else on apology. The amount of responsibility in that moment is incredible because you and your client are at a pivotal moment in that relationship. An apology has a way of testing the bounds of a relationship and advising someone else on an apology does the same thing. The amount of trust and familiarity between the attorney and the client are two critical components that make up the relationship and set the boundaries of how far the attorney, friend, or family member can go in advising the other party on the proper course of action. Submitted by Casey Caton, emphasis added.

4.21 The Lawyer's Pragmatic Analysis

An attorney will hopefully consider the pragmatic analysis about the risks of apologizing and not apologizing. I say hopefully because some defense attorneys have a knee jerk reaction to deny everything and circle the wagons. Their philosophy about the practice of law is to wait and see what the other side can prove. Some defense attorneys are oblivious to the second injury and tragic cycle concepts that are critical to the pragmatic "risks of not apologizing" analysis. This approach is fairly common and can be viewed as part of the culture of the adversarial approach to the practice of law. This adversarial approach is not optional but is embedded in the ethical standards for lawyers.[1] A law student's journal illustrates the point.

I never really thought about the way apologies could apply in a legal context with clients until today, which really challenged the way I personally use apologies. It is ironic that my individual view of apologizing is much different when representing a client in a legal setting. In the car accident hypothetical in class, I honestly would not have advised the sister to contact the driver to formally apologize because it would not be a wise move in the legal and liability sense. However, putting that all aside with no risks or insurance/legal consequences, if I were in her shoes, I would have absolutely apologized for the accident regardless of whether it was my fault or not because that is the type of person I am. Submitted by Chelsea McGrath, emphasis added.

The lawyer's ethical standards include a duty of "zealous advocacy."[2] Zealous advocacy requires lawyers to seek the best possible outcome for their client allowed by law. The adversarial context blinds some lawyers from the possibility of getting the best outcome for their client by telling the truth and taking responsibility. Some lawyers assume they get the best outcome for their clients by not admitting anything. They do not consider that the risks of not apologizing may outweigh the risks of apologizing. Even when liability is clear and easily proven by their accuser, they believe they are serving their client's best interests by being stingy with their admissions.

I had this experience as a young lawyer. I worked in the Office of General Counsel for a US Government agency. My first month at work included an assignment to a complex and significant litigated case. The legal team for the government included the lead litigation attorney who had practiced law for 25 years and two junior staff attorneys. The other staff attorney was one year older than me and had one-year experience practicing law. I was just out of law school and was waiting for my bar results before I would be licensed to practice law. (I learned I passed two months later.)

The other side in the case had submitted written interrogatories asking us to explain certain aspects of our approach to the case. The lead attorney told both junior staff attorneys that he wanted us to write a draft response to each of these questions. We would exchange drafts in a week and then meet to decide how to respond to the lawyers representing the other side.

I concluded the questions were reasonable and that the law required us to provide the information requested. I researched the law and evidence supporting the government's claims and wrote draft responses that explained to the other side the factual and legal basis for the lawsuit we had filed. I had worked hard that week and produced a draft response I was proud of.

When we exchanged draft responses after the week, I was embarrassed for the other junior staff attorney. His proposed draft consisted of objections to every question. In every question, he would focus on one word and claim that it was vague or ambiguous and that he didn't know what it meant. Therefore, he could not answer the question. He had lots of other cases he was working on and obviously did not make the time to do a thorough job on this assignment. I estimated his draft took two hours to complete compared to the fifty hours I had spent.

Imagine my surprise when we met with the lead litigation attorney, and he chose to use all the answers drafted by the other attorney. He appreciated my work and instructed me to save it because we would eventually need to provide a version of those responses to the other side. But for now, we would make what I believed to be frivolous objections to frustrate the lawyers representing the other side.

This stinginess with information is prevalent in the practice of law, but it is not representative of all lawyers. There are many examples of good lawyers encouraging their clients to disclose incriminating information, some of which will be described later in this section.

Lawyers will consciously or unconsciously perform the pragmatic analysis about the risks of apologizing and the risks of not apologizing. But as lawyers, they can conduct this analysis with special knowledge. One aspect of the lawyer's special knowledge is the awareness that the pre-trial legal procedures will require their clients to answer the opposing lawyer's questions under oath at a deposition. The lawyer can help the client tell her story in an as advantageous way as possible, but if the driver was texting while driving and the other attorney asks that question, the client will need to reveal this incriminating fact.

The lawyer also knows that pre-trial procedures almost always involves needing to respond to "Requests for Admissions." Michael Marcus, a retired California State Bar Court Judge, wrote a summary of the legal requirements when responding to Requests for Admissions.[3] Requests for Admissions are designed to simplify the trial process by narrowing the list of contested issues for trial. The California Code of Civil Procedure requires that each response to a request for admission "shall (1) Admit so much of the matter involved in the request as is true, either as expressed in the request itself or as reasonably and clearly qualified by the responding party. (2) Deny so much of the matter involved in the request as is untrue. (3) Specify so much of the matter involved in the request as to the truth of which the responding party lacks sufficient information or knowledge."[4]

Marcus informs parties responding to a Request for Admission that case law in California has created a duty to make a reasonable investigation of the facts which do come within their personal knowledge[5] and that the statute requires the awarding of costs and attorney's fees when a party denies a request for admission and the matter is later found to be true at trial, unless the court finds that the party who denied the request for admission "had reasonable ground to believe [he or she] would prevail on the matter" or "[t]here was another good reasons for the failure to admit."[6] The lawyer considering whether to advise a client to apologize may want to anticipate that they are likely to receive Requests for Admission, and they should consider how they intend to fulfill the legal obligations triggered by such requests. They will need to consult the statutes and case law regarding Requests for Admissions in their jurisdiction.

Another source of special knowledge a lawyer should have is the availability of what Jonathan Cohen describes as the "safe apology" options in their jurisdiction.[7] The safe apology concept describes legal provisions that allow a client to offer a protected apology, which means that the apology CANNOT be used in court against the client. Safe apology options are significant because they can tip the risk analysis balancing test in favor of apologizing.

One safe apology option is to use the laws providing confidentiality of statements made in mediation. Many jurisdictions provide that statements made in mediation proceedings are not admissible in subsequent civil proceedings, arbitrations, and administrative proceedings.[8] Thus, a lawyer who wants his client to benefit from the possible advantages of apologizing, while minimizing the risks of an apology might arrange an early mediation. Some mediations are conducted before lawsuits are filed. Maybe the client can be spared the expense and trauma of a lawsuit by apologizing and offering reparations at a mediation. If the other side is unreasonable and sues the client, the conversation at the mediation was "off the record" and not admissible in the legal proceedings. Mediation confidentiality statutes vary by jurisdiction, including between state and federal law, so the lawyer will need to check the relevant laws for each case.

Another safe apology option is provided by "apology statutes." In the Spring of 2017, thirty-six states in the United States have enacted statutes that protect the admissibility of apologies. For example, California Evidence Code Section 1160 (a) provides,

> The portion of statements, writings, or benevolent gestures expressing sympathy or a general sense of benevolence relating to the pain, suffering, or death of a person involved in an accident and made to that person or to the family of that person shall be inadmissible as evidence of an admission of liability in a civil action. A statement of fault, however, which is part of, or in addition to, any of the above shall not be inadmissible pursuant to this section.

Notice that the California statute applies only to accidents, apparently not being available for a vast range of other disputes including breach of contract or employment matters. Notice also that the California statute specifically states that statements of fault are not protected. Thus, the California statute only protects empathy apologies and carefully worded social harmony or externally motivated apologies. It does not protect the remorse apology where a party admits they were wrong and takes responsibility for their actions.

In contrast, the Apology Act for the State of British Columbia (Canada), c 19 provides:

> An apology made by or on behalf of a person in connection with any matter
>
> (a) does not constitute an express or implied admission of fault or liability by the person in connection with that matter,
> (b) does not constitute a confirmation of a cause of action in relation to that matter for the purposes of section 5 of the Limitation Act,
> (c) does not, despite any wording to the contrary in any contract of insurance and despite any other enactment, void, impair, or otherwise affect any insurance coverage that is available, or that would, but for the apology, be available to the person in connection with that matter, and
> (d) must not be taken into account in any determination of fault or liability in connection with that matter.

Notice that the British Columbia statute covers all types of apologies in all types of disputes. It even goes so far as to override the wording in a contract of insurance to assure that the apology will not affect available insurance benefits. The contrast in these two statutes demonstrates again that the lawyer must be knowledgeable about the apology statutes governing specific cases when considering the safe apology options.

So, a lawyer's pragmatic assessment may conclude that for a given case the risks of not apologizing are greater than the risks of apologizing, especially if the lawyer can arrange a safe apology. Maybe liability is clear and easily provable, so the lawyer sees a benefit in stipulating to that issue. The lawyer understands that admitting the mistake may lessen the likelihood of being sued. The lawyer may also see that denying liability would make the injurer unsympathetic and lose credibility with a judge, jury, or arbitrator. These are pure zealous advocacy pragmatic strategies why a lawyer might advise a client to apologize.

The observations about the civil trial experience provided by a trial lawyer adds to the pragmatic analysis.

> Since I tried my first case – a four-month employment discrimination case involving eleven African-American employees in Fresno – I have tried to describe to people why it is that I struggle to look back at the experience with fondness. The trial ended up being the largest race discrimination case in the country to go trial that year, and I still have the press clippings littered around my office. Most people consider the trial to be a tremendous success. All I can think about, however, are the times I spent in the Residence Inn with my head in my hands. ...

> Too often, I come across lawyers who wax poetic about the beauty of trial and the exposition of justice. Despite the favorable outcome, I did not see justice in our trial. I saw games, cruelty, arbitrariness and isolation. I saw plaintiff's counsel snickering every day that I was a "sell out" for representing "white people." I saw people play games with evidence. And I saw a firm that was more interested in fees than outcomes.

> I have had other trials since that one. None of them have been as contentious; however, they have been equally unfulfilling on a personal level. They have taken me away from my wife and kids –both physically and emotionally, and they have driven some of the joy out of my practice. I think that is why I am pursuing this LLM.

> . . .

> Our clients are more important than our egos and they need to know the financial AND human cost of protracted litigation. To the extent we mentor younger attorneys or JD candidates – they need to hear it too. So that when they counsel clients, they can tell them the truth: In the context of civil trials, justice (for lack of better word) is seldom found and never freely given. Submitted by a student who will remain anonymous, emphasis added.

4.22 The Lawyer's Analysis of Moral Ramifications

Should the lawyer consider the moral ramifications of the decision to apologize? Lawyers knowledgeable about apology will be aware of the psychological risks for clients who do not apologize. They will know that guilt (what I did) can become shame (who I am or what I've become), potentially resulting in a diminished self-esteem.[9] Many lawyers do not consider moral ramifications for their clients because they assume the client wants the lawyer to maximize their financial outcome. The lawyer assumes that clients seeking guidance on moral decisions or their psychological health will reach out to clergy or mental health professionals.

Another one of Jonathan Cohen's articles challenges lawyers to discuss with clients the basic choice of whether to take or deny responsibility.[10] He describes how lawyers sometimes make the mistakes of assuming the client is only concerned about economic interests and/or fear alienating the client if the lawyer raises the possibility of taking responsibility for the behavior. Cohen analogizes physician patient dynamics in two respects: some patients want their doctors to "tell it to me straight;" he also cited a study that concluded a patient's willingness to talk about death with her doctor depended significantly on the willingness of the doctor to talk about it.

Cohen's solution is to remind lawyers that "If it is for the client and not the lawyer to determine the ultimate ends of legal representation, the lawyer must speak with the client and explore what those ends are."[11] Cohen encourages lawyers to "not be overly fearful of alienating the client . . . because the essential goal of legal representation is serving the client's best interests rather than avoiding client alienation".[12] Cohen balances his enthusiasm by concluding:

> "the lawyer's goal should not be 'salvational'-to turn the client into a moral being and persuade the client to make the moral choice. But neither should the lawyer assume the worst about the client's morals. The goal rather is similar to that of much moral counseling: to have a conversation that assists the client in helping him understand the possible ramifications, including moral ramifications, of his choices. The choices are fundamentally the client's".[13]

The question of lawyers considering moral aspects when giving advice is addressed in Rule 2.1 of the Model Rules of Professional Conduct. Pertinent parts of this rule and comments on the rule provide:

> "In rendering advice, a lawyer may refer not only to law but to other considerations such as moral, economic, social and political factors that may be relevant to the client's situation ….
>
> Comment [2] Advice couched in narrow legal terms may be of little value to a client, especially where practical considerations, such as cost or effects on other people, are predominant. Purely technical legal advice, therefore, can sometimes be inadequate. It is proper for a lawyer to refer to relevant moral and ethical considerations in giving advice. Although a lawyer is not a moral advisor as such, moral and ethical considerations impinge upon most legal questions and may decisively influence how the law will be applied.

Comment [3] A client may expressly or impliedly ask the lawyer for purely technical advice …. When such a request is made by a client inexperienced in legal matters, however, the lawyer's responsibility as advisor may include indicating that more may be involved than strictly legal considerations."

Notice that the language in these provisions is permissive, not mandatory. A lawyer may consider moral factors, but she is not required to. Some lawyers will integrate moral factors into their philosophy of practicing law; some will consider it on a case by case basis; and, some will decide that they are uncomfortable and ill-equipped for such a conversation and relationship. Cohen explains that "lawyers who discuss responsibility taking with clients may find a deepened sense of meaning in law practice, a meaning derived from providing a fuller range of service to the client, and, simultaneously from being a member of a profession that fosters moral behavior, social healing and just outcomes."[14]

A journal entry by a practicing lawyer from Brazil provides an example.

> This class is something different than I am used to at a law school and for that I feel curious about it. It is about law and to help our professional practice but at the outset I was trying to understand how this would be accomplished. I know that sometimes people say "I am sorry" with different intentions but I never thought about analyzing it in more depth.
>
> For example, I knew based on my previous background working at the Health Secretariat that an apology from a doctor to a patient would decrease his chances of being sued in a case of malpractice. Moreover, sometimes we had to assist the Press Sector at the Secretariat in answering public notes regarding mistakes of malpractice at state healthcare facilities. However, I never thought under a professional point of view on evaluating types of apologies, or on how to avoid conditional apologies…
>
> At last, I remember that you pointed out that this class might help us deal with our clients while supporting them with issues beyond the legal technicalities. It is interesting that you said that because of a phone call that I received one day later from a close friend talking about a lawsuit she was served that day. The plaintiffs are her cousins. One of the first things that I thought about was that maybe mediation alongside apologies and forgiveness among these people could heal their situation and avoid hurtful court disputes. After talking with this person, I thought that the plaintiff's lawyer could have contacted her before filing suit and tried to negotiate. Submitted by Ricardo L. Sadicoff, some editing for translation and emphasis added.

4.23 Combining Client and Lawyer Apology Preferences

To understand the variety of dynamics between attorneys and clients regarding apology strategies, we need to consider four combinations. The attorney and client are both for apology. The attorney and client are both against apology. The attorney is for and the client is against the apology option. The attorney is against and the client is for the apology option. A visual for these possible combinations is:

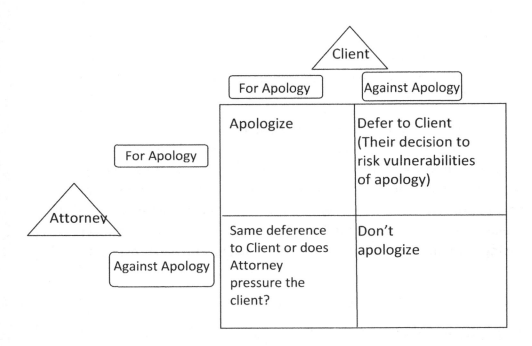

The result is obvious when the lawyer and client agree on apologizing or not apologizing. Good, thoughtful lawyers and clients can come to either conclusion, hopefully after a thorough analysis of the benefits and risks of both approaches. As a lawyer, I hope the attorney is well versed and maybe more knowledgeable about the apology option and willing to assist the client in considering the apology option.

The result is also clear when the lawyer favors apologizing, but the client disagrees. The lawyer's job is to fully inform the client about the apology approach, but the decision and responsibility for such a decision must belong to the client. Regardless of whether the lawyer favors the apology for pragmatic strategic considerations or because of the moral ramifications, there are risks that come with apologizing. If those risks come true and there are costs to be paid because of the apology, the client will be the one paying those costs. After the lawyer fully explains the apology approach, he must defer to his client's decision on this issue.

Maybe the most interesting combination is when the client wants to apologize and the lawyer counsels to the contrary. The first concern is whether the lawyer is fully informed about the apology option. If not, is the lawyer conforming to unexamined professional norms that are not always in the best interest of the client? Cohen observes that such conflict escalating behavior could be unconsciously self-serving for the lawyer because the lawyer benefits financially by the continuation of the conflict.[15]

Tom Gehring's book, *SETTLE IT... and be Blessed*, provides an example when he describes a client asking for his help in settling a class action complaint filed by the client's employees. The client agreed that the managers of his company had not complied with law concerning breaks. A large law firm had been representing him for about a year, and it seemed there was no end in sight. When Gehring started handling the case, he asked the previous lawyers if they had calculated the number and duration of violations and concluded on the amount of damages due the employees. The large law firm had not yet performed this analysis.

Gehring hired an expert and made this his priority. He then shared the results with the attorney representing the employees and accomplished a settlement in short order.[16] It would be unprofessional for the large law firm to intentionally delay settling the case to earn more fees, so I don't believe that was their intent. Rather, they have a certain approach to practicing law that is exactly what some clients want; this approach does not favor prompt and efficient sharing of perspectives necessary to settle a case quickly.

A journal entry reveals one student's view of the influence of law schools.

> The issue of when the client and the lawyer disagree about giving an apology seems to be a huge issue. I see the disagreement as a result of confusion concerning the potential harm that an apology could have on a client's future liability. If I knew that there was a for sure way to allow my client to apologize when they are clearly in the wrong, without receiving any harmful liabilities later, then it is an obvious choice to apologize. A good case was made in class for the potential benefits of apologizing as opposed to the benefits of withholding an apology. It seems in law school; besides ethics class, we are taught that ethics matter but liability and potential suits for malpractice matter more. Submitted by Casey Caton, emphasis added.

A second concern is the power dynamic between the client and lawyer. The lawyer is the professional with experience and wisdom in knowing how to handle the client's problem. A client consulting with a lawyer takes comfort knowing that while this is a novel problem for the client, the lawyer has served many other clients with similar problems. Sometimes there is a built-in deference to professionals out of respect for their expertise. The client suppresses her instincts and values and agrees to follow the lawyer's lead. It takes a determined patient to sign the papers leaving the hospital against medical advice. Likewise, it takes a strong client to instruct the lawyer to proceed with an apology strategy against the lawyer's advice.

A topic for further investigation is the frequency of this scenario. How often does a client approach a lawyer with an instinct to "tell the truth and take responsibility" and the lawyer smiles and says she wishes it were that easy? Based on my experience with law students and mid-career attorneys earning LLMs at Pepperdine, most legally trained advisors are reluctant to encourage apology. They are aware of the risks of apology and minimize the risks of not apologizing. The dominant choice is to conform to what other lawyers do and advise against the apology.

Some will argue that this is a marginal issue for the legal profession because it is the rare client who is inclined to apologize. Most clients feel they are the victim, even when another has accused them of wrongdoing. My focus is on the client who wants "to do the right thing" and the lawyer who perceives his role is to protect the client from himself. I hope the first three chapters of this book begin equipping lawyers for a balanced and respectful conversations about apologies with their clients.

4.3 The Execution of Attorney Assisted Apologies

An analysis of attorney assisted apologies should start by considering a variety of ways to deliver such an apology. Should the client or the attorney be the mouthpiece for the apology? If the attorney will be delivering the apology, how much does he attribute it to the client? If the represented client decides to apologize, there are still lots of decisions about the best way to deliver it. Again, the attorney can be useful to the client in thinking through these issues and possibly by delivering the apology.

4.31 Apologies Delivered by the Client

An example of an attorney assisted apology delivered by the client is Paris Hilton's conviction for repeatedly driving on a suspended license. She had been sentenced to 45 days in jail. Her first attorney complained to the media that the sentence was unfair and filed a notice of intent to appeal. A week later the LA Times reported "Paris Hilton has a new lawyer and a new strategy: public contrition." In a statement released by her new attorney, Richard Hutton, Hilton seeks to "correct what I believe are misperceptions about me … no one is above the law. I surely am not. … I absolutely realize how serious driving under the influence is." Maybe it is a coincidence, but the LA Times and I suspect that the change in attitude by Hilton was the result of Mr. Hutton's counsel. In this situation, the statement of contrition was made by Hilton and released by her attorney. Maybe I am being overly cynical, but I imagine that Mr. Hutton may have assisted in coaching Ms. Hilton on what to say and possibly went so far as to draft his client's statement.

Another case study and collection of insights about attorney guided apologies is provided by Roberta Burnette.[17] She has practiced employment law for more than 30 years representing both the plaintiffs and defendants. The last ten years she has led the employment practice group for a large law firm representing employers. Her strategy is influenced by the following three observations:

1. Most employees who have complaints don't want to sue;
2. Most employees who have complaints are not motivated by money; and
3. Apologies can make a big difference in employment law disputes.

If the apology is before a lawsuit is filed, Ms. Burnette's advice about apology usually includes:

1. Timing is important. She thinks one to three weeks after the incident shows the victim that the apologizer thought about it, but it is not so long as to leave the employee

stewing about it too long;

2. Apologize in writing, but it needs to sound natural; it should not sound forced or like it is written by an attorney;

3. It should not be partial or incomplete and should not throw blame back at the employee ("Sorry you felt that way.")

4. It should not highlight the bad conduct ("Sorry I said you dressed like a slut") or justify the bad conduct (Sorry, but I always talk to my friends like that); and

5. It should talk about the conduct, but not use legal terms or admissions (Sorry I sexually harassed you).

Ms. Burnette generously provided the follow sample apology letters to Pepperdine students and has graciously agreed that they can be published here.

SAMPLE DISTRICT MANAGER APOLOGY

Dear Employee,

I wanted to write to you personally to apologize for my comments last week. I have been thinking a lot about what I said to you. I am so sorry that I used that language and that I upset you.

I am glad that you called me out on my comments because it will make me be more sensitive, both to you and to other employees, and it will help me to be a better manager. In the future if I have a concern about your job performance, I will make every effort to hold myself to the same high standards that I expect of my team.

You are an important member of my team, and I appreciate your hard work. I hope that we can put this matter behind us and work together effectively from now on. If you ever have concerns, please feel free to share them with me.

Sincerely,

District Manager

SAMPLE HUMAN RESOURCE REPRESENTATIVE APOLOGY

Dear Employee,

Thank you for telling me about your recent concerns regarding your District Manager. Please understand that I took you seriously, communicated your concerns to upper management, and an investigation was conducted. You expressed further concerns that you did not know what was happening behind the scenes and felt frustrated and as though I did not listen to you.

I am writing to apologize for not telling what actions we were taking on your behalf. Although there are always privacy issues with personnel matters, I could have and should have kept you better informed about what was happening. For me, working in human resources is always a learning process, and I am trying to improve my skills.

I hope that you will feel free to contact me about any concerns in the future. Please do not hesitate to contact me if you need to talk further about any personnel matters. I look forward to working with you in the future.

Sincerely,

Human Resources Representative

SAMPLE COMPANY APOLOGY

Dear Employee,

Thank you for bringing your concerns to our attention regarding remarks from your District Manager and regarding your transfer. We have conducted an investigation of your concerns. As a result of the investigation, the company reached the following conclusions:

1. The comments made to you were inappropriate. We are taking personnel action with regard to the District Manager as a result.
2. While the comments were inappropriate, we do not believe that the comments were sufficiently severe and pervasive to violate our sexual harassment policy.
3. Your transfer was based on legitimate business reasons and was not prompted by the District Manager's comments or your complaint.

With that said, I wanted to personally apologize to you, as a valued employee, for the District Manager's comments to you. The comments must have been very upsetting. I also wanted to apologize that you were not better informed of what the company was doing to address your concerns. Employees should feel welcome to discuss concerns with Human Resources and should feel their complaints are heard and treated seriously.

I hope that we can move forward from here and that you will continue to have a positive working relationship with our company. I want to emphasize that our company does not tolerate unlawful retaliation, and you will not be penalized in any way for bringing your concerns to our attention. Please feel free to come to me if you have any further concerns.

Finally, I am personally authorizing an additional 3 days (24 hours) of paid vacation time for you. You should see the additional vacation time added to your balance on your next pay stub.

Sincerely,

Company CEO

Clearly Ms. Burnette's advice and sample language for pre-suit apologies give her clients the benefit of her decades of experience. As with Mr. Hutton and Paris Hilton, the apology comes from the client, but the attorney is instrumental in conceptualizing the apology.

Ms. Burnette has the following advice for apologizing after an employee has sued the company.

1. Don't apologize until six to nine months after the lawsuit is filed. The plaintiff is more likely to be tired of the lawsuit; he or she may be psychologically ready to be done with the legal proceedings;
2. An apology is a good way to set the stage for settlement negotiations;
3. It is best if the employer can apologize directly to the employee at a mediation. If necessary, the company can tell the employee's friend who still works for the company; and
4. The apology should come from someone high up in the organization. It should not be in writing.

Again, we see Ms. Burnette sharing with her clients decades of experience about the most effective way to apologize after a lawsuit has been filed. The specificity of her advice demonstrates that there is still a need for expertise and wisdom after a client decides to apologize.

The lawyer assisting the client in apologizing raises some ethical concerns. Cohen suggests that the lawyer is facilitating fraud if she encourages a client "to misrepresent their remorse so as to gain a strategic advantage."[18] Cohen believes that accomplishing a good result for the client by encouraging the client to offer an apology that falsely professes guilt is unethical. Cohen does not discuss the social harmony apology option and how forbearance might be an acceptable substitute for remorse. Staying in the remorse apology paradigm, he accepts that a lawyer can make the client aware of strategic advantages of an apology and ask the client if they have considered making an apology. Whether the reader agrees with Cohen's ethical construct, he has done a service by raising the issue and offering his views. Practitioners should consider when their encouragement of apology would be unethical.

4.32 Clients Apologizing Through their Attorney

Sometimes it is the lawyer who communicates the apology. This is different from above because the client is not communicating for himself; his lawyer is expressing the client's remorse and apology. This approach may be used to avoid a situation where the client might make statements that could be used against him later. The lawyer's apology for the client is probably most often offered privately or in a mediation. Sometimes this is done in the media.

Two examples were recently reported by the press. The attorney for a Dallas-area police officer who was videotaped aggressively restraining teenagers at a pool party held a televised news conference.[19] The attorney told the media that her client was in hiding after receiving death threats and apologizes. She explained that her client had been emotionally unsettled by two suicide calls he handled shortly before responding to the pool party complaint and was not in an appropriate emotional state when dealing with the teenagers.

The other example involves a Southern California man whose attack on an Uber driver was videotaped. After criminal and civil charges were filed against him, his attorneys released a statement that included the following,

> "Mr. Golden recognizes that despite his level of intoxication, he should have never slapped Mr. Caban and is extremely remorseful for his actions .... Mr. Golden accepts full responsibility for his actions and understands the consequences that may occur as a result .... Mr. Golden has worked hard to live a life of compassion, respect, and professionalism and understands the damage that this incident has done .... Moving forward, Mr. Golden will avail himself of all opportunities that will assist him in gaining insight and growth from this experience."[20]

Another example is described by Darci Teobaldi. Darci served as General Counsel for a company that manufactured a device to enable people who have been deaf to hear. The executives and scientists of this company who invented the device were passionate about the mission of assisting deaf people to be able to hear.

Darci describes a situation when a sub-contractor negligently manufactured a component part. The result was that some of the devices eventually malfunctioned, either creating a loud screeching sound or just stopped working. The devices are surgically installed. Thus, the only solution for the malfunctioning device is a second surgery to remove and replace the device.

The company accepted responsibility for the malfunctioning devices. When a patient informed the company that their device had malfunctioned, Darci or her team meet with the patients to assist them in the replacement process and sometimes negotiate a resolution. The company supported Darci in having her explain its heartfelt calling was to help people hear; it knows that the patient trusted this company and the company let the patient down. Darci provided an apology to the patient and their family or caregivers as part of the resolution conversation.

The situation makes sense. Liability is clear. The company wants to take responsibility in these situations. The company's lawyer is sent to resolve the complaint. The likelihood of reaching agreement increases if the company and the lawyer extend an apology.

It may be a nuance, but notice that in these cases, the lawyers are not issuing statements by their clients proclaiming their apology. Rather the attorneys are describing that the client apologizes. This may be done purposefully in live press conferences because the attorney may be gifted at describing the apology, answering follow up questions, and explaining the mitigating circumstances. The client may not have those skills or be in an emotional state to handle such an interview. The possibility must also be considered that this approach is used because the client is not as remorseful as the attorney describes.

Jennifer Robbennolt's empirical research has documented that apologies offered by an attorney are viewed as better than no apology but are not as positively as apologies personally offered by the offender. Her study concluded that apologies offered by attorneys are perceived as being motivated by a desire to avoid litigation and less likely to be accepted by the victim.[21]

My family had a similar experience with an attorney apologizing on behalf of a healthcare provider. An Urgent Care doctor made a mistake and a member of our extended family died. The HMO did a very poor job on two administrative matters after the death. Because I am the only lawyer in the family, they asked me to communicate with the HMO about our frustrations. I met with a physician who is also a lawyer, now specializing in medical malpractice cases, who confirmed that the Urgent Care doctor clearly made a mistake and committed malpractice. This lawyer was eager to represent my family until he learned that the patient was a 79-year-old diabetic; he said those factors meant there would only be nominal damages.

I filed a complaint with the HMO's customer service department. They sent the case to a review committee which found that the doctor's decisions had been within her professional discretion. My family was livid, and we had exhausted our internal grievance procedures. Pursuant to the contracts with the HMO, we submitted the case to arbitration.

The HMO had in-house lawyers represent them in arbitrations, and I began communicating with Richard Phillips, the HMO's lawyer assigned to this case. From the first conversation Richard was empathetic, sharing that his parent had died in a hospital, and he personally experienced many of the same questions being asked by our family and was sorry for our family's loss. After two or three conversations, I shared with Richard the analysis we had received from the physician/plaintiff's attorney and told him that my family would probably be satisfied if they could have a meeting with the Urgent Care Doctor and hopefully receive an apology. He eventually told me that the HMO's experiences when they had arranged such meetings were not good, so they would not agree to such a meeting.

After exhausting all other possibilities, I told Richard that he had been decent and caring throughout our conversations and asked if he would be willing to meet with three members of my family so they could have someone from the HMO to hear their complaints. After checking with his superiors, he agreed. At the meeting, Richard was empathetic and a good listener. He started to be a little defensive once, and I asked him not to contradict the advice we had received from physician/plaintiff's attorney. He backed off and returned to listening to the frustrations of my family members.

He was in full agreement that the two administrative matters after the death were handled very poorly and that the HMO should create protocol to prevent those mistakes from happening in the future. He apologized for those mistakes and promised that he would personally advocate for the protocols to prevent the recurrence of those mistakes with the appropriate committee at the HMO.

After the meeting with Richard, I went to lunch with the three members of my family. They all liked Richard and felt a sense of relief that finally someone at the HMO listened to them and at least partially agreed that our family had not been treated right. They agreed to dramatically drop their monetary demand to a symbolic figure.

After the case was settled and the paperwork complete, I called Richard and thanked him for how humanely he handled this matter. I told him that if I were the General Counsel at the HMO, I would not waste his sensitive bedside manner at arbitrations. I would ask him to meet with every family who initiated arbitration with the HMO to listen to them and show compassion. If he heard things that he believed were not handled well, he would be authorized to apologize and promise that this experience would be used to improve the policies and practices at the HMO. I complimented him on keeping his humanity after three decades of practicing law with a medical malpractice defense specialty.

Notice in this case, the attorney is not reading a statement of apology from the client. Here the client is apologizing through the attorney. The attorney may have the personality and skill to be a conflict de-escalator for her client, sometimes even resorting to be the mouthpiece through which a client apologizes. It is well documented that doctors with a good "bedside manner" don't get sued as often as other doctors because they have good people skills. In a similar way, the strength of some attorneys may be their ability to offer apologies on behalf of their clients.

4.33 Attorneys Apologizing for their Client

There may be some situations when the attorney serves the client by apologizing for the client. This is unique in that the client may not be sorry or able/willing to say he is sorry. The attorney becomes the surrogate apologizer. She apologizes on her own behalf for the bad behavior. While usually the injured party needs the apology from the perpetrator, there may be situations where the attorney's apology for her client assists in reaching a resolution.

Attorney Don Wolfe describes a time in his career where this happened. During the mortgage default crisis in 2008-2010, a prominent attorney from a neighboring state with media outlets and a large public following agreed to represent about 500 clients whose homes were in various stages of foreclosure. The only problem is that his firm did not have the expertise to handle these kinds of cases. After a while, his office was in full damage control mode responding to clients complaining because they wanted to know what was happening with their cases.

The prominent attorney hired Don to advise the firm on handling these 500 clients. Don's priority was to assess exactly what had been done on each case. Don was alarmed to learn that nothing had been done on many of the cases after being represented by the prominent lawyer for almost a year. Don's advice to the prominent attorney was to meet with every client and tell the truth. This meant that some clients would be informed that nothing had been done on their case. The prominent attorney reluctantly agreed to Don's approach but wanted Don to be the one to meet with the clients.

Don met with all 500 clients individually and informed them on the status of their case. He apologized when nothing had been done, gave his cell number to each client, and promised that he would make sure the firm would start doing whatever was possible to help save their homes. The clients were angry at the prominent attorney, but trusted and liked Don. The clients were well served from that point forward and not one of them sued or complained to the Bar about the prominent attorney.

In this case, the attorney's bedside manner worked to the benefit of his client. Don's ability to build trust and rapport by telling the truth, including an apology when appropriate, helped his client to get out of a bad situation. The prominent attorney knew that he had lost credibility and had too much ego to admit a mistake and apologize. He was smart enough to hire Don as his "fixer."

Don shared with Pepperdine students a time when he made a mistake on a client's case. He could have rationalized or done a comparative fault analysis, but instead he simply admitted the mistake to his own client and gave his client the name of a good plaintiff's malpractice attorney. When he invited the client to sue him, the client, who was very angry, suddenly relaxed and said that he didn't want to sue Don. Don's penchant for telling the truth and apologizing is part of his method when he is handling his own affairs, as well as when he is representing others.

4.4 Attorneys Negotiating the Terms of the Apology

Attorneys knowledgeable about apology should consider aiding their clients by attempting to negotiate the terms of an apology. Lazare identifies the following variables that could be negotiated when making an apology.[22]

Who should apologize to who;

How much responsibility the offender and offended each accepts for causing the grievance;

The specificity with which the offender acknowledges the offense;

Whether mitigating explanations are acceptable;

How much remorse, shame, humility, and sincerity the offender must communicate;

The amount of suffering the offender must bear;

The acceptability of reparations;

The timing of the apology;

The opportunity of the offended parties to verbalize their suffering; and

The degree to which the offended parties will acknowledge that their needs have been met and give forgiveness.

This list of variables in the apology equation helps an apologizer to emphasize one or more element that might be particularly important in a certain situation. A perpetrator may be hesitant to deliver the kind of apology he anticipates the victim wanting. But Lazare's list of variables equips the perpetrator to explore with the victim if they can agree on the terms of a mutually agreeable apology. For example, the perpetrator may be willing to make a public apology accepting all responsibility and declaring his remorse **if** there are assurances that this act of humiliation will be accepted by the victim with a public declaration of forgiveness. Without the assurance that the apology will be accepted, the perpetrator would not be willing to publicly apologize.

There may be some cases when the perpetrator and the victim can have the conversation to negotiate the terms of the apology. There are other situations where the injury and reactions to the injury make such a conversation impossible. A significant service is rendered if the perpetrator and victim have representatives who can explore the terms of the apology on their behalf. This happens around the world when a family member or representative of a tribe or village who is removed from the incident has a more objective conversation about the terms of resolution. Attorneys who understand this opportunity and are knowledgeable about apology can serve as the advance team to explore the terms of an apology for their clients.

It is important to note Lazare's observation that reparations without acknowledging wrongdoing is a settlement.[23] This is the common practice and comfortable for lawyers. Reparations with acknowledgement of wrongdoing is an apology. Apologies have the potential advantage of being healing for both the perpetrator (guilt) and the victim (restoration of dignity) individually; apologies also serve as the foundation for resuming the relationship because of the possible assurances of shared values and future safety in the relationship. The lawyer might be able to help the client accomplish some of these benefits if the lawyer successfully negotiates terms of a mutually agreeable apology.

Two student journals provide an overview of concepts and concerns raised in this chapter. The first provides a cross cultural and generational perspective.

> Before coming to Pepperdine, I never realized how different lawyers were portrayed and viewed in the United States compared to Europe, well at least the Netherlands. People would say things in class like "I'm a recovering trial lawyer" and I never really understood what they meant by that and why it seemed to be a funny thing to say. Over time I came to understand that lawyers appear to be perceived as sharks or snakes, people that act in sneaky ways to get what they, or their clients, want without regard for other people.

Though I doubt that this is actually the general view of lawyers in America, and though I doubt even more that American lawyers really act in such a manner, it is interesting that the notion even exists. Last week's class played into this idea that lawyers in America hold different standards for themselves than they do for their clients. Advising your client to apologize seems like an unprofessional thing to do whereas had it been you or your child making the mistake, the first thing you'd do would be to apologize. My take-away from this class is mostly that by allowing yourself to give into the risks of apologizing, you enforce the vicious cycle that leads to the booming litigation culture that makes America unique.

In my mind, apologizing is the only decent thing to do when you make a mistake and even when something happens that is not entirely your fault but that you were involved in. This is how my friends and I were raised, and this is how I thought our society, meaning the Netherlands, worked. I could not imagine that lawyers in Holland would advise their clients not to apologize when they had made a mistake, or that people could be afraid of apologizing because it would increase their liability.

Turns out I was both right and wrong. I talked with my father about this because on the one hand I could not believe that lawyers on different sides of the ocean could be so different. On the other hand, it was hard for me to envision my friends' fathers holding such different standards between their personal and professional life. <u>My father explained that when he was in law school in the early 1980s he was taught to always apologize, even when it was not your clients' fault. This way, when the case actually came before a judge, the judge would know you acted in good faith because at least you apologized. However, this standard is slowly giving way, like so many other things, to the American way of life creating a more fearful atmosphere when it comes to apologizing, even in the Netherlands.</u>

America's influence on the world is in many respects quite positive. Sadly, I think the litigation obsession may be one of the least favorable aspects of American culture and one that I would hate to see travel across the globe. Therefore, I hope to never give in to the risks of apologizing and always keep my own personal standard as a measuring stick for the advice I give to others. Submitted by Majlie de Puy Kamp, emphasis added.

The final student journal for this chapter raises important questions and concerns about attorney assisted apologies.

I liked reading and talking about how apology can be used as a part of a legal strategy. It poses the problem of how to figure out if an apology is ever sincere? We want less to crucify someone for their actions when they recognize their wrongdoing, so why not fake it in order to avoid the potential dire consequences? Taft is right when he says the bargained-for apology is not authentic.

In the example of the (HMO's) atrocious medical malpractice and misdiagnosis, the target was the arrogant doctor that did not apologize, not the doctor who felt bad about what happened and voiced his feelings to the family. Once everyone knows that this little trick could save you from massive lawsuits, people will be dishing out strategic and calculated apologies like candy. I would swallow my pride if I knew it would save me from a lawsuit. One could make an argument that we do not need more insincere apologies in this world, and legally we are encouraging them.

The thing that is most offensive is that the law protects apologies that are not really apologies. These types of apologies can be perceived as insults and almost make the victim even angrier and the situation worse. It is like saying, "I'm sorry you feel that way, but I still refuse to admit I did anything wrong, but I'm sorry." If I was the victim, that apology would not only be insufficient, but it would make me hate my offender even more.

In class, we talked about three ways an attorney could apologize for their client: the attorney can give an apology for their client with attribution, without attribution and the attorney can apologize for himself/herself without any reference to the client. I think that the third option is ridiculous. While it may make the victim feel better that the lawyer for the offender feels bad about what happened and knows that their client did something wrong, it could also further validate the victim's anger and resentment towards the offender. Here is why: not only is the offender not sorry, he or she has done something so bad that even his or her own lawyer disapproves of their conduct, and they still won't give me an apology! I think this type of an apology would make the situation much worse, and make the victim want to go after the offender even more instead of diffusing the situation.

The idea that we have to carefully craft our apologies so that we avoid liability really takes the heartfelt meaning out of an apology in general. We become so focused on apologizing in the right way because we are so terrified that we might say too much and get ourselves into a ton of trouble. We have to try so hard to reach the perfect balance between vagueness and specificity that we apologize enough to validate the emotions of the victim, but not too much that we give them power or latitude to take advantage of our apology.

Our in class exercise this past week focused on how an attorney would advise apologies in certain circumstances. Is this part of our job description? —coaching our clients on how to apologize in the exact correct way to avoid liability. By doing this, don't we completely take away the idea of morality from the apology? Submitted by Caitlyn Peskind, emphasis added.

4.5 Claremont College Crisis Exercise

Background Facts

An anonymous whistleblower alerted the University President to investigate the SAT scores the University publishes for incoming freshmen classes. The whistle blower reported having evidence suggesting they were being inflated, but he/she did not substantiate the accusation. The President referred the accusation to the General Counsel for investigation. An Assistant General Counsel did a spot check of the data for the most recent year and concluded that it is highly likely the published figures were inflated. The General Counsel informed the University's Vice President and Dean of Admissions about the issue and suggested retaining an independent accounting firm to do a thorough audit. The VP/Dean appeared concerned but agreed to the audit.

First Assignment:

You have been retained by the VP/Dean. The VP/Dean admitted to you that he had attempted to boost the University's national rankings by inflating the numbers. He is sure the audit will reach this conclusion. He said he acted alone and is willing to resign. You need to advise him about how to handle this. You have concluded that either no laws were broken or that criminal prosecution is highly unlikely. Should he inform the General Counsel that the audit will not be necessary; he will confess that he inflated the numbers and acted alone? If you advise him to confess, should he try to negotiate for a severance package in exchange for confessing and taking full and sole responsibility for this?

Second Assignment:

You are the General Counsel for the University. Assume the VP/Dean has confessed to you, taken full responsibility because he acted alone, and that he is willing to resign with a moderate severance package. You reported the above situation to the President, who asks for your counsel about how to handle this mess. He specifically asks your advice on the following issues:

1. Should we disclose this situation to the public? If not, should we disclose it to:
    a. The University's Governing Board?
    b. Significant Donors?
    c. Institutions who rank Universities
    d. Faculty and Staff?
    e. Alumni and Students?
2. Should we ask the VP/Dean to resign? If so, will the typical severance package be offered?
3. If we ask the VP/Dean to resign, should we gain a commitment from him to keep his mistake confidential? Should he keep the severance package confidential?
4. If we announce it how should we describe it ... How much do we blame it on a lone rogue employee?

As you consider the second part of the exercise, don't forget that governing board of Penn State University demanded the resignation of the University President and Athletic Director because they participated in covering-up the child abuse allegations against an assistant football coach.

Created based on the LA Times article, "College inflated scores, probe finds" on January 30, 2012 at http://articles.latimes.com/2012/jan/30/local/la-me-sat-20120131.

A student reaction to the Claremont College Crisis is helpful.

> In class, I was the lawyer helping craft a way for my client, who had bolstered SAT scores for a college and been found out, decide how he should go about the situation. The client was remorseful about what he had done but did not know what to do in the situation. My advice was to apologize to the President and have a conversation about taking blame for a smooth exit from the university with a severance package.

> In class we had the opportunity to see what Professor Robinson would do in the situation. I found that particularly helpful. His idea was similar to mine, for the client to be willing to take the blame in return for a graceful exit and severance package, but he went about it more strategically. Professor Robinson would have had lunch with the President's lawyers and spoken in hypothetical terms about what the client would be protected from and/or get if he was to officially apologize. I found that incredibly tactful because it was very much the middle ground in terms of creating the space for the client to apologize if he wants to, but also doing due diligence in insulating the client from some of the potential harm. Submitted by Rachel Hews.

Endnotes

1. *See* ABA Model Rules of Professional Conduct: Preamble & Scope ¶ 2.

2. *Id.*

3. *See* Michael Marcus, "Mediation Message No. 125 RFAs-Important Procedural Requirements," www.marcusmediation.com.

4. California Code of Civil Procedure Section 2033.220, subdivision (b).

5. *See* Wimberly v. Derby Cycle Corp. (1997) 56 CAL. APP. 4th 618, 634

6. California Code of Civil Procedure Section 2033.420, subdivision (a) and subdivision (b)(3) and (4).

7. *See* Cohen, *Advising Clients to Apologize,* 1013.

8. *See e.g.*, California Evidence Code Section 1119.

9. *See* Cohen, *The Immorality of Denial*, 79 TUL. L. REV. 903, 934 (2005), http://scholarship.law.ufl.edu/facultypub/41.

10. *See* Jonathan Cohen, *The Culture of Legal Denial*, 84 NEB. L. REV. 247 (2005).

11. *Id.* at 270.

12. *Id.* at 274.

13. *Id.* at 280.

14. *Id.* at 281.

15. *Id.* at 362.

16. Thomas Gehring, *SETTLE IT ...and be Blessed* (2013).

17. Author's interview with Roberta Burnette and published with her generous permission, on file with author. Roberta Burnette is regularly recognized as a Southern California Super Lawyer in the area of Employment and Labor and led that practice group for the Dentons Law Firm, Los Angeles office from 2012 to Present (2017).

18. Cohen, *Advising Clients to Apologize*, 1065.

19. Matt Pearce, "Former Texas officer apologizes for aggressiveness at pool party, attorney says," *Los Angeles Times*, June 10, 2015.

20. Veronica Rocha, "Uber driver's assailant apologizes after video goes viral," *Los Angeles Times*, November 4, 2015

21. Jennifer K. Robbennolt, "The Effects of Negotiated and Delegated Apologies in Settlement Negotiation," Law and Human Behavior, Vol.37, No. 2, 2013.

22. Lazare, *On Apology*, 205.

23. *See id.* at 64.

Chapter Five

Mediators Facilitating Apologies

5.1 Introduction

5.2 Mediator Orientation and Process Control

5.3 Parties with Conflicting Views About the Need for an Apology

5.4 A Five Continuum Analysis Tool

    5.41 Mediator as Catalyst of Conscience

    5.42 Mediator Assistance in Formulating the Expression

    5.43 Apology Attribution

    5.44 Culpability in the Apology

    5.45 Clarity of the Apology's Meaning

    5.46 Various Combinations of the Factors

5.5 Family Food Truck Fiasco Mediation Exercise

5.1 Introduction

This chapter will explore the appropriate role of a mediator who seeks to encourage an apology. This will be challenging because mediation is a very flexible process that can be designed to accomplish a variety of objectives.

Some parties may need to settle a lawsuit and use mediation to "bargain in the shadow of the law."[1] These mediations frequently focus on the legally admissible evidence and projected outcome if the case goes to trial. Because the facts and/or law are usually contested in these mediations, an apology would be rare.

In contrast, some parties utilize a mediator because they desire to resolve a dispute and maintain some level of relationship. The dispute may involve relationships that are important to maintain like family, business partners, and inter-dependent businesses. Parties hoping to heal the relationship will anticipate and expect the mediator to explore the underlying wounds in the dispute and encourage parties to communicate their perspectives about the alleged offenses. The enhanced understanding between the parties sometimes reveals unintended impacts or heightened awareness that aspects of one and/or another's behavior was inappropriate. The mediated resolution is sometimes facilitated by an apology or sometimes an apology is an essential element of the resolution.[2]

Wedding Drama Case Study

Submitted by an anonymous student

Today we talked about the "eggshell friend," and someone instantly came to mind and I just had to share it. We talked about how the eggshell friend can require an apology even when the supposed offender did nothing wrong. Objective standards of offense are completely irrelevant with an eggshell friend. Often time, in my experience, this is a situation that can call for a social harmony apology. Something I really love about this class is that it gives us words to things that I never had words for. I have always understood the social harmony apology, and known when it is required, but I have never had a word for it.

My husband's Aunt Susan is not an eggshell friend, she is an eggshell aunt! She takes great offense to absolutely nothing. Rob (my husband) has a younger sister named Dori. She has a hard-enough time apologizing when she knows she has done something wrong, but she absolutely will not apologize if she thinks she is in the right. The result? Family drama. Aunt Susan is also not the nicest or most conscientious person on the planet, so it makes it hard for the family to see any convincing reason to persuade Dori to apologize.

At Dori's wedding, Aunt Susan decided she would wear a white dress! Dori was not having that at all. When she made feelings known to Aunt Susan, the real drama started. Aunt Susan said she was not going to the wedding, and Dori was beginning to say maybe Aunt Susan's entire family would not be allowed at the wedding then. Then Grandma got wind of the fiasco and said she would not go to the wedding unless everyone had "made up and were friends again." Aunt Susan would not apologize for proposing (pun intended) to wear a white dress to her niece's wedding, because she believed she was the injured party. Dori would not apologize for hurting Aunt Susan's feelings, because she found that idea ridiculous.

This situation would be a classic mediation role play. We did not have a mediator and I am an outsider, so I did not step in. Everyone in the family was taking sides (mostly on Dori or Grandma's.) It was the most conflict avoidant member of the family that saved the day. Uncle John, Aunt Susan's husband, encouraged her to back down for the benefit of the family. She bought a new dress, Dori was the bride, so she had another crisis to attend to, and Grandma was happy no one was fighting. Uncle John is the last person I would have expected to intervene with any of the angry parties. It would have been best, probably had everyone "made up" by apologizing, because things were still tense. But the wedding went off without a hitch after that!

Maybe a social harmony apology from Dori is too much to ask from a strong-willed bride, and any kind of apology from eggshell Aunt Susan would probably never happen. So, given the personalities involved, this was probably the best result any mediator could have hoped for!!

5.2 Mediator Orientation and Process Control

In addition to considering differing objectives of the participants in a mediation, we need to consider the mediator's orientation about how much the process is controlled by the parties and how much of it is controlled by the mediator. Some mediators define their role as controlling the process while the parties control the outcome. Such a mediator may project her views about the role of apology in a given mediation, regardless of the parties' desires. Such a projection can be to encourage an apology or direct the conversation so that it never comes up. Either way, the role of apology was determined by the mediator.

The style and philosophy of other mediators are to invite the participants to participate in creating the mediation process for that dispute.[3] Mediators with this approach will be more inquisitive about parties' desires and responsive in guiding the mediation. The extent apology is explored will depend on the level of the parties' enthusiasm for such a soul-searching examination and potentially vulnerable conversation.

A description of how these two variables (level of party interest and mediator level of process control) affect the role of apology in a mediation is provided by a Pepperdine Adjunct Professor. He described mediating between three sisters who had inherited the farm where they grew up. One of the sisters and her husband lived on and managed the farm. A conflict arose over some of their management decisions, and it escalated to the point of claims and counterclaims in lawsuits. The adjunct professor was retained to mediate.

He described guiding the mediation to focus on resolving the legal claims. Lawyers for each of the sisters were present and actively participating in these negotiations. Personal issues that were not legally relevant were mentioned, but the mediator did not pursue those comments because he was laser focused on resolving the lawsuits. With considerable skill, the mediator assisted them in reaching an agreement that the farm should be managed by a professional manager in the future and that all lawsuits would be dismissed. The documents were drafted and executed, and it seemed like the mediation was about to successfully conclude.

When all the sisters and their lawyers were together for what they thought would be a closing ceremony, the mediator surprised them. He announced that during the negotiations, each of the sisters had privately told the mediator that this dispute had fractured their family and each of them "wanted their family back." The mediator then asked the sisters if they wanted to continue talking to each other about healing the fractures and reconciling their family and if so, how? The sisters agreed that they wanted to have that conversation that afternoon with the mediator present, but no lawyers. The second stage of the mediation concluded with multiple apologies, promises of forgiveness, and commitments to not allow this conflict to destroy their family any longer.

The case study is instructive on two levels. First, notice that the mediator controlled the focus of the mediation. For either strategic or habitual reasons, he focused on resolving the business dispute first, including the lawsuits and how to co-own the farm in the future. Only after that was accomplished, was the mediator willing to explore if the parties wanted to include the interpersonal dimension of this dispute. This illustrates how a mediator can control the agenda and process. Some mediators are not comfortable with the interpersonal dimension, so they provide a valuable service by simply settling the lawsuits. Apology is not explored in some mediations because the mediator is not comfortable with the personal nature of the topic.

The sisters and farm example illustrate how a mediator can invite, but not require an apology conversation. When the mediator was ready, he did not mandate another round of meetings to discuss putting the family back together. He informed them that each sister had expressed this desire to him privately and invited them to continue with that focus. Any of the sisters could have declined the invitation for a variety of reasons. Maybe she was already exhausted and did not have the energy for that conversation. Maybe she wanted to digest the things she learned at the mediation and would reach out to her sisters in her own way and on her own timetable. The mediator in this case both controlled the mediation and shared control of whether to have the interpersonal conversation that could lead to apologies.

One extreme is the mediator who is so focused on resolving the lawsuit that she does not see the opportunity for apology and/or doesn't allow it unless she deems it necessary and likely to be helpful in resolving the lawsuit. If both sides are making accusations that the other is the "offender," then such a mediator often concludes that a conversation about who owes whom an apology is unlikely to assist in settling the legal claims.

The other extreme is the mediator who has integrated an exploration of apologies into his process and requires parties to reflect and consider if there is anything they have done that should trigger an obligation to apologize. This mediator automatically explores questions that might lead to an apology in every mediation as part of his approach to the process. (Is there anything you did in this conflict that you wish you had handled better? Have you told the other party that you regret those actions or wish you had handled that better? Would you be willing to today?)

A Straus Adjunct provides an example of facilitating an apology to both settle the case and help heal the relationship. The dispute was between two cousins who went into business together. One was very wealthy and contributed the capital. The other was a capable business person and contributed the sweat equity. Over time, it became apparent that the sweat equity partner had stolen from his wealthy cousin. The wealthy cousin brought a lawsuit to recoup the money and prevailed at trial. The sweat equity partner was on the verge of bankruptcy that might include losing his home to satisfy the judgement at the time of the mediation.

The mediator was intrigued when he learned that this extended family was so close that they had a family dinner every Sunday with both cousins and the mothers of both cousins in attendance. The mediator asked the wealthy cousin how the extended family had interpreted the situation. He described how he was viewed as the bad cousin because he didn't need the money but was going to force his cousin and family into financial ruin and out of their home. The mediator asked if it would be valuable if his cousin would publicly apologize and take responsibility for stealing at the next extended family dinner. The wealthy cousin said that it would be priceless and that he would arrange for him to keep his home if he made such an apology.

The mediator worked with both parties as to the content of the apology. At the next family dinner, the sweat equity cousin called for the attention of everyone. He then fully confessed that he had stolen from his cousin and got down on one knee to ask his cousin to forgive him. Forgiveness was granted, and the wealthy cousin's standing as a good member of the family was reinstated!

My goal is for mediators to understand and be comfortable with facilitating the apology process and to look for signals the parties may be open to it. One such signal might be confidential confessions to the mediator acknowledging ways in which a party contributed to the conflict or the escalation of the conflict. (Remorse Apology.) Another signal might be a statement of sadness about losing this relationship. (Social Harmony Apology.) Another signal might be a lament about how much this conflict is going to cost a party. (Externally Motivated Apology.) Another signal might be acknowledgement of the other party's terrible situation combined with declarations that it wasn't the speaker's fault. (Regret/Empathy Apology.)

Another category of signals is when the victim informs the mediator that this case will not be resolved without an apology from the other side. Instead of revealing a reason why the speaker might apologize, the speaker is demanding an apology from the other party. The apology competent mediator can follow up by exploring the terms of the required apology.

5.3 Parties with Conflicting Views About the Need for an Apology

This leads to the discussion of how to handle the situation where one participant clearly wants to include apology in the mediation and the second party does not. The easier case is when a party wants to apologize. Victims may be skeptical and concerned about whether the apology is a crass tactic to "soften them up" so they will accept a lower settlement offer.[4]

The mediator should validate the skeptical party's concerns and help the parties negotiate a solution. If the offender insists on apologizing early in the mediation, the parties could agree to allow that to happen, with an understanding that the victim will be guarded in his reaction until he sees the reasonableness of the settlement offer. Alternatively, the parties might agree to allow the apology after the settlement has been negotiated. While reparations were listed as the last element of a remorse apology, there may be instances when there are good reasons to address this first and include the other elements after reparations are agreed upon.

The harder case is when the victim is demanding an apology and the offender refuses. The mediator should begin exploring the demand for the apology. Why is it necessary? What does it look like? What does it accomplish? Is she okay with a forced apology that isn't sincere? What exact behavior needs to be described in the apology or is a vague general apology acceptable. The mediator is assisting the parties negotiate the terms of the apology. The offender has refused, but he may be picturing a comprehensive, sincere, remorse apology, which would not represent his honest feelings.

The mediator also needs to explore the offender's reasons for the resistance. Does the offender deny doing anything wrong? (Does the mediator agree with this construct or is the offender rationalizing or pretending? Some mediators might ask questions or even make statements if they perceive that the offender needs to take more responsibility.) Does the offender know that she made mistakes, but is reluctant to humble herself before the victim? (Would the offender like the mediator to explore whether the victim will accept the apology and forgive the offender if she apologizes?) Is the offender willing to offer an apology for specific and limited actions (maybe for their reaction to the conflict instead of the origin) or offer a type of apology other than a remorse apology?

If the mediator cannot negotiate mutually acceptable terms of an apology, the mediator can inform the parties that this is the cause of an impasse. If they want to resolve this dispute in this process today, one of them will need to accommodate the other, or they will need to agree to some compromise solution. Sometimes one of the parties really wants or needs to resolve this dispute, so either the plaintiff will drop the demand for an apology, or the defendant will offer a lackluster apology.

So, the goal is for the mediator to be sensitive to signals that could lead to exploring an apology and be capable of following up on those signals. The message is that the scope of the mediation can be expanded to include the exploration of apology, but not in every case.

The rest of this chapter assumes that at least one participant has asked/given permission for the mediator to explore the topic of apology. Now, the question is how much should the mediator do to assist an apology? Are there times when a mediator should decline to assist with the apology?

5.4 A Five Continuum Analysis Tool

Assessing how far a mediator should go to assist an apology is a personal question. Different mediators will have different comfort zones and responses. The author recommends considering five factors and suggests a continuum for each. Each factor will be discussed below. This chart below organizes the combination of factors that either confirms or condemns the mediator's decision to assist an apology. A discussion of the continuum for each factor will follow the chart.

Evaluating the Mediator's Role in Facilitating Apologies

Low_____High

Amount of Mediator Involvement in the Apology

(Catalyst of Conscience)

Low _____High

Amount of Mediator Involvement in the Apology

(Formulating the Expression)

Party _____Mediator

Attribution

	Empathy /	Externally
Remorse	Regret	Social Harmony	Motivated (See Chapter One)

Culpability in the Apology

Clear _____Vague (See Chapter Two)

Clarity of the Apology's Intended Meaning

5.41 Mediator as Catalyst of Conscience

One factor a mediator should consider when assessing how far to go in assisting with an apology is the extent the mediator has been the catalyst of conscience. The category of "catalyst of conscience" describes the extent the mediator played a role in a participant realizing that his behavior was inappropriate. Some parties freely confess to the mediator that they feel guilty about aspects of their behavior that contributed to the conflict. This scenario describes the mediator having a low role on the catalyst of conscience continuum. The party felt bad about their behavior without any prompting from the mediator.

The contrast is when a mediator plays a role in the party realizing that their behavior was inappropriate. The innocuous version of this is when the mediator relays what the other party said about how certain behavior had a harmful impact. Assuming there was no ill intent, the party may feel bad about unintentionally hurting another. The more controversial version of this involves increasing amounts of objective confrontation. Examples of questions a mediator might ask from less to more intrusive are:

1. Would you handle this situation in the same way again? (Remorse)
2. The other person is really hurting; does that matter to you? (Empathy)
3. I wouldn't wish the other person's predicament on my worst enemy; do you feel bad that they are in this situation? (Regret or Empathy)
4. Do you feel any regret or guilt over anything you have done in this conflict? (Remorse)
5. Do you think that most people would be sympathetic about the other person's complaint?
6. I don't think you intended to hurt the other person, but I understand why they are offended-- can you?
7. I am surprised that you don't feel responsible for the other person's situation. Can you explain to me why you aren't responsible?
8. I am personally appalled at what you have done and believe you should apologize.

The more the mediator escalates to trigger the party's conscience, the greater concern that the mediator is usurping the party's self-determination and becoming too involved in the apology dynamics. The more involved the mediator was in triggering the awareness of wrongful conduct, the less likely the apology reflects the party's conscience as opposed to the mediator's conscience.

An example is provided by another Straus Adjunct Professor. A woman accused a very successful doctor of sexual exploitation. He regularly attended professional functions with a series of beautiful women half his age. He privately told the mediator that there is an understanding that beautiful women exchange their beauty to be with men who have money and power.

The mediator asked the doctor to consider whether he was objectifying the women. The doctor just laughed and told the mediator that this is the way the world works. Regardless of the outcome, the mediator felt the need to at least ask the doctor to reflect on his behavior. Had the doctor responded to the mediator's suggestive question with an apology, there would have been a concern about the depth of the conviction beneath the apology.

When considering this factor, a mediator should be much more comfortable assisting the apology when she has a lesser role in serving as the catalyst of conscience. The more she has been involved in getting the party to realize his misdeed, the more concerned she should be about assisting the apology. In fact, a student journal strongly condemns this role.

> <u>Mediators should be able to pick up on subtle hints that either party wants to apologize and help the parties expand that desire. However, mediators should never try to be a "catalyst of conscience" and convince either party they need to apologize. That is beyond their role. The mediator's role is to help the parties better articulate an apology they want to give.</u>
>
> In class, I served as the mediator in a family dispute involving a young food truck owner and his aunt who had funded the venture. The young food truck owner wanted more money after the truck had been vandalized, but the aunt had already lost money and was unwilling to invest more. The young owner took offense and they were in sort of a stalemate. I found it morally compelling as a mediator to ask both parties if they had any regrets about what had happened in the past, or if they felt bad about the current situation.
>
> Both parties to some level recognized they had disrespected the other or misled the other. I as the mediator was able to help them better articulate that to each other. Even though the aunt only had a regret apology, she was able to articulate it in a way that was pleasing to her nephew. The nephew was able to see where he had been disrespectful and somewhat entitled. He was able to articulate a remorse apology.
>
> The positive thing about being a mediator is that you can help facilitate a relational healing process if the parties want to do that. It can be difficult if the parties have no intent on apologizing because mediators cannot be a moral conscience. They simply help facilitate the intent that is existent within the parties. Submitted by Rachel Hews, emphasis added.

5.42 Mediator Assistance in Formulating the Expression

Mediators regularly assist parties in expressing their thoughts, feelings, beliefs, or arguments. One of the ways mediators add value is to allow parties to practice what they will say to the other party and offer objective feedback. Sometimes the mediator's feedback is focused on whether the other party will be able to hear the intended message the way the person is expressing it. Sometimes the mediator's feedback helps the speaker articulate his message more clearly.

Whenever a mediator is engaged in this activity, care must be taken to maintain the speaker's true message. Especially when the mediator is suggesting ways to express the message, the mediator should preface the suggestion with, "Only use this phrase if it is true for you."

Sometimes the mediator suggests replacing accusatory language with expressions of how the speaker felt or was impacted by the other. This is done to decrease the likelihood that the listener will respond with a defensive counter-accusation. An example is replacing "You misrepresented the monthly revenue of the company" with "I was panicked and really afraid when the monthly revenue of the company was only half of your forecasts the first three months after I bought the company." The balance is to remove the toxin but remain true to the speaker's message.

This mediator assistance is appropriate when a party is in full attack mode or when one party is simply not articulate. Some parties are not good at expressing vulnerable feelings. When a mediator asks that party in private to explain her motives, she may only respond with curt phrases. In the ensuing conversation the mediator attempts to explore and add depth to the conversation. Sometimes the mediator even suggests ways for a party to explain their feelings. Again, the concern is that the mediator must be very careful not to provide a script written by the mediator that is not an authentic message from the party.

When evaluating a mediator assisting with an apology the extent the party needs assistance in articulating various elements of an apology is a factor. I am less concerned about mediator coaching about things like vague or conditional apologies. In fact, I encourage mediators to assist parties in delivering a better apology. If a speaker cannot describe the offense that is the subject of the apology, the mediator needs to be concerned about whether the speaker has shared values about the behavior. If the speaker needs help articulating remorse, again the mediator needs to be concerned about whether the speaker feels remorse.

Notice that is possible that the speaker has shared values regarding the behavior and is genuinely remorseful. He may just not be able to articulate those intimate/personal feelings and beliefs. The mediator should proceed with assisting this speaker to deliver an effective apology. This factor in the evaluation system does not preclude proceeding. It simply alerts the mediator to be aware that they have needed to offer a lot of assistance in articulating the apology. The more the party needs the mediator's assistance in articulating the apology, the more the mediator should be concerned about its authenticity.

5.43 Apology Attribution

The variety of sources of attribution of the apology is another factor a mediator should consider when assisting with an apology. The presence of the mediator creates a variety of the delivery systems for the apology. Which of these delivery methods is selected by the offender may affect whether the mediator is willing to assist the apology. Some of the ways an apology might be delivered are so removed from the offender that the mediator might resist assisting the apology, especially if some of the other factors raise authenticity issues.

The attribution issue is not complicated when the offender delivers her own apology in joint session. She delivers her own message that she is sorry. The message is clear: the offender declares her sorrow for the behavior. If the victim wants to ask clarifying questions or engage in dialogue, the offender is present and available for this purpose. The offender is the one delivering the message in the event she chooses to be vague or otherwise hedge the expression of acknowledgement or remorse. The face to face delivery allows the victim to assess the tone and body language to judge the depth and sincerity of the apology. An offender speaking for himself directly to the victim is the best form of apology attribution. A mediator should have fewer concerns about facilitating the apology in this situation.

The next best form of attribution for an apology is when a mediator relays the apology to the victim for the offender. Sometimes an offender agrees with the apology but is unwilling to deliver it himself. Humbling himself directly to his adversary is just too difficult. The offender might readily confess his guilt or regret privately to the mediator but also inform that he will not disclose this to the victim. He may ask the mediator to deliver the apology for him, or the mediator may ask permission to relay the message. Either way, the mediator ends up being the "mouthpiece" that delivers the apology to the victim on <u>behalf of the offender</u>. This is an apology by the mediator attributed to the offender.

Mediators regularly deliver messages for the parties in the shuttle diplomacy dimension of mediation. This practice is accepted so long as the message is generally accurate. The danger is that a well-meaning mediator may filter the message to be more acceptable to the recipient. An example in the apology context is the mediator who "cleans up" a reluctant apology so that it does a better job of meeting the victim's needs. The offender's bare whisper of regret is delivered by the mediator as a deeply held conviction of wrongdoing. Of course, this distortion can be managed because the mediator can control the accuracy when she carries the message.

When a mediator is delivering a sensitive message, like an apology, the mediator and party being spoken for should consider having the party in the room to observe how the mediator is communicating on the party's behalf. The party receiving the message can look for a nod from the party being represented to validate that the mediator gave an accurate summary.

An indirect approach regarding attribution is when a mediator tells the victim that the offender has not said it, and the mediator believes the offender knows he made mistakes and is sorry. In this instance, the mediator is trying to fill the victim's need to know that the offender is aware of and regrets the offense, when the offender is not willing to say it or allow it to be said for him. Sometimes a party confesses to the mediator but forbids the mediator from telling the other side. Other times the mediator comes to her own conclusion that the offender knows and regrets the offense, without the offender saying the words. In either event, some mediators will assure the victim that the mediator believes the offender is aware of and regrets the offense. This is indirect because we have crossed a line where the mediator is giving her opinion and is not delivering a message from the offender. This technique can meet the victim's needs if the victim trusts the mediator's assessment.

A more controversial approach regarding attribution is when a mediator apologizes for the offense. This is problematic because it is generally accepted that only the offender has standing to offer a remorse apology. Still it may meet some of the victim's needs if others, including a mediator, offer an empathy apology.

An example is Retired Marin County Presiding Superior Court Judge Lynn Dupree, who is now a panelist for JAMS. She describes how she handled the initial greetings when conducting a settlement conference for a lawsuit involving a catastrophic loss like the death of a loved one. She often hugs the plaintiff and says she is sorry for what happened. She attends to the look of terror in the defense attorney's eyes fearing that the judge has abandoned neutrality by following up with a statement that today's meeting will involve scrutiny about assigning responsibility for causing the tragedy. For her, the starting point is to acknowledge the plaintiff's suffering. When questioned by other judges at a mediation training program, she explained that she does not abandon her humanity when she puts on the judicial robe.

In extreme cases, a mediator may even offer a surrogate remorse apology. An example would be the mediator in a divorce matter responding to one party's description that they learned that the marriage was over when they walked in and observed their spouse in the act of adultery. While the mediator needs to be neutral, authenticity might also result in a statement by the mediator condemning this way of ending a marriage and saying that they are sorry. This is like an empathy apology, except it includes a statement condemning the behavior and saying that this should not have occurred.

A mediator should consider who the apology is attributed to as one of the factors that might affect whether he is willing to assist with the apology. The more the apology is attributable to the party, the easier it is for the mediator to facilitate the apology.

5.44 Culpability in the Apology

Chapter One already described the various amounts of culpability in the following spectrum of apologies.

Remorse	Regret	Social Harmony/Empathy	Externally Motivated

--------/----------------------/------------------------------/--/

The type of apology being offered is another factor a mediator may want to consider when deciding to assist with the apology. If private conversations with the offender convince the mediator that the apology is externally motivated, the mediator may have concerns about providing assistance. In contrast, the mediator might be enthusiastic about providing assistance if he is convinced that a party is genuinely remorseful.

A mediator who is willing to assist with apologies should know about the different kinds of apologies and how an apology can be used to manipulate a victim. An unsuspecting mediator can unintentionally become part of an exploitive apology. More problematic, a mediator may be the originator of the apology strategy to accomplish a settlement. Such a practice might be acceptable if the victim is not misled about the amount of culpability represented by the apology. This legitimacy analysis begins with the mediator knowing the various types of apologies and determining the offender's intentions in a proposed apology.

5.45 Clarity of the Apology's Meaning

Chapter Two described the issue of clarity in an apology. There are instances where every type of apology can be clearly explained without offending the victim. There are also instances where the victim will want a remorse apology and the explanation of other types of apologies will further frustrate the victim because the offender is denying responsibility and/or remorse. This creates the temptation to disguise the actual meaning of some types of apologies and hope an unwitting victim will accept it, even if they mistakenly interpret it as a remorse apology. The mediator who assists with apologies should monitor the clarity of the apology and be cautious about becoming a part of the apology "sleight of hand" to the victim.

There is room for a variety of ethical constructs for apologies. I believe that all types of apologies can have legitimacy if they are delivered with full disclosure. Especially when something less than a remorse apology is being offered, the speaker can fully explain the meaning and limits of the intended message. The ethical danger of misleading and potentially re-injuring the victim is anticipated and avoided by the emphasis on apology clarity.

Mediators should assess the extent of clarity in the proposed apology when considering their willingness to assist in its delivery. The more clarity, the more enthusiastic the mediator should be in assisting. Lesser degrees of clarity will need to be evaluated in the totality of the circumstances, considering the factors of the type of apology, attribution, mediator assistance in formulation, and mediator as catalyst of conscience.

5.46 Various Combinations of the Factors

The five continuums are constructed to reflect the author's view that assisting the apology is more acceptable when that factor is rated on the left-hand side of the continuum. Any factor rated towards the right-hand side of the continuum should raise a yellow flag to caution the mediator. The yellow flag does not disqualify from the mediator from proceeding, but she should be aware that the situation is not ideal. How many and which combination of yellow flags should cause the mediator to decline to assist with the apology will depend upon that mediator's goals, philosophy, and moral orientation. The chart is an attempt to assist mediators in understanding and articulating why they are uncomfortable.

Evaluating the Mediator's Role in Facilitating Apologies

Low_____High

Catalyst of Conscience

Low_____High

Formulating the Expression

Party_____Mediator

Attribution

Remorse _____ Regret _____ Social Harmony/Empathy _____ Externally Motivated

Culpability in the Apology

Clear _____Vague

Clarity of the Apology's Intended Meaning

Some sample combinations will illustrate.

If all factors are on the left-hand side of the chart, the party entered the conversation able and willing to articulate the condemnation of certain aspects of their behavior. The party has genuine remorse and wants to use the mediation to clearly explain his remorse directly to the victim. The mediator should be comfortable assisting in facilitating this apology.

Now assume the mediator played an active part in helping a party understand how his behavior was inappropriate and played an active part in helping the party articulate the apology. I was in this situation when mediating between a film producer and his client.

The film producer was demanding the client pay for costs that exceeded the contract budget. During the mediation, the producer revealed that he had produced a second film for himself using the same talent and rented equipment. He explained that he had asked everyone to donate their time and materials for the second project. He was oblivious to the possibility that the second bootlegged project might have contributed to the cost overruns. After being confronted by the client and private prodding by the mediation team, the producer admitted it was wrong for him to not disclose the second project to his client and that some of the costs may have been inflated to account for the additional time and effort.

For me, active mediator involvement in the first two factors does not necessarily disqualify the mediator from assisting with the apology. If the mediator believes that the party has genuine remorse and is willing to directly and clearly communicate that remorse to the other party, the mediator may still conclude she is comfortable facilitating the apology.

Let's assume a more complicated situation. What if the defendant denies all wrongdoing, but the plaintiff demands an apology as a prerequisite to any resolution? The defendant sees an opportunity to resolve the complaint for less than attorneys' fees if the case proceeds to trial. Because the plaintiff has demanded an apology, the mediator is probing what the defendant might be willing to apologize about. It becomes clear that the defendant has no remorse, but he asks the mediator to deliver an externally motivated apology to the plaintiff, without revealing that it is just to appease the plaintiff and get the complaint resolved. In this situation, the combination of yellow flags regarding type of apology, clarity, and attribution may cause the mediator to decline to participate in actively deceiving the plaintiff.

How does the mediator react if everything is the same as the immediately preceding example, except the defendant asks the mediator to arrange a joint session where the defendant will deliver a vague externally motivated apology? Does the plaintiff's demand for an apology provide enough notice that any subsequent apology may be coerced? Is the mediator relieved of responsibility for the authenticity of the message because the defendant is speaker for herself directly to the plaintiff? Does the face-to-face exchange put the burden of assessing the authenticity of the message on the plaintiff? Mediators often know things disclosed in private that are not fully disclosed in joint sessions.

What is the mediator's role if the defendant asks assistance in delivering a vague externally motivated apology? Should the apology educated mediator offer pragmatic counsel about the likelihood of such an apology being well received? Should the apology savvy mediator suggest ways to enhance the apology to improve the likelihood of its effectiveness? Should the mediator assist the recipient in accurately interpreting the apology? Should this interpretation assistance only occur if the recipient asks for the mediator's thoughts? How does a mediator balance any interpretive assistance with confidential insights learned in caucus with the defendant? Mediators knowledgeable about apology will need to make myriad decisions about how to appropriately use this understanding.

Another Straus Adjunct had a case illustrates the mediator's potential role in helping to reveal a dubious apology. The mediation concerned generational planning for a family business. The parties were two sons in their early 20s and their father. The father disappeared and the boys were largely raised by their grandparents. When it came time to decide who would control a family business upon the grandparents' death, the father reappeared and wanted to be in charge. He reached out and asked to reconcile with his sons if he could run the company. A tentative compromise was reached where the father and his two sons would serve as the board to run the company. The mediator was concerned that the young men had significant expectations about having the father they always wanted but never had back in their lives.

The mediator wanted to check the dynamics between the father and the boys by having the first board meeting within a few days, with each party's lawyers observing from the back of the room. As the mediator suspected, the father did not play nice at the board meeting. When the sons and their lawyers saw him try to bully his sons, they took a timeout and renegotiated the business relationship. After that, the father was not interested in reconciling the family.

The discussion about mediators assisting with apologies should conclude with a reminder that Professor Taft's article titled, "The Commodification of Apology"[5] specifically cautions mediators about assisting apologies that risk re-victimizing the victim. He admonishes mediators to consider apologies as part of a sacred space.

A student comment integrates many of the above concepts.

> I don't believe it's our role as mediators to convince someone that they are in the wrong, but we can remind them of their interests. I feel we should concentrate on external motivations such as making or saving money, repairing business relationships, and securing good PR. As a facilitative mediator who is uncomfortable the deeper I dip into evaluative waters, I would be less comfortable being a "catalyst for conscience" who tries to make someone feel remorse or guilt.

> I am thinking back, in particular, to a case I mediated in Santa Monica that involved a petitioner, a school bus driver who was suing for defamation after having been falsely accused, by the defendant, of child molestation. I don't feel that the defendant truly felt guilty, but in order to settle the case without a large cash payment, she knew that she would have to apologize, in writing, to the plaintiff, satisfying his deeply-felt need to see her brought low.

> The motivation of this apology was extremely external. It lacked motivation in even the "social harmony" or "empathy" columns. The plaintiff was an English-speaking African-American male and the defendant a Spanish-speaking Hispanic woman. Neither treated the other like a fellow member of a cohesive social group. The defendant made an informed decision based on a calculation of the risks and rewards of apologizing vs. those of going to trial.

> My co-mediator and I took our roles as "agents of reality" who ensured process fairness (not necessarily substantive fairness.) We reminded her that the risk of losing money at trial was greater than the risk of losing face in a private apology that, in truth, she would probably forget about after going home. For the plaintiff, the sincerity of the defendant's apology mattered less than the sense of power and control it gave back to him.

In crafting the written apology ("formulating expression"), we advised the defendant to sculpt away the justificatory language she would have preferred, giving the plaintiff the language he needed to gain satisfaction. We also made sure both sides understood not just the language, but the intent and motivation behind the words (clarity), and that the plaintiff attributed the apology to the defendant and not to us. In the end, the plaintiff had no illusions and fully understood the defendant's motivation for apologizing to him was entirely selfish ("culpability"), but the defendant understood why he needed the satisfaction of her apology. Submitted by Jonathan Andrews, emphasis added.

5.5 Family Food Truck Fiasco Mediation Exercise

Family Food Truck Fiasco Mediation

Role for Investor Partner

You are a mid-50s lawyer who is financially comfortable, but not wealthy. At your nephew/niece's request, you became a partner in a food truck business. Your nephew/niece graduated from a reputable chef's school and worked in a food truck business for three years. You have eaten his/her food at many extended family gatherings, and everyone agrees it is outstanding. He/she described that the food truck business is a can't lose money making machine. He/she asked if you would provide the $50,000 start-up money to buy a truck, get the licenses etc. The written partnership agreement you prepared specified that you would be an equal partner and receive 50% of the profits. He/she would contribute sweat equity by working the truck and sharing the expertise to earn his/her 50% of the profits.

You agreed to do this because you have a close relationship with your nephew/niece. You made it clear from the beginning that you are already overcommitted and that 100% of the effort and expertise for this enterprise would need to be the nephew/niece's responsibility.

The business exceeded expectations the first month, generating a net profit of $10,000, so pursuant to the partnership agreement, you and your nephew/niece each received $5,000. The next two months your share of the net profits was only $2,000. You could tell that your nephew/niece was becoming frustrated with the long hours and modest return on his/her labor. You wondered if he/she was not working as hard as the first month when he/she was so excited but would never suggest this because you know it would seriously damage your relationship.

Early in the fourth month, disaster struck. The food truck was catastrophically damaged by vandals in the middle of the night. Your nephew/niece had insured the truck for liability, but not for vandalism. The damage was so extensive that the truck would require $30,000 in repairs to resume operations.

Your nephew/niece was shocked when you declined to pay the money to have the truck repaired. You aren't sure this venture will generate enough profit to be sustainable. Your thought is to sell the truck "as is" for about $10,000. Since you paid the money to buy the truck you assume you should receive the $10,000 from liquidating the business. You prefer to cut your losses at a little more than $30,000 than to invest more money in what you now believe to be a very risky endeavor.

Your nephew/niece is upset and insists that you fix the truck so that the truck can make "serious money during the busy summer season" to make this whole thing worth the effort. He/She now explains that he/she always considered you the deep pocket that would make additional investments in an emergency. You were unaware of this expectation and in fact promised your spouse that you would not invest any additional money in this business. When you informed your nephew/niece about this, he/she lost his/her temper and called you cheap, stupid, and under the thumb of your spouse.

A mediator has asked you to think about if you are sorry for anything in this situation and be ready to share your response privately in an upcoming caucus. You have reflected and decided to share that you are sorry for the following things with the connected qualifications.

1.   That the truck was vandalized without insurance, but that was not your fault.

2.   That your nephew/niece's dream is collapsing before your eyes, but again, you don't feel responsible. You fulfilled your commitment and the failure of the business is not your fault.

3.   That there is a misunderstanding about the extent of your commitment to this business, but again you don't believe you did anything to lead your nephew/niece to believe that you would provide additional money if needed.

4.   That you will end up losing more than $30,000, but you knowingly took that risk and do not have hard feelings about the outcome.

5.   That this incident may be the ruin of your relationship with your nephew/niece and maybe others in the extended family.

If the mediator suggests it might help heal your relationship if you offered your nephew/ niece an apology for the things you described above, you are willing. You want to make sure your nephew/niece understands that you are not taking responsibility for the things that led to the closing of the business. You may want a chance to practice your "apologies" with the mediator before delivering them to your nephew/niece.

Family Food Truck Fiasco

Role for Sweat Equity Partner

You are a late 20s chef who is financially stable but living financially month to month. You graduated from a reputable chef's school and worked in a food truck business for three years. You have seen how food trucks are very lucrative and asked your Uncle/Aunt to be your partner in a food truck business. Everyone inside and outside the family who has eaten your dishes raves that they are incredible. You described that the food truck business is a can't lose money making machine.

Your Uncle/Aunt is a mid-50's lawyer who is financially well off. You asked your Uncle/Aunt to provide the $50,000 start-up money to buy a truck, get the licenses etc. The written partnership agreement your Uncle/Aunt prepared specified that he/she would be an equal partner and receive 50% of the profits. You would contribute sweat equity by working the truck and sharing expertise to earn your 50% of the profits.

You asked your Uncle/Aunt to do this because you have a close relationship since you were little. Your Uncle/Aunt made it clear from the beginning that he/she was already overcommitted and that 100% of the effort and expertise for this enterprise would need to be your responsibility.

The business exceeded expectations the first month, generating a net profit of $10,000, so pursuant to the partnership agreement, you and your Uncle/Aunt each received $5,000. The next two months your share of the net profits was only $2,000. You were becoming frustrated with the long hours and modest return on your labor. Since you worked in the industry, you were not alarmed because all the trucks make reduced income during the colder winter months, but really make a killing during the longer days and warm evenings all through the summer.

Early in the fourth month, disaster struck. The food truck was catastrophically damaged by vandals in the middle of the night. You had insured the truck for liability, but not for vandalism. The damage was so extensive that the truck would require $30,000 in repairs to resume operations.

You were shocked when your Uncle/Aunt declined to pay the money to have the truck repaired. Your Uncle/Aunt isn't sure this venture would make enough profit to be sustainable. It was really upsetting when they suggested selling the truck "as is" for about $10,000. He/she explained that since he/she paid the money to buy the truck he/she was expecting to receive the $10,000 from liquidating the business. Your Uncle/Aunt explained that he/she preferred to cut his/her losses at a little more than $30,000 than to invest more money in a very risky endeavor.

You are upset and insist that your Uncle/Aunt fix the truck so that the truck can make "serious money during the busy summer season" to make this whole thing worth the effort. You always considered your Uncle/Aunt to be the deep pocket that would make additional investments in an emergency. Your Uncle/Aunt claims he/she was unaware of this expectation and in fact promised his/her spouse that they would not invest any additional money in this business. When he/she told you about this, you called him/her cheap, stupid, and under the thumb of their spouse.

A mediator has asked you to reflect on whether you are sorry for anything in this situation and be prepared to share your response privately in an upcoming caucus. You reflected and decided to share with the mediator that you are sorry about the following.

1.   That the truck was not insured to cover the vandalism;

2.   That your Uncle/Aunt will end up losing more than $30,000;

3.   That you lost your temper can called your Uncle/Aunt "stupid, cheap, and under the thumb of your spouse."

4.   That this episode may create an awkward distance between you and your Uncle/Aunt and others in your extended family.

If the mediator suggests it might help heal your relationship if you offered your Uncle/Aunt an apology for the things you described above, you are willing. You may want a chance to practice your "apologies" with the mediator before delivering them to your Uncle/Aunt.

Family Food Truck Fiasco

Role for the Mediator

You are in the middle of mediating a family dispute involving a business partnership concerning a food truck. The Uncle/Aunt is a mid-50s lawyer who invested $50,000 to acquire a truck and the licenses so that his/her nephew/niece could start a food truck business. The nephew/niece graduated from a reputable chef's school and worked in a food truck business for three years. He/she told the Uncle/Aunt that the food truck business is a can't lose money making machine. The written partnership agreement prepared by the Uncle/Aunt specified that they would be equal partners, and each receive 50% of the profits. The nephew/niece would contribute sweat equity by working the truck and sharing the expertise to earn his/her 50% of the profits.

The Uncle/Aunt agreed to do this because of a close relationship with the nephew/niece. The Uncle/Aunt made it clear from the beginning that 100% of the effort and expertise for this enterprise would need to be the nephew/niece's responsibility.

The business exceeded expectations the first month, generating a net profit of $10,000, so pursuant to the partnership agreement, each partner received $5,000. The next two months each partner's share of the net profits was only $2,000.

Early in the fourth month, disaster struck. The food truck was catastrophically damaged by vandals in the middle of the night. The nephew/niece had insured the truck for liability, but not for vandalism. The damage was so extensive that the truck would require $30,000 in repairs to resume operations. The nephew/niece was shocked when the Uncle/Aunt declined to pay the money to have the truck repaired. He/she wants to sell the truck "as is" for about $10,000 and receive the $10,000 from liquidating the business.

The nephew/niece is upset and insists that the Uncle/Aunt fix the truck so that the truck can make "serious money during the busy summer season" to make this whole thing worth the effort. The nephew/niece always anticipated that the Uncle/Aunt would make additional investments in an emergency. The Uncle/Aunt was unaware of this expectation and in fact promised his/her spouse not to invest any additional money in this business. When informed of the situation, the nephew/niece lost his/her temper and called the Uncle/Aunt "cheap, stupid, and under the thumb of his/her spouse."

As the mediator, you asked both parties to take a few minutes privately and reflect on whether there is anything either of them is "sorry for." You are about to meet with each of them privately in caucus to learn their responses. While you need to confirm this in caucus, you sense that there is a history of closeness in this family and that both sides are concerned about this conflict creating a lasting breach. If so you intend to suggest that apologizing for things either of them are sorry for may help maintain positive relationships. If they agree to apologize, you would like to let them practice with you first in private.

A student's reaction to the Food Truck Fiasco exercise is interesting.

> I played the role of the mediator who was responsible for facilitating and crafting the apologies between the two parties. <u>Initially I did not think that the exercise, specifically coaching the parties to apologize, would feel as unnatural as it did. I thought that the parties would be more willing to apologize to each other to resolve the dispute. In retrospect, however, that view is more indicative of my own underlying principles regarding apologizing.</u> I felt like more of a therapist because I repeatedly asked the parties how they felt and how they wanted to proceed. I wanted to make sure that the apologies were sincere and parallel to their positions. I heavily factored their feelings into the mediation, instead of just considering their best interests. It felt very odd, as the practice of law usually does not seem to incorporate emotion into the equation.
>
> I was also surprised how much the parties needed coaching in order to formulate a proper apology. Their apologies were consistent with our Class One discussion of apologies, specifically the apology phrased like, "I am sorry if you took it that way..." (I think it is easier to assess quality of an apology from an objective perspective though.)
>
> I think the apologies set up the potential for a possible reconciliation between the parties, but it did not lead to a total settlement. While the parties were able to apologize to each other, they were unable to settle the dispute primarily at-issue: sell the food truck and give the proceeds to the aunt. Both parties remained adamant in their positions regarding that major issue. While the apologies helped diffuse the minor issues (i.e. the insults, the impact on the aunt's marriage, the previous miscommunication, and a resolve to communicate better in the future), the apologies did not dissolve their differences on the financial matters. However, there could have been a different outcome if we had more time. Submitted by an anonymous student, emphasis added.

Endnotes

1. *See* Robert H. Mnookin and Lewis Kornhauser, *Bargaining in the Shadow of the Law: The Case of Divorce*, 88 YALE L.J. 950-97 (1979) (describing how disputants reach agreements by anticipating the outcome if the dispute was resolved through the courts).

2. *See* Lelah Love and Eric Galton, *Stories Mediators Tell*, (Chicago: American Bar Association, 2013).

3. *See* Robert D. Benjamin, Considering, "Mediation What Lawyers and Clients Should Know," AMERICANBAR.ORG, November 7, 2001, https://www.americanbar.org/newsletter/publications/gp_solo_magazine_home/gp_solo_magazine_index/benjamin.html.

4. *See* Lee Taft, *Apology Subverted: The Commodification of Apology*, 109 YALE L. J. 1135, 1135-60 (2000).

5. *See id*. at 1159-60.

Part II

Forgiveness

Chapter Six

Defining Forgiveness

6.1 Introduction

How does forgiveness work for you? The premise of this question is that people have different forgiveness experiences. The goal of this book is to assist the reader in mapping out how a person lets go of grudges and heals from emotional injuries. Experiencing emotional injuries is inevitable. No man is an island, and offenses small and great are part of cohabitating with imperfect people. This book will advocate for healing from these injuries by forgiveness.

This book will **NOT** prescribe a certain approach to forgiveness. It seeks to develop a better understanding of forgiveness, and it allows the reader to explore a variety of paths to recovery. Not only will this enhanced understanding of forgiveness equip the reader to advance their own healing, it will empower the readers to assist their circle of influence to advance their healing. A personal circle of influence might consist of family and friends. For lawyers, therapists, mediators, and clergy it might be a professional circle of influence. There is usually an overlap between circles of influence as well.

The study of forgiveness is difficult on a personal level because it returns us to times when we have been hurt. Forgiveness is more difficult to process than the study of apology because forgiveness causes us to focus on the times we have been unfairly injured. In contrast, apology requires us to process guilt and to accept our failings when we have been perpetrators. While the apology study is not an easy task, the study of forgiveness is harder because remembering and maybe reliving painful events causes us to be vulnerable.

This first chapter will explore a variety of definitions and meanings of forgiveness.[1] The words "I forgive you" can communicate a multitude of messages depending on the context and the intentions of the speaker. The process by which a person comes to utter those words can be equally varied. The following excerpts from two student journals provide a rich picture of the importance and complexity of forgiveness.

> This affects my life right now, as well as generally, because forgiveness is such an important element in our lives. I think that not forgiving people has and continues to take a toll on my health and wellbeing. … At one point when I was thinking about forgiveness I thought, "I don't think I've forgiven anyone for anything ever," and that really scared me because I don't want to be someone who holds on to grudges and never lets things go. I was glad we mentioned in class that forgiving does not mean forgetting, because part of the reason I have trouble forgiving is because I don't want to feel like a fool if and when the person does something else that needs my forgiveness as well.

I don't want to continue to forgive people only to have the same behavior continue. Therefore, I don't forget so that I can be aware and alert for things that might indicate that behavior is coming up or is going on. Because I don't forget, I have trouble forgiving because when I remember certain incidents, I get angry, and I can't forgive anyone. How are forgiving and forgetting related? Are they? One student in class mentioned that it's interesting how this class made us realize how unforgiving we are, and that's what makes it difficult to talk about forgiving. After thinking about it, I think I am a very unforgiving person, but I will try to improve some of that throughout the course of this class. Submitted by an anonymous student, emphasis added.

I had never thought of apology and forgiveness being not only separate concepts but separate processes. Even after four weeks of studying apology knowing we would study forgiveness next, it didn't register for me. Last week during class as we started looking at the forgiveness process in its own right and I started to really see the way I view apology and forgiveness as concepts.

I can define each differently. I can separate apologizing to someone or receiving an apology from forgiving someone or being forgiven by someone. And yet, I see that my assumptions and personal mental filing system have the processes tangled together.

There are many reasons why apologies and forgiveness can be difficult and trying. But the more I've thought this week, the more I think this entanglement in my mind of one process instead of two adds to dissatisfaction and difficulty in both processes. I often don't want to accept or give an apology until some forgiveness has occurred. At the same time, often an apology starts the forgiveness process. I think this problem of depending on each for the other to start complicates things for me.

Being able to see apology and forgiveness are related but different, and have different requirements and needs, makes it easier for me to engage in each process separately. They inform each other but don't rule each other. It helps me to see that I can and should apologize separate and apart from forgiving. And helps me practice accepting apologies separate and apart from forgiveness. Knowing and practicing this doesn't take away the complications that my emotions, memory, and past history bring in. But it does help me actively attempt to balance logic and feeling, to balance knowing and doing. All of these things (feelings, structure, technique) are a necessary and important part of both of these processes. Submitted by Stacy Rouse, emphasis added.

6.2 Characteristics

How does forgiveness work for you?

Is it a decision or is it based on a feeling? Is it driven by the rational part of your brain or is it the culmination of the healing of your emotions? A purely rational approach to forgiveness explains why a person might say, "I forgive you, but I am still so mad at you that I never want to see you again." If you were to receive such a statement of forgiveness, would it make sense, and would you understand? In contrast, a purely emotional approach to forgiveness might explain why a person might say, "I want to forgive you, but I can't right now because I am too hurt and still very angry." We begin our consideration of forgiveness by asking if the epicenter of forgiveness is in the rational mind or the emotional heart. This tension is illustrated by an anonymous student's journal.

Once I broke up with … because the long-distance relationship became too difficult to bare, we continued to speak. While we weren't technically "together," in my mind we were, and I loved her deeply. Then one weekend she bumped into her ex-boyfriend. They ended up catching up with one another and at the end of the night, they kissed. She confessed to me two days later and I was heart-broken in a way I had never previously experienced.

She apologized over and over and over again. And I thought about it over and over and over again. Weeks went by but I couldn't allow myself to forgive her. I wanted to forgive her. I was sick of feeling enraged and sad, but I just couldn't. Not after the way she betrayed me. She was so frustrated, pleading with me constantly, begging for my forgiveness, and asking me what she could do. The truth was that there was nothing she could do.

I wasn't capable of forgiving her until three months later. It was not my choice but rather when my emotions allowed me to do so. While we can take certain measures to control some of our emotional experience, at the end of the day, it is not up to us.

Is forgiveness an event or a process? Sometimes people describe a moment when they forgave. For example, "Last night I forgave you!" This suggests that forgiveness is an event that happened at a particular time. Other times people describe that they are working on forgiving with explanations like, "I have not forgiven you yet, but I am working on it." This language suggests that there is a process of forgiveness that culminates in a forgiveness event. Sometimes people describe being so hurt that for them forgiveness consists of a daily prayer to ask God for serenity and for the strength to live that day.[2] This could describe forgiveness as a continuous process. Three students reacted to this in their journals.

I think that forgiveness is both a will and a feeling. You can't forgive unless you have both. You need to WANT to forgive, and you must be READY to forgive. You can be ready but if your heart doesn't let you, your forgiveness won't heal. It's kind of like the idea that your heart and head have to be aligned. I think that this is what makes forgiveness so important and complex. With apology, it is easy to find a way to apologize. There are many external and internal motivators. With forgiveness, I think it's more of a personal decision. Someone can force you to apologize, but no one can really force you to truly forgive. Submitted by Monica Ryan, emphasis added.

I believe that forgiveness is both a process and an event. I believe that the event occurs when you formally offer someone forgiveness. It is an outward step in the healing process and puts the other party on notice that you are prepared to rebuild the relationship. In many ways, I believe that it is indicating to the other party that you are ready to begin the *process* of forgiveness. I think it can be easy to say that you forgive someone, but much more difficult to actually forgive someone in your heart.

With that said, I believe that each step in the process of forgiveness is a choice and is driven by both will and emotions. If you choose to see the bad in the other person and choose to see how he or she is failing in his remorse, then it is much easier to hold on to the emotional resentment that often accompanies being wronged. If, however, the person who offers forgiveness chooses to see the offender's efforts to strengthen the relationship, then she too will subconsciously work toward true, inner forgiveness. Submitted by Maura Kingseed Gierl.

Forgiveness. Is it a process or event? Decision or feeling? … I think the answers to all of these questions is, "Yes, and …" The reality of this concept of forgiveness is there are too many realities. Reactions, feelings, people, and situations are all varied and determinants in the forgiveness process. One question this concept raises for me is, "Is there a 'best process' for coming to forgiveness?" Or is it more important for individuals to move at their own pace in their own journey towards forgiveness? The ultimate goal is forgiveness, so however you get there works? … So, I guess my question is, how much will power is involved with our own forgiveness process and can we empower others in how they forgive? Submitted by Ansley Waller, emphasis added.

Is forgiveness dependent on an apology by the offender or is it a unilateral act? Some people explain that they do not forgive unless the offender gives a sincere apology. I once heard a preacher at a Christian church teach that God requires confession before He forgives our sins, so we should have the same requirement before we forgive those who sin against us. (I do not agree). Others describe that they have the power and prerogative to forgive independent of any behavior of the offender. Can a person forgive in isolation or is it inherently relational? A student gives a good description of this.

Forgiving someone is a difficult task. We are only human and when someone hurts us we hold on to the pain and resentment and carry it with us. We tend to dwell on the pain and bad memories and replay them whenever we can, bringing up the hurtful events over and over again like a broken tape. This helps us justify why we are angry with the other person, why they deserve to not be forgiven. This attitude is unhealthy and is one that is hard to let go of.

I, in my past have been wronged by someone who I thought I loved and loved me. This person hurt me emotionally more than anyone ever has and has made me bitter. I swore I will never forgive this person for what they have done to me and would dwell on the pain and bad memories to refresh my anger and resentment towards this person.

But understanding forgiveness is just as important as understanding the act of apologizing. We can forgive someone whether there has been an apology given or not. Forgiveness surprisingly is a separate act from apologizing. Forgiveness is for us and about us and not the offender.

By looking at the situation itself, at the person who hurt us and understanding that the pain we carry can be removed, can be extinguished and can result in a happier, better us, we can look at forgiveness as an alternate way out of the darkness that we surround ourselves. Forgiveness means taking back our power, and not giving that power to the offender over us. …

This is what freed me at the end. I let go of the painful feelings and the hurt this person caused me and moved on. <u>This person never apologized to me for what they have done, and I am ok with it. I forgave them for what they have done because I wanted to take control of my life and feelings. Now being happy, truly and genuinely happy, is better than any other revenge I could think of.</u> Submitted by Keren Kogan Barash, emphasis added.

6.3 Meanings

What does it mean when a person forgives? There are three basic variables that define the meaning of an act of forgiveness. They are presented in the following graph:

Animus

Wish Them Well	Neutral	Wish Them Harm

Reparations

Waived	Partial	Full

Future Relationship

Trust is restored. The forgiver is vulnerable again.	The forgiver is willing to allow the offender to be close enough to re-earn trust.	The forgiver is not willing to ever interact with the offender again.

The first variable might be a reduction of animosity. A person's immediate response to an injury might be to wish the offender harm.[3] When that person forgives, they may be describing that they no longer wish that person harm. They may be neutral about the offender or they may have gone so far as to wish them well. Thus, one measure of the meaning of forgiveness might be the extent a person has moved to the left of the animus continuum.

Animus

Wish Them Well	Neutral	Wish Them Harm

Notice that forgiveness might describe a reduction in animus, but not necessarily mean the forgiver wishes the offender well. Some people may feel they have forgiven when they still wish the offender harm, but not as much harm as they wished before they forgave. For example, "I used to wish for your slow and painful death; now, I just wish for you to spend the rest of your life in prison." Context matters, and we may be able to think of a situation where a person forgives without a reduction in animus; however, that would be an exception to the norm. An anonymous student's journal illustrates a reduction in animus.

> While listening to the lecture, I was thinking about my relationship, or lack of relationship, with my father. With the new terms and concepts that I have learned in class and really delving into what forgiveness is and the different forms, I learned that I really have never forgiven my dad for all the pain that he has put my family through. This realization hit me like a brick wall because I thought I had put this all past me when I was fifteen.
> I learned that I only said to myself that I forgave him as a way to let myself heal. I have released my expectations that I had for him as a father, but I don't think I can ever forgive him because he has never stopped doing what destroyed our family and has been more than a repeat offender. While I do not have as much anger towards him as I did when I was growing up, I am not sure if I can ever forgive him…. Submitted by an anonymous student, emphasis added.

A second variable in the measuring the meaning of forgiveness is the issue of reparations. What does it mean when I forgive someone who has not repaid a $500 loan? Instead of focusing on the level of animus, let's focus on whether forgiveness includes a release of a claim for repayment. Does it make sense to say, "I forgive you, but still expect repayment?" If you are told that you are forgiven for not repaying a loan, would you assume that payment was no longer expected? One element of forgiveness that could be measured is the extent that reparations are or are not expected. Thus, we can measure the meaning of forgiveness on the following reparations continuum.

Reparations

Waived	Partial	Full

Making reparations means taking responsibility for making the injured person whole. In the case of an unpaid debt, it means paying the debt. In the case of losing or ruining a borrowed item, it means providing the owner with a similar replacement. In the case of negligently damaging another person's car, it means paying for the repairs to return the car to its condition before the accident. Forgiveness may or may not include a waiver of reparations because, ultimately, the need for reparations depends on the needs of both parties and their relationship. For example, it is common for an act of forgiveness to communicate that even though you are not mad at the offender for the injury (reduction in animus), you still expect them to make you whole (full reparations).

A student expressed a strong opposing opinion on this topic.

> It has been said that one can say, "I will forgive him, but I want him to be punished for what he has done." There is a thought that one can forgive and still want reparations on another. I do not believe this is true. I believe that true, full forgiveness is something that comes without reparations. In order to fully forgive, one needs to accept the person's wrongdoing and not wish anything of them. If reparations are a condition to the person's forgiveness, then they have not forgiven the wrongdoer. Full forgiveness is when a person forgives whether or not reparations are imminent. To me forgiveness is irrevocable.
>
> Let's look at a hypothetical situation. A person forgives the murderer who killed their son, under the condition that the wrongdoer must go to jail for the rest of their life. The person forgives their son's murderer and the murderer goes to jail. Then for some reason the murderer gets out in a year. Can the father/mother take back their forgiveness? I do not believe this is possible. Forgiveness is something that can only be reached within one's self and it cannot be conditional with reparations. Submitted by Jamie F. Goldman

A third variable in the measuring the meaning of forgiveness addresses the issue of a future relationship. This spectrum illustrates how vulnerable or trusting the forgiver is willing to be toward the offender. Some forgiveness models require reconciliation as part of forgiveness. According to these models, offering forgiveness means that the forgiver reinstates the offender to the position they were in prior to the offense.

Recognize that some approaches to forgiveness do not require the restoration of the relationship.[4] These approaches are especially helpful at encouraging forgiveness as a healing experience in situations where it would be unwise for the victim to be vulnerable again. An example where most people would encourage "boundaries" is chronic domestic violence. Forgiveness is flexible, and forgiveness may be possible without the victim being vulnerable to the offender in the future.

A student shared a poignant example in a journal.

> During our fourth class session were introduced to the components relating to forgiveness, as well as the three general models of forgiveness. While reading about and discussing these concepts in class, I couldn't help myself from considering them in light of my personal experience, particularly my experience with forgiving my mom for her neglect in the upbringing of my brother and me. For the majority of our childhood, and probably the majority of her life, my mom struggled with addiction and substance abuse. Drugs took over her life, and at the expense of our family.

My dad, frightened by the idea of raising two boys without their mother in the picture, tried to save the marriage and family on multiple occasions. Unfortunately, the addition got the best of my mom and she overdosed for a third time, resulting in a stay at the hospital and another failed attempt at rehab. Soon thereafter, my parents were divorced, and my dad had full custody of my brother and me.

Years later, mom finally apologized. I wish I could remember exactly how she did it and what was said, but I can't. But I do remember the long process it took for me to finally forgive her. When I think about this event in my life in light of the three components of forgiveness, I better understand my feelings towards my relationship with my mom and the future that I see going forward.

I have no animus towards her. She is my mom. She gave me life and I will always love her. I want her to be happy and healthy. I expect no reparations from her. I want her to be able to live her life guilt free, and not feel she has to make-up for the past. How could she repay us anyway? The time is lost, our youth is gone. Will I trust her in our future relationships? That's a tough one to answer. I can't bring myself to fully trust her. The history of drug abuse and neglect went on for the vast majority of my youth. The memories are vivid. I am cautiously close to her nowadays, providing her the opportunity to earn some of my trust back, but I just can't shake the thought that always lies in the back of my mind. Submitted by an anonymous student.

The resulting continuum from these contrasting approaches to forgiveness allows us to measure the meaning of forgiveness on the following "Future Relationship" continuum.

Future Relationship

Trust is Restored. The forgiver is vulnerable again.	The forgiver is willing to allow the offender to be close enough to re-earn trust.	The forgiver is not willing to ever interact with the offender

The meaning of a forgiveness could be diagrammed by marking the forgiver's intended meaning on each of the following spectrums. The left-hand side of each continuum is designed to be the most generous meaning of forgiveness. Thus, in this methodology, the most generous meaning of forgiveness would be an offer of forgiveness consisting of the extreme left hand of all three continuums. The tool is intended to help people understand their intended meaning of forgiveness when at least one measure is not on the extreme left of one or more continuums. The tool is intended to provide a system for understanding a multitude of understandings of forgiveness—without judgment.

Animus

Wish Them Well	Neutral	Wish Them Harm

Reparations

Waived	Partial	Full

Future Relationship

Trust is restored. The forgiver is vulnerable again.	The forgiver is willing to allow the offender to be close enough to re-earn trust.	The forgiver is not willing to ever interact with the offender again.

Context is critical, and the potential combinations are extensive. In one situation, a person may decide to wish the offender well, but still expect full reparations and not want to see the offender again. In contrast, I have heard people express that they will forgive someone in the sense of not expecting reparations, but they look forward to the offender being humiliated someday when the truth comes out.

The tool helps the reader understand that forgiveness is complex and can legitimately assume a variety of meanings.[5] This tool is on a single page so it can be copied and the responses can be discussed with others.

6.4 FORGIVENESS MEANING INVENTORY AND SURVEY

Forgiveness can be defined as consisting of three components. Each component is presented on a continuum below. The sequencing and interrelationship between the three components can vary depending on context and personal values.

Animus

1_____10

Wish Them Well   Wish Them Harm

Reparations

1_____ 10

None   Some   Full

Future Relationship

1_____ 10

Trust Again   Allow them to   Never trust or be

Vulnerable   eventually re-earn trust   vulnerable again

Please rank each of these variables on a scale of 1-10 in the following situations:

1. Car accident with an uninsured negligent driver with an annual salary of $10,000. Your car suffered a scrape that would cost $500 to repair, but not affect the functionality of the car.

    Animus _____ Reparations _____ Future _____

2. An immediate family member who has substance abuse problems borrowed $2,000 and didn't repay you.

    Animus _____ Reparations _____ Future _____

3. A trusted employee of a business you own embezzled $200,000 and quit,
    a.   But   the   company   will   survive.
    Animus _____ Reparations _____ Future _____
    b.   Which caused the company to collapse.
    Animus _____ Reparations _____ Future _____

4. Your roommate borrows your three-year-old iPad with permission and for no reason, it stops working.

    Animus _____ Reparations _____ Future _____

5. Your spouse with whom you have three minor children is unfaithful.

    Animus _____ Reparations _____ Future _____

6. A co-worker knowingly does not fulfill his responsibilities in such a way that he looks competent and you look incompetent to your boss.

    Animus _____ Reparations _____ Future _____

An anonymous student's assessment of her measures of the three elements of forgiveness is helpful.

> Forgiveness. This past summer in June my parents told my brother and me that they were getting a divorce. They have been married for 27 years. My father is the one who wants the divorce, while my mom wanted to try to work through their issues with counseling. … Over the months I started to resent my father and felt angry at him. I spoke to him that night after the exam and told him everything that upset me with his actions in this situation. He apologized, but I didn't feel like his apology was meeting my needs, perhaps it was his explanations that did not make sense to me. He is my father, so I love him, but his current actions upset me, and I am struggling to forgive him. …
>
> When I place my numbers on the different spectrums of forgiveness, I realize I am at a three with wishing my father well on the animus scale. Again, he is my father, and I love him. He has provided my family and me with a beautiful life, and that came from his many (and ongoing) years of working hard. … It is complicated because I am angry at him, but I still love him. As for reparations, I am at a three as well, because my father is a generous man and I truly believe not a malicious man. … He has made it clear that he wants my mom to keep the home and will keep supporting my brother and me. … Finally, on the future relationship spectrum, I am at a solid five. My father and I will have work on building trust again and anticipate this will take time.

6.5 Three Models of Forgiveness

When I first started investigating forgiveness, I quickly observed that various authors conceptualized forgiveness differently.[6] Most authors present their approach without explaining the alternatives. I probably read fifteen books on forgiveness until I was finally exposed to an explanation of three distinct definitions of forgiveness and how to forgive. This section will present the three approaches to forgiveness without preference so readers can consider when they might utilize different approaches.

6.5.1   Therapeutic

The therapeutic approach to forgiveness is based on the premise that the objective of forgiveness is to advance the happiness and serenity of the forgiver. The need for forgiveness arises when a person experiences an unfair violation. A common reaction to the injury is an internal objection, resentment, and anger. Most authors writing about forgiveness agree that this reaction is healthy.[7] They also agree that this is **not** a healthy long-term response.[8]

Forgiveness is one way to describe the releasing of this anger and resentment. The suggestion is that people are happier and healthier if they release their anger and resentment through forgiveness. Dr. Fred Luskin's book *Forgive for Good* provides a good presentation of therapeutic forgiveness and many of the descriptions for this approach are summaries of his writings. [9]

Therapeutic forgiveness is a unilateral process in which a person perceives s/he has been the victim of an injustice and ceases to allow the injustice to dominate his or her thoughts and feelings. Rather the person moves forward unburdened by the negative emotional reactions associated with past events and is free to enjoy future experiences. This person forgives for the sake of his or her own future happiness. The unilateral nature of this approach reveals that the perpetrator does not participate. It is not conditioned on an apology. In fact, the perpetrator(s) may have died. This concept of forgiveness is accomplished by the victim in isolation and purely for the victim's benefit.

All approaches to forgiveness emphasize that forgiveness is not condoning, accepting, or minimizing the injury or the behavior that caused the injury. Some observe that if such was possible forgiveness would not be necessary. Rather, forgiveness is honest about what happened and the effects it had. Therapeutic forgiveness is a commitment not to stay in the wounded victimized state.

Therapeutic forgiveness, as described by Luskin, is a decision and a choice for the wounded person.[10] The wounded person chooses to overcome the injustice and not remain a victim. Everyone has had some unfair experiences in life. Each of us consciously or unconsciously decide how long we will allow that experience to define who we are. This explains why some people have horrific childhoods and are affected by it 50 years later. Other people have the same tragic experience but do not allow it to define them throughout their adult lives. Luskin suggests that people who say that the injury was so great that they cannot forgive have simply not been given an adequate incentive to forgive.

So, one could conceptualize that therapeutic forgiveness is choosing to relinquish being a victim in exchange for a happier outlook. Forgiveness enthusiasts must recognize that this may not be an easy decision. Being a victim comes with benefits. Victims have the moral high ground because they did not do anything wrong. Their moral high ground might be in comparison to the person who unfairly hurt them, or it might be compared to reasonable expectations. A victim of an unfaithful spouse can identify the person who hurt them. The parents of a baby who dies from Spontaneous Infant Death Syndrome (SIDS) are victims of a more amorphous set of circumstances. In either case, the person who suffers an injustice has the moral high ground that should result in sympathy and support. If the support is robust and satisfying, relinquishing the attention and sympathy may be an obstacle to the decision to forgive, but it could also help the person adjust and move on.

This description of therapeutic forgiveness presents a model that leans more toward the decision approach rather than toward a feeling approach. But we will see that feelings are an integral part of Luskin's process to get to therapeutic forgiveness in the next chapter. Many people perceive that forgiveness is a gift of grace to the perpetrator, but therapeutic forgiveness describes a gift the victim gives herself. Three students described experiences that support this approach to forgiveness.

> In my view, Luskin is correct that when the injured party decides not to be a victim any longer and realizes that the harm of resentment outweighs the benefits, the person can engage in the act of forgiveness which ultimately heals the victim. While apology from an offender may help bring about forgiveness, it is not necessary for the process to occur.
>
> Several years ago, my mother and a sibling were staying at my home, when I began a conversation with my mother about her eating habits because her doctor had recently warned her that certain foods could be extremely detrimental to her. My sibling, without invitation, jumped into the middle of the conversation, used several expletives to describe me and stormed out of the room. I did not speak to this sibling for the remainder of their stay, and further did not engage in any conversation for the better part of two months, mainly because I was waiting for this sibling to apologize to me.
>
> This sibling, who is both overly sensitive and indignant never apologized. <u>For the better part of those two months, my inner angst ate away at me, and as Luskin notes, I was physically affected. One day, I simply woke up, told myself that I was not going to hold the grudge any more, let the feelings go and called my sibling. The apology never came, but I was able to find inner peace and move on with my life</u>. I did not need the apology to forgive. Submitted by an anonymous student, emphasis added.

> I do not like to hold grudges and no matter what someone else has done to me, it is important that I forgive them and move forward instead of holding on to the pain of the situation. <u>Forgiving is a way for me to move on and heal. When you choose not to forgive someone, you are deciding to keep the pain you feel and are hindering any chance of moving on. For me, keeping a grudge against someone who has wronged me by not forgiving them, hurts me in the long run.</u> It means that emotionally, mentally, and even spiritually, I am choosing to relive an experience that affected me adversely. Deciding not to forgive someone keeps these negative vibrations within you and hinders you from moving on from the situation. Therefore, I always choose forgiveness, even when it is hard. This does not mean that I automatically choose to forgive right away. Sometimes it takes time for me to forgive and ultimately move on, but I believe that if you eventually forgive then that is what is important. Submitted by Jenieva Abner, emphasis added.

Growing up I was often told that holding a grudge against someone does not hurt that person, it only hurts myself; that it is like taking poison myself and hoping that the other person dies from it. But I always found it so hard to truly forgive someone else just for my own sake. It never seemed like it was possible. It is hard to forgive someone who never actually asked me for forgiveness and who may not even be sorry. I told myself that I would forgive that person so that I could move on myself, but I do not think I actually forgave them because that person never apologized; it felt like I was just trying to trick myself.

But Eva's documentary showed me that someone really can forgive another person who never asked for forgiveness to achieve their own inner peace and mental health. It takes a lot of strength to be able to do that. It takes more strength than I ever would have thought because you have to choose to forgive and move on even though that person may not have asked for it and may not even deserve forgiveness. That is not something that is easy to do even if it will benefit you in the end. Submitted by an anonymous student, emphasis added.

6.5.2 Relational

Some writers approach forgiveness from a perspective that is inherently relational. The assumption is that the objective is to restore a broken relationship. This approach to forgiveness equates forgiveness with reconciliation. (Compare with Therapeutic forgiveness, which enables a victim to grant forgiveness and choose whether to reconcile.) The affected relationship could be interpersonal between the perpetrator and victim, or it might be for the well-being of a team or community. In either case, forgiveness is granted so that relationship can be restored or protected.

Tian Dayton describes forgiveness as being "relational in nature."[11] She describes forgiveness as a process to restore a connection with others or within ourselves.[12] She starts with the need to accept that "No one is perfect."[13] Forgiveness is necessary to accept our own and others' imperfections. She defines forgiveness as a healing that happens when we "deal with whatever issues are blocking our ability to relate (to others) or to be comfortable with our own insides."[14] Dayton observes that long-term relationships require learning to forgive the predictable injuries perpetrated by others and ourselves.[15] Thus, she describes forgiveness as "an atmosphere, part of each day."[16]

Dayton weaves together the internal (maybe therapeutic) and external aspects of forgiveness by observing that our identity is in the context of relationships.[17] "(T)hus, when we choose to forgive others, our identity is also affected."[18] Dayton describes forgiveness as grieving the wrong, recognizing the impact that wrong had on us and "honestly exploring the effect they had on forming who we are today."[19] She describes forgiveness as the by-product of doing the work of therapy to understand where you hurt and letting it go.[20]

If the goal of relational forgiveness is the restoration of an interpersonal relationship, notice that both parties must be interested. The victim's desire to heal the relationship may be thwarted by an offender who is unwilling to acknowledge any wrongful behavior or even to engage with the victim. The victim may accomplish a unilateral healing, which is more in the category of therapeutic forgiveness.

David Augsburger distinguishes therapeutic forgiveness from relational forgiveness in the following excerpt.

> "Go to your brother," said Jesus, "and if he will hear you, you have regained your brother." For Jesus, this is the goal—the central focus, the true meaning of forgiveness. The primary issue is not inner peace for oneself, not moral rightness with one's own conscience, not assurance of one's own salvation. These are self-centered, narcissistic goals that are only further evidence of the fact that one is still giving primary care to one's own needs and secondarily—if any—care to the relationship or to the pain in the other.
>
> In the modern Western world, writing on forgiveness is almost exclusively focused on the process within, the virtues of the freedom found by the forgiver. [21]

The interdependent nature of the relational approach to forgiveness changes some of the concepts and language. Augsburger cautions about what he calls "One Way" or "One Up" forgiveness.[22] He expresses concern about the message behind the frequently used phrase of "I forgive you" because if the goal is the restoration of a healthy relationship with equal standing and mutual respect, the phrase is suspect. Augsburger's concern is that forgiveness is being framed as a one-way street where the saint forgives the sinner.[23] This construct could create residual dynamics where the forgiver is superior and the forgiven is forever indebted for having been forgiven, which Augsburger describes as "one way" resulting in "one up" forgiveness.[24]

Augsburger uses an example describing a husband who has been unfaithful and wants his marriage to continue; however, his wife refuses his request to forgive him, causing him to believe that the marriage is over.[25] His wife explains that she wants the marriage to continue also, but not with her in a superior position as the victim of his affair. She requests a forgiveness process where both of them consider how they contributed to the affair; they forgive each other for their contributions; and they forgive themselves.[26] The sensitivity to ensure that the method of forgiveness is relationship enhancing highlights the contrast between therapeutic and relational forgiveness.

Two students affirm relational forgiveness in their journals and one student refuted it.

> The topic of forgiveness came up again in an indirect way this past week when I went to the funeral service for my friend's dad. We remembered my friend's dad, who had just lost a two-year battle with cancer. The speakers at the funeral all spoke about the preciousness of life, how valuable it is, to live each day to its fullest, and to cherish each moment we are alive. The service caused me to become incredibly introspective, thinking about how fleeting life is and how sacred of a gift we are given.

The people in our lives are our richest treasures, not the money we make or material belongings we own. We often get too caught up in the trivial matters in life that in the long run do not matter to our happiness, our existence. On the spectrum of different types of forgiveness, I tend to relate most closely to the idea that forgiveness is a gift of reconciliation for both the offender and the offended. I view forgiveness as being relational, working to fix and preserve relationships with the people most important to us. Submitted by Andy Nguyen, emphasis added.

The model of therapeutic forgiveness is not forgiveness at all. The idea that you choose to let go of harms and injuries that you have experienced for your own happiness is a great thing to do for your mental health and well-being. However, it is not forgiveness. This type of "forgiveness" often includes cutting yourself off from the wrongdoer. The reason being that you do not forgive the wrongdoer, because if you had, you would still value the relationship. Again, I believe that it is very healthy sometimes to move on from an injury, come to terms with the damage, and move on with your life. But, if you burn the bridge between you and the wrongdoer, you are doing so because you do not truly forgive that person.

I would label this kind of "forgiveness" self-healing. In this kind of situation, you are coming to terms with the fact that you can no longer live with a certain injury, either because it has become debilitating or you have made a conscious choice. Either way, you have decided to help yourself instead of reaching out to the wrongdoer. The wrongdoer cannot heal you from the wound, and therefore, you decide that it no longer has power over you. This is why individuals do not forget when they undergo this type of self-healing, and they do not let go of wanting justice.

Accordingly, to truly forgive someone is to practice the relational model of forgiveness. When you truly forgive someone, you have decided to remove all anger toward that wrongdoer because you want to continue a relationship with that person. This type of forgiveness requires both parties to acknowledge that a harm was committed, and both parties must acknowledge that they are moving forward and away from that harm. This type of forgiveness requires that the wrongdoer give a remorseful apology for his or her actions. It is after a remorseful apology that the victim can forgive. The victim can actually let go of the pain and no longer wish justice or revenge on the wrongdoer. Submitted by Sean Olk, emphasis added.

In class we discussed the relational model that stresses equality in a relationship and the necessity of forgiveness to be done in the right way to not make the other person indebted forever to the forgiver, but I think that model tries too hard and ignores reality. The reality is that when someone hurts someone else, the parties are unequal, the injured party is less than the aggressor. When the aggressor apologizes, the roles reverse, and the victim is now above the aggressor who wants and needs forgiveness. When the victim forgives the aggressor, the parties are now on equal footing and the past is in the past, but the relational model suggests that the forgiver is still in an elevated position because they are the benevolent forgiver.

As I suggested in class, I think this is wrong because we all know that we all need forgiveness because we are not perfect beings. This perpetual messing up causes us to be sensitive to the needs of others to be forgiven because we have the need to be forgiven. We must be humble whether we are in the right or the wrong, and whether we are the forgiver or the forgiven. Practicing humility is the key for forgiver and forgiven to be on the same level footing. Submitted by Casey Caton, emphasis added.

6.5.3 Redemptive

The assumption behind the redemptive approach to forgiveness is that some people must forgive to live consistently with their value system. A value system can be religious or moral beliefs that are important to an individual so much so that it influences their day to day decision making. The title of "redemptive" for this approach to forgiveness reflects that many of the world's religions teach that the Creator will forgive a person in the same measure as the person forgives others. Thus, the reason to forgive is because the people want God to forgive them the way they forgive others. The act of forgiving is a part of their spiritual journal and religious practice and related to God's redemption of them.

I can describe it best in the context of my religious tradition of Christianity, and I have been assured by international students from across the globe that other world religions have similar understandings. When Jesus taught his disciples to pray (The Lord's Prayer), he included the phrase: "Forgive us our trespasses (debts) as we also have forgiven those who trespass against us (our debtors)."[27] Later in the Sermon on the Mount, Jesus teaches "For in the same way you judge others, you will be judged and with the measure you use, it will be measured to you."[28] After Jesus told Peter to forgive 77 times, he taught the following parable of the unmerciful servant:

> Therefore, the kingdom of heaven is like a king who wanted to settle accounts with his servants. As he began the settlement, a man who owed him ten thousand talents was brought to him. Since he was not able to pay, the master ordered that he and his wife and his children and all that he had be sold to repay the debt.
>
> The servant fell on his knees before him. 'Be patient with me,' he begged, 'and I will pay back everything.' The servant's master took pity on him, canceled the debt and let him go.
>
> But when that servant went out, he found one of his fellow servants who owed him a hundred denarii. He grabbed him and began to choke him. 'Pay back what you owe me!' he demanded.
>
> His fellow servant fell to his knees and begged him, 'Be patient with me, and I will pay you back.'

But he refused. Instead, he went off and had the man thrown into prison until he could pay the debt. When the other servants saw what had happened, they were greatly distressed and went and told their master everything that had happened.

Then the master called the servant in. 'You wicked servant,' he said, 'I canceled all that debt of yours because you begged me to. Shouldn't you have had mercy on your fellow servant just as I had on you?' In anger, his master turned him over to the jailers to be tortured, until he should pay back all he owed.

This is how my heavenly Father will treat each of you unless you forgive your brother from your heart.[29]

The theological concept is that when the God forgives us for our significant failures in honoring him as Creator of everything, he expects us to forgive when we are the victim of another person's comparatively insignificant failure to extend the honor (love) due to us as created beings.

Presenting redemptive forgiveness in a religious context is not meant to diminish the experience of people who are not religious. I have had many students explain that they are not religious people, but they have a life philosophy that calls them to forgive. Being "true to themselves" creates another version of redemptive forgiveness in a non-religious context.

This approach to forgiveness intertwined with one's spiritual and religious journey is illustrated in a poem often referred to as Mother Teresa's Poem. A version of it was written on the wall of Mother Teresa's children's home in Calcutta and contained minor modifications of Kent Keith's Paradoxical Commandments.[30] Various versions have circulated, and Mr. Keith has expressed some reservations about the "Final Analysis Version" of the poem titled, "Anyway."

The poem reminds the reader of many people's deficits: they are unreasonable, selfish, make false accusations, jealous, opportunistic, and ungrateful. Yet it encourages the reader to forgive and be generous and kind "anyway." The final line provides the rational,

"You see, in the final analysis, it is between you and God;

It was never between you and them anyway."

The redemptive model describes a forgiveness that is granted because the forgiver understands that it is what is expected of her by the Creator or by her own life philosophy. Six students shared insights about this from different traditions.

No Sacred Text

Although I do not follow a strict sacred text, forgiveness is central to my belief system. I forgive because I am aware of the blessings and rewards of forgiveness, both morally and personally. I do not forgive because I am told to do so. I forgive to advance my sense of self, and my ability to connect and empathize with others. This comes from the many experiences that life has provided me.

It is hard to consider forgiveness as a concrete idea. To me, it is abstract. It is flexible. It is transformative. Forgiveness is a combination of models, perceptions, and insights. I do not believe that forgiveness is correlated to fairness. Forgiveness is a personal journey. In my opinion, there is not one reason to forgive. But rather, it is a balance of personal, emotional, and spiritual beliefs. I hope that with continued education and practice, I will be better able to understand my forgiveness model. Submitted by Alexis Harris, emphasis added.

Islam

In my opinion, how to forgive depends on the religion and culture. Because culture and religion control most people's behavior. So, if anyone wants to forgive, he or she will follow one of these two things. <u>In my religion, Islam always asks for forgiveness between people. It tells them that you have the right to not forgive but if you want to get something in return from God, the fast way to get it is forgiveness.</u> Also, in my culture, when people forgive, they will announce that in front of people to make it official and to close any door that may be a way to revenge. Sometimes people forgive for a reason like money …. For example, when someone killed your son you have the right to ask the court to kill the killer or you can forgive the killer for an amount of money. Submitted by Abdullah Sulaiman Alluhaydan, emphasis added.

I think that my religion has definitely influenced my attitude toward forgiveness. <u>Islam teaches us to forgive others, whether they are deserving of it or not, in order to give ourselves peace, give others peace, and so that G-d forgives us.</u> We're taught that if we want G-d to excuse our behavior in this world, we must treat others with generosity and rest assured that our reward will be with Him in the hereafter. This perspective has allowed me to move past situations that could have otherwise consumed me. Submitted by Pashtana Abedi, emphasis added.

Forgiveness and reconciliation in Islam help maintain community harmony. "Dispute resolution in the Middle East is guided with an overarching principle of collective interests of the family, the tribe, the community, and the country." So, though there is a history in Islam of *sulha,* where "injustice to one tribe was matched a similar injustice to another, the strong preference was for forgiveness, often symbolized by a *diyya* (monetary compensation) that served to "maintain communal peace and restore trust." Islam prefers forgiveness. <u>"While the Quran permits certain retribution and self-defense, forgiveness is the spiritually superior option."</u> Submitted by an anonymous student, emphasis added.

Buddhist

The Tibetan Buddhist teacher and writer, Pema Chodron, once took her children to visit a great Tibetan master. She explained that her children were not Buddhists and asked the master to say something to them. Without hesitation, he remarked: "You will die someday. And when you do, the only thing you will take with you will be your state of mind."

<u>Forgiveness permits us to live and die in a state of contentment, instead of a state of suffering.</u> If the perpetrator is someone with whom we desire a continuing relationship, such forgiveness can benefit us both. If the perpetrator is someone asking for forgiveness, we can reduce his/her suffering in conjunction with ours by granting such forgiveness with grace. If there is not a perpetrator present to deal with, forgiveness permits us, as Eva Kor stated, to be the person each of us wants to be and to experience the abundance of joy life offers. Submitted by Z. Zeller, emphasis added.

Catholic

Learning about the redemptive model of forgiveness also made me think about the impact that my religion plays in my willingness to forgive someone. I was raised in a Catholic household and I regularly attended mass. At a young age, I learned that forgiveness is one of the values that the Bible preaches. As an adult, I stopped attending church on a regular basis and even though I still consider myself to be Catholic, I do not think that I subscribe to everything taught by the Catholic religion. I like to think my religion does not influence the way I think.

Even though I do not think that my religion necessarily impacts the way I think, this reflection made me look at the difference between my sister and me. While I identify as a Catholic, my sister identifies as Atheist. I started to think about common experiences that we have gone through with our family and how she is less likely to forgive than I am. <u>Although our differences in willingness to forgive might be attributed to other causes or reasons, I thought that religion does play at least a small part in this difference between us. I feel something inside me that says that I have to forgive people and move on</u>, and when the offense is not as great, it is easier for me to forgive and move on. On the other hand, my sister is always more reluctant to forgive. This lack of forgiveness prevents her from being at peace with herself.

These differences were not only noticeable between my sister and I, but between my sister and my mother. They too have a lot of shared experiences, but my mom is more willing to forgive what happened than my sister is. I do think that a large part of it is because her religion dictates that this is what she should do in order to be at peace with God. Submitted by an anonymous student, emphasis added.

6.5.4   Venn Diagram of Combinations

The therapeutic, relational, and redemptive models of forgiveness are intended to describe three different meanings and approaches. Each model explains how and why some people forgive; however, people are complex and often do not fit neatly into a defined package or model. Many people will relate to a combination of the characteristics of the various models when they unravel their personal approach to forgiveness.   A three-way Venn diagram is a helpful tool when deconstructing the models to acknowledge that a combination of factors may be in operation.

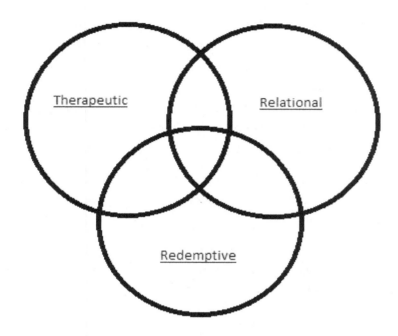

The overlap between the therapeutic and the relational models describes the person who forgives for both their own mental health and to preserve some aspect of a relationship or community. The relative strengths will vary between individuals and situations. It may be 80% out of concern for the relationship and 20% because they do not want to be an angry victim or vice versa.   If the motivation to forgive includes some percentage of both concerns, the forgiveness should be considered a hybrid of the two approaches. The person is unconcerned about conforming to any belief system.

The overlap between therapeutic and redemptive models describes the person desiring to conform to a belief system that expects her to forgive and who also wants to release her anger and be happy. These two factors may reinforce each other. The belief system expects the practitioner to forgive and it also encourages inner serenity and a love for one's enemies that is rarely possible when a person has unforgiven anger.

The purely redemptive forgiver extends forgiveness (release of reparations and maybe even a reduction in animosity) in obedience, but still carries the weight of anger and resentment in their heart. This might be the result of external (or internal) pressure to conform to the value system. When both therapeutic and redemptive factors are operating, the forgiver is practicing another hybrid approach. This person's goal is to obey his or her belief system and protect his or her own heart from becoming resentful and angry. Notice these objectives might be accomplished unilaterally and, therefore, this person may be entirely unconcerned about restoring relationships. I am not proud of it after studying relational forgiveness, but I am acutely aware of two significant relationships in my life where I practiced this form of forgiveness.

The third two-way hybrid approach is the combination of relational and redemptive forgiveness. Again, a person's value system expects him or her to forgive, but the person is also driven by a concern for some dimension of the relationship. My spouse hurt my feelings. I forgive to be consistent with my value system and because I do not want to create walls in my marriage relationship. The emphasis on loving other people and unity among family or others with the same value system is an example of how these two themes may reinforce each other. As in the other two-way overlaps, this person is unconcerned about their internal anger and bitterness.

David Augsburger argues that for Christians, the redemptive forgiveness requires relational forgiveness.[31] He convincingly presents Jesus' example and teachings as always seeking the goal of restoring a relationship and regaining a brother.[32]

The three-way overlap diagrams the situation where a person is motivated by all three factors, their mental health, relationships, and belief system. The percentages of each may vary case to case, but the person relates to all three appeals to forgive.

Some people's approach to forgiveness may fit one of the models or one of the hybrid-models every time. Most people have shifting applications. Certain types of injuries are often processed in one model or hybrid, and other types of injuries are processed in another model or hybrid. Even the same type of injury might be handled differently based on the context, history, or relationship.

A student's journal is illustrative.

> Although I have not thought about my forgiveness style or why I forgive, I now realize that much of forgiving for me is relinquishing myself of hurt and negativism, and wanting to be more positive, self-healing and have or continue relational positivity. I tend to be very introspective and analytical, and as I stated above, in developing my forgiveness thinking, I incorporate the reasons, what my responsibility is in the relationship, what forgiveness may mean for me in the future and how I can continue to be direct, honest, and forward thinking.

Human interactions and relationships between family, friends, and colleagues are extremely important to me while I maintain positivity and diminish ill-will. I am not a grudge-holder and tend not to hold onto blame or guilt. Building relationships while maintaining honesty, sincerity, dependability, affirmation and mutual fondness is at the root of my relational forgiveness mindset.

Redemptive forgiveness is important to me, not only based on my Jewish practices and upbringing, but also on my personal value system. I rely on my religious values, belief in G-d and righteousness as a source of information, healing, and forgiveness. I also rely on my values and strong sense of self and confidence to direct me to treat others with openness, fairness, honesty, devotion, caring, and selflessness.

Although the different types of forgiveness appear to be distinct entities, in actuality <u>my forgiveness is a combination of all three areas with emphasis placed on certain areas more than others, depending on the issue or problem at hand. In general, I probably emphasize and think most clearly about therapeutic forgiveness, then relational forgiveness and always have redemptive forgiveness as a basis to make decisions as it is part of my being, belief system and guidepost on how to live my life.</u> Submitted by Dr. Alan Nager, emphasis added.

The main objective of our first chapter in the study of forgiveness and the introduction of these models is to try to understand the roadmap in our heads/hearts that gets us to the point of forgiving. It is a personal journey unique for each of us and influenced by a collection of factors. I am not qualified to judge between these approaches. I am satisfied if the reader has a better understanding of the possibilities and their instincts regarding forgiveness. A student's journal describes her journey implementing this material.

I had to think that if this was how much energy I was giving to an insignificant event, how much energy am I giving to truly significant events? If I am renting space in this area that evoked in me so much emotional after being cut off, how much space am I renting to serious events in my life? Well, it became clear to me that I was giving up PREMIUM rental space without even knowing it. It also started to become clearer that if I was able to physically manifest this amount of anger, how much anger and resentment was still within me?

Then, I realized that I had to consider what kind of space I wanted to continue to let these bad memories occupy. But here is the bad part, in order to clear out my mind, I would have to deal with events that I had been successful in previously avoiding. It is like <u>cleaning a closet that has not been cleaned for years. When you first start cleaning, it is going to get really, really messy. Before, at least everything was locked away and out of sight. But the only way to clean a closet is to get everything out, decide what you want, throw out what you don't, and organize what is left. That is what I realized I had to do with my own mind and my memories.</u>

I would have to reflect on what pain I am still holding onto, decide what I will allow to continue to rent space in my mind, forgive in order to throw out what I don't want, and then recreate the memories that I do want to hold onto. This is no easy task. If you have seen my closets, you will see why. I tend to hold onto things. But I know that I will need to do the work if I want to be happier and healthier. I am committed to do it. However, today is not that day. It seems to me that this is a great task that I am going to have to start with little by little. While the task seems daunting, I know it can be done. I will do it. Submitted by Beatriz Paleyo-Garcia, emphasis added.

Endnotes

1. *See infra* sections 1.2-1.5

2. See e.g., Beliefnet.com, http://www.beliefnet.com/prayers/protestant/addiction/serenity-prayer.aspx (last visited Sep. 5 2018) (written by Reinhold Niebuhr (1892-1971).

3. *See e.g.*, Dr.DianeMahoney.com, http://drdianemahoney.com/bad-intentions-and-mean-spiritedness/ (last visited Sep. 6, 2018) (exploring why humans from a young age wish bad upon others).

4. *See Focus on the Family*, https://www.focusonthefamily.com/marriage/divorce-and-infidelity/forgiveness-and-restoration/forgiveness-what-it-is-and-what-it-isnt, (last visited Sep. 6, 2018) (**"Forgiveness is not the same as reconciling**. We can forgive someone even if we never can get along with him again.")

5. A simple search on google for "types of forgiveness" reveals websites claiming three, four, two, and six different types of forgiveness.

6. *Compare* Lewis B. Smedes, Martha Minow, David Augsburger, Dr. Fred Luskin, and Tian Dayton.

7. *See generally id.*

8. See id.

9. *See* Fred Luskin, *Forgive for Good* 105-67, (2002).

10. *Id*. at 63.

11. Tian Dayton, *The Magic of Forgiveness* 3-14, (2003).

12. *Id*. at xvii-xxiv.

13. *Id*. at 4.

14. *Id.*

15. *Id.*

16. *Id*. at 9.

17. *Id*. at 10-11.

18. *Id.*

19. *Id.*

20. *Id*. at 63

21. David Augsburger, *The New Freedom of Forgiveness* 25, (2000).

22. David Augsburger, *Caring Enough to Not Forgive* 9-12, (1981).

23. *See id.*

24. *Id.*

25. *Id*. at 9-12.

26. *Id.*

27. Matthew 6:12.

28. Matthew 7:2

29. Matthew 18:21-35.

30. Kent M. Keith, *Anyway*, (2001).

31. Augsburger, *New Freedom of Forgiveness,* 20.

32. *Id.*

Chapter Seven

How to Forgive

" I've found the secret to forgiveness is to get revenge first. "

7.1 Introduction

Now that we have identified three distinct models of forgiveness, it should not come as a surprise that there are three approaches to how to forgive. If the forgiveness is different, the path to that forgiveness will also be different. If you are unsure about your intuitive forgiveness approach, maybe examining the paths to various types of forgiveness will help clarify your unconscious forgiveness journey. Taking a journey without a map is sometimes an enjoyable adventure and sometimes a dangerous endeavor. This chapter provides a map for navigating through an injury to reach the desired destination of forgiveness.

This chapter will summarize suggestions for how to practice the three approaches to forgiveness. This oversimplifies the forgiveness journey because people are complex and do not fit neatly into the models; however, it is still possible to provide structure and direction to aid people in this journey. Studying the techniques is still valuable because it deepens our understanding of the forgiveness experience.

Exploring how to forgive also raises the question of *when* to forgive. Some authors suggest that forgiveness should be utilized to recover from all of life's hurts and disappointments.[1] Lewis Smedes' book *Forgive and Forget* suggest that forgiveness be reserved for deep, personal, and unfair offenses.

We may need coping mechanisms for responding to annoyances and disappointments, but Smedes suggests saving the big gun of forgiveness for instances of disloyalty, betrayal, or brutality.[2] He also challenges us to only use forgiveness when people have injured us because only people can be held accountable for their actions, which means that only the injured person has standing to grant forgiveness.[3] Lastly, Smedes asks us to reserve forgiveness for instances of unfair pain that we do not deserve or is not necessary.[4] He differentiates between losing $50 on a fair bet and getting mugged.[5]

Smedes' proposed boundaries for forgiveness raise interesting issues. We don't need to agree with him or each other on those boundaries, but awareness of them might be helpful as we dissect various approaches to how to forgive.

One student's journal shares how her parents' example inspires her to forgive and another student's journal describes a commitment to begin the journey.

> Before I was born, my parents lived in a house in San Gabriel with my grandmother and my older sister. My uncle had the deed to the house in his possession because he was my parents' real estate agent, not to mention they trusted him completely because he was family. One day, my parents get a knock on the door. Strangers stood at their front door telling them that the house was now theirs and my family had to move out. It turned out that my uncle had sold the house to obtain money to fuel his gambling addiction. He didn't even have the decency to let them know. My dad had to find out from strangers rather than his own brother that his house was sold, and he had to leave right away.

Because of this incident, my parents were forced to leave and find a new house to live in. By borrowing money from other family members, my parents were able to buy a new house where they have been living ever since. Because of their huge amount of debt owed to family members, my parents struggled financially. ... Fortunately, my parents are hard workers and were able to climb out of the huge mountain of debt they faced.

The forgiving aspect of this story is that my parents forgave my uncle. Of course, forgiving him didn't mean they condoned his actions. But because he was family, they used the relational model of forgiveness and forgave him. I admired my parents for being able to forgive my uncle because the rest of the family hasn't forgiven him yet. It's been over 25 years, but my uncle is still barely invited to family gatherings. He had borrowed other family members' money or stolen their possessions to fund his gambling habit. My other aunts and uncles remember all this and still hold a grudge against him.

<u>I told this story to a friend before, and he told me that he would never be that weak. He said if someone ruined his life to the extent that my uncle ruined my parents' lives, he would never forgive the offender. He said he would find a way to exact revenge rather than forgive. But I don't think this makes my parents weak at all. On the contrary, I think it makes them very strong and loving.</u>

My parents could have easily shunned my uncle and never spoken to him again. But they were bigger people in this whole situation. After learning about the various models in this class, it's clear to me that my parents used therapeutic and relational models of forgiveness. They forgave my uncle to restore their relationship with him so that he would have at least one family member who still cared about him from his side of the family. They also forgave my uncle because they couldn't change the past. The offense had already occurred, and there was no way to turn back the clock. To make their present happier instead of holding a grudge against my uncle, my parents forgave him for themselves as well.

Any time I feel very offended and like I'm going to hold a grudge against somebody, I remember how my parents were so strong in being able to forgive my uncle. When I remember that they could forgive someone like that despite what he did, I find that my problems are trivial and forgivable as well. Submitted by an anonymous student, emphasis added.

One could say that I do not forgive easily. But the subject of today's class has had a profound effect on my ole curmudgeon soul.... And like many skills, it takes work before it becomes easy and instinctive. As one Professor I know often says, today, "I drank the Kool-Aid." Now begins the hard part of laying some internal foundation, however small the footage, and allowing it to live and grow within me. It is strange that I have always thought of myself as a forgiving person. Who knew that I may be a fraud, or, at least, less than honest about owning this quality.

It never occurred to me to consider forgiveness as one more actor in my personal Broadway show I refer to playfully as, "Veracity and Values," starring me. I have no doubt that practicing forgiveness will redeem me from the burden of carting around annoying demons. The lesson learned today is that forgiveness is not passive but active, designed to move one forward to an even better and more meaningful life. Forgiveness has the capacity to help one on their journey toward the ever-elusive goals of peace and happiness. Submitted by Carole Helfert Aragon, emphasis added.

7.2 How to do Therapeutic Forgiveness

Psychology professor Fred Luskin, Director of Stanford University's Forgiveness Project, describes a series of a very practical steps to experience therapeutic forgiveness.[6] This summary of some of Luskin's suggestions on how to experience therapeutic forgiveness makes more sense when remembering that Luskin's approach is built on the idea that forgiveness is a choice.[7] A student's journal describes a transformation in his understanding of forgiveness.

> I will be brutally honest, … my general opinion on forgiveness was that it was a majorly overrated conceit. I definitely understood the importance of apologies and displaying remorse to a victim. Clearly for the sake of peacekeeping and dispute resolution, an apology is an essential tool in the toolbox. However, I always perceived forgiveness as something that only benefits the person in the wrong. In my mind, it was just a magic word that's only purpose was to release the villain of guilt and culpability. Operating under that negative perspective, my belief was basically that if I got the apology, why give the perpetrator the satisfaction of forgiveness. Why not deny them that and continue to punish them? …

> I now realize that, as crazy as it is for me to believe, the purpose of forgiveness is not to release the perpetrator of their pain and absolve them of the burden of their guilt. Rather, the purpose of forgiveness is to release the victim of their pain and absolve them of the burden of their own suffering. If the perpetrator truly is sorry, they will never be fully released of the guilt and pain no matter the degree of sincerity of the forgiveness offered. Nor does the forgiveness erase the wrong that has been committed or "even the score" so to speak.

> It takes a lot of work and effort to be angry and sad. It's a role that requires a full commitment and breaks are not available. It's a commitment that comes with great sacrifice as it forces you to deny everything that makes life worth living, including joy, hope, and peace of mind. Metaphorically speaking, it is a giant boulder attached by a chain around your leg that you are forced to drag with you everywhere that impedes your freedom, exhausts your will, and serves as a constant reminder of what you have lost. Unfortunately, forgiveness is the only way to break that chain. Submitted by Andrew Duncan, emphasis added.

The first of Luskin's practical techniques we will examine is, **"Take Responsibility for your Feelings."**

The first choice Luskin identifies is to take responsibility for your feelings.[8] We are not responsible for the injuries inflicted by others, but we are responsible for how we react to them.[9] Our feelings are determined by what we think about, so we can manipulate our feelings by exercising control or choice about what we think about. If we dwell on how people have disappointed or hurt us, we will be sad or angry. We can choose to fill our mind with more positive things, creating feelings of gratitude and happiness. Luskin uses the picture that your mind is a TV and your will is the remote control to describe deciding what to think about. [10]

Most forgiveness authors acknowledge the need to think about and feel the reality of the injury, rather than denying the reality of the injury. This concept is reinforced by William Faulkner's famous phrase from Requiem for a Nun: "The past is never dead. It's not even past."

Rather than forget or deny the injury, Luskin asks us to take responsibility about how often and how long we think about and feel the injury.[11] He explains that we will be too angry to forgive if we continue to dwell on and relive the injury multiple times a day. But, if we choose to fill our minds with images of beauty, gratitude, and love, we will manipulate our feelings to be more positive and open to forgiveness and moving forward into a brighter future. Examples of beauty, gratitude, and love include remembering positive experiences with the person who hurt you, thinking about a time when someone did an act of kindness and sacrificial love for you, or visiting an inspiration nature site like the Grand Canyon.

As a person who has no formal training in psychology, this was a new concept. I thought that our feelings are what they are, and we do not have the ability, much less the responsibility, to control them. If my wife is unfaithful, my feelings of anger and despair are the natural response to experience. The wisdom of Luskin's approach is found in asking how long to stay in that state.[12]

Some people never recover from a betrayal. A decade later it is still the defining moment in their life, and they are still angry about it. They have never recovered from the incident; they have never forgiven. The beginning of Luskin's forgiveness intervention is to challenge them to think about the injury less and fill their minds with thoughts of better experiences.[13] If people exercise this self-control, their feelings will be more positive and maybe support a forgiveness experience.

Notice how this concept contributes to our exploration about whether forgiveness is a feeling or a decision. Is the forgiveness experience driven by the heart and emotions or by the head and ration? Taking responsibility for your feelings acknowledges the role feelings play in the forgiveness journey, and the role of rational thought in deciding not to allow our thoughts to dwell continually on the wrongdoing. This concept is summarized by Luskin's point that forgiveness is about not allowing the unfair injury you suffered to "rent anymore space in your head."[14]

A student described her mother's experience with "controlling your feelings."

> When my father cheated on my mother it's true that letting go and forgiving gave her more peace than she had felt when she held onto her feelings of anger and hurt. <u>However, forgiving him was not easy for her to do even though she understood the therapeutic value. Knowing that it's possible to take control of your feelings and doing so are two different things.</u> Even when my mother understood early on that someone who would do that to her was not someone she even wanted to share a life with, the fact was that they *had* shared meaningful time together. They were married in front of family and friends, they had a child together, and there was a significant history there, and my father had disrespected that.
>
> Time was the crucial element that finally allowed her to forgive. Ultimately if you asked her today, I believe she would tell you that forgiveness is the way to go and that is what she taught me. However, she would also tell you that it was that anger and pain that motivated her to persevere and come out more successful and stronger than before. Submitted by an anonymous student, emphasis added.

Next, we explore Luskin's second practical technique of **Taking Your Hurts Less Personally**.

This concept challenges injured people to reconstruct their expectations so that the injuries are less devastating. It encourages people to relinquish their "unenforceable rules."[15] An unenforceable rule describes a demand of life or others that is beyond the control of the person making the demand; yet, the person insists it must be a certain way.[16] Examples include: my friends must be loyal to me in my absence; my spouse must be faithful; my children must be high achievers; and my employer must be fair in assessing and giving credit for my work.

Framing our expectations as unenforceable rules sets people up to be devastated when they do not happen. Thinking that something beyond my control "must" be a certain way, does not leave room for me to adjust when it doesn't happen the way I am demanding that it should. Some people don't forgive because they are either still trying to conform the world to their wishes or because they haven't yet recovered when their deeply held worldview is contradicted. They interpret the violation of the unenforceable rule as a personal attack or affront.

The vulnerable part of an unenforceable rule is that its focus is on something beyond the control of the rule maker such as other people or life. Other people and life do not always conform to our expectations. When we recognize that we cannot control other people or life, we realize the foolishness of creating unenforceable rules. Sometimes the obstacle to forgiveness is that the victim demanded certain behavior that was beyond his control.

This technique does not require us to have low or no expectations of others. Instead our expectations are constructed slightly differently, but with a large impact. We recognize our inability to control others when we frame our expectations as aspirations and hopes, instead of demands. "I HOPE my spouse will be faithful" recognizes that there is a possibility it will not happen.

This way of thinking combines high expectations with acknowledgement of other people's autonomy. If my understanding of how I should be treated in this situation is violated, I am not as devastated because I recognized this possibility from the beginning. If I didn't recognize this possibility from the beginning, maybe I can adjust my expectations after the violation so that I am not taking it so personally.

The expectation may be reasonable and appropriate. The violation of that expectation created an unfair injury. As the victim seeks to recover from this injury, possibly through forgiveness, she can continue to hold on to her standards and expectations, but also have the wisdom to accept that others may not have the same standards or always live up to those standards.

The Serenity Prayer is another way to consider this technique:

God grant me the

Serenity to accept the things I cannot change,

Courage to change the things I can and

Wisdom to know the difference.[17]

This aspect of the therapeutic approach to forgiveness can be described as the victim accepting the things that cannot be controlled and having the courage and determination to heal and recover so that the victim can be happy again.

A student journal highlights trying to control things beyond our control.

> Honestly, I'm not very good at any level of forgiveness as I tend to hold a grudge, particularly if I don't receive an apology for a transgression. Truthfully, one rarely receives an apology, so forgiveness is a skill which I hope to develop. However, Luskin's metaphor of unenforceable rules was very helpful for me just as a way to manage stress and create inner peace. I tend to get frustrated with things that are out of my control – traffic and weather are good examples. Sometimes I also complain too much about problems that seem large but are actually minor when compared to what others go through. I often personalize problems not realizing that what I'm experiencing is part of life and many others have the same experiences. While I think Luskin's model is healthy, at times I question if he was speaking of forgiving or forgetting. Submitted by an anonymous student, emphasis added.

The third of Luskin's practical techniques is to **replace the victim story with a hero story**.[18]

A victim story describes the wrong suffered by the victim. The hero story describes the victim overcoming the injustice. One way to diagnose which kind of story you are telling is to assess the percentage of the story that describes the injury compared to the percentage of the story that describes overcoming the injury.

If the emphasis is on the overcoming of the injustice, you are telling a hero story. Another way to diagnose which kind of story you are telling is to identify the main figure in your story. If it is the perpetrator, you are telling a victim story. If it is you overcoming the injury, you are telling a hero story.

Luskin finds that the stories we tell ourselves and others have significance.[19] These stories not only relay facts, but they also contain interpretations and meaning. Like Luskin's first concept of taking responsibility for your feelings by controlling what you think about, here, Luskin challenges us to control how a negative event will affect us by creating a story about how we overcome the event.[20] The most important story we tell is *to ourselves*. We will minimize the impact of the negative event if we construct how we have or how we will overcome this setback.

In the example of an unfaithful spouse, does the injured party's story consist only of a litany of details about the affair and lack of character of their spouse? Or, does the story largely focus on what the injured party did or will do to recover from this tragedy? Does the injured party describe what efforts they made or will make to meet new people and love again? Does the injured party describe what they learned from this chapter and how they will be a better person because they experienced this deep sadness? Does the injured person describe how they are committed to recovering from this and being happy and healthy in the future?

The victim or hero story we tell ourselves and others about the injustices we suffer is an indication of where we are in the forgiveness process. This practical technique suggests that creating a hero story can be a part of advancing the healing and forgiveness.

Two students described situations where they or their family focused on the hero story.

> I struggle with forgiving my abusive ex-boyfriend as well as myself for remaining in a dangerous relationship. Unbeknownst to me before this class, I am in the process of healing myself through the therapeutic process because I am forgiving him for my own selfish reasons – I have dwelled on the past for too long and I want to be happy again. ... While I aim to take responsibility for my feelings, it is hard to not get fixated on feeling like the victim and, consequently, develop a victim's mentality. When I first went to therapy after a major incident this year, I hated the fact that the therapist called me a "victim." In fact, I asked him to not call me that because I consider myself to be a resilient person. It is difficult to reconcile those two contradictions.

> Changing the victim's narrative is very beneficial. Dwelling and obsessing on the past is unhealthy, as it cannot be changed. I have realized that firsthand and determined that happiness is a choice. We can either choose to stay in the past and be unhappy or we can choose to focus on how we overcame that adversity. Over the past year, I have chosen to make my narrative one about how I survived and thrived, despite the odds. My decision was based on the time that I spend being unhappy and hating my ex. I do not believe that our battles define us. Submitted by an anonymous student, emphasis added.

The story of Japanese-Americans during WWII provides us with an example of coping. My great-grandfather, a doctor in the small town of Hilo, Hawaii, was taken to a military camp for internment. Many of my grandparents' older siblings were taken to internment camps across the United States, even if they were all American-born citizens. The story of the Japanese-American internment is one of injustice but also resilience. Once Japanese-Americans were released after years of imprisonment, they went back to their homes that were looted, vandalized, and ruined. Many struggled with their identity and the psychological damage caused by years in an internment camp and living in the country that so wrongly imprisoned them.

However, Japanese-Americans coped with their circumstances and took the necessary steps to make a successful living. Japanese-Americans exhibited advancement in the years and generations to come. For example, they now surpass even Whites in average income and educational attainment. Refusing to let an unfair injury define their identity, Japanese-Americans stepped out of a downward cycle and decided to write their own narrative. ...

Although this event was traumatic and historic, my grandparents never talk about it. I only recently discovered that two of my grandmother's older brothers were taken to internment camps in California, when she nonchalantly mentioned it over coffee and pancakes. ... When I asked my grandmother about her reaction to the internment of her family, she said she was not upset. ... I think that culturally, Japanese-Americans look back at the event with shame and would much rather focus on all the success we have had since then. Submitted by Emily Tanaka, emphasis added.

To summarize, Luskin identifies the building blocks of therapeutic forgiveness as taking responsibility for your feelings, relinquishing your unenforceable rules, and creating a hero story.[21]

7.3 How to do Relational Forgiveness

If the goal is to construct a forgiveness that is not one way or one up, we cannot accept a simple construct that one is the wrongdoer and the other is the victim. (Often, we think and organize things this way when considering forgiveness and apology.) We need to be willing to create a more comprehensive narrative that allows all participants to be both the victim and villain. A student's journal description is helpful.

> I don't like being in a position to forgive because I feel like it can come off looking entitled and as though I think I am superior. That is why whenever someone apologizes to me, whether I feel like I deserve it or not, I tell them it's not necessary and that we can act like it never happened.

I'll sometimes return their apology with an apology and tell them I'm sorry they felt like they needed to apologize. It helps when both of us stay on the same level. I find that it helps create trust and new ground for the future of the relationship. Submitted by Pashtana Abedi, emphasis added.

One technique to creating a more comprehensive narrative is to "complicate the story."

When I am hurting, my defense mechanisms cause my interpretation of the events to emphasize the wrong committed by the other person. If forgiveness occurs when I am in this state, I am the saintly forgiver. As I hopefully heal over time, sometimes I look back and accept partial responsibility for the events. To avoid Augsburger's one-up or one-way forgiveness, we need to resist the temptation to rush to a saintly forgiveness and instead take the time to consider our roles in the conflict so that forgiveness can be mutual. A student describes how she does this in a journal.

> In class we discussed forgiveness and that we should complexify the victim's story. When I tell a story to someone about something that happened between me and another person, I tend to completely simplify the other person's side of the story and simplify what happened because I just want it to be over with and do not like talking about it. But when I simplify the victim's story, I belittle them and what they experienced in this situation and I belittle the situation in my mind; this makes me not care about what happened anymore. It makes me feel like the other person acted completely irrationally and therefore it was their own fault and I did not do anything.
>
> When I start to do this, I stop myself and there are certain things I do to complexify the story or just tell the story like it actually happened. One thing I need to do that is hard for me to do and that I rarely do is to consider my own contributions to the situation. I tend to dismiss the whole situation and the other person and just think that I did not really do anything wrong and the other person overreacted. I also need to feel empathy for the other person and remember that he or she is a human being who makes mistakes and may have upset me or hurt me, not on purpose, but because of his or her own needs or frailties. I have to humanize that person which I often forget to do. ... I should also remind myself of the mistakes I have made myself and remember the times that I needed and received genuine forgiveness. Submitted by an anonymous student, emphasis added.

One easy way to complicate the story is to expand the time frame of the incident. As a father of twins, I accidently experienced this. When they were in their early adolescence, one of them came to me complaining about a hurtful act committed by the other. I agreed that this behavior violated the expectations for how we treat family members and summoned the perpetrator.

In front of the child who initiated the complaint, I asked the alleged perpetrator if the allegations were true and, if so, why she acted this way. After confirming the offense, the second child explained that the first child had done something to her earlier in the day that purposefully embarrassed her in front of friends. I asked the first child if this was true and, if so, why she did that. She confirmed it was true and explained that yesterday her sister had revealed a confidence to a mutual friend.

We kept digging trying to find the beginning of the downward spiral without success. The expansion of the time frame for assessing how they were treating each other resulted in my concluding that I was disappointed with both of them and that they needed to spend some time in their rooms thinking about whether they wanted our family to undermine or to support each other.

A student describes her experiences with others encouraging her to expand the time frame.

> Analyzing my experiences has allowed me to see the benefit of expanding the timeframe. Expanding the timeframe allows people to analyze their own behavior and not just focus on what the other person did to upset them. It allows them to see how every action has a reaction and how that person's behavior could have been a reaction to something that they did. Therefore, expanding the timeframe can result in a person becoming more self-reflective, which in turn makes him or her more aware of how their actions affect others.

> Expanding the timeframe when emotions are high is very difficult to do. I have had people try to do that to me when I am very upset and all it has done is anchor me into my position even further and say things that I don't mean. It narrows my vision and makes me only see how I was wronged. However, when a person I trust is the one who is trying to help me see the bigger picture, he or she knows what points to implement that strategy and it is almost always effective. It helps calm me down and makes the situation seem a lot less serious than it is. Expanding the timeframe on my own, however, is more difficult to do. It takes much longer for me to analyze the situation and see both sides without an outside objective voice. Submitted by Pashtana Abedi, emphasis added.

Simple stories are easy and can be contained in one sentence sound bites for campaign speeches or in the evening news. Complex stories require more effort and work, and they are more realistic because they include subtleties and nuance.

Consider how Hawaii became a US possession. The quick story is in the 1890s the US Ambassador to the sovereign nation of Hawaii requested a US Admiral to bring his battleship into Honolulu harbor and dispatch the US Marines to depose the Queen. Clearly, the US was in the wrong and the nation of Hawaii and its Queen were the victims.

I recently visited the Queen's former palace and its museum in Honolulu. I learned that five years before he died, Hawaii's prior monarch, the Queen's brother, agreed to a revised constitution for Hawaii that relinquish a lot of power to Hawaii's legislature. Shortly before she was deposed, the Queen created a constitutional crisis for Hawaii by unilaterally nullifying the existing constitution and replacing it with one she created; unsurprisingly, the one she created returned much of the government's power to her. Leaders in Hawaii's legislature asked the US Ambassador to use the US military to intervene to avoid a civil war.

Determining who was right and who was wrong depends on many considerations. Did the agreement to a new constitution by the prior King make the Hawaiian legislature the legitimate governing body? Should the US Ambassador have waited for the Hawaiian legislature to formally act as a body? Even if the legislature had acted, should the US have stayed on the sidelines and allowed the Hawaiians to resolve this internal power struggle between the monarchy and the legislature? Does it make a difference whether the US Ambassador was interested in good governance for Hawaii or was influenced by the US business community with interests in Hawaii? Did the Queen participate in creating this situation by unilaterally announcing a new constitution that gave her much more power? The US Government accepted Hawaii as a "Protectorate." Would it have made a difference if the US Government had restored order and then reinstated the Hawaiian legislature as the legitimate government?

In matters of both international affairs and interpersonal squabbles, we choose between constructing a simple story that affirms the rightness of our cause or a complex story that acknowledges the perspectives and equities of all participants. Instead of expanding the time frame, we complicate the story when our narrative includes the needs and reasons behind the behavior of all participants. Often people who hurt or dominate others have tragic backgrounds where they were hurt or dominated. For example, I recently saw a documentary about the life of Charles Manson and felt very sad about his tragic childhood.

A student described his views about this in a journal.

> In this class discussion, we began by discussing forgiveness and the concept of "complicate the victim story." Aspects we discussed include expanding the time frame, considering your contribution, and visualizing the perpetrator as hurting you because of his/her history, needs, and frailty. Although expanding the time frame is important, it is the other two aspects that truly stuck out to me.
>
> When someone commits an action that leaves you feeling hurt, it is easy to automatically focus in on the damage caused, the anger and hatred you have towards the person who caused you the pain, and the revenge you would like to enact upon the architect of all of your pain. However, by solely focusing on the other person and how they caused your pain, I believe a better approach would be to utilize what I have called a "blame pie."

In a blame pie, one hundred percent of the blame is divided amongst several perpetrators. The pie is similar to a pie chart. The only rule of the blame pie is that there can never be a one-hundred-percent–to–one-person pie. Even when it can appear that a perpetrator was the only person who caused you pain, in reality, there was probably someone in the past that caused him to become the person who would eventually cause you pain, or at least there might have been a person who could have prevented the incident and the damage from ever occurring. Therefore, there are no one hundred percent blame pies. By using the blame pies, you can both consider your own contribution to causing the incident as well as visualize the perpetrator hurting you because of their history/needs/frailty, and therefore understand where the damaging incidents gain their inspiration.

In addition, other aspects of "complicating the victim story" <u>include compassion for the pain of being a perpetrator and visualizing a time when you have needed forgiveness. I believe that these two aspects are very important and key to the forgiveness process. They also might be two of the most difficult aspects to accomplish. For example, when visualizing a time when you have needed forgiveness, that process involves remembering an awkward and painful time. You would have to have caused a person some form of injury, and then you would have to suffer enough to warrant a request for forgiveness.</u>

<u>The empathy, the awkwardness, and the pain are all emotions that one would most likely avoid and never experience again, so it is hard to remember those times so you can better forgive a perpetrator.</u> However, by briefly reminiscing on the emotions around your own request for forgiveness, you can quickly understand the perpetrator's situation and be more likely to provide forgiveness. Finally, finding compassion for the pain of being a perpetrator plays into both visualizing a time when you needed forgiveness as well as the concept of the blame pie. Submitted by Patrick Simpkins, emphasis added.

A Theologian's Steps for Relational Forgiveness

David Augsburger served as professor of pastoral care and counseling at Fuller Theological Seminary for more than 20 years and writes persuasively about relational forgiveness. Augsburger attributes to John Patton the concept of forgiveness as something we discover.[22] After a conversation with Patton, Augsburger provided the following summary:

> Forgiveness is not something we do; it is something we discover. I am able to forgive when I discover that I am in no position to forgive. I am more like those that hurt me than unlike them, more similar than different. Forgiveness is not the act of canceling a debt or erasing an act of wrongdoing; it is the discovery of our similarity.[23]

Augsburger describes three prerequisites to beginning the path to relational forgiveness. The first is "the search for an understanding heart."[24] He explains, "[b]eyond the discovery that we can refuse to turn the other person into a monster lies a second discovery. We can see the other as blind, yet still invited into the light; as a doer of evil, but as more than the evil he has done."[25]

Augsburger's second prerequisite is "valuing the other."[26] He suggests that all perpetrators are human, and thus have innate value.[27] As a theologian, he ascribes value to every human being because they are created by God and God values them.[28]

Augsburger's third prerequisite (and the first of his five steps of forgiveness) is to love the other, which he defines as "seeing the other as precious regardless of the wrong done or the injury felt."[29]

Augsburger summarizes the prerequisites for what I am calling relational forgiveness as:

> Understanding, valuing, and loving are all steps toward forgiveness. They are not yet forgiving, but the prerequisite steps towards forgiveness. The real work of forgiving begins when an attitude of love has been restored. Then the negotiations of trust can begin resolving anger, suspicion, and resentment, and reopening the future. This is the difficult task that gets bypassed when forgiveness is made cheap, private, and one-way.[30]

To accomplish a renewal of trust and a reopening of the future, here is a brief summary of Augsburger's steps:

1. Restoring the attitude of love.
   "To love another is to see that person as full of worth and precious regardless of any wrongdoing."[31]

2. Releasing the painful past.
   "I am not my past; I am a person capable of repenting, changing, and turning away from past patterns of behavior. You are not your past; you are equally free to change if you accept the freedom that is within you. To affirm that freedom is the first step of forgiveness."[32]

3. Reconstructing the relationship.
   "To review the pain of offense within each of us and between the both of us is not easy, but it is the way to healing. As we work through our anger and pain in reciprocal trusting and risking, at last we come to recognize the genuineness of each other's intentions. Our repentance needs to be authentic, honest, and as complete as possible at the moment. That is the central work of forgiveness."[33]

4. Reopening the future.
   "The relationship may return to a civil participation in community with mutual respect, or to a new level of friendship resulting from the depth of encounter that has taken place; or it may mean a return to or the beginning of profound trust and willingness to risk. In each case, the future is reopened to whatever level of relating is appropriate to the two participants. Not every relationship should be pursued."[34]

5. Reaffirming the relationship.

> "We must touch each other as deeply as is possible in our release of the pain and then celebrate the mutual recognition that right relationship has now been restored or achieved."[35]

These steps demonstrate Augsburger's definition of forgiveness. "Forgiveness is the mutual recognition that repentance is genuine and that right relationships have been either restored or achieved."[36]

Augsburger's approach resonated with one student.

> Augsburger writes of the difference between one and two-way forgiveness in the "Don't Forgive" section of his book. He posits that it is better not to forgive at all than to merely forgive without engaging the forgivee with the goal of removing the pain and offense between the two parties. Forgiveness that takes place only within the mind of the forgiver, who accepts the burden of the offender's sins and reconciles himself to suffering alone, is not constructive and misses the point of true forgiveness.
>
> The superiority of the two-way, shared problem-solving approach rings very true to me. I can relate to the frustration that festers inside the one-way forgiver who, although he personally absolves the offender of his wrongdoing, constantly bears the burden of the wrongs committed and of the responsibility to keep the resentment private. I believe Augsburger's suggestion to include the forgivee in creating a solution whereby the two parties work as equals in removing the obstacles between them is a far better method. Submitted by John Stanley, emphasis added.

A Mental Health Therapist Describes Five Stages to Relational Forgiveness

Tian Dayton is a mental health therapist who describes a five-stage journey to relational forgiveness in *The Magic of Forgiveness*.[37] Her practical advice and explanations of each stage merits a careful study. For the purpose of this forgiveness overview, I will use excerpts and summarize parts of her approach. I categorize her approach as relational because she defines forgiveness as restoring, "our ability to make new kinds of emotional connections and emotional freedom that most people value far more than their resentments."[38]

Dayton uses the phrase "Waking Up" to describe her first stage.[39] She explains that this is when we realize that "resentment is costing us more than it is worth. Forgiveness is blocked by our fear of being hurt again. We are scared of the feelings of helplessness and powerlessness."[40]

Dayton's second stage is anger and resentment. Forgiveness writers regularly acknowledge that anger is an important and healthy reaction to an injury.[41] Jane Bolton goes so far as to suggest that if we don't experience anger when we experience an injury, we may lack self-respect.[42] Dayton explains that anger can feel empowering and that some people are more comfortable experiencing anger at feeling violated.[43] She also cautions that this can be addictive because "[g]iving up the anger can feel like giving up a part of yourself."[44]

The third stage in Dayton's journey is hurt and sadness. She explains that before we can heal, move on, and trust again, we need to feel the pain and sadness caused by having our trust shattered.[45] She suggests that if we deny feelings of grief and sadness, those feelings are displaced from the past to the present, and we end up asking future relationships to carry those emotions.[46] If we don't feel our pain and link it to where the wound began, we may unconsciously withdraw and isolate ourselves by creating distance or erecting walls.[47] Dayton encourages us to link our pain to the where the wound began; grief separates the past from the present.[48] Dayton concludes that real grief cleanses us from the pain of the past.[49] It is difficult to feel hurt and sadness and avoiding these feelings may be a reason people avoid this approach to forgiveness.[50]

Acceptance, integration, and letting go are the fourth stage of Dayton's practical path. This stage involves getting past our defenses and experiencing a growing understanding and compassion for our own and other people's frail humanity.[51] We experience forgiveness for our self (feelings of victimization or wrongdoing) and others and "gain new insights as to how circumstances of our lives have impacted us and why . . . We still remember, but the poison and sting will be gone and replaced by a kind of wisdom and acceptance . . . Releasing the past is a by-product of acceptance."[52] She concludes her description of this stage by the following expanded definition of forgiveness.

"So, forgiveness is a by-product rather than an act of the will. It is a letting go or releasing of something we no longer wish to carry—rather than a moral decision."[53] This echoes another place in her book where she describes forgiveness as a by-product of doing the work of therapy to understand where you hurt and letting it go.[54] This sounds similar to Augsburger's concept of forgiveness as something we do not do, but something we discover.

Dayton's final stage is to reorganize and reinvest. She describes this as adopting "a more realistic picture of what we can and cannot expect from a particular person" and being "able to reinvest in what is actually possible to expect without burdening the relationship with expectations of what it is not likely to offer."[55] She describes being able to "free ourselves to receive the good that is possible in that relationship."[56]

7.4 How to do Redemptive Forgiveness

This section will largely describe how to do redemptive forgiveness from the perspective of my religious tradition, Christianity. Journal entries from students will describe insights from other traditions. I will provide the students' insights from non-Christian traditions first because they are much shorter than the detail I describe from a Christian perspective.

Buddhist

Toward the end of the class, we discussed feelings about the arsonists who burned Eva's museum. In a Buddhist philosophy of identity, we believe that humans are inherently good, which is one of the major reasons why Buddhism and Confucianism melded together so beautifully in China. Yes, I initially felt anger toward the perpetrators, but I also knew immediately that they were not happy people. It is not a matter of the head and the heart to me, but a matter of <u>the head and the belly,</u> or <u>"hara." The head is a great rationalizer, whereas the belly always lets us know —if we are listening—when our thoughts are harming us.</u> Thus, the perpetrators may be thinking, "I did it! I ruined that stupid place!", but I will always believe that their bellies are telling them otherwise. Over time, the *stress of this cognitive dissonance* is grinding just below our conscious thoughts in our bellies. This stress will ruin our happiness and health if we do not pay attention and take care of it. Submitted by Z. Zeller, emphasis added.

Judaism

Atonement on Yom Kippur … can occur as many times and for the same repeated transgression. I do not agree that if you atone and confess you can return for the same wrong every day. However, G-d forgives and forgives, and forgives. If someone continuously returns for the same transgression is this truly atonement? Another question, another time. The point, man to man, it would not work if you came back daily for a repeated transgression. Clearly, we are not made like G-d where we keep forgiving the same transgression over and over again. To me, that would appear to be an apology with no remorse

<u>Often times, when I am upset about something and can't believe someone did something, I remember that on Yom Kippur, we say the attributes of G-d as forgiving, kind, slow to anger, etc. And even when it is hard for me to forgive, I do anyways,</u> and I forgive on my own. If I get an apology, that is great. Submitted by Dr. Amora Rachelle Magna, emphasis added.

Islam

Has forgiveness as a part of a faith been diluted through culture? Has the abundance of it made people disregard it? Muslims tend to ask for forgiveness on the hour from God. In a story taught in all schools in the Middle East: Once a man asked the prophet if God can hear them or if they needed to shout for his attention. The prophet replied that God is close to all people, even closer than the neck arteries. Hence a true devout Muslim considers every action to be candid and God is always overlooking.

Nevertheless, revenge has been an ongoing issue where Islam is dominant; where tribes fighting can hold grudges for decades and even sects with the religion are kept strong with the message of revenge; non-existent forgiveness is rampant. So, the question that always looms around when visiting my native country is: *Why is forgiveness mentioned so often when the lack of it is still a major part of some traditions and cultures?* Does the presence of tribalism and social equality that is rampant within societies in the Middle East advocate intolerance and bias?

The answers to the many questions in this journal have been answered within me; forgiveness is a choice that all societies should promote. <u>In my understanding of forgiveness in Islam, God forgives all sins. When a person wrongs another, he/she should do an equal right to those they have wronged and ask for forgiveness from the victim and then from God. And even if the victim did not accept and forgive, God is the final word of forgiveness. Some Islamic scholars have also promoted accepting all apologies because in the end of the day we will be judged in front of God.</u> Submitted Hussain Alkazemi from Kuwait, emphasis added.

Tonight's class had me reflect on forgiveness within my own cultural and religious beliefs. I'm Afghan and Afghanistan is a very tribal system. I belong to the Pashtun tribes of Afghanistan and the Pashtuns operate under a code of conduct called the Pashtunwali. Pashtunwali is paramount to the Pashtun identity. It is an honor or behavior code amongst the tribal Pashtuns that's used to govern relationships between people and increase one's honor. There are three concepts that constitute Pashtunwali: *melmastia, badal, and anawati. Melmastia* is hospitality, *badal* is revenge, and *nanawati* is asylum, submission, or forgiveness.

For this journal I'll discuss only badal and nanawati. Badal, or revenge, allows injured people to retaliate against anyone who has caused them harm and it is ideal to cause harm greater than the initial offense. Alternatively, in order to protect himself and his family, the aggressor can offer nanawati, which is a formal apology that shows symbolic submission by the culprit to whomever he or she has harmed. Nanawati can also be offered on behalf of the injured party in order to put an end to a conflict. Therefore, nanawati can flow in both directions. A person who accepts or offers nanawati as opposed to opting for badal is considered very honorable within society.

I believe that my understanding of nanawati is what has made me somewhat good at offering apologies along with reparations when I have made a mistake as well as accepting people's apologies or requests for forgiveness. ... Furthermore, sometimes I find myself giving a person forgiveness to save face and increase honor despite not being ready to do so deep down inside. I'll decide to bear it in order to avoid seeming petty or to make the other person feel better, regardless of whether or not they deserve it.

In addition, Islam also holds a generous attitude toward forgiveness. Muslims are constantly reminded in the Qur'an and from the Prophet Muhammad's (pbuh) tradition to forgive others, regardless of whether they deserve it or not, if we want to be forgiven by G-d on Judgment Day. Even if a person repeatedly offends us, we're encouraged to forgive them each time keeping in mind how often we want G-d to forgive us. However, forgiveness isn't seen as a ticket for automatic reentry. We're taught to take heed with those who exhibit certain patterns of behaviors and characteristics that are not ideal to put up with. We're encouraged to forgive even those who we could never trust again but are not taught to have to deal with them after; that is at our discretion, but we're told to keep lessons learned about them intact. … I believe that the concept of nanawati is influenced by Islamic principles of forgiveness. Submitted by Pashtana Abedi, emphasis added.

No Sacred Text

As we looked around at the other ways to find forgiveness, it occurred to me that no one has told me about any tools to use to find forgiveness. Since I am not a religious person and have no religious faith background to draw upon, I am floundering to find my own path to forgiveness that does not include Luskin's visualization exercises. In retrospect, I do think we were a little too harsh on Luskin. There is very little other literature out there that seems to offer such a specific model of cognitive therapy.

There aren't many practical steps to forgiveness outside of the religious context. And for most of us, myself included, I feel like there is a sense that forgiveness should be culminated around sort of event or process. You should know when you forgive someone, especially when you were a serious victim. The reality of forgiveness, which I think (another student in class) articulated well when she mentioned how she had forgiven an ex-boyfriend for cheating on her without realizing it, is that most of us do forgive, or at least let go, many offenses over time.

Perhaps accepting that habits of anger and hurt are hard to break is the first step to working with Luskin and allowing yourself to change channels gradually over time. In fact, I find myself thinking about people in my life who I have already forgiven or anger that I have already let go of and realizing that somehow, I managed to change the channel on my own. Perhaps the visualization should be more personally tailored to the victim. For myself, visualization of Big Sur or other grandeurs of nature was not as useful but visualizing all of the good that has ultimately come from some negative experiences and situations is a visualization that I find meaningful. Submitted by Emma Williams Phan, emphasis added.

After discussing the transformed life model of forgiveness, I believe that this model could be the most powerful and comprehensive form of forgiveness. On the continuum of why we forgive, we put belief systems before healthy reconciliation. However, I believe the transformed life model of forgiveness is potentially the highest point on that spectrum because the forgiver not only forgives the wrongdoer, but the forgiver does it for pure reasons.

If someone forgives merely because of a lack of self-respect or as a gift to others, then the forgiver is forgiving either to avoid conflict or because the forgiver believes that he deserves the harm that he received. If the forgiver truly forgives, not just because of his belief system, but because he truly feels and believes that he has so much for which to be grateful, then that forgiveness is pure and not tainted by selfishness or a lack of respect for oneself. This pure form of forgiveness can then rub off on the person receiving the forgiveness, and it may make that person think twice about what he did and the gift of forgiveness that he received.

The transformed life model of forgiveness sends a signal to the forgivee that there is so much in life for which to be grateful, and that whatever the forgivee did to the forgiver has no power over the forgiver. I believe that forgiveness such as this has a powerful indirect impact on the person receiving forgiveness.

I also want to say that I believe a person can exercise the transformed life model of forgiveness without a faith-based background. I am not a religious person. Yet, I still know what is moral and what is ethical. I am also grateful for this life that I have and the **wonderful experiences and relationships this life has provided me. These things are more** important to me than holding grudges or living in hate. I therefore believe that implementing the transformed life model of forgiveness based on a general gratefulness for life and what it provides is definitely possible. I hope to utilize this form of forgiveness in my life because it focuses on things for which we should all be grateful instead of focusing on hurt, pain, and resentments. Submitted by Sean Olk, emphasis added.

Christianity

Jesus summarized all his teaching in the two greatest commandments: "[l]ove the Lord your God with all your heart and with all your soul and with all your mind and with all your strength," and "[l]ove your neighbor as yourself."[57] Jesus defined who a neighbor is by dismissing the political and religious rivalries used to limit "neighbor" through the parable of the Good Samaritan.[58] He told his followers "be perfect, therefore, as your heavenly Father is perfect" after challenging his followers to "love your enemies and pray for those who persecute you."[59] His teaching that his followers should forgive others in the same way they want God to forgive them removes any question that loving others, even our enemies, includes forgiving them.[60]

How then are Christians supposed to live up to these extraordinary standards? Jesus' good news is that he recognized that it is humanly impossible. He died as a sacrifice to pay the price for our inherent selfishness (between each other) and rebellion (declaring our independence from God.) People who accept Jesus' payment for our brokenness, are not only forgiven, but God's Spirit enters that person to change his or her heart from dead (cold, judgmental, and unloving) to alive (warm, forgiving, and loving.) The Christian faith is literally life giving. Jesus described this when he taught, "[n]o one can enter the kingdom of God unless he is born of water and the Spirit. Flesh gives birth to flesh, but the Spirit gives birth to spirit."[61]

The obligation to forgive in the Christian community is executed in two ways. The first is when a person is very hurt and angry but offers forgiveness as a matter of obedience. This is a forgiveness grounded in rational thinking and a decision of the will to comply with a prior commitment to a set of values. For the Christian, even his rational mind remains acutely aware of Christ's sacrifice for and forgiveness of him. The victim may still be devastated, but they know their sacred text teaches that they must forgive, so they overcome their feelings and live their values. This honors their faith commitment because they choose to obey and trust that the feelings will come later.

An example is Corrie ten Boom's description of her forgiving the German that guarded her in a concentration camp during World War II. When the guard asked her to forgive him when she gave a talk after the war, she describes the following thought process:

> And still I stood there with the coldness clutching my heart. But forgiveness is not an emotion—I knew that too. Forgiveness is an act of the will, and the will can function regardless of the temperature of the heart. 'Jesus, help me!' I prayed silently. 'I can lift my hand. I can do that much. You supply the feeling.'[62]

A student journal gives another illustration for how a person might forgive in this way.

> What stood out most to me was our discussion of the decision and feeling in a religious context as it defines forgiveness. Since our first day of class, I have constantly come back to one situation that is still stuck with me. I dated someone in college for three years, only to find out he was unfaithful and lying to me for quite some time. He is still with the same girl to this day. Faith has helped me in so many ways and I know I would not be where I am today without God's gentle presence. I know that as a Christian, I should forgive wholeheartedly whether or not an apology was provided. I often think to myself, "God has such an amazing capacity to forgive billions of people, every second of every day. Thus, I should be able to forgive this small instance." So, I have set my mind to forgive and I am on good terms with my ex-boyfriend.

> Yet, my emotional battle with this is constant. I think about it every day and often wish harm upon him, debate whether he gave a remorse apology, and often struggle with general trust. I feel constant guilt because I know I should turn the page of this book, forgive and move on. Yet this feeling contradicts that.

The final words of Mother Teresa's Poem eloquently say, "you see, in the final analysis, it is between you and God; It was never between you and them anyway." What a profound thought. I am imperfect: that is how God created me and that is what makes faith so inherently beautiful. I have limited perspective as does my enemy. The idea of a decision to forgive by redemptive religion and then feelings to *follow* is an essentially reassuring concept that I will hold close in my journey with forgiveness. Submitted by an anonymous student, emphasis added.

The contrasting execution of forgiveness in the Christian community is when a victim is experiencing so much love and forgiveness from God that they feel genuine love for the person who hurt them and forgive from the heart. This person's faith commitment is honored because he or she is experiencing the release of God's forgiveness in the moment and extending the grace he or she is experiencing to those who injure him or her. These two types of redemptive forgiveness highlight the question at the beginning of chapter one about whether forgiveness is based on a rational decision or an emotion feeling.

Ken Sande's book about Christian dispute resolution, *The Peacemaker*, includes a practical approach to Christian forgiveness.[63] Sande suggests that Christians consider the following four promises when seeking a Biblical approach to forgiveness, and he clearly states that this approach to forgiveness is based on a decision and not on feelings.[64]

Sande's first forgiveness promise is, "I will no longer dwell on this incident."[65] The value of this promise is like taking control of what we think about in therapeutic forgiveness. The strategy is that the negative feelings will dissipate as we cease thinking about the hurtful incident. Unilaterally promising to no longer dwell on the incident is Sande's first step towards a level of forgiveness.

Sande does something unique because of the Christian context. He identifies three more promises but instructs that they should only be given if the perpetrator repents. His concern is that within the context of the Christian community, I may need to confront my brother until he repents so that my brother is restored.[66] This blends in with relational forgiveness because my motive for confronting my brother is to win him back and restore him to right relationship with me, with others in the Christian community, and with God. This uniqueness is the collective community seeking to follow God, including duties of encouragement and accountability. It would not be loving if I neglected to pursue my brother who I believed acted contrary to God's will.

If the person who injured me repents, then I promise that:

I will not bring up this incident again and use it against you;

I will not talk to others about this incident;

I will not allow this incident to stand between us or hinder our relationship.[67]

Sande emphasizes that these promises remove the penalty of separation and restore the relationship if the person repents.[68] If the person does not repent, Sande encourages us to cease from dwelling on the incident. This does not mean that the issue is closed. We may need to confront the perpetrator about it again, request others in the Christian community to assist in confronting the perpetrator, and possibly diminish the relationship with a person claiming to be a Christian but who is living inconsistent with that claim and not acknowledging and repenting of his wrongdoing. Sande's approach echoes Augsburger's definition: "[f]orgiveness is the mutual recognition that repentance is genuine and that right relationships have been either restored or achieved."[69]

The essence of the redemptive approach to forgiveness is the belief that forgiving or not forgiving has eternal consequences. Jesus taught that

> anyone who is angry with his brother will be subject to judgment … But anyone who says, 'You fool!' will be in the danger of the fire of hell. Therefore, if you are offering your gift at the altar and there remember that your brother has something against you, leave your gift there in front of the altar. First go and be reconciled to your brother; then come and offer your gift.[70]

Notice that this passage challenges the reader to seek reconciliation for our brother's eternal well-being. It is your brother who has something against and may be angry with you. He is in jeopardy. Pursuing forgiveness is not only part of my spiritual experience with possible eternal consequences it may have eternal consequences for the one who is injured and angry. My pursuit of reconciliation takes priority over my worship—I should only give my gift at the altar after I have sought reconciliation.

A student's journal describes her views.

> My longtime boyfriend from high school essentially "cheated" on me while in college (There is still some disagreement on the term cheated.) He showed no remorse and offered no real apology, but I decided after a long time of wallowing in my own self pain that I needed to forgive him for myself and move on. Up to this lecture I had really thought I had forgiven him out of my own ambitions, but since looking deeper I realize I have never even been close to forgiving him. What he did is still a scar on my heart, impacting every relationship I have had, and all I have really done is pushed it from my mind.

> The more I studied and reflected on this material, the more I realized the redemptive model is much more viable in terms of actually finding healing. I know I have a very biased perspective, coming from a religious foundation and background, but I think having some form of higher power or ideology being the root and power behind your forgiveness is the only way to find true healing.

Atheists would have a serious problem with this statement, however, <u>I think this world is so broken, and pain runs so deep, that we simply do not have the ability to push the pain out of our heads, to forget about what we have just experienced, but in order to look at pain and wrong doing straight in the face and choose to give the offender mercy and grace takes something stronger than human will power.</u> Submitted by an anonymous student, emphasis added.

Endnotes

1. *See generally* Dayton, *The Magic of Forgiveness.*
2. Lewis B. Smedes, *Forgive and Forget* 13-19, (1984).
3. *Id.* at 3-14.
4. *Id.* 18-19.
5. *See id.* at 13.
6. *See* Fred Luskin, *Forgive For Good*, (2002).
7. *Id.* at 63.
8. *Id.* at 110.
9. *Id.* 110-16.
10. *See id.*
11. *Id.*
12. *See e.g., id.* at 13-14.
13. *Id.* at 19-12.
14. See *id.* at 7-11.
15. *See id.* at 46-59.
16. *Id.*
17. See e.g., Beliefnet.com, http://www.beliefnet.com/prayers/protestant/addiction/serenity-prayer.aspx (last visited Sep. 5 2018) (written by Reinhold Niebuhr (1892-1971).
18. Luskin, *Forgive for Good* 147-53.
19. *Id.*
20. *Id.*
21. *See generally id.*
22. John Patton, *Is Human Forgiveness Possible? A Pastoral Care Perspective,* (1985).
23. David Augsburger, *The New Freedom of Forgiveness* 36, (2000).
24. *Id.* at 38.
25. *Id.* at 39.
26. *Id.* at 40.
27. *Id.*
28. *See id.*
29. *Id.* at 40-43.
30. *Id.* at 42.
31. *Id* at 48-49.
32. *Id.* at 49.
33. *Id.*
34. *Id.* at 49-50.
35. *Id.* at 50.
36. *Id* at 48.
37. Tian Dayton, *The Magic of Forgiveness*, (2003).
38. *Id.* at 57.
39. *Id.* at 59.
40. *Id.*
41. *See id.* at 59-60.

42.   Jane Bolton, PSYCHOLOGYTODAY.COM, *Is Anger Good or Bad For Self Esteem?*, https://www.psychologytoday.com/us/blog/your-zesty-self/200908/is-anger-good-or-bad-self-esteem (last visited Sep, 13, 2018).
43. Dayton, *The Magic of Forgiveness* 60.
44. *Id.*
45. *See id.*
46. *Id.* at 60-61.
47. *Id.* at 61.
48. *Id.*
49. *Id.*
50. *See generally* id.
51. *Id.* at 62-63.
52. *Id.* at 63.
53. *Id.*
54. *Id.* at 63.
55. *Id.* at 64.
56. *Id.*
57. Deuteronomy 6:5 and Mark 12:29-31.
58. Leviticus 19:18 and Luke 10:25-37.
59. Matthew 5:43-48.
60. Matthew 7:1-5 and 6:12.
61. John 3:3-6; *see also* Ephesians 2: 1-10; Ezekiel 11:19.
62. Corrie ten Boom, *Tramp for the Lord* 55-57 (1974).
63. Ken Sande, *The Peacemaker,* (2006).
64. *See id.*
65. *Id.* at 209.
66. *See id.* at 186-97.
67. *Id.* at 209.
68. *See id.*
69. David Augsburger, *The New Freedom of Forgiveness* 48.
70. Matthew 5:22-24.

Chapter Eight

Advising Others (and Yourself) to Forgive

"I think you should forgive and forget, instead of leaving wet towels all over Dad's grave."

CartoonStock.com

8.1 Introduction

This chapter will discuss advising others to forgive. It will include an examination of reasons to choose forgiveness that will be useful when navigating your own decision to forgive. It will also consider the alternatives to forgiveness. This chapter's focus will assume a person has been unfairly injured and is being encouraged by a family member or close friend. Roles professionals such as lawyers and mediators will be addressed in later chapters.

Encouraging others to forgive is hard for three reasons. First, the person is already hurting; he or she is the victim; and he or she has already suffered an unfair injury. It does not seem fair to ask the victim to fix the situation. For an advisor to challenge the victim to take responsibility for healing seems like kicking a person when they are down. Shouldn't he or she be allowed to wait for an apology to facilitate the healing? But some of our definitions and approaches to forgiveness are initiated by the victim alone.

The second reason it is hard to encourage another to forgive is concern about pushing my values to the point of violating the victim's autonomy. As the advisor, I may be a forgiveness zealot, believing it is the path to health and wealth, and I am free to forgive generously and reap the benefits of doing so. But just because I choose to live my life this way, does not mean another person is interested in following suit. The person encouraging forgiveness must leave room for the victims to elect or reject forgiveness. We must respect their right to decide how they want to handle the situation. The forgiveness encourager can make victims aware of the forgiveness option and its advantages, but the decision must be left to the victims.

A third reason it is difficult to encourage another person to forgive is to respect anger as part of the grieving process. Each person will have his or her own timetable for when he or she is ready to hear and respond to the possibility of moving on from the unfair injury. My wife needs more time to recover from a small spat than I do. Sometimes I will apologize and ask if we are okay, and she tells me she needs some time before we are back to normal. Being sensitive (understanding) and respectful of another person's recovery process requires the person encouraging forgiveness to accept that timing is everything and the victim may not be in an emotional place to forgive.

About a month after my Mother-in-Law died, my wife and I attended a previously scheduled weeklong retreat with our young children. One day at lunch the organizers announced that the afternoon optional activities would include the opportunity to meet with a husband and wife therapy team. My wife reluctantly agreed to do this together to discuss our recent loss and grieving. I will remember forever when one of the therapists described that her mother died a few years earlier and that other people don't understand that you never get over it. A few months after her mother died well-meaning friends had asked her, "Are you over it yet?" I am so grateful we received that advice because I know that I would have been a well-meaning husband asking the same thing. I have made many mistakes in my marriage, but not that one!

Now that we have explored various kinds of forgiveness and paths to forgiveness in chapters six and seven, we are able to possibly encourage people we love to heal through forgiveness, but this role needs to be exercised carefully. The advice in chapter three on Advising Others to Apologize to recognize the amount of rapport and whether the advice has been requested applies equally when encouraging others to forgive.[1] The matrix that summarizes those concepts is provided below as a refresher:

	Advice Requested	**Advice Not Requested**
High Rapport	Advise Freely	Ask Permission
Low Rapport	Advise Cautiously	Don't Advise

A student's journal describes how these factors impact her willingness to advise others to forgive.

In my own life, I find it difficult to tell someone to let go of their hurt and forgive the person that has harmed them or someone close to them. In general, if someone comes to me to ask for my advice on a situation, I will happily give it to them. But many times, people simply come wanting to vent and to satisfy their need of feeling heard. I have no real issue with that, as long as the same person does not continue to complain about something over a long period of time. What is difficult for me though, is advising someone to forgive when they are not open to the idea of it. Although a large factor of my willingness to advise forgiveness comes from the relationship I have with said person, another large aspect of my comfort stems from the type of forgiveness I am advising.

I possess very strong religious beliefs and convictions, so I do not find it difficult for me to advise another Christian on forgiveness based on redemptive motives. I feel like as a sister in Christ, I have both the authority and the obligation to guide another believer toward forgiveness.

I also think it would be easy to persuade someone to forgive from a therapeutic standpoint. Part of my personal understanding of the world is the idea that people are naturally self-centered. This does not necessarily mean that people are selfish, but humans as a species instinctually think about their own needs first. Therefore, it is rather simple for me to tell another person to forgive if I show them how it benefits them and makes their situation better.

What is difficult for me is advising others on relational forgiveness. Like a remorse apology, relational forgiveness requires a person to reflect on their involvement and wrongdoing in a given situation. While I think this may be one of the richest forms of forgiveness that has the best potential outcome for individuals and groups of people, it is hard for me to tell another person that they also are at fault.

People like to have a positive self-image, which is often why many people find it difficult to offer a remorse apology and confront their negative actions, and therefore <u>it is hard for me to try to get another person to admit their fault in a situation. Again, the type of relationship I have with the person I am supposedly advising makes a great difference. I have an easier time telling my best friend that she should look at herself in the mirror than I do telling someone I do not know as well.</u>

While relational forgiveness is the most challenging in my opinion, I also think it is the richest form of forgiveness. Apology, forgiveness, and reconciliation are responses to conflict and wrongdoing, but they don't just need to be tools to cope or recover from harm. When we put the relationship first in any situation, we can turn conflict into a positive way to improve our relationships. I think if I reframe how the person understands conflict, I will have better luck in guiding them toward forgiveness and possibly toward reconciliation. Submitted by Rachel Yoshimura, emphasis added.

There is value in exploring a variety of concepts and thoughts when encouraging others (and yourself) to consider forgiving. But the concerns in this introduction remind us to be *patient* and *respectful* of the full range of emotions and reactions resulting from an unjust injury. We should be aware of the following menu of ways to encourage forgiveness but not apply them mechanically or simplistically.

8.2 Options After an Unfair Injury

The option of forgiving should be considered in context. What are the alternatives to forgiving? How satisfying are those alternatives? Forgiveness may not appear attractive at times, but the victims need to compare what will they do if they don't forgive.

The options after experiencing an unjust injury fall into three categories: forgive, sulk, or seek revenge. This section explores the costs and benefits of sulking or seeking revenge so we can compare them with the costs and benefits of forgiving, which will be presented in the next section.

Benefits and Costs of Seeking Revenge

A positive aspect of revenge is the assertion of the right to be treated fairly. Standing up for yourself when treated unfairly could be viewed as a healthy expression of self-respect. Philosopher Jeffrie Murphy argues against forgiveness when it is based on a lack of self-respect.[2] A person has to believe that he is worthy of being treated decently to recognize that degrading behavior is not appropriate. The person who chooses revenge as a way to defend their self-respect at least has self-respect. A student's journal provides an example.

> A phase I hadn't heard in a long time was, "anger is a healthy response to injustice." I was particularly struck by this phrase because while doing the Forgiveness Inventory and Survey, I remember having a very different answer than nearly all of my classmates for one of the scenarios based on an experience I had. ...
>
> Someone I had a very close relationship with broke my trust in a substantial way and it was not in my distant past but close enough to that time where it was very relevant for me. I guessed that most of my classmates' answers were very different than mine because they had not experienced this type of thing first-hand. However, what bothered me most was that I did not actually feel the level of anger that I thought should have been appropriate for this type of thing. I was worried about my own emotional health, and whether I had any self-respect for not feeling enough anger and actually forgiving this person. It wasn't until just about a week ago that I was thinking about it and actually got mad –finally. Submitted by Shelby Warwar, emphasis added.

A benefit of revenge is the deterrent message it sends to the perpetrator and observers. Game theorists recommend the tit-for-tat strategy as a way to avoid exploitation.[3] Demonstrating willingness to return the injury may cause some potentially opportunistic predators to look for an easier mark. Sometimes the desire to create such a precedence is targeted at the perpetrator. Other times the message targets the extended community that this person or organization is not to be trifled with. For example, an institutional defendant, like an insurance company, will sometimes spend more money vigorously defending a claim than it would have taken to settle the case to discourage other plaintiffs with similar kinds of claims. Again, a student's journal paints a picture of this.

> In discussing forgiveness in class, I have been reflecting on my life experiences and how quick I have been to forgive. Although I come across as stubborn at times, my heart is soft and once someone demonstrates any form of remorse to me, it is very difficult for me not to forgive them. ... Another issue that comes with the territory of forgiveness is boundaries. I have suffered from a deplorable lack of boundaries in my past, and this is something I've been recently very conscious of.

When one forgives too easily or too quickly, she signals to the offender that the behavior was acceptable. When one is stingy with their forgiveness, they signal not only that the offense was egregious, but possibly that they are stubborn and uncompromising. Thus, the sweet spot in between is the area that I would like to elevate towards. <u>In the past, because of my naturally forgiving tendencies, I have forgiven transgressions that have resulted in very thin boundaries between myself and others. For that reason, those who I had consistently forgiven ended up reoffending, each time to a stronger degree.</u> Submitted by Elica M-Zadeh, emphasis added.

There might also be situations when taking revenge has social rewards. The LA Times reported the results of a Russian who went to Switzerland and killed the Air Traffic Controller responsible for the mid-air collision of two planes resulting in the death of his family.[4] He was released after eight years in prison and returned home to a hero's welcome.[5] He was revered in his community as a man who defended his family's honor and memory, and the local government even gave him a well-paid cushy job.[6]

These positive aspects of revenge must be balanced by the negative consequences. The most immediate negative consequence is that the victim becomes a perpetrator. She repeats the behavior she condemns. Thus, she lowers herself to the original perpetrator's level. She loses her moral high ground and exclusive victim status. She is now the second perpetrator, and after taking revenge, both participants are victims and perpetrators.

A danger of revenge is that it is hard to get it right. Our attribution bias includes perceiving our own suffering as worse than that of others.[7] Thus, our retaliatory tit-for-tat becomes a tit-for-tat plus. The concept of proportionality is violated, and we become the worse perpetrator. Many have commented that the "eye for an eye" principle was designed to put limits on consequences.[8] If the perpetrator causes me to lose one eye, I am not entitled to inflict any worse punishment on him. Should my revenge exceed the scope of the original injury, the original perpetrator is now the greater victim and entitled to even the score.

On a macro level, revenge continues a downward cycle. Disrespect and denigration are exchanged in an escalating series that goes back and forth. Affected relationships and the observing community are damaged in increasingly large concentric circles that emanate from the damaged core. Acts of revenge are almost always noticed by others and become a part of a communities' narrative of values and meanings. Victims considering responding with revenge should consider how such a decision will affect their spouse, children, and friends. The private personal choice to take revenge often communicates a message that the world is harsh and non-gracious to a broader audience.

A third reason to reconsider the urge to take revenge is that it does not provide the victim with satisfaction. Many people believe they would feel better if they could take revenge. Sometimes this is not an option because the perpetrator has more power than the victim or the perpetrator is no longer living. When revenge is not possible, victims need to learn to recover without revenge. Sadly, the availability of revenge distracts the victim from evaluating whether it will be satisfying.[9]

A student journal uses the cinema to explain a nuanced understanding of forgiveness.

> However, it got me thinking about how revenge is portrayed in the media. I am a huge cinema fan and one of my all-time favorite sub-genres is the revenge film. ... There's just something immensely satisfying about watching someone that has been wronged beyond one's wildest imagination go on a crazed, single minded, killing spree in an attempt to settle the score at all costs. Thinking about this more, I now realize these movies tend to breakdown into two broader philosophical categories.
>
> The first grouping I would label as the "wish fulfillment" revenge category. This is the category that depicts revenge as people wish it to be. Specifically, that the person exacting revenge is always totally justified, the villains are unrepentant, and that the act of revenge concludes in a sense of closure and satisfaction greater than could have been achieved by any other means. A great example of this is Ridley Scott's *Gladiator* in which not only is the former Roman general able to avenge his own betrayal and the murder of his family by killing the unrepentant evil emperor, he's able to do so in front of an entire coliseum full of people cheering him on with approval.
>
> The second grouping I would label as the "somber existential" revenge category. This is the category <u>that depicts revenge as it actually is. Specifically, as a scenario where there is rarely a true hero and villain, the process of seeking revenge forces the protagonist to compromise their own moral integrity, and after taking revenge the protagonist is left feeling even more empty and damaged.</u> A great example of the "somber existential" revenge film is Steven Spielberg's *Munich*. In this film, an idealistic young Israeli agent is recruited in the wake of the Munich massacre to be a part of an off-the-books government sponsored hit squad targeting anti-Israel terrorists. As the character progresses on his mission he is confronted with the surprising humanity of some of his targets, watches in despair as his sacrifice does little to actually prevent further terrorism and becomes a disillusioned empty shell that is no longer able to look his wife or child in the face.
>
> *Gladiator* was a huge box office success and *Munich* was perceived as one of the few major financial disappointments for the otherwise bulletproof Spielberg. So, what happened? I believe forgiveness is one of the hardest things anyone can do and that nobody likes to wallow in pain. And so, Hollywood does what it has always done. It finds people's most appealing inner fantasy, in this case that they can be greatly wronged and not have to forgive in order to heal and sells it back to them in the form of popular entertainment. Submitted by Andrew Duncan, emphasis added.

Benefits and Costs of Sulking

Some people easily reject revenge, but they also reject forgiving. Instead, they accept and maintain a perpetual victim status. They carry the memory of the harm done and the resentment of those responsible for their suffering.

The first benefit of resentment is that it is a form of punishment the victim delivers to the perpetrator. The victim's rejection of future relationship including coldness and distance is a small piece of punishment he can impose on the perpetrator. The victim may not be able or willing to deliver overt revenge, but the ongoing suffering lets the perpetrator know the depth of the injury he inflicted. Should the victim heal and get over it, the perpetrator may assume the victim has given the perpetrator permission to forgive himself. If the victim refuses to forgive, the victim may have power over the perpetrator and over whether the perpetrator forgives himself.

A second benefit of being a victim is the availability of sympathy and support. Hopefully everyone has people in their lives who are sympathetic and supportive, especially after suffering an unjust injury. When you learn that a friend has betrayed a serious confidence, your team should come to your psychological aid with sympathy and support. Your team might consist of a spouse, adult children, your family of origin, other friends, members of your faith community, and/or mentors. This support is appropriate and important.

The duration of this support will depend on the quality of your relationships, the number of times you have called on that system for support, and the seriousness of the injury. Support systems often experience fatigue. Even for serious injuries, many people will eventually choose to avoid spending time with a person caught in a victim mentality. Supporting another person's emotional pain is often emotionally draining. Usually, at some point if the victim doesn't learn to heal, much of their support system will drift away, and they will need to ask new relationships to be sympathetic and supportive.

Some people never recover from the unjust injury and are defined by that experience. Twenty years later the event still dominates most conversations. This identity is difficult to redefine because it stimulates a sympathetic response for the benefit of the individual being a victim.

I recently experienced this when I telephoned someone who had been married to a close friend, but the marriage ended twenty years earlier. We had shared interests and enjoyed trips and events together, but I hadn't spoken with her for fifteen years. I called because I wanted her professional opinion about how to handle a situation. Before I could explain my purpose for the call, she started complaining about my close friend and describing how he had contributed to the alienation between her and her adult kids. She asked me to tell her kids that they should try to have a relationship with her. I was surprised that twenty years after the divorce and fifteen years since I had spoken with her, the wounds were still deep and the only thing she could talk about with me.

The benefits of holding onto the injury come with a price. Lewis Smedes describes the cost of resentment.[10] He proposed that nurtured anger grows into hatred, and that hatred hurts the hater and is self-destructive.[11] The result is a bitter, negative, and hostile person. While this is sad, some may be willing to pay the price *IF* it had the desired impact of punishing the perpetrator. Maybe most tragically, hate hurts the hater and often has no effect on the perpetrator.

Fred Luskin, and many other authors, remind us that anger and hurt are appropriate responses to painful events.[12] But anger and hurt do not improve with age, and they are not healthy long-term strategies. Luskin documents the medical studies showing how ongoing anger and hostility are harmful to physical, psychological, and emotional health.[13] His description for emotional well-being consists of "more hopeful, less depressed, less anxious, less stressed, more confident, learn to like themselves more."[14]

While we examined the benefits of the revenge and resentment responses to an unjust injury, we also summarized serious costs of both those options. Choosing to forgive is often not easy, and while the alternatives may seem easy at first, they do not allow a person to heal in the long term. This section proposes to people in the despair of deep personal pain that there are no easy exit strategies.

A student's journal provides a description.

> About twelve years ago, a colleague of mine offended several people, including other colleagues, my father and me. Although he was targeting me, he created a conspiracy theory and alleged in an email forwarded to tens of associates that a large group of people was trying to benefit me and harm him. Years later, I learned that the offender was having severe trouble with his mental health. He got divorced and lost his friends, and his professional behavior went down.
>
> He never apologized for the damage he inflicted. I was entirely sure that I never wronged him and that my and my father's reputations were severely damaged. … <u>In the first days after the offense I was planning for revenge, but soon realized that this ill feeling was hurting me more than the offense. Afterward, I went to the sulking stage, but I still was hurting from the attack.</u> Years passed without him addressing the incident. I was hurting and angry not only because of what he did to me but also —and especially- because of what he wrote about my father.
>
> Nothing changed even when he seemingly recovered from his mental issues. No more offenses to anybody, but no apologies as well. Suddenly I decided to move on. It was time to overcome from all the pain by myself. I took years to forgive him apparently, but, as I learned from the last class, I did not forgive the perpetrator. I just let the pain go.
>
> Indeed, I could forgive him for what he did to me, even without an apology offered. However, I was, and I am not able to forgive him for what he wrote and said about my father. … The way I found to survive this was to let the pain go. Submitted by an anonymous student, emphasis added.

8.3 Reasons to Forgive

This section will suggest some of the concepts that can be used to convince others (and our self) to relinquish their right to justice and replace it with forgiveness. The description of an internal debate with pros and cons of forgiving may be an inappropriate projection of my experience. In any event, the discussion helps to map a variety of internal journeys from victim to victor. This chapter will provide some new arguments to reinforce your mental and emotional tool kit to encourage forgiveness.

Reasons to forgive are related to the type of forgiveness being extended: therapeutic, relational, or redemptive. This discussion will seek to organize most of the reasons so that they relate to those three approaches to forgiveness. A "catch all" category will be included for reasons that do not fit neatly into the three categories.

Reasons to forgive therapeutically

- ❑ To give a gift to myself. To stop reliving the injury and hurting from it. To focus on being happy and positive and not angry and negative. For my emotional health because resentment and bitterness are not positive feelings. For my physical health because resentment and bitterness take a toll on my physical body.
- ❑ I recognize that revenge is not possible or satisfying. Resentment hurts me and does not hurt the object of my disdain.
- ❑ I see this incident as an opportunity for me to grow in learning compassion, empathy, and kindness. These traits tend to be exercised when we experience unfair injuries. I want to be a kinder and more loving person.

Reasons to forgive relationally

- ❑ I need or want a relationship with the person who hurt me.
- ❑ The person who hurt me needs or wants a relationship with me, and I don't want to abandon him.
- ❑ I know that I hurt people unfairly and need them to forgive me. It is only right that I forgive them back. This is especially true if I have unfairly injured the very person I am now forgiving, such as a spouse or sibling. The burden to forgive is also greater when the person who hurt me knows times when I needed forgiveness from someone else in a shared community, like a family, workplace, or community of worship.
- ❑ I accept that people are complex, with both bad and good characteristics. I forgive the bad because of the good.
- ❑ If I push away everyone who hurts me, I will be eventually be isolated with very few close relationships.

❑ I look beyond the injury to the heart of the person and history/context of the situation and ask why did she do this? This exercise may shed light in two dimensions:

First, seeking the history and context of the situation gives me an opportunity to consider if I played any part in creating this situation. Did I instigate or contribute to the offense in anyway? Even if I didn't, could I have prevented the injury by defusing the situation earlier in the transaction? Was the ultimate injury to me the climatic act in rounds of escalation in which I intentionally or negligently participated? My willingness to forgive relationally may be part of a realization that my hands are not entirely clean.

Second, even if I believe my hands are clean, I may want to explore the childhood and early influences of the perpetrator. What did her culture and environment teach her about people like me? How did she become so angry, hateful, or insensitive? For example, when I learned about Charles Manson's horrific childhood, it didn't excuse his killing others, but it did cause me to have empathy for him. Martin Luther King Jr. encouraged victims of racial injustice to recognize that their oppressors were also victims of the social institutions of their times that taught and encouraged racism and bigotry.[15] This exercise in expanding the horizon and depth associated with the anti-social behavior often helps us see the perpetrator as also a victim, scared, hurting, weak, or needy; furthermore, they needed our help, support, and comfort before and after the injury.[16] This emphasizes the role of the systems, collaborators, and neglect of the people who should have prevented the injustice.[17] I accept that I might act the same way if I had the same history.

❑ For the good of a group. Feuds affect others. Types of people who might suffer collateral damage include children, spouses, siblings, cousins, in-laws, teammates, and observers. I forgive so innocent bystanders will not be hurt by my vengeance or sulking.

Reasons to forgive redemptively

❑ My belief system includes the recognition that every human being has innate dignity and that I am called to love my neighbor and even my enemy. ("But I tell you, love your enemies and pray for those who persecute you.")[18]

❑ I believe that my selfishness and independence have damaged my relationship with God much worse than what the person did to me and that God has forgiven me. God's forgiveness comes with an expectation that I will be a steward of His forgiveness and pass it on to others.

❑ I believe that what goes around comes around. Somehow Karma or something works it out so that I will be treated with the same kindness or harshness with which I treat others.[19]

❑ I know that I am not qualified to fairly judge the situation. As an injured victim, my objectivity has been compromised. Smedes wrote that "to expect two people caught in mutual hate to sort out their pains is like asking a child to calculate the national debt."[20] I will trust others (God or the government) to address the situation from an objective perspective.

Reasons to forgive that relate to all three or none of the forgiveness themes

❑ Forgive to be an example to others.[21] People who have suffered unjust injuries can recover, heal, and be happy. Shattered relationships can be restored. Faith or a life philosophy can inspire a person to forgive. Observers notice and may gain hope from your forgiveness.

❑ Forgiveness is fairer.[22] Some people don't forgive because it is not fair to allow the perpetrator to get away with something; the final score will be perpetrator one, victim zero. Revenge results in both being perpetrators, making the score perpetrator minus one, victim minus one. The only way to avoid perpetuating the unfairness is to rise above it and refuse the temptation to take revenge or stay bitter. The better fairness is to overcome evil with good.

The website for the Quotes of Martin Luther King Jr. provides his explanation.

"I am convinced that love is the most durable power in the world. It is not an expression of impracticable idealism, but of practical realism. Far from being the pious injunction of a Utopian dreamer, love is an absolute necessity for the survival of our civilization. To return hate for hate does nothing but intensify the existence of evil in the universe. Someone must have sense enough and morality enough to cut off the chain of hate and evil, and this can only be done through love."

❑ Forgiveness is a better risk.[23] Some people do not forgive because they do not want to risk the perpetrator repeating the behavior. But not forgiving leaves the victim tasked with remembering and re-living the pain from the past. Forgiveness is a better risk because there is the chance that the victim might heal individually and maybe relationally. Forgiveness might lead to a healthier future.

❑ Philosopher Jeffrie Murphy argues that Forgiveness should only be given for a moral reason; otherwise, the victim lacks self-respect.[24] He suggests five possible moral reasons:
   1. he repented or had a change of heart;
   2. he meant well (motives were good);
   3. he has suffered enough;
   4. he has undergone humiliation (the apology ritual of begging for forgiveness); and
   5. because of old times' sake (he has been a good and loyal friend.)[25]

A student's journal reacts to one of the reasons some people don't forgive.

> I think one of the saddest things I've seen … is when a person knows they have the ability to forgive but fail to do so out of a fear of what people will think. <u>People sometimes refuse to let go because they're afraid that they will be perceived as weak and unprincipled. However, forgiveness makes one strong and principled because they took control of their own well-being</u> as opposed to giving someone else that power over them
>
> If people do judge you for doing the right thing, then it's probably better that those people are not in your life anyway … Letting someone's perception of you control your internal happiness strips you of your autonomy and assumes that that person cares more than they really do. Submitted by Pashtana Abedi, emphasis added.

This section of Why Forgive can be summarized by a continuum ranging from least to most admirable. The value assessment of these reasons could be personal, so the reader can make personal modifications.

Why Forgive Continuum

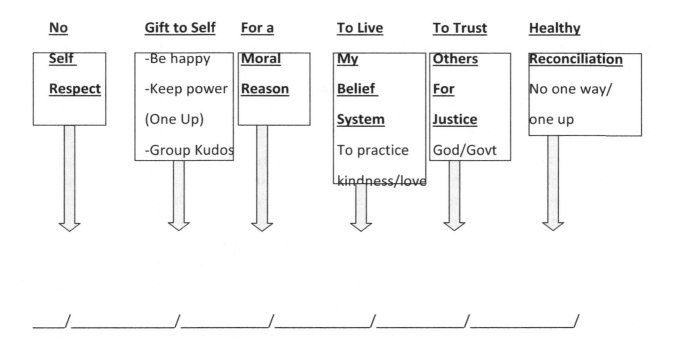

Remember, the forgiver is not discounting the injury or excusing the actions of the injurer. The literature agrees that forgiveness must be honest about both of these aspects.

A student's journal provides an example of using the conceptual building blocks to critically analyze an approach to forgiveness. She examined the idea of forgiving by trusting others (God in her journal but I believe the same could be said for the government) for justice.

> I found last class' discussion on forgiving rather interesting. It seemed as if many people said they were able to forgive if it was not up to them to "do justice." That it is easier to forgive because they knew that ultimately their offender would have to account for his actions to God. I can completely follow this logic and I understand how that would work internally for a person. My problem though is that if your forgiveness is based on someone else's responsibility to render a judgment, are you then really forgiving? Or are your merely shifting the responsibility to deal with the offense from you to whatever higher being you believe in? And why is justice part of your forgiveness?
>
> My definition of forgiveness is that you actually, honestly, and wholeheartedly forgive someone for his actions. It feels hypocritical to me to say you forgive and then rely on God to punish him. <u>If you are still looking for punishment for your offender, you are still high on the reparations scale and if you forgive but assume that God will point him in Hell's direction you are, in my humble opinion, still quite high on the animus scale. Those combined don't seem to translate into a true forgiveness.</u> Submitted by an anonymous student, emphasis added.

8.4 Forgiveness and Grief

One of the introductory caveats for this chapter was to respect the importance of timing. The experts agree that anger after unjust treatment is appropriate and healthy. The question is how long should an unfairly injured person be allowed to wallow in their anger and self-pity before encouraging themselves (or being encouraged by a caring friend) to forgive? An anonymous student's journal provides a powerful lesson on this point.

> Talking more about how to advise people on how to forgive is still a subject that I am trying to put an opinion on in this class. I think I have trouble with it because growing up I was encouraged to forgive people to the point where it was forced and premature. This ended up hurting me the most out of all the parties involved because my voice was being taken away from me and giving someone a peace of mind that our battle has been mended, when in reality it was not. My oppressor was being given a free ride and I was being even more scarred from not being able to fully process my emotions and being given the time to heal in my process of forgiveness.
>
> This mainly happened with instances with my dad. Growing up my mom was so worried that I was going to turn out like him, so her plan was to make sure that I forgave him, so I wouldn't be like him. This didn't really make sense to me, but I did see her point in trying to forgive him so I would not be resentful of him. To be honest, I have detached all expectations from my father and am not mad at him. … What has really damaged me the most out of the "forgiveness process" is that I was still hurting, and my feelings were being invalidated because I was being told that they needed to go.

> When I am using my degree for encouraging people to forgive, I want to make sure that I am not giving people an ultimatum and that they are ready to do so. I am a strong believer that premature forgiveness is unhealthy and that it can cause more damage since someone is mitigating their true emotions due to someone else's advice on how they think they should handle the situation.

Insight about this question of timing occurs by comparing the forgiveness process to the grieving process. Forgiveness can be thought of as a type of grieving. The victim expected to be treated fairly and instead was unfairly injured. The victim's expectation of fair treatment has died, and the victim grieves the death of how he thought he would be treated. The grieving could extend to the victim's beliefs that the perpetrator is a good person. The perpetrator's actions have proven otherwise, and now the original view of perpetrator might need to be abandoned and grieved.

The Kuber-Ross explanation that grief is a process that includes recognizable stages is helpful when trying to construct how people forgive.[26] The stages are denial, anger, bargaining, depression, and acceptance.[27] There is a general sense that they happen in a sequence, but it is also accepted that the stages may not be linear and that the cycle may need to be repeated in part or in whole.[28] It is generally accepted that it is wise for a person who has suffered loss to allow themselves to experience all of these stages.[29]

A student's journal describes relating to this description in her forgiveness experience.

> I am the kind of person who needs to fully examine a situation where I got hurt. I need to put myself in the shoes of the offender. I also need to put myself in the shoes of someone else in my situation. It takes me a long time to forgive, and no matter how hard I try, I need to get angry and ruminate, and mourn. I think forgiveness is most comparable to the stages of loss. The five stages of loss are a common model for grief. The stages include: denial, anger, bargaining, depression, and acceptance. I feel like forgiveness is what happens at the end, and that it is most analogous to acceptance. Sometimes I just equate acceptance and forgiveness.
>
> This is a model that occurs naturally in one's personal psychology, and I think it is appropriate to talk about forgiveness in terms of grief. But I think that all of these must run their due courses, and that time is a necessary component, more so than sheer willingness to forgive. However, being conscientious about the problem and trying to direct one's mind in a way that will help cope with these problems can help the person move through these stages. Submitted by Heidi Simavsky, emphasis added.

This chapter focuses on assisting others to forgive. Forgiveness enthusiasts are well served to view the forgiveness journey as like the grief journey and to encourage victims of unfair injuries to experience all the steps on the journey.

I experienced this when my adult daughter was in a serious car accident. She was driving on the freeway when a car spun out as it entered the flow of traffic and ended up driving in the wrong direction. My daughter was driving the speed limit but could not avoid the oncoming car. The collision was significant and young children in the other car were not in car seats or even wearing seat belts. A few of them were ejected from the car and suffered very serious injuries. My daughter later learned that the driver of the other car was driving with a suspended driver's license.

My daughter was very angry when she learned that her insurance company had offered to pay the maximum amount of her insurance policy even though they said the accident was not her fault. The insurance company explained that if she was found only one percent responsible for the accident, she could be found liable for the injured children's significant medical expenses. She argued that she wasn't one percent negligent, but the insurance company insisted on pursuing settlement to avoid the risk and exposure. A few months later, her insurance company let her know that the lawyer representing the other driver was asking my daughter to disclose her personal assets, so they could decide if they would demand payment from her beyond the insurance policy limits.

My daughter was very angry at the other driver for being so irresponsible (driving on a suspended license, losing control of her car and driving against traffic, and not having her children properly restrained in the car) and then expecting my daughter and her insurance to pay for the consequences. She was very expressive about her anger. After three weeks, I asked her how long she was going to allow herself to be angry and when would she start to forgive.

She said that she knew she would need to forgive for many of the reasons described above, but she just wanted to be mad for a few more weeks. I applauded her recognition that she would need to eventually forgive and agreed to be patient. After she began forgiving, she learned that the other driver and her lawyer signed the papers with the insurance company settling for the full amount of the policy without including any payments from her personal assets.

8.5 Archbishop Desmond Tutu's Forgiveness Model

Archbishop Desmond Tutu was the chair of South Africa's Truth and Reconciliation Commission. He is probably the world's most famous and recognized advocate for forgiveness. His articles and publications on the topic are extensive. In *The Book of Forgiving* that he co-authored with his daughter, Mpho Tutu, he provides the following model for forgiveness that contrasts a "Revenge Cycle" with a "Forgiveness Cycle."

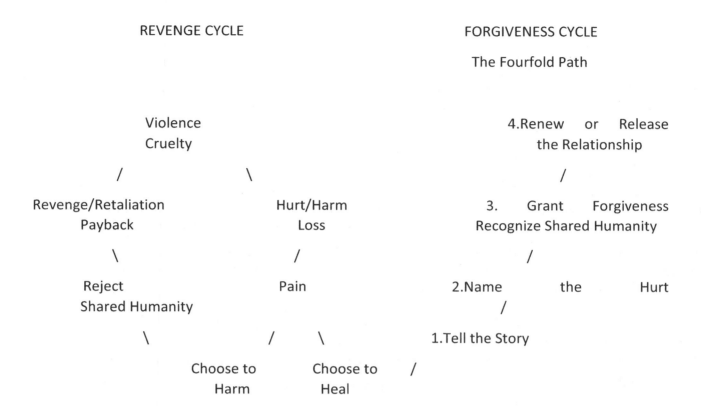

This flow chart simplifies Archbishop Tutu's work to encourage forgiveness but is useful because it is easy to understand and apply. Like in Luskin's model, the direction an individual takes boils down to whether he chooses to heal or harm. Tutu's method of "Telling the Story, Naming the Hurt, Recognizing Shared Humanity, and Renewing or Releasing the Relationship" is a preview of some the material in the chapters ahead addressing reconciliation.

8.6 Forgiveness Therapy

The discussion of assisting others to forgive is greatly enriched by Robert Enright and Richard Fitzgibbons' excellent book *Forgiveness Therapy*.[30] Their definition of forgiveness combines elements that have been presented in each of the three models. Their observations about mental health strategies is way beyond my qualifications. Their nuanced presentation of how a mental health professional might possibly include forgiveness in the therapeutic experience is brilliant. This section will consist of extensive excerpts from their book because a summary will not do this topic justice.

I.   Definition of Forgiveness

Enright and Fitzgibbons define forgiveness as when a person determines that they have been treated unfairly and choose to "willfully abandon resentment and related responses (to which they have a right) and endeavor to respond to the wrongdoer based on the moral principle of beneficence, which may include compassion, unconditional worth, generosity, and moral love."[31]

Morality of Forgiveness (Justice and Mercy)

Enright and Fitzgibbons believe that "[f]orgiveness is centered in morality, which in its simplest form is concerned with the quest for the good." The authors find that forgiveness is a communal process because when "people seek good, they do so in relation to others," which shows that it is not self-satisfying. "Forgiveness is the merciful response to this injustice" because the victim recognizes that they have been wronged and chose to offer forgiveness rather than revenge that most people would believe they are entitled to.

A forgiver is a giver of a gift that the other person does not deserve. Enright and Fitzgibbons point out that it is possible for a person to both forgive and perform justice at the same time. Just because someone is forgiven does not mean that they do not face the natural consequences that result from their behavior such as having to return stolen money.[32]

Transformation

Forgiveness has the ability to completely change a person's life because it "shifts perspectives, feelings, attitudes, behaviors, and interactions." The transformation is evident when a new course is charted from "judgmental to understanding, from resentment to loving, from anxious to more relaxed, from conflicted to a willingness to cooperate."[33]

Forgiveness is Not . . . Self-Centering

There is a misconception floating around that forgiveness equates to looking out for the wellbeing of the forgiver with little attention if any being given to the forgiven. Self-centering may be a useful and necessary part of the healing process, but it is not forgiveness because forgiveness is an action of compassion that actually does take into account the individual needing forgiveness. The act of forgiveness is allowing the other person's humanity to come into focus while offering compassion to heal the situation.[34]

Forgiveness is not . . . Reconciliation

It is important to distinguish forgiveness from reconciliation because sometimes these two are confused. Forgiveness does not necessarily mean that reconciliation will happen, but for reconciliation to occur some form of forgiveness must have taken place. As previously discussed, forgiveness is a choice by one individual to no longer resent the other person and adopt a more friendly attitude towards the wrongdoer. Forgiveness can be a one-way street that is not dependent on the wrongdoer's response.

Reconciliation on the other hand is more of a business negotiation between the parties to determine what it would take to get the two parties back working together. Forgiveness can be mostly internal while reconciliation is external changes being made to rebuild a working connection.[35]

II. Definition of Forgiveness Therapy

Forgiveness Therapy is the process of walking through the situation with the client to reexamine the totality of the circumstances that gave rise to the harm so that the client can better understand why the event occurred. The end goal of this process is for the client to begin understanding the event from the perspective of the wrongdoer, to slowly release the anger directed towards that person, and eventually make a "moral response of goodness towards the offender." This can take a short or long period of time.[36]

A. Compared to Other Therapeutic Approaches

Surprisingly the forgiveness conversation is lacking in the healing process of many clients going through various types of therapy today. Many times, clients show up for therapy because they have been treated wrongly and unfairly by others. Forgiveness therapy is unique because it focuses on this fundamental element of a person's healing process which deals with injustice by working through the "anger to attain emotional health."[37]

As long as the therapy session is willing to address the issues of right and wrong, mercy, and justice, it will be compatible with forgiveness therapy, which delves into those issues. If a therapy labels itself as "value free" it will most likely not work with forgiveness therapy because the counselor must be able to analyze the behaviors as right and good or wrong and bad to move forward. ...

> Once anger has been uncovered, many therapists have tended to rely on its expression as the primary method for dealing with this emotion. ... As anger was expressed, depressive symptoms were believed to abate ... [O]thers failed to experience improvement in their depressive symptoms after giving vent to their anger ... We hope that after reading this book, therapists who make decisions about treating anger in their patients will consider the use of forgiveness.[38]

B. Forgiveness Therapy as a Process

Forgiveness Therapy takes time. The process includes figuring out where the client is in the timeline of the event and what the path forward looks like. In each situation, the client must discover what forgiveness is and must have the free will to choose it on his or her own. The process includes the potential forgiver seeking to view the perspective of the wrongdoer by analyzing the circumstances leading up to the event. The forgiver will then need to discover a "newly emerging identity" of the wrongdoer and perhaps himself after the act of forgiveness.[39]

III. Phases of the Forgiveness Process

1. Uncovering Phase

First, the client must look deeply into the original unfairness, how he or she responded to it, and if that response was appropriate. "Before Forgiveness Therapy can be successful, the client or patient must accurately conclude, 'I have been wronged, it hurts, and I wish to do something about this.'"[40] The counselor's duty is to determine if the client's defenses are stopping the client from logically analyzing the situation. The counselor should aid the client in understanding what actually happened and who was unfair.[41] The client must be notified that the solution (that is forgiveness) is coming and that insight by itself will not resolve or heal the pain from the injustice.[42]

2. Decision Phase

As it sounds, the decision phase is the moment when the client decides to forgive. In this phase, the counselor should determine which strategies are working and which ones are ineffective and experiment with alternative coping strategies.[43] The client should have the opportunity to explore forgiveness as an option and decide either to accept or reject forgiveness.[44]

The next step is committing to forgive the offender, which is different than actual forgiveness. This step is simply testing the waters of forgiveness with a toe because it is a refrain from seeking revenge or having vengeful thoughts. People tend to first decide in the minds to forgive, test how it feels, and then move towards actual forgiveness. After the commitment is made, the more difficult task of making it a reality begins. Exercising this right to choose allows the client to understand that he or she actually does have control over how to respond. One way to nudge a client in the right direction is for them to rank the level of effectiveness and satisfaction of the previous methods they have tried for the same unfair situation.[45]

3. "Work Phase"

Reframing the situation begins the work phase. This step is simply seeing the situation with clear eyes through rethinking and reconsidering the first impressions of the event. A good way to do this is by asking certain questions that challenge the initial view of the offender so that the humanity rather than evil can be seen by the forgiver. Enright and Fitzgibbons include the following questions and advice:

> What was it like for the offender as he or she was growing up? (Reframe who the offender is, perhaps someone who is vulnerable, scared, or confused.)
>
> What was it like for the offender at the time of the offense?
>
> Can you see him or her as a member of the human community?
>
> Is it possible that the client may have contributed to the offender's objectionable behavior? But be careful that clients do not blame themselves for another's moral failure.

Reframe the relationship. If their interactions are typically civil and respectful, the victim may see the perpetrator in a new light.

Reframe the cosmic perspective. This is where the client's worldview/ religious beliefs enter. If the client is from a monotheistic tradition, one might ask, "[i]s the perpetrator a child of God? May he/she be granted salvation? Will I see him/her in heaven some day? Is he/she loved by God to the same extent that I am loved?

A study determined that clients found reframing as the third most difficult unit to accomplish. This likely is because of the tension between anger and seeing the personhood in the one who caused the anger.[46]

Showing Empathy/Compassion

After reframing, the goal is that the client begins to discover the existence of empathy and compassion within himself. This can take a long time depending on the trauma and pain experienced by the individual, and while the therapy can help and support this discovery, it cannot be forced.

Empathy means the client is able to see who the other is, without distortion. Distortion can take two forms: One is over deprecation, whereas the other is over adulation. In both cases the client fails to distinguish the person from his or her actions.

Over deprecation—the client judges the person's worth in light of harmful acts.

Over adulation—the client equates the person's acts with his or her worthiness, concluding that the acts must be fine if the person is of value.

If the client is condemnatory about the person rather than his or her acts, then reframing has not yet progressed sufficiently.

Empathy, in other words, is not some automatic step devoid of complication or even danger. The therapist needs to provide guidance to a client who empathizes with a perpetual abuser but then does not assess the abuser's trustworthiness. Empathy can work on the side of forgiveness, but it can also work on the side of enmeshment and enabling. This is why reductionism must be avoided in our forgiveness models.

Empathy, as part of a total program including the understanding of forgiveness, reconciliation, and reframing, can be an aid to psychological improvement. Isolated from these other features of forgiveness therapy, it can work against the client's best interests.[47]

4. Deepening Phase

a) Finding Meaning

When a client can find rational meaning through a narrative that they create surrounding the event, the client is moving in the right direction by recognizing that suffering is "an inevitable part of the world." But the client will make great progress by using the suffering to grow a benefit as a person through an enhanced sense of self-understanding in areas such as maturity and tranquility.[48]

A student's personal experience provides a good application for the material about the decision to forgive.

> The more we study forgiveness, the more I am convinced of its complexity. Whereas the apology literature contained numerous yet similar definitions as to what constitutes a good apology, the discussion about forgiveness contains many differing opinions as to its definition. Is it a process of healing oneself emotionally and psychologically as Luskin suggests? Or is it a five- step process similar to grieving? Furthermore, does the offender even need addressing for forgiveness to occur? Because of an offense that was committed against me that I only learned of last week, I think I am starting to gain some clarity on the issue.

> As I mentioned in prior journals, in entering the Straus program, I simultaneously left my former law firm and began my own practice. In doing so, I would occasionally perform some work for my former firm on a contract basis, as I believe that we had a good relationship. Last week, I was speaking with one of my fellow associates at the firm when he advised me that one of the partners had "thrown me under the bus" in a declaration to a Federal Court in a matter in which I had performed no work.

> I think my time at Straus has changed the way I view the world, because I was surprisingly calm at learning this fact. Upon returning home, I checked the PACER website to see exactly what had been written about me. My former boss had initially submitted a motion claiming that he was late in filing a court ordered document because he was attempting to meet and confer with the other side in the case. Then upon receiving the opposition papers, he submitted a reply declaration, whereby he completely changed his story, and using me, by name, claimed that the reason the document was not timely filed was because I had failed to file it before I left the firm. Tellingly, in her order, the judge called out my former partner on his inconsistencies, labeling his attempt to blame me for his failure as "undecorous."

> Having studied forgiveness for the past few weeks, I immediately began analyzing whether I would forgive my former boss for his conduct.

> From a Luskin standpoint, I will move forward, I will think about other things, and I will find inner peace. To me, however, this is not forgiveness, but me showing an ability to live in the moment and to not let the past dictate my future.

What this incident caused me to realize is that <u>true forgiveness consists of relieving the offender from two things: (1) the act, and (2) any ill will toward the offender himself. Here the act was inexcusable. He lied and tried to blame me for his own failures in a capacity that could potentially have professional consequences for me. Moreover, in doing so, he has revealed his true person to me, and has shown me that I no longer want a relationship with him</u> in either a professional or social setting. While I can release myself from the anger caused by his conduct, in no way am I willing to release him from his wrongful acts. Submitted by an anonymous student, emphasis added.

8.7 The Event/Process and Decision/Feeling Forgiveness Matrix

The matrix below helps organize how many of the relational and redemptive forgiveness models, including methods described by Tian Dayton, David Augsburger, and Enright and Fitzgibbons respond to the questions about whether forgiveness is an event or a process and whether it is a decision or feeling. Notice that there may be only limited application of this matrix for therapeutic forgiveness.

The matrix is organized to begin in the upper left quadrant and rotate counter-clockwise.

	Decision	Feeling
Event	The First Stage is a DECISION to Forgive – an EVENT	Fourth Stage is when the empathetic FEELING is strong enough to create a forgiveness EVENT
Process	Second Stage is a DECISION to Engage a PROCESS: -Control what you think about -Create a hero story -Create a more complicated story -Focus on your beliefs and values -Embrace the stages of grieving -Reframe your understanding - Humanize the perpetrator	Third Stage is When whatever PROCESS you engaged creates empathetic FEELINGS for the perpetrator

8.8 The HOA Forgiveness Advice Exercise

A friend for 20 years emails you and asks if you are willing to discuss a problem she is having with her Home Owners Assn. The friend is about 70 years old and lives in a retirement community that was built 20 years ago with about 1200 homes in the HOA. You became friends when you were the Director of a Christian Mediation Program and she was the Director of Human Resources for one of the Christian Universities in your region. The two of you partnered as co-mediators on a few cases and have stayed in contact since she retired about 7 years ago. You call and learn the following:

About a year ago her HOA informed the members that it was concerned about some of the 20-year-old trees having "invasive roots" that will seek out and rupture the sewer lines between the homes and the street. The HOA is responsible for maintaining the front yards of all the homes and thus will be removing and replacing the trees in question. The problem is that they are removing 20 years old trees which are at least 20 feet high with 24-inch trunks and replacing them with one-year old trees six feet high and with one-inch trunks.

Your friend has gone to considerable lengths to object to the HOA's plan. She believes that less drastic measures can be taken. Cameras could be sent down the sewer lines to see which of them are showing signs of be compromised by roots and only those trees could be removed. She also believes that protective barriers could be put between the trees and the sewer lines. She also believes that trees that need to be removed could be replaced by more mature trees. She may be willing to pay half the cost of planting a more mature tree in front of her home.

Her considerable efforts include more than 30 emails to the HOA Board of Directors, some of which threaten suing the HOA. The HOA's attorney wrote a long letter documenting the HOA's legal right to take its actions and informing her that if she sues the HOA and loses, she will need to pay the HOA's attorney's fees. She found a statute that requires the HOA board to meet with a disgruntled member if the member requests a meeting in writing. She asked for a neighbor to attend the meeting as a witness. A member of the board and the board's attorney attended the meeting but were uncooperative. At the end of the meeting the attorney encouraged her to sue the HOA, because if she loses, she would need to pay the HOA's attorney's fees. Your friend admits that she totally lost her temper because of their stubbornness and disrespect. She ended up yelling at them, using foul language, and again threatening to sue them in small claims court. They refused her demand that they not replace the tree in front of her house until after she dies.

She did research and found that the Charter for the HOA Board's Landscaping Committee states that if a tree must be replaced, it must be replaced by a tree similar in size and kind; the next sentence says that replaced trees will be 15-gallon trees (six feet high and one-inch trunks). The board member told the neighbor who witnessed the meeting that lots of members are complaining about the tree replacement program.

Your friend asks your advice about going to small claims court and for any advice you may have.

Endnotes

1. *See* Chapter Three, *Advising Others (and Yourself) to Apologize.*

2. Jeffrie Murphy, "Forgiveness and Resentment," *Midwest Studies in Philosophy*, vol. 7, ed. Peter French, Theodore Uehling, and Howard Wettstein (Minneapolis: University of Minnesota Press, 1982), page 504 (condemning forgiveness based on a lack of self-respect).

3. Robert Axelrod, "The Emergence of Cooperation among Egoists," *The American Political Science Review*, vol. 75, No. 2 (June, 1981), pp. 306-318.

4. Megan K. Stack, "Russian's revenge begets rewards," *Los Angeles Times*, February 2, 2008.

5. *Id.*

6. *See id.*

7. Hanna Brycz, "Perception Accuracy of Biases in Self and in Others," *Institute of Psychology*, vol. 1, no. 3 (Sep. 2011) pp. 203-215.

8. See e.g., Christopher Townsend, "An eye for an eye? The morality of punishment," JUBILEE-CENTRE.ORG (March 1997) http://www.jubilee-centre.org/an-eye-for-an-eye-the-morality-of-punishment/.

9. *See* Karyn Hall Ph.D., "Revenge: Will You Feel Better?" PSYCHOLOGYTODAY (Sep. 15, 2013) https://www.psychologytoday.com/us/blog/pieces-mind/201309/revenge-will-you-feel-better. (Finding that "[r]evenge can be a strong urge, but you may not feel better if you act on it."

10. Lewis B. Smedes, *Forgive and Forget* 13-19, (1984).

11. *Id.* at 106.

12. *See* Fred Luskin, *Forgive For Good*, (2002).

13. *Id.* at 77-81.

14. *Id.* at 78.

15. *See* "The King Philosophy," THEKINGCENTER.ORG (2018) http://www.thekingcenter.org/king-philosophy.

16. Smedes, *Forgive and Forget* 99-104.

17. *See id.*

18. Matthew 5:44.

19. *See* Galatians 6:7 ("Do not be deceived, God is not mocked; for whatever a man sows, that he will also reap. For he who sows to the flesh will of the flesh reap corruption, but he who sows to the Spirit will of the Spirit reap everlasting life.")

20. Smedes, *Forgive and Forget* 105.

21. *See generally id.* at 122-49.

22. *Id.* at 125-33.

23. *Id.* at 134-37.

24. *See supra* note 2.

25. *Id.*

26. Kuber Ross, "The Five Stages of Grief," GRIEF.COM (last visited Sep. 18, 2018) https://grief.com/the-five-stages-of-grief/.

27. *See id.*

28. *Id.*

29. *See id.*

30. Robert Enright and Richard Fitzgibbons, *Forgiveness Therapy,* (2015).

31. *Id.* at 26.

32. *Id.* at 25.
33. *Id.* at 26.
34. *Id.* at 49.
35. *Id.* at 44.
36. *Id.* at 6.
37. *Id.* at 10.
38. *Id.* at 17-18.
39. *Id.* at 7.
40. *Id.* at 59, 61.
41. *Id.* at 63.
42. *Id.* at 67.
43. *Id.* at 69.
44. *Id.* at 70.
45. *Id.* at 70-71.
46. *Id.* at 72-73.
47. *Id.* at 74-75
48. *Id.* at 79-81.

Chapter Nine

Lawyers Encouraging Forgiveness

9.1 Introduction

9.2 Between Vengeance and Forgiveness

9.3 The Opportunity for Lawyers to Encourage Forgiveness

    9.3.1 A Unique Relationship

    9.3.2 Lawyer Qualifications

    9.3.3 For the Benefit of the Client

    9.3.4 For the Benefit of the Lawyer

9.4 Full Disclosure About the Legal Process

9.5 Lawyer Advising Client About Forgiveness at the End of a Personal Injury Case

"RECONCILIATION? ARE YOU CRAZY? THINK ABOUT ALL YOUR PAIN AND SUFFERING! THINK ABOUT MY RETAINER!"

9.1 Introduction

This chapter explores how lawyers can encourage forgiveness. This topic is especially pertinent to plaintiff lawyers serving victims. It is also important when lawyers are representing parties who are well acquainted with their opponents. People sometimes sue strangers, but often are in conflict with people who have been important in their lives: family, partners, employers, and long-term vendors. Readers will examine how a modern legal system can both alleviate and consume victims seeking justice.

Encouraging forgiveness will be presented as an opportunity, but not a requirement, for lawyers. The ultimate question for a lawyer considering this opportunity is, "what kind of a lawyer does he or she want to be?" Reasons for encouraging forgiveness will include benefiting both the client and the lawyer. Finally, lawyers will be encouraged to consider a "full disclosure approach" when encouraging clients to consider forgiveness in their journey seeking justice.

An experienced family law attorney's journal is illustrative.

> When we discussed the role of the lawyer and the numerous options that lawyers have and/or that their clients want their lawyer to play, I immediately thought of a case that I was just in court for two days prior to class. A former client contacted me in April about a situation that occurred which he did not handle very well. The client acknowledged that he let the situation get out of control. We discussed the events leading up to the incident, and while I understood the client's frustration, I was sure to let the client know that this type of behavior could not happen again in the future, but that the client could not ignore the situation either.

> I counseled the client to document the incident in writing to his ex-spouse, to explain what his actual frustration was really about, to acknowledge that he didn't handle the situation the best way, and to avoid attacking or rationalizing his behavior by attacking the ex-spouse's new boyfriend. The client said he would take my advice, and I did not receive an update from him.

> Five months later, the client contacted me and asked to retain my services because his ex-spouse filed a motion. In the motion, the incident that occurred in April was included along with a myriad of other allegations from over two years ago, a diatribe degrading my client, and a concern that my client has anger management issues. As I read through the motion, I realized that it was meant to provoke my client and make him look bad in front of the judge.

> While I was waiting for my client to give me his specific response to the motion, I reached out to the opposing counsel with an offer to settle all of the issues. The settlement included an agreement to the majority of what Mom requested in her motion, with the exception of three smaller issues that I felt my client would prevail on at court.

Mom, unfortunately, decided to counter with some unreasonable demands, which I could not understand because we were in agreement with the majority of her requests, which could help the parties avoid future conflict. I specifically informed opposing counsel that I did not think going to court when we had the majority of issues resolved would help future conflict, but his client would not back off a few of her requests.

Therefore, when I wrote my opposition and countermotion, I specifically focused on my client's willingness to adopt conflict reducing solutions. I informed the court of all the issues that were agreed upon, and instead of responding to each of mom's attacks, or engaging in the same type of behavior (the tit-for-tat), I wrote the following:

> Dad has no desire to engage in a "bashing contest," but believes it is telling that Mom would set forth such allegations against him in a public pleading, copies of which the children may one day see, as adults. The majority of issues that Mom mentions in her motion are from 2015 – over two years ago. Dad attempted to come to an agreement as set forth in his Exhibit "B" –the court can clearly see that nothing has changed from Dad's agreement to resolve the issues to this opposition.

> The only thing that can come from forcing this matter before the court is to further degrade Dad and increase the level of conflict between the parties. This office purposely did not put any time in addressing or responding to Mom's allegations in an effort to avoid bickering and to limit the amount of attorney's fees that Dad incurs.

Of course, when my client saw Mom's rejection of his settlement offer and re-read her motion, his immediate response was to tell me that he had all kinds of information and text messages to show exactly how Mom has acted badly. Dad gave me some of the information and asked that we fight fire with fire.

I calmly explained to Dad the reasoning behind the approach that I was taking and further told him that I believed Mom was trying to bait him, and that he shouldn't take it. When everything is all said and done, I asked what his goal was. To continue having conflict with Mom, or to reduce the conflict so that the children are not affected, and he no longer has to worry about these types of allegations or accusations in the future.

My client decided to trust my advice and allowed me to file the opposition and countermotions and maintain my argument in court – that Dad's actions showed his desire to decrease conflict, while Mom's insistence on moving forward with court showed the exact opposite. This indeed worked, and while the Judge did not ignore his concerns about my client's actions from April, he agreed that the best course of action was to put certain orders in place that would reduce conflict between the parties and to reduce the contact at exchanges.

The parties voluntarily agreed to enroll in a cooperative parenting class for high-conflict cases so that they could learn the tools they need to have more effective and open communication, and so that hopefully moving forward, they will be on the same page.

We are not just lawyers, we are also counselors at law – I take that title seriously, especially because_my job does not just affect my client, it affects the other party and in cases like this, it also affects children; children who did not ask to be raised in two separate homes with warring parents. Submitted by Audrey Beeson, emphasis added.

9.2 Between Vengeance and Forgiveness

In *Between Vengeance and Forgiveness*, Martha Minow focuses on violence associated with the wholesale breakdown of a community.[1] She describes how the re-establishment of a legal system and/or other government investigatory commission, like a truth and reconciliation commission, relieves victims from the need to personally retaliate (a measure of forgiveness) with an expectation that justice will still be accomplished.[2] A functioning legal system can be seen as a social institution to allow citizens to trust that bad behavior will be punished without them executing personal revenge. Thus, civilized citizens can abandon vendettas and feuds and trust their grievances to the state's justice system.

One positive aspect of this model is that justice is done without the victim becoming a perpetrator. The victim does not decide whether or how much to punish the perpetrator. The justice system takes that responsibility. The justice system is in a superior position to accomplish better justice because it is objective and has not been biased by the experience of being victimized by the perpetrator. The community disciplines bad behavior by administering a sanitized revenge.

This description is accurate in the criminal law arena. The government has the responsibility to prosecute complaints against criminal defendants. The offense is viewed as an offense against the state as opposed to the victim. Victim's rights groups argue that this approach has been taken to an extreme and advocate that the criminal justice system should allow more participation by victims. Still, if my family member is murdered, the government accepts responsibility to accomplish justice, and my only role is to serve as a witness; however, victims can give an impact statement after the verdict is in.

A victim's ability to passively defer to the legal system for justice is different for injuries that are not criminal in nature but are reserved for the civil court system. Victims are required to play an active role when asking the legal system to award compensation from perpetrators for a long list of non-criminal unfair injuries such as negligent driving, sexual harassment, breach of contract, and professional malpractice.

In civil cases, the government supplies the courthouse, its personnel, and the laws which determine whether the perpetrator will be required to compensate the victim (liability) and the amount of that compensation (damages). This apparatus for the delivery of justice in disputes between parties is helpful, but it is not a self-executing justice system. The civil legal system utilizes an adversarial model where the victim must bring the claim and establish certain elements while the perpetrator must defend against the lawsuit. The civil court system requires active participation by the victim.

In the civil system, the victim files a complaint and becomes the plaintiff. As the plaintiff in a civil lawsuit, the victim is required to:

1. articulate a legally actionable offense;
2. gather the facts to prove all the legally required elements of the case by a preponderance of the evidence; (the judge or jury must be convinced that the legally required facts are more likely to have occurred than not to have occurred);
3. prove that the offensive behavior was the proximate cause of legally recognizable damages and the amount of those damages;
4. refute and disprove any countervailing explanation or version of the facts advanced by the perpetrator (defendant) that would avoid liability or decrease damages; and
5. present themselves as sympathetic and deserving so that the judge and/or jury is inclined to find in his favor.[3]

A student's journal describes an important contrast.

It is also very interesting that typically part of the healing process involves telling a hero story, as we learned earlier. However, the litigation process and the way the entire trial scheme is set up makes it seem very victim-story oriented! It may be a part of strategy for the victim to induce a "pity" emotion from the jury, therefore hoping that those emotions would be favorable to the case. There, the entire litigation process in and of itself is one that keeps the victim in a state of victimization! They constantly focus on the victim story and not the hero story, and continue to remain in their state of anger, disgust, etc. But how much of this is really necessary? Is it *always* necessary to play the victim card in order to win at trial?

These questions are so intriguing because they make me think outside the realm of what I expect lawyers to do. From my perception based on what the media shows me, it is always good to make the jury feel sorry for the victim, and therefore it is assumed it will be good for the victim- because in the end they will win the case. But psychologically, this can actually be *bad* for the client! I do believe that lawyers can help the client by telling them that yes, we (the lawyer) can help you (the client) get justice, but we should let you know that it may be a polarizing and adversarial process and our counsel is that you don't necessarily *have* to do that! Submitted by Andrew Kahng, emphasis added.

In the civil court system, the victim is actively seeking vengeance (compensation to make themselves monetarily whole), often requiring a considerable investment of time and money. The victim is agreeing to defer to the community (courts, judge, and jury) to assess whether and, if so, how much the perpetrator should be required to compensate the victim based on the severity of the injury and the wrongfulness of the conduct. Thus, the civil justice system is a hybrid model. The community will decide whether to punish the perpetrator and the extent of punishment. But the victim is required to prosecute the complaint usually including a significant investment of resources to fund the qualified professionals. Sometimes those professionals include expert witnesses and almost always the professionals necessary to prosecute a civil case includes lawyers.

Most people know someone who was wrongfully injured, had grounds for pursuing a civil lawsuit, and chose to forego his or her legal rights for a variety of reasons. One reason for not pursuing a civil lawsuit is that the victim does not want to pay one or more of the variety of prices (financial, emotional, relational and/or opportunity costs) necessary to hold the perpetrator accountable through the civil court system. Peg Healy's column titled, "A Lesson in Forgiveness" in the April 1999 edition of the *California Lawyer* describes this from a very personal perspective.

> The last time I saw my eldest brother, Stevie, alive, I was six years old, and he was ten. He came out of his bedroom, saying, "I feel sick. My stomach hurts," and disappeared down the hall in the direction of my mother's room. … That evening, my father told us that Stevie was in the hospital, and my mother was staying with him. The next morning, Saturday, my parents were a little more cheerful as they dropped us with friends and went back to the hospital. Stevie was in a coma, but the doctors had learned he had diabetes, and insulin was going to make everything fine. But everything was not fine. Stevie never came out of the coma. He died Sunday night. …

> Information came trickling in after the autopsy, and my father explained it to us carefully. Stevie had died of a blood clot in his brain. The blood clot came from a heart infection. The heart infection was connected to the rheumatic fever he'd had after he and Robbie had strep throat the previous year. …

> My father never talked about his work at home, certainly not to his children, but I knew he was a lawyer. He liked to help people who were hurt, by suing other people for them. I don't know how many times my parents said that if Stevie's initial strep throat had been treated by our doctor with penicillin, which was still a new-fangled drug then, instead of sulfa drugs, he wouldn't have gotten a rheumatic heart. Or that my mother had previously asked the doctor about Stevie's mysterious ongoing symptoms, which proved, in hindsight, to point to a missed diagnosis of childhood-onset diabetes. But at some point, in callow adolescence, I asked my mother directly, "Why didn't you sue the doctor, if he made so many mistakes?" …

My mother sighed. "You know," she said, "the doctors at the hospital were worried that we would sue when they learned that your father is an attorney. But what they didn't know is that an attorney's family is the *least* likely to bring a lawsuit." She smiled at my surprise and continued. "A personal injury lawyer's family knows better than anyone else how long and painful and expensive and miserable a lawsuit is. It goes on for years before anything gets resolved, and you have to keep thinking about it and caring about it, and you keep on hurting. We didn't want to do that. It wouldn't bring Stevie back." She paused delicately. "The doctor was very bright, but he was overworked. He went back to school to train for a specialty. I don't know for sure, but I think the medical association put pressure on him to get out of general practice."

That was a lesson in generosity I have never forgotten: that my parents, after such a devastating event, could forgive someone else for being fallible, could choose to move on and start healing: that in the middle of mind-numbing grief, you can refrain from revenge.

They didn't teach me this in law school, but perhaps good lawyers could be candid and educate their new clients about the emotional costs of litigation before clients have to decide if it's worthwhile to prolong their pain.

9.3 The Opportunity for Lawyers to Encourage Forgiveness

9.3.1 A Unique Relationship

This section assumes that the victim meets with a lawyer to consider civil litigation. When discussing lawyers encouraging forgiveness, it is essential to remember the variety of understandings and meanings of forgiveness.

The lawyer might want to explain that it is possible to forgive and still pursue justice. Many clients might equate forgiveness with a full relinquishment of reparations, leaving the client confused as to why a lawyer would encourage forgiveness and not want to advocate for justice. Likewise, some clients might equate forgiveness with reconciliation. Usually clients consult with a lawyer when they feel wronged and can't imagine trusting the perpetrator again. It is essential that the lawyer encouraging forgiveness explain that she is focusing on the client's emotional recovery (Therapeutic Forgiveness) and not reconciliation.

A student's journal describes this well.

Forgiveness can be a very good thing for lawyers to bring up to a client. I think of therapeutic forgiveness in the context of a lawyer-client relationship. Sometimes clients can get so caught up in the minutia of the dispute, (especially if it goes to litigation) they forget what the dispute was over in the first place. Sometimes litigation brings out the worst in people and makes an otherwise resolvable dispute unresolvable by virtue of the fact that these parties are in conflict for a longer period of time, money is inevitably involved, and parties see each other as adversaries, as opposed to friends, business people, or family in conflict.

Therapeutic forgiveness might help the client see through the messiness of litigation when he or she is confronted with the idea of forgiveness. Bringing it up in the context of therapeutic forgiveness shifts the focus from the offender to the victim. If the victim forgives the offender without a formal apology (because she is forgiving for herself), it might help to stop or resolve the dispute.

I do think, however, that it is important for the lawyer to assess the situation and the client to see if it is appropriate. The concerns we mentioned in class are valid and it is important for the lawyers to consider the context before bringing in the concept of forgiveness. Therapeutic forgiveness is probably the safest form of forgiveness to bring up because it does not involve "forcing" a client to forgive. It simply acknowledges the benefits of forgiveness in the context of helping the victim grow. For these reasons it might be more appropriate than the other models of forgiveness. Submitted by Lauren Guccione, emphasis added.

If the lawyer is sloppy in his execution of encouraging a client to forgive, the result might be the client's decision to not pursue the lawsuit because she forgave (waiving reparations). A similar result may be the client rejecting forgiveness because the client can't imagine being vulnerable and trusting the perpetrator again (reconciliation). The client may decide to pursue a civil action, but not retain the lawyer who encouraged forgiveness because the client perceives the lawyer is a pacifist and doesn't have the temperament to fight for her.

A paradigm the lawyer may want to use is that there are two dimensions to the injury: financial and emotional. The lawyer suggests that the recovery also needs to be both financial and emotional. The lawyer will accept responsibility to get the client financial justice according to the law. The client can relinquish the duty to defend his or her self-esteem, and the lawyer will assure that the perpetrator will be held accountable for the wrongful injury to the full extent possible under the law.

A student journal describes this in another voice.

> Advising someone else to forgive can be a daunting task, but as attorneys, we may have to nudge a client toward the idea of forgiving a wrongdoer. When doing so, however, we must be careful not to insult a person's victimhood and feelings of hurt. It is natural and okay for a person to feel that he or she is a victim. When we are injured, part of the healing process is to acknowledge that there is an injury. Sometimes, we also need to grieve for the injury and feel pity for ourselves. Nonetheless, this process cannot go on forever.
>
> In our legal system, there are only so many remedies that we can provide for a client that has been wronged. Most of the time, the remedy is money. Money will almost never be a direct substitute for what has been lost due to an injury, but it is usually the best substitute available. In order for a client to understand this, he or she might need to get past his or her victimhood and move toward forgiveness. I believe that if a victim can forgive, then a large part of the emotional injury can be healed. At that point, the victim can then focus on his or her legal remedies.

We encountered a similar problem in the roleplay we did last class. The victim was not ready to let go of the injury and was not ready to settle. Not only was the victim not ready to settle the matter, but also, the victim did not know what to do with the money offered. The victim could not wrap his head around the fact that the money could not replace what was lost. In order to get past this dilemma, I encouraged the victim to think about forgiveness.

I recommended therapeutic forgiveness, which I described as self-healing. This explanation allowed the victim to think of forgiveness as something to help heal himself, instead of taking blame away from the wrongdoer. Moreover, I described to the victim that we could help heal his emotional pain through therapeutic forgiveness, and then we could pursue his legal remedies through the settlement process. This separation of the two concepts helped the victim move past his trepidation toward setting the matter. Submitted by Sean Olk, emphasis added.

The client can start working towards emotional healing. He doesn't need to wait for the legal proceedings to conclude. The legal proceedings will require her to relive the injury for the next one to five years, but she will not need to nurse the resentment for that period. She can begin therapeutic forgiveness by healing in small steps as soon as she is ready. She can begin to redirect her mind from the pain of the offense and focus on things that bring her joy and happiness. Lawyers can explain these benefits to the client so that the client can make an educated choice about which path she will travel.

A journal from an experienced family law attorney describes how she does this.

Attorneys can be part of a revenge system. Lawyers are at risk of becoming the tip of the revenge spear, agent of revenge. In the family law arena, the most difficult and unsuccessful negotiations for settlement involved opposing counsel who took on the emotion of the client. Those attorneys may do better to avoid the role completely and refer clients to other resources to help with the emotional fallout of their situations. On the other hand, for the attorney who objects to encouraging clients to address the emotional aspects of their case, including forgiveness, consider the concept: Attorney and Counselor at Law.

Instead of being a part of the revenge system, the lawyer's role could be dual track. The lawyer could counsel the client in relation to the emotional impact of the event. In addressing the impact, the counselor at law might introduce therapeutic letting go, overcoming, re-directing anger, managing, even if the perpetrator does not apologize, or the client believes that the apology was inadequate. However, I would not use the word forgive or forgiveness. The word itself conjures such personal and individual connotations, that it can actually be very presumptuous and intrusive for the attorney to use the term, forgive. For me, it is best left described, but unsaid. Submitted by Nancy Nager, emphasis added.

The theoretical result is a client who is an inspiring human being: a person who stands up for justice and accountability from a place of serenity rather than from a place of brokenness filled with anger and hatred. If the client's forgiveness has included a reduction in animosity, the client may wish the perpetrator well. Recent historical examples of this approach include Dr. Martin Luther King Jr. and Mahatma Gandhi.[4] Both led movements that confronted oppression, but they instructed their followers that resisting out of bitterness and hate is not the better path. The better path is to recognize that even the oppressors are human and therefore their followers owe them a duty of treating them with consideration and dignity.

From a Judeo-Christian perspective, this is consistent with Jesus' instruction to "love your enemies."[5] Micah 6:8 answers the question "[w]hat does the Lord your God require of you?" with the well-known summary of "[d]o justice, love mercy, and walk humbly with your God." Theologians and philosophers have wrestled with the proper balance of justice and mercy.[6] My observation is that contemporary Christian practice is to be merciful first, and then resort to justice if the bad behavior persists. If Micah 6:8 advocates for the simultaneous practice of justice and mercy, the client who holds perpetrators accountable, while forgiving and wishing the perpetrator well, is complying with the teaching.

A lawyer is in a unique position to encourage the client to consider simultaneously pursuing both justice and mercy. The lawyer's pursuit of justice for clients might enable some clients to begin pursuing mercy and begin the journey of overcoming their resentment and bitterness and to find happiness.

Two international students do a good job of describing this in their journals.

> In my opinion, society depends on the lawyers to make their clients' life better without revenge. In my country (Saudi Arabia), this depends on the lawyers because they are looking for their clients' benefit. So, if the lawyer encourages the client to forgive, the lawyer will not get anything. Sometimes they encourage their clients to forgive if the client will still get a benefit like an amount of money. <u>Judges normally ask the lawyers if they talked to their client about forgiveness because sometimes they forget to do that</u>. Also, Islam asks people to talk to the other and encourage them to forgive. In the exercise, I learned a few ideas that may help me explain to the client and encourage him or her to forgive. Submitted by Abdullah Sulaiman Alluhaydan, emphasis added.

> In addition, the attorney in civil cases can become the "tip of the revenge spear." This is true when someone hires an attorney, they want a fighter to administer what the client thinks is justice. Nevertheless, the attorney can be fine being the tip of the spear or can engage in meaningful conversations with the client exposing his limits of being part of the revenge cycle.

The benefits for attorneys to encouraging forgiveness is not related to professional success measured by cases won. The benefit for the attorney is personal, is beyond the legal matter, it is changing someone's path of destruction (revenge) or being stuck (sulking) and pointing towards self-healing and moving on with their lives. Submitted by Fabio Franco, emphasis added.

9.3.2 Lawyer Qualifications

Some law students and lawyers in my classes have objected to the proposition that lawyers might encourage clients to forgive. They explain that they don't feel qualified. This concern for emotional healing appropriately belongs to mental health professionals. Law school and professional development programs have not equipped lawyers for this role. They reason that this is not the lawyer's job, and the most the lawyer should do is encourage or require her clients to be under the care of a licensed mental health professional. A law student's journal expresses this concern... but her experiences as a lawyer changes her perspective.

> However, in a legal dispute, the desire to get revenge and the anger that comes with it can be a hindrance. I think the exercise we did in class where we determined the best way to get a client to settle when they're holding a grudge/can't move on shows how important forgiveness is. You end up hurting yourself in the long run if you cannot give up on being a victim and cannot find a way to move on and live life.

> If you are too engrossed in trying to find revenge, you can overlook what could be the best outcome for you in order to find the worst outcome for your wrongdoer. I think it's very important that attorneys try to push for the best outcome possible for their clients, and if that is settlement, and the desire to fight and get revenge is what is preventing that, moving on should also be advocated.

> I do not think that forgiveness is something that is necessary to settle a suit or move on. Because forgiveness is such a personal decision, I think an attorney would not be the best person to push that on a client. But, presenting it as an option is appropriate, and advising the client to seek a therapist or other outside help in coming to a decision would also be appropriate. An attorney is not trained in psychology and shouldn't attempt to take on that role. Submitted by Jaime Verducci in 2012, emphasis added.

In 2019 Ms. Verducci added these comments while emailing the author permission to use her journal.

> "I now practice civil litigation and the anger/resentment factor of settlement is huge! I have seen more than one plaintiff reject a good settlement offer because of emotion/anger and end up with nothing. I am always impressed by the mediators and attorneys who have the skills to trouble shoot the forgiveness component."

I respond by asking whether it is appropriate for an experienced lawyer to notice and then share his observations about how some clients have recovered from similar injustices. Some clients never recover from a tragedy, while others find a way to rebuild their lives and recover. If a lawyer's legal specialty means that he repeatedly serves clients who suffer catastrophic losses in car accidents, whose marriages are ending, who have been wrongfully terminated or sexually harassed, or who have been victims of professional malpractice, I believe he has observed productive and unproductive coping mechanisms over the course of his career.

Is it appropriate for the lawyer to share the productive coping mechanisms with future clients in similar circumstances? The productive coping mechanisms may be menu of a variety of things that different clients have said or done to help heal. If the lawyer has observed thought processes and emotional responses that have been unproductive, should she also make clients aware of those potential dangers? If an experienced lawyer has gained wisdom about a better way for clients to emotionally navigate their wrongful injury, is he unqualified to share that wisdom with clients? A student's journal describes how she would like a lawyer to treat her.

> Is it wrong for an attorney to engage her client in a forgiveness conversation? By engaging a client in a forgiveness conversation, does an attorney overstep her bounds? My initial reaction is no—it is not wrong for an attorney to engage her client in a forgiveness conversation and it is not overstepping bounds. I arrive at this conclusion because if I was a client, I would be thrilled if an attorney engaged me in holistic thinking like this. I am always looking for ways to learn and to better myself in the process. I would come to an attorney because of her expertise and would not even question her if she brought up a forgiveness conversation.
>
> Since I have this holistic mindset, I was very surprised when other people in class mentioned that they would be offended, feel belittled, or think that the attorney was crazy if she mentioned forgiveness as an option for healing. I had never thought that an attorney taking a holistic approach by suggesting forgiveness could be interpreted as pushing personal values onto a client. Since so many people are concerned that this could be pushing the boundary, it becomes evident that an attorney or mediator should use caution when bringing up the forgiveness option.
>
> Even though I would be very receptive and open to a conversation about forgiveness, when we were doing the role-play this week (I was the client) I couldn't help but become a little bit nervous when the topic was brought up. In fact, I thought that it was very interesting that my "attorney" was nervous to bring it up too. <u>She did not actually say the word "forgiveness" until I practically said it myself. My attorney described all of the requirements and steps to forgiveness so well, that I found myself coming to the conclusion that forgiveness may be an option without her even uttering the word.</u>

After the role-play was over, it was interesting to hear my attorney's feedback. She mentioned that she was very nervous to bring up the topic of forgiveness and dreaded using the actual word "forgiveness." She was worried about how this suggestion would be perceived. Would I take it as an insult? Would I feel as if I had been understood? Would I feel belittled and angry? I felt none of the above, but I can definitely understand how some people could.

In addition to the possibility of pushing personal values onto a client by suggesting forgiveness, there is a danger that the client will view forgiveness as a burden put on them to fix the situation at hand. There is also a possibility that the client is not ready to forgive. Forgiveness is not just something that can be switched on and off. It takes time, and right now may not be the best time. …

Forgiveness conversations can be tricky, but for those clients who are willing to engage, the results can be outstanding. Therefore, I would encourage attorneys to at least mention the concept to their client's when and if the timing seems right. Submitted by Brittany Wiser, emphasis added.

We will discuss below when and how to share such wisdom, but it seems cold and uncaring for lawyers not to share observations that might help their clients emotionally recover. This question needs to be considered on a case-by-case basis depending on the lawyer and depending on the client's openness to the lawyer's observations.

The concern about qualifications raises the issue of whether lawyers are ethically allowed to provide this type of counsel. The question of lawyers considering non-legal aspects when giving advice is addressed in Rule 2.1 of the Model Rules of Professional Conduct. Pertinent parts of this rule and comments on the rule provide:

> In rendering advice, a lawyer may refer not only to law but to other considerations such as moral, economic, social and political factors that may be relevant to the client's situation ….
>
> Comment [2] Advice couched in narrow legal terms may be of little value to a client, especially where practical considerations, such as cost or effects on other people, are predominant. Purely technical legal advice, therefore, can sometimes be inadequate. It is proper for a lawyer to refer to relevant moral and ethical considerations in giving advice. Although a lawyer is not a moral advisor as such, moral and ethical considerations impinge upon most legal questions and may decisively influence how the law will be applied.
>
> Comment [3] A client may expressly or impliedly ask the lawyer for purely technical advice …. When such a request is made by a client inexperienced in legal matters, however, the lawyer's responsibility as advisor may include indicating that more may be involved than strictly legal considerations.

Notice that the language in these provisions is permissive, not mandatory. A lawyer may consider non-legal factors, but she is not required to. Some lawyers will integrate forgiveness into their philosophy of practicing law; some will consider it on a case by case basis; and some will decide that they are uncomfortable and ill-equipped for such a conversation and relationship. Lawyers do not have a duty to open the Pandora's Box of involvement in clients' emotional recovery.

Individual lawyers should feel free to assess their comfort level in this sensitive area and decide what kind of lawyer they want to be. Jonathan Cohen's analysis about potential rewards to the lawyer who encourages clients to take responsibility and apologize may apply in the realm of encouraging forgiveness.[7] Cohen explains that "lawyers who discuss responsibility taking with clients may find a deepened sense of meaning in law practice, a meaning derived from providing a fuller range of service to the client, and, simultaneously from being a member of a profession that fosters moral behavior, social healing and just outcomes."[8]

A student's journal reacted to this material.

> As mentioned in class, there is a deeper sense of meaning in law practice. Lawyers are perceived as trusted advisors to the client and therefore lawyers should consider clients more than just a job. Throughout my time as an extern, I have seen many lawyers who literally consider the client to be nothing more than a case. I have seen lawyers who reject cases because they are 50/50 without even considering who the client is. I have even seen lawyers who don't compromise with the client on a price even though the client is just short financially.

> Thankfully, my supervising attorney this semester has been anything but disengaged in her moral compass. I have seen her stand pat against clients who have brought fraudulent and maliciously motivated claims. I have seen her pull the truth out of lying clients and decline higher pay for representation.

> The combination of law school and my externship experience has led me to realize that lawyers are more than just individuals who represent their clients in the face of the law. When a client comes to your office, they aren't just bringing a case or an issue of law, but they are coming for help. It's our duty to listen to them, assess their issues, and effectively communicate to them how we can help. Submitted by Daniel Yesayan, emphasis added.

A good friend and excellent lawyer who practices family law is clear with new clients when he tells them, "you need an emotional support system and that is not my role." He does an excellent job of assisting his clients in acquiring their legal entitlements. His clients know that will be the extent of his professional and personal services. I know he is a very emotionally insightful and compassionate person, but he doesn't see that as part of the attorney-client relationship. I respect him and have referred clients to him.

The purpose of this chapter is to encourage lawyers to consider if the bifurcation of financial and emotional recovery is the only way to practice law. I know some lawyers who describe professional satisfaction from assisting clients with emotional recovery by coaching and counseling clients based on their experiences with similarly situated victims.

Important variables may include whether the lawyer regularly serves clients who have suffered traumatic injury and whether the lawyer has a one transaction relationship with the client, like a personal injury lawyer, or whether the lawyers is part of a collective conscience role for the client, like an in-house General Counsel. Every lawyer needs to decide their approach and philosophy regarding the practice of law. Some lawyers' strength may be their willingness to coach traumatized clients into a healthy response that includes both justice and mercy.

A journal from a student who decided to forego law school and later earned his Ph.D. in Couple and Family Counseling provides a different perspective.

> What I heard a lot of tonight was abdicating responsibility. I cringed as one student described how she would only fit her responsibilities in the nice, tight little attorney box. Anything outside of that realm, well, that's up to 'others' to decide what may be appropriate. Basically, this is the Pilate Process; a quick fix to a bigger problem and a washing of our hands as it pertains to the humanness of anything related to apology, forgiveness, or reconciliation. The important question we posed is how does one define 'in the client's best interest'? Is it only monetary in nature, or does it include the individual and her psychological state at this particular point in time? I believe this is the main hold up for me ever attending law school; that the majority of institutions leave the conversation of law at the professional level without ever giving considerable regard to the people it affects. Submitted by M. Hunter Stanfield, emphasis added.

9.3.3 For the Benefit of the Client

A lawyer's analysis of a client's benefits from forgiving might depend on when and how the lawyer encourages forgiveness. The benefit to the client of forgiving can be articulated different ways at various times in the life of the attorney-client relationship.

Timing

Lawyers desiring to encourage their clients to forgive should be thoughtful about when such encouragement is likely to be well received and effective. Careful timing can reflect the lawyer's appreciation of the client's need for healthy anger and the other stages of the grief/recovery process. Each client is different, and the lawyer should be sensitive to the need of that client. The following observations will be general concepts to consider when formulating an individual plan for a specific client.

This discussion will simplify the question of when a lawyer might encourage her client to forgive to three-time frames: early, middle, and end. The dangers and motivations for encouraging forgiveness is different in each of those stages. The risks to the lawyer are greatest in the early stage.

If a lawyer encourages forgiveness in the intake interview, he risks losing the potential client because the client doesn't like that the lawyer encouraged the client to forgive the perpetrator. In contrast, the risks are minimal in the end stage. The lawyer has little to lose if she encourages forgiveness in the exit interview with the client after the conclusion of all issues. The graph below provides a visual for this relationship.

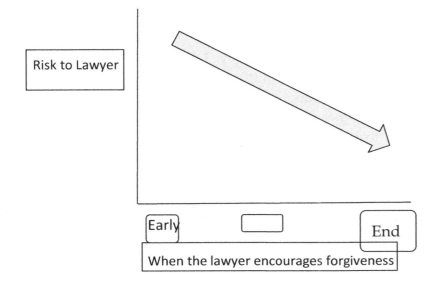

Encouraging Forgiveness at the Conclusion of a Case

Because the risks are least in the end stages of the attorney-client relationship, we will start there. How does the lawyer counsel the client who has received justice according to the legal system, but expresses that he is still very unsatisfied? Friends who practice in this area of the law have relayed stories about clients who receive significant compensation and still say, "[t]his doesn't make everything alright!"

The lawyer who has not broached the issue of forgiveness earlier in the relationship might find it easier to raise the topic at the conclusion of the case. The lawyer can explain to the client that the various proceedings associated with the lawsuit have required the client to relive the wrongful injury. The client had to be prepared to describe the incident and feelings associated with the incident in response to interrogatories, in depositions, at status conferences with the judge, at mediations, and at the trial. The client could not begin the emotional healing until the conclusion of the lawsuit.

A lawyer friend described this phenomenon while representing a plaintiff. Two years had passed since the plaintiff had been mistreated at work. At the mediation seeking to settle the case, the plaintiff calmly described the incident in a private session with the mediator. After the mediator left the room, the lawyer reminded the client how outraged and indignant he and his wife were at the time they first came to his office. He instructed his client to remember that trauma and pain and communicate it with passion the next time the mediator came into their room. The client had healed over the two years and the lawyer needed to scrape the scab off the wound to convince the mediator of the seriousness of the impact of the bad behavior.

The lawyer encouraging forgiveness at the conclusion of the legal proceedings can inform the client that they can now begin the emotional healing from the incident. Now that the legal system has determined their financial recovery, they can focus on other things that bring them joy like their family, hobbies, nature, travel, or future goals. The lawyer can encourage them not to think as much about the wrongful injury for their own mental health—therapeutic forgiveness. The lawyer can encourage the recovering victim to find a new purpose or goal related to preventing the kind of injury suffered by the victim, to save others from similar injuries, and/or to change the system that supported or allowed the injury.

Ask the client if s/he has a belief system, religious or otherwise, that helps him or her find peace, contentment, and joy. Affirm that the client has suffered but also share hope that others have found ways to survive and even thrive after similar circumstances. S/he may not be ready today because s/he is in the various stages of a grief like process, but the hope is that the individual will find a time to begin the journey of emotional recovery from the injury.

The client who receives this kind of encouragement from her lawyer in the exit interview may perceive that the lawyer understands the emotional aspect of the injury and the client's possible desire and need to continue to relive the injury during the life of the lawsuit. She may perceive that the lawyer is concerned for her well-being and like it. On the other hand, the client may become angry because the lawyer does not understand and is minimizing the emotional pain. The client may also become angry because the lawyer encouraged the client's resentment during the legal proceedings, but now that the case is over and the lawyer has been paid, the lawyer is encouraging healing. The lawyer who intends to consider the possibility of encouraging forgiveness at the end of a case, may want to forewarn the client at the intake interview that they will need to stay emotionally invested and focused on the painful incident during the legal case.

Lawyers open to encouraging forgiveness at the end of a case need to assess the rapport with the client and where the client is in the grief-like healing process. Some lawyers will only encourage forgiveness when they anticipate an appreciative or receptive reaction from the client. Some lawyers will encourage forgiveness at the end of a case regardless of the client's reaction; these lawyers accept the client's anger as part of the client's "waking up" process when the client realizes that the resentment is costing the client more than it is worth.

Encouraging Forgiveness at the Beginning of a Case

Some attorneys may want to include the description of financial and emotional recovery in the client intake interview. The attorney may inform the client that beginning the forgiveness process is optional or is a necessary component of the lawyer's approach to the practice of law. The client doesn't need to complete the forgiveness process but must accept that the lawyer will be encouraging steps towards forgiveness/healing from the beginning as part of the lawyer's concern for the whole client. The client can decide whether she wants a lawyer who encourages the client to take steps towards forgiveness while working diligently for the client to receive the full compensation available under the law.

I have a lawyer friend who specializes in representing people suing their physicians for medical malpractice. My lawyer friend advertises on Christian radio stations. I asked him to speak to my class about how he encourages clients to forgive. The advice he gave the law students was to be selective in who they represent. He has chosen to not represent people he perceives to be vengeful. He warned students that people with a personal vendetta against their physician are also likely to become people with a personal vendetta against their lawyer. He didn't have much to say about how he encourages his clients to forgive compared to his warnings about representing people who are hateful. This illustration suggests that maybe the lawyer should celebrate when a client rejects a lawyer because they don't want to be encouraged to emotionally recover.

An experienced divorce lawyer and a law student's journals are instructive.

> In class we talked about the role of the lawyer when an aggrieved person seeks the assistance of a lawyer after they have been wronged. This led me to think about the <u>literally hundreds of times I said to potential divorce clients that a courtroom is the wrong place to attempt to extract revenge against your soon to be former spouse. I explain that if that is what they are seeking from me or from the court they are going to be very disappointed. I further explain that my goal is to put them in as good a position as possible to move on and to succeed</u> in their lives post-divorce. This is because divorce is not a morals contest. It doesn't matter which spouse was the "better spouse." In fact, even attempting to define what a better spouse is would be nearly impossible as many people have different criteria for the same. Submitted by Frank Toti, emphasis added.

> In our discussion about advising others, I can see how difficult it can become when the client and the advisor have different views of how to approach apology or forgiveness. I personally agree most with letting the client be the final say on whether forgiveness should be given. However, I think it is really important to have an honest conversation with your client on forgiveness and its benefits. In the end, it is your client's case and their subsequent relationships with the ones they are in conflict with so they should be the ultimate decider, but really discussing forgiveness could be helpful.

Despite the possibility of losing business, or smaller settlements, I don't view the job of the lawyer as the "tip of the revenge spear." I identify closer to the "justice" role that a lawyer has. I think that differentiating between pandering to a vengeful audience and trying to advertise services of zealous advocacy is a more difficult subject. But I really liked what was said in class about having difficult conversations with the client at the beginning of a representation rather than later on. It would be a good tool for calming a client down in order to move them from a revenge mindset to a more justice mindset. Clients should be in the same boats as attorneys and "rise above the drama." Submitted by Maetha Jacobe, emphasis added.

Encouraging Forgiveness in the Middle Stages of a Case

An experienced plaintiff's trial lawyer explained that he encourages clients to forgive before trial. He believes that juries and judges prefer survivors over victims. When a person has suffered a serious loss, juries and judges have more respect and appreciation for that person telling a "hero story" compared to a "victim story." Luskin describes that the emphasis of a hero story is on the victim overcoming the unfair injury.[9] This lawyer coaches his plaintiffs to at least appear to have begun the emotional healing before trial so as not to alienate the jury or cause the jury to be suspicious.

This rationale for encouraging forgiveness is pragmatic and within the job description of most lawyers. One reason to forgive is to maximize your financial recovery from the legal system. Few cases actually go to trial in most jurisdictions. I asked prominent plaintiff trial attorney West Seegmiller if the same rationale applies before a deposition. He replied that it may, because the defense attorney and claims adjuster will be assessing the extent this plaintiff is "likeable" to the prospective jury. Thus, a lawyer could encourage the client to be a hero in the deposition.

This middle stage timing may be easiest for the lawyer to deliver and easiest for the client to receive because it is for pragmatic financial reasons. Do the means matter so long as a good end is accomplished? Does it matter if the lawyer tells the client to forgive just enough to make a good impression or if she equips the client with a robust package of forgiveness tools? Either way the lawyer is encouraging the client on a forgiveness journey.

How

An important variable in discussing forgiveness with a client is the accompanying degree of obligation. A lawyer can mention it as an eventual possibility. This may plant a seed that may not take root for months or years afterwards, but the client may remember the lawyer's encouragement to forgive and heal. Forgiveness zealots may want to be more forceful in the need to pursue emotional healing. The literature is clear that a victim needs to have the freedom to choose or reject forgiveness.[10] A lawyer who is concerned for the whole client may encourage forgiveness but should not demand it.

An experienced litigator's journal is affirming a lawyer's role and caution.

> I would never try to step in someone else's shoes and browbeat them in to offering forgiveness, but I think acknowledging the concept of forgiveness is a healthy part of any counselor's role in analyzing a dispute. While withholding forgiveness can be empowering in its own, it has a price. It forces you to stay rooted in the event and connected to the perpetrator in a way that you may not want to. Indeed, offering forgiveness can allow you to finally break free from the perpetrator and focus on healthier pursuits.
>
> As we discussed in the readings and in class, the tricky thing with forgiveness is that it has to cycle through the appropriate stages before it can manifest itself fully. When people forgive too soon, it may be their attempt to distance themselves from the pain –to shut down. Or it may be due to a lack of self-esteem or self-worth. People need to understand the impact an event has had upon them so that they can make the appropriate decision concerning the importance of an apology and the potential for forgiveness. Submitted by Jonathan Andrews, emphasis added.

Another factor affecting many lawyers' willingness to discuss emotional healing and forgiveness is the extent that the client initiates this more intimate conversation. Did the client make a statement about the money not meeting all his needs? Such a statement might trigger a follow up question by the lawyer about whether the client is referencing the need for emotional healing. Some lawyers will be more willing to enter the conversation about emotional healing and forgiveness when the client opens the door to that conversation.

If the client doesn't provide an entry point to the conversation, some lawyers might be willing to ask the client if they have considered the need for emotional recovery from the injury. They will assess whether to offer suggestions to support that effort depending on the client's response. The lawyer's willingness to discuss forgiveness at the beginning, middle, or conclusion of the legal case may depend upon the client's willingness.[11]

The following chart combines the factors of timing and who initiates the conversation about forgiveness.

	When to have the Forgiveness Talk		
	Early	Middle	End
Client	Acknowledge Legal System's Limits	Encourage Patience & Concurrent Paths	Encourage Closure & Healing/Therapeutic Forgiveness
Atty	Optional or Part of the Lawyer's Approach to Practice	Prepare for Best Impression	Suggest Possibility of Healing/Therapeutic Forgiveness

Who Initiates the topic of Forgiveness

Two students' journals urge caution on the topic of lawyers encouraging forgiveness.

I think one reason people struggle so much with the concept of forgiveness is that they may not really know what it is and what it is not. I think it is important for people to know what forgiveness entails. They should also know that it is a process and not just an event. While advising a client to forgive can be difficult for a variety of reasons, I think it is very important in order for them to heal. I worry that I would come off as too patronizing. I think if you let the client control the conversation and only advise when asked, then that mitigates any concerns about being patronizing. I also think it is helpful to relate to the client so that he/she feels heard. Submitted by an anonymous student, emphasis added.

I was oh-so uncomfortable while Peter was talking about the lawyer helping his client learn to forgive. The transformative lawyer! My problem was twofold: (1) how dare the lawyer assume s/he knows the "better" response to the situation than the client; and (2) I don't know anyone who goes to a lawyer to obtain advice on being a happier person. Isn't that what clerics are for? Or therapists? Surely not a lawyer at those outrageous rates! ...

Peter's response to my concerns dealt with the vast majority of these concerns. ASKING the client if they would like to hear your views as a result of your experiences eliminates the "I know what is good for you" concern, and also offers the client the option to say, "Keep your opinions to yourself." The only other concern I have remaining is this: Is giving this type of advice something the lawyer should bill the client for? If this ends up being a 30-minute discussion, should the lawyer bill his full rate? To me, it would be appropriate for the lawyer to provide a substantial discount to his rate (i.e., 50%) to reflect the fact that this discussion is not within her/his primary area of expertise .... Submitted by Z Zeller, emphasis added.

9.3.4 For the Benefit of the Lawyer

My lawyer friend who advertises on Christian radio stations is motivated by his own best interests when creating a policy that he will not represent potential clients he perceives as vengeful. In addition to concerns about the client eventually suing the lawyer, he also mentioned that the hateful client will sometimes expect the lawyer to adopt the client's hate.

Understanding forgiveness dynamics help the lawyer keep perspective and not become an angry person. We cannot say that the lawyer forgives the perpetrator because the lawyer is not the victim and only the victim has standing to forgive.[12] Nevertheless, the lawyer who understands forgiveness can recognize when her client is in an angry stage and when the lawyer is adopting the client's anger as her own.

Do the lawyer's clients expect or need for the lawyer to be angry too? Is hating a drunk driver who hurt your client part of serving the client? We already discussed how the lawyer can take responsibility to accomplish justice under the law for the client. Is it necessary or appropriate for the lawyer to share the client's indignation and disgust for the perpetrator or is it better for a lawyer to have a cool and level head as he plans for the best course of legal action to take?

In any conflict it is easy to villainize the other side. In the adversarial legal system, it is necessary. Does a lawyer do a better job for the client if he is equally emotionally invested? Alternatively, does the lawyer do a better job if she adopts a more objective and moderating voice for the client? Taken to the extreme, can a lawyer be that inspiring person discussed earlier who works diligently for justice while having mercy and love for the perpetrator? Do people want a merciful lawyer, or do they want the raging bull who joins in the client's hate for the perpetrator?

An admonition in a journal from a Brazilian judge is instructive.

> Sometimes the Lawyer gets involved in the client's case. Many times in my court I tell the attorneys: "Counsel, remember that the case is your client's, not yours." Because they sometimes act with great emotion towards the other party and the other attorney, as if taking the case personally or seeking revenge for their client. Submitted by Doroteia Mota.

Maybe the merciful lawyer will lose some clients, but maybe save her own soul. Leaders of the legal profession are concerned about job satisfaction and civility among lawyers.[13] One author noted, "[i]t is hard to be an SOB all day at work and then leave it in the office."[14] Attorney and author Joseph Allgretti argues that if lawyers accept the hired gun model of lawyering, we abdicate moral responsibility for our actions.[15] In *The Betrayed Profession*, the Sol Linowitz argues that lawyers lost their professional satisfaction when they ceased exercising their personal judgement and simply started doing whatever the client wanted.[16] Linowitz observes a shift in the professional role during his lifetime from when lawyers would tell clients what to do and when lawyers largely agreed to follow their clients' instructions. [17]

9.4 Full Disclosure Regarding Litigation

Lawyers who are reluctant to actively encourage forgiveness should consider at least providing full disclosure regarding litigation for potential clients trying to decide between forgiveness and litigation. A potential plaintiff without prior litigation experience may have myriad misperceptions. Some lawyers leave the client in the dark and let them learn some of the ugly truths about litigation as they unfold. Other lawyers may want to magnify the challenges and limitations of litigation at the outset, so the client isn't surprised and is prepared.

The victim is angry about his injuries and wants justice; he is also possibly frustrated because the perpetrator has resisted the victim's efforts to hold the perpetrator accountable. If necessary, the victim may be willing to force the perpetrator to be accountable by suing.

A tragedy is that most clients are unhappy with their litigation experience. [18] Even when they prevail, clients often perceive that litigation is a brutal experience that is expensive and takes a lot of time and energy.[19] Lawyers who provide full disclosure at the outset enable clients to make an informed choice between some version of forgiveness and litigation. Many potential clients will be so angry they will not be able to hear it, but at least the lawyer will have forewarned the client about the emotional and financial costs associated with litigation.

Lawyers are well acquainted with the processes described below. I have presented how these processes might affect the client. I will focus on the plaintiff because he is the one deciding whether to initiate litigation. A student journal describes this.

> It was interesting to learn about the different roles a person may have with counseling someone to forgive. I think forgiveness is something that is important to discuss with clients, especially in certain areas of the law, such as family law. If someone has been wronged, learning to forgive the offender and learning to forgive him or herself is crucial to the healing process.

> When discussing forgiveness and apology, it is important to discuss the topic of revenge. When people are hurt, they often think that they want revenge and revenge will make them feel better. However, revenge will not help the healing process, and ultimately, it is not what the victim truly wants. Revenge will not truly satisfy the victim. It is important with being a lawyer that you discuss this with your client. They likely want to have their day in court, yet ninety-five percent of cases settle. Dragging out the legal process can often ruin relationships, when the relationships have the potential to be fixed with an apology and forgiveness.

> I do not think that the lawyer should be an agent for vengeance. While it <u>is important that the lawyer do what the client wants and be a zealous advocate, revenge is not necessarily being a zealous advocate. It may be important for the lawyer to tell the client that whatever amount of money he or she asks for will never be enough to heal him or her</u>. If the case does go to trial, it is important that the client understand the jury system and how critical jurors may be. Submitted by Melanie Cockrum, emphasis added.

The Pre-Trial Process

Litigation begins when the victim (plaintiff) files with the court and delivers to the offender (defendant) a written description of the alleged wrongs perpetrated by the defendant and the injuries suffered by the plaintiff as a result of those wrongs (Complaint.) Clients should be forewarned that the legal system is adversarial. From beginning to end, this is a contest and a fight.

In the process of drafting a complaint, the lawyer educates the client that the law only recognizes certain kinds of wrongful behavior, so the client's story needs to be translated into those standards. For example, a misunderstanding between businessmen becomes negligent misrepresentation or fraud, which requires the plaintiff to allege and prove that the defendant neglected to disclose information he was required to disclose or knowingly made false statements with intent to deceive.

The legal system's binary task of deciding whether the defendant is liable reduces the likelihood of the plaintiff telling a more complicated story that includes both side's contributions to the dispute. In litigation, the plaintiff presents a total victim story attributing the worst possible motives to the defendant, and the defendant, at best, asserts that they have been wrongfully understood and accused. The judge and/or jury decides which story they believe is more likely, by a preponderance of the evidence.

The preponderance of the evidence standard means that it is **more likely than not** to have happened that way. If the jury believes that it is 51% likely to have happened that way, that side wins. The legal system often does not leave room to integrate the 49% of likelihood that the truth lies somewhere in between.

The adversarial system polarizes the parties and escalates the conflict. The legal contest often exacerbates the conflict. The polarization and exacerbation of the conflict often hurts the participants and seriously damages any chance of a positive future relationship. Examples of escalating the conflict are myriad.

When requesting to be the primary parent in a divorce proceeding, your lawyer will ask you to articulate the parenting inadequacies of your spouse, times when he lost his temper and maybe even spanked a child in anger. Even though these may be exceptions to the norm, these instances will help convince the judge that the children are better off with you as the primary parent. And we need to have these instances at the ready because your spouse very well may submit evidence of the instances when you were not at your best as a parent. The adversarial system translates, "I am the better primary custodial parent" into "My soon to be ex-spouse is a dangerous parent."

Another example involves siblings who inherit a farm. One of the siblings lives on and manages the farm and the net profits are periodically distributed to all the siblings. The manager of the farm regularly makes judgement calls and makes a string of decisions that were wrong in hindsight. For example, the price of soybeans went up in the summer so we shouldn't have sold our inventory in the spring. One sibling complains to the sibling manager and other siblings that the manager should be replaced by a professional farm manager. The sibling manager becomes angry and defensive and the other siblings express support for sibling manager. When the disgruntled sibling consults a lawyer, he learns that the law will empower him to replace the sibling manager only if the disgruntled sibling alleges and proves incompetence or negligence.

Likewise, in medical malpractice cases. The law will only compensate a victim if the doctor's mistake is the result of negligence. The plaintiff must allege and prove that the doctor did not exercise the standard of care that the reasonable doctor would have in the same circumstances.

When the plaintiff's lawyer writes the complaint, the victim may feel a sense of relief to see his victim story eloquently presented in writing. He may hesitate because the description of the situation has been escalated to meet legal standards, but the escalated version satisfies the anger he feels from being victimized. The process of memorializing the injury requires him to relive the victim experience. This is the exact opposite of taking responsibility for his feelings by controlling the remote control in his mind to focus less on the injury and more on things of beauty, kindness, and love. Even if the lawyer has encouraged the client to start recovering emotionally, the process of memorializing the injury in the legal complaint requires the client to re-create the incident. For many clients, the pending lawsuit rents so much space in the client's mind that it becomes a long-term anchor tenant.

The defendant's lawyer assists the defendant in constructing reasons why the wrongs did not occur or were not the defendant's fault and why the damages were not related to the defendant's behavior. For a plaintiff needing to emotionally forgive the offender, it is often devastating when the defendant denies the allegations in the lawsuit and may even counter-sue alleging that the victim was at fault in the situation and owes compensation for the defendant's damages. The inexperienced plaintiff didn't anticipate how the defendant's lawyer will resist any possible legally required element and that she will need to fight to prove her version of the dispute.

The law requires litigants to provide copies of all relevant documents in their possession related to the dispute and requested by the other side, including copies of contracts, memoranda, correspondence, emails, social media posts, and medical records.[20] The plaintiff should be forewarned that he will need to take the time and emotional energy to review all of these sources for documents that are relevant to the lawsuit. Plaintiffs should also be aware that some defendants frustrate this information exchange by providing access to warehouses full of documents, the vast majority of which they know are irrelevant. The plaintiff's lawyers may need to invest the resources to comb through hundreds of boxes of files looking for the pertinent documents, often at the plaintiff's expense. Likewise, companies may need to be hired to manage and store electronic files that are disclosed by the defendant.

Lawyers often disagree about the scope of these required disclosures and file motions with the court for rulings. Some courts are so congested that the judge doesn't have the time to rule on these "discovery disputes" and appoints a retired judge or experienced lawyer to serve as a discovery referee, with the hourly costs for the private judge paid by the parties.

The law allows participants in a lawsuit to submit written questions to each other that must be answered under oath (Interrogatories.)[21] These interrogatories can ask questions to the other party about the facts and legal theories that would support or disprove their case. Likewise, the law allows litigants to submit written "Requests for Admissions" which are sent to the opponent requesting the opponent to admit specific facts.[22] The plaintiff should expect to respond to a barrage of interrogatories and requests for admissions by the defendant's attorney. A plaintiff working closely with her lawyer may be excited about how the interrogatories and requests for admissions will require the defendant to disclose information supporting the plaintiff's case.

Lawyers are famously reluctant to provide information to their opponents because information is power. The law allows lawyers to object to interrogatories and requests for admissions on the grounds that the requests themselves are ambiguous or because the requested material is privileged or confidential for example. [23] Lawyers regularly disagree about whether interrogatories and requests for admissions are worded in such a way as to be deserving of response. This category of discovery dispute is also the subject of motions to the court and often referred to a private judge to serve as a discovery referee, at the clients' expense. The client's excitement about submitting questions to the opponent is rarely satisfied by the answers, potentially creating another round of frustration and injury because their opponent is not being transparent.

The law allows parties to a lawsuit to question people with information relevant to the lawsuit under oath (a deposition) and have the questions and responses recorded by a licensed court reporter. The transcripts of these depositions are admissible in court if a witness contradicts his deposition testimony in the trial. Witnesses usually seek to testify consistently so they won't lose credibility by having contradictory responses under oath. Thus, these depositions usually establish a witness's likely testimony at the upcoming trial.

Often the key witnesses in a lawsuit are the plaintiff and defendant. The lawyers know the importance of these depositions and spend extensive time preparing their clients in anticipation of their depositions. Standard advice is that the law requires parties to answer the question, unless the client's lawyer objects, but do not volunteer any additional information. Information is power. For example, the plaintiff's lawyer may ask, "Did you abruptly swerve from the slow lane to the fast lane while driving?" The answer should be, "Yes." Do not volunteer any additional information or explanation, such as the need to swerve because a pedestrian stepped into the slow lane. It is the plaintiff's lawyer's job to ask the follow up question, and, if she neglects to ask, she doesn't earn the information. The result is often a cat and mouse conversation game with the lawyer seeking to tie down the testimony and the witness being as coy as possible while seeking to appear credible to a potential jury.

Also, if the witness does not have clear recollection about the information requested in the question, the witness should testify, "I do not recall." The plaintiff has the burden to prove certain facts to win the lawsuit. The defendant's lawyer does not want the defendant's deposition testimony to assist the plaintiff in proving his case. If the defendant has any doubt or confusion about the information requested, the correct answer is, "I do not recall." Again, the result is a cat and mouse conversation game.

At the plaintiff's deposition he should expect the opposing lawyer to scrutinize every possible relevant aspect of the plaintiff's allegations. The deposition of the plaintiff usually comes after the defendant has conducted a thorough investigation and received responses to requests for production of documents, interrogatories, and requests for admissions. The opposing lawyer is very knowledgeable about the case and seeks to discredit various aspects of the plaintiff's story to disprove the alleged wrongful behavior, prove that the plaintiff contributed to creating the situation, or diminish the amount of damages arising from the defendant's wrongful behavior. The defendant's lawyer may ask questions out of chronological order in an effort to test the consistency of the plaintiff's testimony. The defendant's lawyer may try to get the plaintiff to open up and share information by being nice. Plaintiff's need to anticipate that the defendant's lawyer may twist things he said and impute the worst possible interpretation.

Many cases require the testimony of "expert witnesses" who can express opinions.[24] If a witness is not an expert, she can testify only to things she experienced. Only experts can testify about a variety of relevant aspects of many cases that are not observable, such as how most doctors would handle a certain situation or the likelihood that an injury will require additional surgeries years later. The plaintiff will be impressed by the expert witnesses recommended by her lawyer. She takes relief from feeling supported by a capable person with excellent credentials. In contrast, the plaintiff will feel bewildered when the defendant's expert witnesses testify at depositions in ways that threaten or diminish the plaintiff's claim. Here is another equally capable person with excellent credentials whose opinions undermine the plaintiff's case. The adversarial approach to civil litigation extends to lawyers knowing which experts to hire to testify as desired. The plaintiff may panic when she realizes the outcome of her case may depend on which of these usually equally capable and credible expert witnesses the jury believes is 51% more believable than the other.

Ninety Percent of Cases Settle Before Trial

As the legal process unfolds and information is revealed through the above discovery processes, the information is evaluated through the lens of its evidentiary impact on a jury. Inexperienced plaintiffs may start to mistakenly believe and expect that there will eventually be a trial and the evidence will be presented to a jury. In contrast, lawyers know that in the United States only 5-10% of civil lawsuits ever go to trial.[25]

US Supreme Court Justice Anthony Kennedy observed that the ADR movement in the US started in the 1930's when the Federal Rules of Civil Procedure established the pre-trial discovery mechanisms described above so trial lawyers could predict the outcome of a hypothetical trial.[26] Also, he observed that this pre-trial robust exchange of information makes the trial unnecessary because experienced lawyers get a preview of the evidence that would be presented if there was a trial.[27] Armed with this preview, experience lawyers can usually agree on a comparatively narrow range of likely outcomes if the case were tried.[28] The pre-trial discovery process is designed to assist the lawyers in assessing how much power they have in the settlement negotiations. This system works reasonably well for the government because it doesn't need as many judges and courtrooms. This system is usually viewed by citizens as too expensive and time consuming.

Some plaintiffs are relieved when they realize, either early or late in the case, that they will not need to testify at trial. Other plaintiffs may feel cheated. They have expended considerable time and money to hold the defendant accountable. They have an emotional need for their day in court where they can describe how they have been victimized. The litigation process has made them work hard to earn the right to a public process where their story will be shared with the community and the community can deliver justice.

After enduring all the scrutiny, skepticism, and lack of transparency by the defendant and his lawyer, some plaintiff's feel cheated when on the eve of trial their own lawyer strongly encourages settlement. Their own lawyer knows that the defendant's settlement offer roughly approximates the probably result of a trial, but the lawyer also knows that trial witnesses and juries are unpredictable. The lawyer urges settlement to avoid the risks of a worst outcome at trial.

There are two potential aspects that make settlement difficult for a plaintiff to accept. First, the settlement almost always consists of only money. This is an extension of the legal system. If the case went to trial, the law monetizes almost all injuries. A plaintiff's reputation was wrongly impugned, money is awarded. A plaintiff's physical appearance or abilities have been diminished, money is awarded. A person the plaintiff trusted like a physician or business partner betrayed her trust, money is awarded. The legal system acknowledges a plaintiff's monetary losses and expects this acknowledgement to address the emotional aspect of the injury.

Because lawyers often "bargain in the shadow of the law" the context of the settlement negotiation is the amount of money the plaintiff would be likely to receive at trial.[29] If we approximate that outcome, the trial is not necessary. The plaintiff's desire for interpersonal recognition and acknowledgement through gestures such as apology or simply admitting is usually unfulfilled in settlements because they are absent at trial and/or are too hard for the defendant.

This leads to the second aspect of settlement that is difficult for the plaintiff to accept. Settlements usually include a declaration by the defendant that the settlement is NOT an admission of wrongdoing. The news is full of stories about companies paying millions and sometimes hundreds of millions of dollars while declaring that this is **NOT** an admission of wrongdoing. The plaintiff is not only expected to accept only money, but the defendant reserves the right to explicitly deny that they treated the plaintiff badly.

The defendant may deny any wrongdoing because the defendant has come to believe his lawyer's defensive construction of the situation. Regardless of the reason, the failure to accept responsibility for wrongful behavior is recognized in apology literature as a second offense.[30] This denial of wrongdoing is often hurtful to the plaintiff and a hurdle she will need to overcome to accept the settlement. The plaintiff's desire for acknowledgement and recognition is rarely addressed in settlements. The plaintiff's dream of public vindication at trial is transformed into a private monetary settlement with a non-disclosure clause and a complete denial of wrongdoing by the defendant.

I wonder how many plaintiffs know the likely result when they decide to initiate litigation. I wonder if they would have a more objective reaction to all the ups and downs of pre-trial discovery procedures if they knew that the result would be a private settlement without an admission of wrongdoing. I wonder if the victim's emotional recovery through some version of forgiveness could start earlier if he was forewarned about the likely result of litigation.

The journal from a Swiss lawyer describes a case where the law firm could have become entangled in the client's obsession with revenge.

> I remember a case we had in our law firm which was about this topic. A former employee of our client, a steel trading company, ultimately owned by a rich guy from Russia, embezzled a huge amount of money by paying himself excessive commissions to his private account. There was a criminal proceeding pending for already some years, when I started in this law firm and I received this case when I started working there. ...

> However, this research and looking for further culprits and perpetrators (even of foreign companies) started to become an obsession of the client and my boss supported him wherever it was possible. I remember that he used to go for lunch with the client and always after lunch (and probably having one or two glasses of wine) he was super enthusiastic and told me to write another submission or do further research. After a certain time, I started to ask my boss why we do that, and this client is exceeding everything reasonable since the prosecutor finally initiated first steps and the criminal proceedings were going forward. In my view, this should have been satisfaction enough and the client will receive restitution due to the fact that the mansion of the former employee was seized, and the embezzled amount was saved.

But they did not stop and wanted to have more and more. It was not about the money anymore. It was about honor. Because the ultimate owner wanted to have revenge, nothing else but revenge, and wanted to ruin this guy's life. Repayment of the embezzled amount was not enough. …

This was an impressive example of a person who will probably never be able to forgive due to their own cultural honor pattern. And this shows how individual forgiveness is and how much it depends on your culture. In this case, in the end it was the decision of my boss to further work for this client and to fulfill its revenge wishes. I would probably not have gone so far and I would have tried to explain to the client that enough is enough and justice has a limit. I would probably not have provided my services for revenge. Submitted by Rahel from Switzerland, emphasis added.

9.5 Lawyer Advising Client About Forgiveness at the End of a Personal Injury Case

One of the partners in your firm asked you to join him for a meeting with a client when he recommends she accept a settlement. The client was distracted by a phone call and stayed parked for about two minutes when a traffic light turned green. It was late at night with little traffic until a drunk driver plowed into the rear of her car. She has permanent injuries that will result in a slight limp and chronic pain the rest of her life. The drunk driver has enough insurance to cover her damages. Your partner has successfully negotiated with the insurance company so that he is recommending she accept their offer of $800,000. You agree that this is a very good outcome because this is a generous valuation of her damages and assumes no comparative negligence; she could be found to have some comparative negligence for staying parked at the green light.

She is extremely angry at having the limp and is worried about how much pain she will experience. She is also very angry because the driver was drunk. (He was returning from a wedding reception where he claimed to have two beers and had blood alcohol of .09. This is his first DUI; he has pled guilty to the criminal charge and received a suspended sentence of six months, and probation for three years. He will only serve the time if he is convicted of drunk driving again within the three years of probation. He must also complete a substance abuse treatment program and pay restitution to you.)

When the partner first described the proposed settlement to the client, she was reluctant to settle the case. She liked the idea of not settling the case and reporting to the criminal court that he failed to pay restitution and should serve time. You think she is also resistant to the idea of being done with this dispute. (She has been the kind of client who liked to miss her receptionist job to spend time in depositions and meetings with your partner and sometimes your partner and the judge for status conferences about her case.) She appears to like the attention and seemed to love the TV interview your partner arranged in your office commenting on the light sentence from the criminal case. Your partner arranged for the interview to strengthen his negotiations with the insurance company, and it worked.

You believe that $800,000 is a very good outcome for the client, and now she needs to accept it. Before she asked to use the restroom, she asked you and your partner:

> "How do I go on? Is this money supposed to make everything okay? Am I supposed to be happy now? I liked my life before all this happened. I hate him for doing this to me! How do I get my old life back?"

Your partner has asked you to be a part of this conversation because you are known at the firm as being the person who is good in this type of situation. While the client is out of the room, the partner turns to you and asks you to "do your forgiveness thing with her." You have two minutes to plan what approaches you will use.

A student had an interesting reaction to this exercise

> During class, we split up into pairs and worked on an attorney forgiveness exercise. I was paired up with a fellow student that has a lot of life experience as a practicing family law attorney. A fair amount of her practice includes dealing with difficult clients that at times are seeking to extract vengeance on the other party. In this exercise, she filled the role of a client that had been injured by a drunk driver, but she also could potentially face some comparative negligence for her own actions. ... She expressed her hate for the drunk driver and the desire to see him suffer and punished.

> This exercise was fairly challenging, given my partner's background and ability to pose what seemed to be realistic concerns, questions, and obstacles to a negotiated agreement. In order to get the client to agree to the terms of the settlement, I had to first recognize her pain and validate the emotions she was feeling. I also had to explain to her the rationale for why I thought this was in her best interest, primarily I had to explain to her the law pertaining to comparative negligence, and that if she didn't take the offer she would expose herself to comparative negligence in court, resulting in a smaller damages award from a jury. Ultimately, cooler minds prevailed, but it wasn't easy. ...

> I think this exercise was probably one of the most beneficial thus far, primarily due to the fact that human emotions are often difficult to deal with. Submitted by an anonymous student, emphasis added.

Endnotes

1. *See generally* Martha Minow, *Between Vengeance and Forgiveness,* (1998).

2. In the following excerpt Minow describes how the legal process provides victims with some assurance that wrongdoers will be held accountable, freeing the victim from the need to exercise personal vengeance: In theory, forgiveness does not and should not take the place of justice or punishment. Forgiveness marks a change in how the offended feels about the person who committed the injury, not a change in the actions to be taken by a justice system. Philosopher Jeffrie Murphy explains, '[b]ecause I ceased to hate the person who has wronged me it does not follow that I act inconsistently if I still advocate his being forced to pay compensation for the harm he has done or his being forced to undergo punishment for his wrongdoing—that he, in short, get his just deserts.' Advocating punishment for a wrongdoer one has forgiven in fact is well supported by reference to the impersonal processes of a justice system, inherent operations of a theory of deserts, or a commitment to treat offenders as full members of a community that demands responsibility by autonomous actors for their actions. Forgiveness in this sense need not be a substitute for punishment. Even the traditional Christian call to forgive rather than avenge accompanies faith that vengeance will come—through the Divine. Id. at 15.

3. *See* "What to Expect - A Lawsuit Chronology," FINDLAW (2018) https://litigation.findlaw.com/filing-a-lawsuit/what-to-expect-a-lawsuit-chronology.html.

4. *See* "The King Philosophy," HEKINGCENTER.ORG (2018) http://www.thekingcenter.org/king-philosophy; "Mahatma Gandhi," HISTORY (Jul. 30, 2010) https://www.history.com/topics/india/mahatma-gandhi.

5. Matthew 5:44.

6. *See* e.g., Fr Dwight Longenecker, "Pope Francis: Balancing Justice and Mercy," ALETEIA.ORG (Sep 10, 2015) https://aleteia.org/2015/09/10/pope-francis-balancing-justice-and-mercy/.

7. Jonathan R. Cohen, *Advising Clients to Apologize*, 72 S. CAL. L. REV. 1009, 1014-23 (1999), available at http://scholarship.law.ufl.edu/ facultypub/648/.

8. Jonathan R. Cohen, *The Culture of Legal Denial*, 84 NEB. L. REV. 281-82 (2005) Available at: https://digitalcommons.unl.edu/nlr/vol84/iss1/5/.

9. Fred Luskin, *Forgive for Good* 137-53, (2002).

10. *See generally* Robert D. Enright and Richard P. Fitzgibbons, Forgiveness Therapy, (2015) .

11. *See supra* note 7 at 1043-44.

12. *See* Walker, M. U. (2013), *Third Parties and the Social Scaffolding of Forgiveness*, J RELIG ETHICS, 41: 495-512. doi:10.1111/jore.12026. *But see* Glen Pettigrove, *The Standing to Forgive*, THE MONIOT, Vol. 92, Issue 4, 1 October 2009, Pages 583–603, https://doi.org/10.5840/monist200992432 (arguing that 2nd and 3rd parties may also have standing for meaningful forgiveness).

13. *See* J. M. Organ, *What Do We Know About the Satisfaction/Dissatisfaction of Lawyers? A Meta-Analysis of Research on Lawyer Satisfaction and Well-Being*, 8 U. ST. THOMAS L. J. 225 (2011); L. S. Krieger & K. M. Sheldon, *What Makes Lawyers Happy? Transcending the Anecdotes with Data from 6200 Lawyers*, 83 GEO. WASH. L. REV. 554 (2015).

14. *See e.g.*, Marianne Stenger, "Private Is Private—4 Ways to Keep Your Personal Life Out of the Office," CAREERCONTESSA (Apr. 24, 2017), https://www.careercontessa.com/advice/privacy-work-life-balance/ (explaining the effort needed to keep your private life separate from a potentially harmful work life.)

15. Joseph G. Allgretti, *Lawyer's Calling: Christian Faith and Legal Practice* 14-17 (1996).

16. Sol M. Linowitz, The Betrayed Profession, 35-37 (1994).

17. *Id*. at 1-4.

18. *See* Relis, Dr. Tamara, "Civil Litigation From Litigants' Perspectives: What We Know and What We Don't Know About the Litigation Experience of Individual Litigants," Studies in Law, Politics and Society, Vol. 25, pp. 151-212, 2002.

19. *See id.*

20. *See* Fed. R. Civ. P. 26.

21. *See id.*

22. *Id.*

23. *See* Rule 26(b)(5).

24. *See* Rule 26(b)(4).

25. *See* Patricia Lee Refo, "The Vanishing Trial," Litigation online, vol 30 no. 2, 2004.

26. *See* Harry N. Mazadoorian, "SCOTUS Supports Arbitration; But What About Congress?," law.com (July 12, 2018) https://www.law.com/ctlawtribune/2018/07/12/scotus-supports-arbitration-but-what-about-congress/?slreturn=20180827112743.

27. *See id.*

28. Justice Kennedy, Speech dedicating the Western Justice Center in Pasadena, 1995.

29. Mnookin, Robert H., and Lewis Kornhauser. "Bargaining in the Shadow of the Law: The Case of Divorce." The Yale Law Journal, vol. 88, no. 5, 1979, pp. 950–997.

30. *See* Jonathan Cohen, *Advising Clients to Apologize*, 72 S. Cal. L. Rev. 1009 (1999).

Chapter Ten

Mediators Encouraging Forgiveness

"She can forgive Nixon, but she can't forgive me."

CartoonStock.com

10.1 Introduction

This chapter discusses how mediators can include healthy approaches to forgiveness in their mediations. Because clients retain mediators to assist in resolving a conflict, exploring the possibility of forgiveness is within the scope of anticipated mediator behaviors. Yet forgiveness is a sensitive topic that may feel like a bridge too far for angry clients. Thus, the mediator's willingness to enter this terrain depends on the context of the mediator's practice, the likelihood of future relationship between the parties, and mediator's level of training about and experience with forgiveness. This chapter seeks to provide mediators with more information about forgiveness so that they will feel more comfortable in assessing if, when, and how to integrate it into their practice.

Conceptual tools to equip the mediator for forgiveness conversations include various elements (animus, reparations, future relationship) and, philosophical understandings (therapeutic, relational, redemptive.) Mediators also need to be aware of the approaches toward forgiveness such as the (responsibility for feelings, hero story, complicate the story, humanize the perpetrator, focus on systemic causes, recognition of our own need for forgiveness, and belief that I will receive the same measure of forgiveness I grant to others). The motivations for forgiveness also play an important role (gift to self, gift to others, live consistent with a belief system). The goal is for mediators to be nimble enough to create a forgiveness conversation that is guided by a particular client's needs.

A student who is a psychologist described in her journal the expansive application of assisting others to forgive as a mediator.

> I enjoyed this class tremendously. I have never spent time analyzing this topic of apology and forgiveness, although I have spent significant time talking about it with clients and in relationships. This class provided instrumental information in the process of forgiveness, the elements of apology and forgiveness, and the explanation of why people forgive.

> This topic comes up all the time and I never really had the proper identifying variables of the process to communicate effectively about it. I also could not verbalize well enough to someone when they were offended, why they might not be able to forgive the offender but how they could forgive and move on regardless of the position of the other, or whether an apology existed or not.

> Since this class, I have used the opportunity in mediation to open up the floor for apology and forgiveness. I have enjoyed this as it has brought depth and more meaning to the relational mediations I have conducted. When no one wanted to come together and speak, the topic of forgiving without an apology was introduced and that was helpful in allowing parties to move past the principles of the situation and find resolution and move on.

In my professional life, I think back to a case I was a therapist on remembering how difficult it was for the wife to move past the painful experience of her husband's affair. She wanted to do the work but did not know how. I assisted her in this process, and we saved the marriage. Looking back on it, while we succeeded, we never discussed apology and forgiveness itself. We discussed building trust, strategies for communication, boundaries, etc.... However, there was not much discussion of apology and forgiveness. Perhaps had I had the knowledge of the process and elements, I could have identified earlier on what was missing for her to work through that issue or address it so that we could build stronger bridges. Submitted by Dr. Amora Rachelle Magna, emphasis added.

10.2 Various Goals of Mediation

Mediation organizations and some individual mediators advertise that a certain percentage of their mediations have been successful. This raises the issue of the criterion they are using to measure success. What was the goal of mediation that was successfully accomplished?

When I ask this question to groups of mediators there is uniform consensus that the criterion behind the success statistic is whether the parties reached an agreement. This makes sense, especially in a commercial case with an imminent trial where the parties settle their lawsuit and avoid the costs and risks of trial. But mediation can occur in a variety of contexts, and this criterion may not always be appropriate for the parties or fair to the mediator.

10.2.1 Success Criteria Pyramid

From the filter of respecting party autonomy and self-determination, the mediation has been successful when the party determines what will be required to settle this case, the costs and risks of going to trial, and then makes an informed decision whether to proceed to trial. Mediators should feel the mediation has been successful when they have done their job of helping the parties communicate and negotiate and make an informed decision. The parties' informed decision should consider whether the proposed settlement serves their interests better than allowing the conflict to continue and/or resolving it through some adjudicatory process.

Notice that the result is a different criterion for mediation success. Did the mediator assist the parties in understanding each other better, explore mutually acceptable solutions, and consider all the consequences of not reaching an agreement? These criteria allow the mediator to drive home from a mediation that did not reach an agreement and congratulate herself for having practiced her craft at the highest level! The mediator masterfully delivered the process and the parties made their choices. I will refer to this criterion as "Enhance Understanding and Explore Consensus Solutions." Because this is within the mediator's unilateral power to deliver, I will suggest it is beneath the criterion of "Settle the Case" in a hierarchy.

The foundation of a Success Criteria Pyramid is:

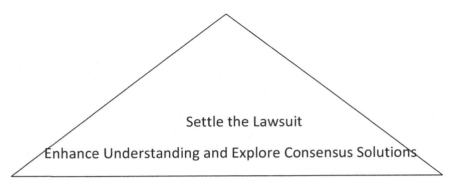

I have mediator friends who have told me that have grown weary of serving on court annexed mediator panels. They complain that the only thing the lawyers want is to settle the case. The parties arrive hating each other. The mediator is disheartened when after reaching an agreement to settle the case, one side asks the mediator to stagger the leaving times so the parties will not need to see each other in the elevator or parking lot. The case is settled, but the parties still hate each other because the conflict is not resolved. My friends became mediators because they wanted to help people resolve underlying conflicts, not just settle lawsuits. So, another criterion could be "Resolve the Underlying Conflict." Because this is usually a more difficult task that is not guaranteed, I will rank it higher on the Success Criteria Pyramid.

All three of these criteria could be accomplished without addressing the topic of forgiveness. While "Resolving the Underlying Conflict" could include forgiveness, I have experienced situations where the "conflict is resolved" and one or more parties are still hurt. Workplace colleagues can agree on the terms to be civil and get along, but the negative history is still a cause of pain for at least one of them. The next criterion for success is "Helping Individuals Recover and Heal."

Forgiveness could be one aspect to helping people recover and heal. One of my mediator friends who earns $7,000 per day and works three to four days per week (she earns more than $1,000,000 per year) says that the most rewarding part of her practice is the letters from participants thanking her for helping them to emotionally recover and move on with their lives. Most lawyer and retired judge mediators view this as an even more difficult task, so I will rank it even higher on the Success Criteria Pyramid.

A student described how this occurred in a mediation.

> After we spoke about apology and then began on the topic of forgiveness, Max Factor also spoke about apology and forgiveness in the mediation clinic. The following week I was at the Courthouse in Compton during my TRO's (Temporary Restraining Orders). I had several cases and situations that presented what seemed like an opportunity to explore the topic. ...
>
> Then there was the case of the neighbors living on the same floor next door to each other in Compton. They were friends and then issues began and Plaintiff claimed Defendant attacked her and filed for a TRO and called the elder abuse hotline. She was extremely emotional. She wanted an apology. She felt she had been wronged and felt unsafe and wanted Defendant to apologize.
>
> Defendant was not apologizing. Her story was that Plaintiff was crazy and did several things to create this situation. I finally had to break it to Plaintiff that she was not getting an apology. So, we moved into the discussion of forgiveness. I shared with her that <u>she could forgive her for what she did for herself. That holding onto the pain was only hurting her and that she could forgive without an apology. She liked hearing that and said, "Your right, thank you.</u>" Submitted by Dr. Amora Rachelle Magna, emphasis added.

Now the pyramid of success looks like this.

Finally, I have some mediator friends who don't believe the mediation has been successful unless there has been sincere interpersonal healing of the relationship. Their goal in mediation is reconciliation and restoration of the relationship. If the mediation concludes with anything less than sincere contrition and robust forgiveness, the mediator has ambivalent feelings about whether the mediation was a success. I will refer to this criterion as "Reconciliation" and put it at the top of the pyramid because it requires the highest participation by all the participants.

The resulting completed Success Criteria Pyramid is:

10.2.2 Case Study

I mediated a case that provides a picture of various criteria for success. I was at my office at Pepperdine Law School when I received a phone call from a judge. He said that he was just concluding a status conference on a case with an out of state party. He believed that they could settle this case today if I was available to lead a mediation.

A few hours later I was meeting with a 45-year-old physician and his lawyer and a 23-year-old woman and her lawyer. She worked in his office for three years before resigning and claiming a hostile work environment form of sexual harassment. We started in joint session and both lawyers laid out their client's legal cases. I asked the principals if they wanted to share how this incident had affected them personally, and both declined.

At the first caucuses I asked again about how this affected them. The woman said this had devastated her. She described the last day she worked in the office and how she went home for lunch and collapsed. Her husband found her in a fetal position five hours later. The reason she lives out of state is because driving past the doctor's office and advertisements would trigger panic attacks. This had been a turning point in her life.

In caucus, the doctor said he was livid about this situation. He said the sexual harassment claim was a pure redistribution of wealth mechanism. He described hosting the office holiday party at his home and the plaintiff complementing the décor and asking the cost of various items. From his perspective, she observed a lifestyle she could not afford, and this lawsuit was her demand that he shares the wealth. He said that this event changed the direction of his professional career. After his lawyer informed him of all the potential liabilities of being an employer, he decided to close his practice and join the staff of a hospital. He will let the hospital be the employer.

We remained in separate rooms exchanging offers for about two hours until we reached a deal. The doctor would write a personal check for $30,000 today, and they would put the settlement on the record with the judge today.

In the final caucus with the doctor, I informed him that the young lady accepted his last proposal. There was a clear sense of relief that the lawsuit would conclude that day. I told him that I intended to have a final joint session where the terms would be recited before going back to court. I then reminded him that he was in a healing profession and asked him if he wanted to say anything at the final joint session that might be healing. I observed that she lives out of state, that this may be the last time he ever sees her face to face, and that this is a unique opportunity. The doctor calmly declined the invitation. His lawyer was more adamant, exclaiming, "What are you doing? We have settled the case. Declare victory and be done!" I responded that the doctor declined the invitation anyway, so it didn't matter.

I then went into the final caucus with the young woman again explaining that I intended to have a final joint session to recite the terms before they return to the court. I reminded her that she would probably not see the doctor face to face after today or she may run into him at a store while visiting her family and asked if she wanted to say anything to him to go their separate paths in peace. She calmly declined. Her lawyer was also incredulous, asking, "What are you trying to do? We have settled the case. You have done a good job. Let's be done with this!" I said it didn't matter because his client didn't want to say anything anyway.

At the final joint session, I recited the terms and said that the judge confirmed he was available to put the settlement on the record that afternoon and was waiting for them. I congratulated them on making what I believed were good decisions to do what they each needed to do to put this matter behind them and move on with their lives. I was just about to thank and dismiss them when the doctor interrupted me.

In a very high-pitched emotion filled voice he said he would like to make a statement. I was nervous because I did not know what he would say. He might offer an emotional olive branch, or he might make one final incendiary characterization about her greed. If he used this opportunity to attack her, she might get mad and the deal would evaporate before our eyes. I had asked in caucus if he wanted to say anything to get a preview which would have given me the opportunity to possibly help craft the message and, if the message was negative, get permission from and prepare the recipient of message. He declined the invitation in caucus so now I was working without a net!

I quickly processed three options. If preserving the deal was paramount to me, I could decline his request to make a statement, explaining that the judge is waiting, and we need to respect his time and get there as quickly as possible. On the other hand, my criterion for success in a mediation could be for parties to understand each other better. In which case I could be indifferent about whether parties choose to settle or to scuttle a settlement at the last minute. If that was my approach, I would give permission for the doctor to speak in joint session letting the cards fall where they may. My final option is to state that we need to go to caucus so I can preview the doctor's statement.

Having a full-time job as a professor means that I am not dependent on mediations to earn a living. I have the luxury of being able to define success in mediation differently from how the lawyers define success. If these lawyers never hire me again (and they haven't), I can still pay my bills and have lots of interesting work to fill my days. I accept that my friends who mediate for a living (most of whom make a lot more money than me) need to be more sensitive about satisfying the lawyers' definition of success in a mediation. All of this explains why I allowed the doctor to make his statement in joint session without getting a preview in caucus.

The doctor could have blown everything up by venting his frustration about her greed. If he had, I would have asked if she wanted to respond. When their conversation had run its course, I would have returned to caucus and asked both sides how they were feeling and if they still wanted to proceed with the settlement or if there were other things they wanted to discuss or integrate into the settlement. I didn't need to do any of these things because I got lucky.

The doctor didn't make eye contact with me or the young woman. He looked into his lap and in a high-pitched emotion laden voice said the following:

> I grew up in rough neighborhood in Chicago. The coarse language I used around the office is just how I grew up and who I am. I talk the same way around my home with our young children. I never intended to hurt anyone by talking that way, and I am sorry I hurt you. This lawsuit has made me realize that I need to change, and I want you to know that I am going to change. I am glad this is over, and I wish you and your husband well.

I waited and the room was silent for about 30 seconds after he made this generous statement. Out of the corner of my eye I could see the doctor's lawyer fidgeting, and I imagined that he was thinking, "Am I supposed to share my feelings now?" Eventually I told the doctor that was a very kind and generous statement and thanked the doctor. I was just about to thank everyone and dismiss them when the young woman interrupted me.

She looked into her lap, started to cry, and said she wanted to make a statement. I was faced with the same dilemma. If I let her speak without a preview, she could still blow everything up. She could reject the doctor's apology and say that he knew he was hurting people and didn't care. If she had, I would have asked the doctor if he wanted to respond. After the conversation had run its course I would have met in caucus and asked each side how they were feeling and if they still wanted to settle the case or if there were other things they wanted to discuss or integrate into the settlement. I didn't need to do any of these things because I got lucky again.

Looking into her lap and through her tears the young lady said:

> I was raised by my Mom and never knew my dad. I started working for you when I was 20 and in many ways, you have been a father figure to me. Watching how you lived your life I learned a lot about discipline, hard work, compassion, a healthy marriage, and two parent family. I have stayed in touch with other women on your staff and know that you are changing the way you talk around the office and that you are closing your practice. I believe you are a good and decent person and thank you for settling the lawsuit today. As we wind this down, I want you to know that I wish good things for you and your family.

I waited about 30 seconds and allowed silence to accentuate the moment. Again, I could sense the lawyers' discomfort with not knowing what is supposed to happen next. I eventually said that her statement was also generous and kind and thanked her for making it. I asked if anyone wanted to say anything else. When everyone nodded no, I dismissed them to go to the court to put the settlement on the record.

This case study is intended to demonstrate the variety of ways the success of a mediation can be measured. Either party could have decided to conclude the meeting with a tirade and not settle the case, in which case, the parties would have left the meeting with a greater understanding of how the other person is feeling and viewing this conflict. The parties could have chosen to settle the lawsuit and not discuss their feelings and views of each other. Either party could have unilaterally communicated that in addition to settling the lawsuit he or she is now wishing good things for the other party, which is a picture of healing for an individual participant. Both parties could exchange expressions of wishing each other well and begin a process of rebuilding trust and vulnerability on the way toward reconciliation.

The reconciliation that occurred in this case study is rare in my experience. I will share more about that at the end of the chapter. The important aspect is that the mediator can invite parties to unilaterally heal as part of the mediation process. This is where forgiveness competency for mediators is necessary. This competence includes encouraging forgiveness, but also respecting a party's decision about whether they are interested in forgiveness and ready for it.

Notice that I inquired of each party in private whether he or she wanted to say anything that would be healing. Both declined my invitation, and I accepted that they were only ready and relieved to settle the lawsuit. If that would have been the end of it (and it usually is for me) I would have felt great about the mediation. As it happened, maybe my suggestion in private planted a seed that germinated ten minutes later when the doctor changed his mind in joint session. If the mediation had ended after his generous statement, I would have felt great about the mediation. Maybe the combination of my suggestion and the doctor's generous statement created a tipping point where the young lady decided that she wanted emotional closure with the doctor, and this was a safe place to be vulnerable. When both parties release their anger and hurt as part of the mediation that also is a great outcome.

The journal by an international student who is a judge gives an illustration.

> In my last Apology class, I learned a powerful option: to continue a mediation after settling the dispute. Indeed, the only approach to post-mediation I was aware of before last class was the follow up if the parties did not reach an agreement. Now I see that even after a deal, parties might be interested in something more. By something more, I mean not only apology, forgiveness, and reconciliation but other ramifications such as the restoration of a relationship, for example. It is fascinating how the subjects approached in the AFR course have drawn my attention to some aspects of mediation that I have thought about before.

> In Brazil, employment <u>courts measure the efficiency of the judges according to several data. One of the more important is the number of conciliations (cases settled by mediation) and legal decisions. There is no difference between these two results</u>, but sometimes a judge can clearly determine that one or both parties are not so happy with the outcome. I guess that condition has led me to think about the mediation process only until the written agreement stage. ...However, sometimes the parties might be able to not only reach an agreement but to also deal with some ramifications that do not need to be written down. That is the case of apology, forgiveness, and reconciliation. Submitted by Fernando Hoffman, emphasis added.

10.3 Mediators Help Parties Communicate About Forgiveness Related Issues

One of the core roles for all mediators is to facilitate communication between the parties. The content of the communication can be limited to predicting the outcome of a potential trial, which allows the parties to "bargain in the shadow of the law."[1] Mediators often expand the bandwidth of communication to include the parties' underlying "interests" including the feelings, values, goals, motives, and fears related to the conflict.[2] The discussion of underlying interests opens the door to conversations about forgiveness when the focus is on the feelings created by the conflict and the feelings associated with the resolution of the conflict.

10.3.1 Feelings Related to the Conflict

Mediators lay the foundation for forgiveness when they facilitate discussion about the feelings created by the conflict. Ken Cloke proposes that the desire for revenge is "often a cover for a deeper desire to communicate our pain and humiliation to the person who caused it."[3] Mediation provides the opportunity for participants to describe how they felt when they thought they had been treated unfairly **if** the mediator guides or allows the conversation to expand to this topic. Lawyers discussing the likely outcome of a lawsuit is one level of how a person has been treated unfairly. For participants who are willing, the mediator might lead the conversation to a more personal level of describing a participant's "pain and humiliation" from the incident.

The mediator may encourage this to happen in joint session so the mediation becomes a forum where disputing parties can directly exchange accounts of how the conflict hurt them. This is a source of concern for some mediators because this conversation often reveals participants' anger. Every forgiveness author including Cloke encourages mediators to remember that anger is a healthy reaction to injustice.[4] Cloke encourages mediators to assist parties in learning how to express it constructively, understand the reasons that created it, and transcend it through dialogue. [5]

A student's journal explains how a guest lecture from Ken Cloke affected his mediation technique.

> One particularly interesting portion of lecture was Ken Cloaks' five step method to reaching forgiveness. These are steps mediators should take when attempting to get clients to forgive. They include: <u>asking the least power party (victim) to explain what happened, and how it made them feel; asking the most powerful party (perpetrator) to do the same; uncovering what is obstructing forgiveness from all parties involved; asking each party to accept responsibility for their past, present, and future; and asking the parties to let go and embrace forgiveness.</u>

> This was especially interesting to me because it was applicable to prior mediations I conducted. In some of those mediations where family members were entangled in disputes, it was clear in hindsight that forgiveness might help clear up impasse and may open the doors for negotiation to continue. Had I applied Cloak's approach, I believe the chances I would have overcome some of that impasse would have increased.

> Parties typically have different perspectives regarding incidents that occurred, so it is important to hear all points of view. It is also important to understand how the parties feel, as that may contribute to their ability to overcome the disputes. Accepting responsibility is an important part of the process, which can be made much easier by understanding how the parties felt, why they felt that way, and the obstacles they had to overcome.

> Further, although it is important not to overstep my place as a mediator by taking actions that could destroy neutrality, there may be opportunities where I can uncover vital information without doing so. In those situations, applying Cloak's method would be helpful. It allows the parties to go through the process of self-reflection that they may not have taken the time to do. Also, with the mediator present, there is a third party that can facilitate the process in cases where emotions escalate. Thus, it provides the parties with a relatively safe environment, where they can express how the conflict affects them, in hopes of resolving it. Submitted by Henry Gereis, emphasis added.

Through the mediation dialogue, participants may be able to accomplish Aristotle's following instruction about anger.

> Anybody can become **angry** —that is easy,
>
> but to be **angry** with the right person
>
> and to the right degree
>
> and at the right time
>
> and for the right purpose,
>
> and in the right way—
>
> that is not within everybody's power and is not easy.[6]

Such a personal exploration about a participant's anger may need to include some private conversations with a mediator. In joint session, a participant's expression of his or her hurt is likely to take the form of an accusation of the other participant and is likely to be not accepted by the other party. That is why there is a conflict. The other party has a different perspective and is unwilling to accept the accusation. Expressing one's pain, embarrassment, and anger to the other participant, even if the accusation is rejected, may still be a helpful step on the forgiveness journey.

In private session, a mediator can provide considerable assistance by being empathetic and letting the injured person know that someone has heard and understands his anger. Caucus may also be a better place for the mediator to aid in reframing the issue so the participant can satisfy more of Aristotle's standards in his or her anger. Finally, in caucus the mediator may be able to coach the participant to express his hurt in "I messages" to decrease the defensiveness of the other participant.[7]

A Saudi Arabian student's journal provides an international perspective.

> In this class we will discuss the mediator's roles and how it can be a way to make people able to forgive. … In my opinion, when people go to mediation, they have agreed to resolve their dispute in a calm way, so it is the best place and time for the mediator to encourage them to forgive. For sure <u>the mediator cannot ask the parties for forgiveness from the first time or when they are in a joint session because they will think it will affect their dignity. But the mediator should talk to the parties separately</u> because that will not let anyone affect the party's mind and will give the mediator a freedom to talk deeply about the dispute.
>
> In my country, the Imam or leader of the tribe will do the mediator's job because mediation is not popular in my country. During the meeting with the Imam or Leader they will read something from the Quran and Hadith to make the parties more flexible and willing to forgive. Sometimes we use old people to talk to the parties and to make them respect their elders to forgive. Submitted by Abdullah Sulaiman Allyhaydan, emphasis added.

Aristotle's conclusion that it is "not within everybody's power" to do anger well, triggers Folger and Bush's fundamental mediation themes of "empowerment and recognition."[8] The immediate connection here is to empower the participant to do anger well, but Folger and Bush challenge mediators to empower parties to simultaneously "stand up for themselves" and "experience and express concern and consideration for others."[9]

Folger and Bush propose empowerment is necessary because

> disputing parties are typically unsettled, confused, fearful, disorganized, and unsure of what to do ... They are empowered in mediation when they grow calmer, clearer, more confident, more organized and more decisive. If a party has taken the opportunity to collect herself, examine options, deliberate, and decide on a course of action, empowerment has occurred regardless of the outcome.[10]

Likewise, their theme of recognition is explained as

> in the heat of conflict, disputing parties typically feel threatened, attacked, and victimized by the conduct and claims of the other party . . . focused on self-protection; they are defensive, suspicious and hostile to the other party, and almost always incapable of looking beyond their own needs ....

> They are empowered in a mediation if they voluntarily choose to become more open, attentive, sympathetic, and responsive to the situation of the other party .... Recognition must be freely given. If that decision is the result of pressure, cajoling or moralizing, it is only self-preservation. A mediator who thinks that only large degrees of recognition count will be sorely tempted to force things .... The mediator must understand that the parties must determine the degree of recognition they genuinely desire to give .... Recognition must be based on empowerment.[11]

There is considerable application of Folger and Bush's mediation framework for mediators interested in encouraging forgiveness. A mediator can provide the forum and then empower a participant to express the personal hurt and anger well. The ability to recognize and be sympathetic and responsive to the situation from the other party's perspective is integral to complicating the conflict in the relational approach to forgiveness. The caution against mediators pressuring participants beyond the recognition they genuinely desire to give reminds mediators to allow the participant to choose the type, degree, and extent of forgiveness they want for this situation at this time.

Allowing the participants to discuss their feelings of hurt and anger arising out of the conflict lays the foundation for forgiveness because the hurt person has the satisfaction of knowing that she acted within her power. If she has a religious tradition or life philosophy that encourages her to be honest with others when they hurt her, she has lived her values by sharing her victim experience with the perpetrator.

The type and extent of forgiveness may depend on the perpetrator's reaction. If the perpetrator refuses to tell the truth and take responsibility (apologize), the victim will need to decide whether to recognize that the "perpetrator's" perspective has validity and adjust her victim story, or she may need to resort to therapeutic forgiveness. If the perpetrator apologizes, the victim can decide whether it is healthy to explore relational forgiveness and begin the process of restoring trust. The act of communicating with the perpetrator allows the victim to better assess her forgiveness options.

10.3.2 Feelings Related to the Resolution of the Conflict

If mediators can include interests related to the conflict, it is not a big jump to discuss interests related to the resolution of the conflict. Whether mediations conclude with agreements, the victims will need to decide what to do with their emotional reaction to the injustices. If there is an agreement, the participant can have the opportunity to decide the scope of the agreement. The mediator might make the participant aware of the Mediation Success Criteria Pyramid or a similar tool to help the participant understand the menu of possible outcomes in a mediation. Some parties may desire individual or relational healing that allows the mediator and participant to explore various understandings and approaches to forgiveness.

If the mediation concludes without an agreement, the mediator can inquire if the participant would like to know about tools that would assist in processing the emotional dimension of the dispute while continuing to seek justice. The mediator might be able to assist the participant move closer to that perfect human being who can purse justice from a place of mercy and love instead of anger and hatred. Mediators should recall Folger and Bush's admonition that these matters cannot be forced and inquire and assist participants in accomplishing the outcomes THEY desire.

A student describes her approach when mediating civil harassment cases, which usually involve parties who know each other and one of them is requesting a restraining order.

> I have found that in difficult civil harassment matters, encouraging a <u>mediated settlement often *includes* the introduction of concepts of apology, forgiveness, and understanding of one another. This helps the mediator to identify the underlying needs and interests of the parties</u> which may have given rise to the dispute and will help to resolve the conflict. By the time the parties reach an accord, there is a framework for some form of reconciliation. But the mediator needs to guide and suggest and point the way. Almost as if the mediator is silently saying, "I don't judge you; I hope you forgive yourself." THEN, people begin to "reopen their hearts" and "transcend what caused [the conflict]" to "become fully reconciled with their opponent."
>
> I would give so much to revisit the parties in six months to see if our efforts toward reconciliation and forgiveness have come to bear. It is my hope that the parties find sincere peace, so their dispute does not have the opportunity to reoccur. Submitted by Carole Helfert Aragon, emphasis added.

10.4 Mediators Assisting Parties to Assess Their Choices Regarding Forgiveness

In contrast to the *exploring interests* paradigm as an avenue for mediators to address the possibility of forgiveness, mediators should consider their role in assisting option generation and helping participants make good decisions. Jim Craven, a Pepperdine Adjunct Professor and full-time commercial mediator from Spokane, uses making better decisions as a core theme in his approach to mediation. He explains to parties that conflict creates distortions in their perceptions. His job is like an optometrist in providing a variety of lenses for the participant and asking which lens provides a helpful focus. His goal is for the mediation process to help participants make the best possible decision about their options.

The mediator who is competent in forgiveness is willing to ask the victims what they intend to do about their anger. The responses may be: stew, seek revenge, or forgive. The mediator should ask the participant if they have another strategy, but these three are the main options for most people. Forgiveness is a difficult choice, so it may be helpful for the mediator to ask the victims if they recognize that the other options have consequences. Here is a quick reminder from earlier chapters:

Revenge

Psychology studies confirm that revenge is not satisfying.[12]

Revenge makes the victim the same as (and hopefully not worse than) the perpetrator.

Revenge causes the victim to lose the position of moral high ground.

Revenge continues the cycle of harm.

Revenge focuses on the past and punishing the perpetrator diverting attention from the future, change, and solving the problem.[13]

Taking a dispute to court can be a type of revenge, and most people are not happy with their court experience.

Stewing

Victims get sympathy from their support system, but it usually wears thin over time.

Stewing is not emotionally or physically healthy for the victim.[14]

Will time heal this wound on its own or does the victim need to eventually initiate a process?

Is the victim refusing to forgive to punish the perpetrator and is the perpetrator oblivious, so the victim is choosing to be miserable without the hoped-for benefit?

Forgiveness

Participants may be more open to forgiveness if the mediator empowers the victim to define the source (decision/feeling, process/event, and unilateral/mutual) meaning (animosity, reparations, future relationship) and approach (therapeutic, relational, or redemptive) that fits for them at this time.

Most mediators accept the role of helping participants understand their choices and make good decisions. The requirement that the victim needs to make the decision when and what kind of forgiveness to experience is consistent with mediation's core value of participant autonomy and self-determination. The mediator does a valuable service to help the participant realize that choosing not to forgive leaves the victim with revenge, stewing, or attempting amnesia.

A student's journal reinforces this concept.

Today we concluded our study of forgiveness with a look at forgiveness as it relates to the role of the mediator. This proved to be a provocative topic because seeking forgiveness, or even suggesting forgiveness, is beyond some people's understanding of the role of a neutral. Some believe that delving into the world of forgiveness is dangerous territory for mediators. What became clear through our discussion however, is that regardless of whether a mediator should encourage forgiveness, a mediator should understand forgiveness.

For me, a mediator's job is to empower the parties. A mediator should help the parties understand that they have choices. A mediator should help the parties evaluate their options so that when and if they decide to make a choice, it is well thought out. Forgiveness can be part of this evaluation. Forgiveness is always a choice, and in some cases, it is a choice that should be considered carefully. This is especially true where *failure* to forgive will limit a party's future choices.

Failure to forgive can limit a person's emotional strength and can keep a person trapped in a negative emotional state. Failure to forgive can also damage a person's relationship with the offender as well as their relationship with others. In these cases, forgiveness is an attractive alternative to not forgiving. Parties also need to understand that forgiveness can be a choice; forgiveness can be a gift that one gives to oneself.

For mediators it may be important to point out to a party that they have three choices: 1) hold onto their anger, 2) forget about their anger, or 3) engage in forgiveness. For many simply forgetting about their anger is impossible.

Moving on from a powerful emotion, such as anger, often takes time, healing, and rebuilding of trust. Therefore, most people will come to see that they can allow anger to consume their lives or they can make the conscious decision to proceed down a path of forgiveness. Obviously, forgiveness is not a switch that someone can flip on or off. Rather it may be valuable to think about forgiveness as a process that takes time and should be worked at. Submitted by Brian Murray, emphasis added.

10.5 Mediators Assisting Parties to Define the Source, Terms of, and Approach to Forgiveness

Forgiveness has been described and presented in all the prior chapters without endorsement or judgement to create maximum flexibility. This flexibility is designed to equip mediators to assist parties in customizing a personally acceptable version of forgiveness. The mediator fluent in forgiveness can adapt to the party who approaches forgiveness as a matter of a decision based on his or her values as well as to the party who approaches forgiveness as a matter of feelings based on his or her desire to experience peace of mind. The mediator needs to defer to the party's construct on how forgiveness works for them in that situation.

A student's journal reinforces the ideal that the mediator allow the parties to choose to forgive.

> But perhaps what I enjoyed most about the presentation was Ken Cloke's advice on how to encourage forgiveness. Indeed, it is overstepping and awkward to ask parties to forgive one another. Additionally, that this process is best executed under circumstances where all the parties are making their own conscious decisions (and not being coerced), makes it more important that at these critical junctures the mediator wisely takes his hands off the wheel and lets the parties do the driving. Instead, I like his idea of asking parties questions that get to the forgiveness process. I was especially struck by this because I have done this in a mediation before. However, his advice about how to approach the situation was much more skillful and masterful than the words I ended up using.
>
> Namely, I was much more evaluative. I remember telling the woman that this conflict is something that has weighed heavily on her and that this is an opportunity for her to relieve herself of this tremendous burden. As with most tactics in mediation, I likely would have gotten more out of her if I posed it as a question – it would be her coming to her own realization instead of me imposing my version of the events on her. Instead, I should have said, "This looks like something that is really weighing on you. Is there anything that you believe you could do to help yourself feel better about the situation?" I will never forget this lesson and will strive, when possible and wise, to use that phrase. Submitted by Benjamin Reccius, emphasis added.

The mediative approach makes a party aware of various approaches to forgiveness and lets the participants define the approach to forgiveness they want to experience, if any. The mediator may want to avoid using the word forgiveness because the parties may reject the concept based on the meaning they are attaching to the word. For example, a mediator can let parties know that they can define forgiveness where they are less hateful to the other party and still expect full reparations and do not need to reconcile the relationship.

The mediator might assist the party to understand the participant's personal view of forgiveness with the following variables. This might be done by presenting these variables to the participant and allowing them to react or it might be done internally by the mediator through conversation.

How any potential forgiveness would work for this participant in this situation?

> Decision vs. Feeling
>
> Event vs. Process
>
> Unilateral vs. Mutual

What would be the elements of a potential forgiveness for this participant in this situation?

Little Animus --------------- High Animus

No Reparations ------------ Full Reparations

Restore Relationship ----- No Future Relationship

What would be the motive and approach to a potential forgiveness for this participant in this situation?

Peace of Mind for the Participant ---------------------------- Therapeutic Forgiveness

Restore the Relationship ------------------------------------ Relational Forgiveness

Consistency with the Participant's Value System ---------- Redemptive Forgiveness

10.6 Mediator Techniques for Encouraging Forgiveness

I have observed a variety of approaches to how mediators encourage forgiveness. My initiation to the mediation field was as the Director of the Christian Conciliation Service of Los Angeles (CCS.) This faith-based organization was created to provide a forum where people who shared the Christian faith could seek resolution of their disputes through mediation and arbitration within the Christian community and consistent with Christ's teachings.

Christ clearly taught that his followers should forgive others in the same way that they want God to forgive them. Parties participating in mediations administered by the CCS gave explicit permission to include conversations about forgiveness in the process. The CCS organization is an example of a mediation organization (or mediator) that clearly declares that forgiveness will be addressed as part of the mediation process. The clients who use that organization or individual know that the topic of forgiveness is integrated into the mediation process.

But the way forgiveness was encouraged was not uniform. In the late 1980s there were 30 CCS chapters loosely affiliated with the Christian Legal Society in many major cities across the US. The annual national CCS conferences were fascinating discussions/debates about the various approaches. I observed a CCS mediation in another city where the mediators instructed the parties that they must forgive each other that evening because their Christian faith demands it. In contrast, the board of directors and I in Los Angeles believed that it was our role to remind participants of what Christ taught, including on the topic of forgiveness, and then allow the participants to decide when, where, and how they would respond to those teachings.

I resigned from the CCS after five years and then served as the Associate Director and then Managing Director at Pepperdine Law School's Straus Institute for Dispute Resolution for 28 years. I mediated many cases after leaving CCS, sometimes within the Christian community and sometimes in a non-religious context. It was interesting to realize that I often explored some level of forgiveness/healing as demonstrated by the earlier case study of the physician and young woman who worked for him. My wording and explanations were different depending on my assessment of rapport and anticipated receptiveness.

Phrases like "bury the hatchet" and "let go of the anger and move on with your life" replaced the words forgiveness and reconciliation. I tried to always let the participants decide what they wanted to do with this issue, but I often brought it up for them to make a conscious decision. I found it interesting to realize that I was illuminating a dimension of the conflict because of my values and beliefs. I didn't push or require it, but I would look for ways to encourage healing of hearts bruised by conflict. At CCS, it was advertised and expected. In many of my post CCS mediations, it was subtle and camouflaged.

The contrast is important because mediators interested in encouraging forgiveness need to decide the degree of transparency about this aspect of their mediation approach. Some may try to describe it as an option in their promotional materials, but I suspect that it will sound too unrealistic to most people in a conflict serious enough to hire a mediator. The less transparent approach is to have it on the mediator's radar and use mediator discretion as to when to explore the sensitive topic of forgiveness. Again, the mediator may disguise the conversation by using phrases that might describe forgiveness without ever using the word forgiveness.

A mature student who mediates and teaches mediation for prisoners in the LA County Jail describes concerns and reactions about her exploration of the mediator role.

The roleplay today really brought to a fore my concerns about "helping" the parties to forgive. Zena Zumeta (who had just taught an advance Family Mediation Course at Pepperdine) strongly emphasized the role of the mediator as a facilitator – as distinguished from an *expert*. She continually told us not to slip into the role of the expert, which is often much more comfortable for those of us with graduate degrees and an existing habit of relying on our expertise for power. As someone who has always relied on expert power, I always try to be mindful of avoiding the "expert trap" with which I feel so comfortable.

When I start to tell people why they should forgive, what the benefits are of forgiveness, etc., etc., I am assuming the mantle of the *expert*. The expert says: "I know this should be done in order for you to feel better." Or "I know how you should behave in this process for the optimal results. Because of my experience and expertise, you should do what I say." I am in the process of training myself to recognize the feeling of "power!" and of control that accompanies a shift into the expert mode in mediation. When I can SEE what I am doing, I can then back off and, once again, give the parties center stage.

So how can I use this newfound information about apology and forgiveness without assuming the aura of the expert as mediator? My partner is a playwright, and I merely need to follow her advice on writing to find a solution here: don't TELL them, SHOW them. Get into each party's current feelings of anger, and then ask him/her to tell me what the discussion is doing to his/her heart and feelings of stress. Do such feelings seem healthy?

I can then ask them to imagine (a' la Ken Cloke) an even meaner revenge than is being sought, to then talk about those feelings. And, finally, I can ask them to describe an alternative. With inmates who are really STUCK in feelings of anger or revenge, I ask them to use their imagination to come up with a scenario that explains how they would have taken the same actions as the perpetrator. I encourage them to think wildly, think out of the box, but to come up with a realistic story where they might have behaved in the same manner.

I believe it is possible, with time, to allow the parties to experience first-hand the physiological changes inherent in different emotions. To see for themselves what their feelings are doing. I also like to quote the 12-step maxim: "Resentment is like drinking poison and waiting for the other person to die." When I ask whether that statement makes any sense to the angry party, the response is usually a sheepish smile. If the party is NOT ready to understand this point and let go of their anger, my role as a mediator is then to help them find an agreement within the confines of their anger and desire for revenge.

With the roleplay today, my goal (without a co-mediator) would have been only to *talk them all back into coming back at 10AM the next day to make the decision.* I really liked Peter's comments today about the importance of letting people sleep over things before making difficult decisions; in this situation, I think exhaustion has a very negative factor.

Getting a commitment to show up at least briefly the next day is not the same as a commitment to continue mediating after a long and stressful day. The next morning, I'd ask: "What have you got to lose?"

We spend a fair amount of time discussing the futility of two emotional parties trying to convince the other that his/her version of reality is correct. Here I am reminded of what brain scans show when people are thinking about religion or politics: the limbic area or emotional center of the brain lights up, while the cerebral cortex or logical area of the brain is fast asleep. In other words, we CAN'T convince the other party to see our perspective because their emotions have shut down the logical capabilities of the brain. It is emotional reaction (disagreement) talking to emotional reaction (disagreement) … and the inevitable result is more disagreement. Submitted by Lisa Z Zeller, emphasis added.

Timing could be another variable for mediators interested in encouraging forgiveness. CCS puts the issue front and center from the beginning. In contrast, some mediators may bring up some approximation of forgiveness after a deal has been reached by doing things like asking if they would like to meet to shake hands or thank the other person for helping to settle this matter.

This is like the discussion about whether it is better to sequence the conversation so that the feelings are addressed first and then address the business issues or vice versa. Some parties find it easier to reach agreement on the tangible terms after their emotions have been expressed and acknowledged. Other parties don't want to discuss their feelings until they learn what the other party intends to do about the tangible terms. Best practice is for the mediator to understand the difference and seek to create a flow of conversation that meets the participants' needs.

A student describes his approach in a journal.

> From my experience with a court-annexed family mediation program in Sao Paulo, Brazil, the idea of forgiveness is an important step for the settlement. The concept of forgiveness can be universal, and for the purpose of describing my experience, forgiveness was a mix of willingness to forgive and apology; this often resulted in a don't-wish-ill type of reconciliation. For the family mediations, the parties arrive hurt and angry because of the dispute. They were not ready to talk about settlement, since the emotions and personal history would interfere. The interference to the settlement often presented itself as an impediment to an important issue of one party by the other. This happened as a way of revenge, hurting someone during the mediation. Therefore, to reach the negotiation stage, most of the time, the first stage was starting the healing process of the parties.
>
> The mediator had to plant the seed of forgiveness in the beginning of the mediation. Generally, to try to encourage forgiveness in family mediation, there was a common goal. Most of the cases were about a custody battle, and the love and care for their children was something that allowed the parties to consider starting to forgive.

After some time, generally in the second session, it was visible that forgiveness was growing. Carefully noticing that growth, the mediator could start the settlement negotiation. Nevertheless, sometimes a misunderstood or misspoken word could end all the progress that was made. Submitted by Fabio Franco, emphasis added.

In his chapter titled "Dismantling the Desire for Revenge," Ken Cloke encourages mediators to avoid judgement and apply a "deep listening" and empathy for situations when a party is hurting to the point where they choose not to forgive.[15] He encourages mediators "locate the urge to violence and destruction within ourselves."[16] He acknowledges that this is often unnatural and uncomfortable for mediators.[17] His suggestions for mediators include:

- ❏ support revengeful parties in communicating their pain, fear, and guilt;
- ❏ ask them to focus on what they want for their future;
- ❏ articulate a choice between revenge and some attractive alternative, such as a child's emotional well-being;
- ❏ suggest redirecting the revenge energy toward a socially beneficial form, such as supporting people who have been similarly injured;
- ❏ suggest hatred freezes and simplifies our opponents while forgiveness makes them more fluid, complex, and changeable;
- ❏ broaden the desire for revenge to include destroying the dysfunctional system that gave rise to it, or to help all victims who suffered in the past, or halt all perpetrators in the future; and
- ❏ broaden the culpability to include not just the individual opponents but their allies and supporters and the system that permitted it, the people who knew about it and did nothing, and the people who should have known about it.[18]

A student's appreciation for Cloke's approach is instructive.

Ken Cloke's method of revenge is extremely interesting. Prior to this course, I had never thought about the concept in relation to mediation. I did not consider revenge to involve communication, but I now understand that revenge is a desire to communicate how it felt to be treated improperly and/or unfairly. Mediation provides an opportunity to communicate revenge in a safe environment.

However, as a mediator, would I be able to empathize with the desire for revenge? It is one thing to say, "I understand why you feel that way," but it is another to encourage or heighten feelings of revenge. Although it is counterintuitive, it may also prove effective. Anger is a natural and important emotion. Anger and pain must be expressed in order to begin the healing process and move toward a better future. Cloke advises mediators to encourage parties to come to terms with anger, pain, suffering, grief, and loss of expectations.

Cloke understands that mediation is not merely a settlement on a piece of paper, but a deeply felt conflict between two people. But what is the boundary between mediator and psychologist? How is a mediator to know whether anger will lead to catharsis or chaos? The theory calls for more than non-judgment. It calls for a response of support, a sense of understanding, and a feeling of negative emotion.

In addition, Cloke understands that forgiveness can only come after the primary issues have been resolved. It is nice to think that forgiveness is a matter of will, but the concept that forgiveness cannot be achieved until there has been communication and/or resolution must be considered. This is a natural human need. It is only then that energy can be invested toward the future instead of the past. Submitted by Alexis Harris, emphasis added.

Finally, some victims want the perpetrator to apologize before forgiving. The mediator who is knowledgeable in the apology language could explore with the perpetrator whether an appropriate apology is possible. If so, the mediator needs to assess whether it is productive for it to happen in joint session where the victim can see and hear the perpetrator and possibly ask about the meaning of the apology. For example, "[a]re you admitting you were wrong, and this conflict is your fault?"

In contrast to the joint session apology is shuttle diplomacy in which the mediator delivers the apology on behalf of the perpetrator. The mediator may choose this delivery method when the perpetrator is frustrated and hurting and willing to itemize and apologize for his mistakes only to the mediator and allow the mediator to carry the message. If confronted face to face, the mediator believes the perpetrator's frustrations will surface and the conversation will become unproductive.

A student's journal describes how a mediator set up the possibility for forgiveness.

In my practice as an attorney, I am often a Daily Settlement Officer, volunteering my time at different courthouses. ... In this one particular mediation, a couple was divorcing. They were reaching amicable agreements, although there were times when the wife would give a harsh quip or a sarcastic laugh. At some point, it stopped being conducive to finishing this process, so I separated the husband and wife.

Speaking first with the wife, I asked her what was wrong. She let me know that she was still very hurt about his affair and that although he was "trying to act like the good guy now," she believed that he was still trying to hurt her. We talked about what it would take for her to move on. She could not give me any response. It seemed to me that she had never thought about it. In fact, she was so caught up in the pain that she could not even see herself in the next moment. Everything until now was about her "divorce."

Then, I let her exit and I spoke with the husband. He acknowledged the affair and that he hurt his wife. He knew he could not fix his marriage anymore, but felt he was really trying to do the right thing in his division of assets and support. He just could not understand why his wife took every opportunity to make him feel bad. He felt that for the rest of his life she would constantly remind him of his great error in this marriage.

I spoke with him about the possibility of an apology. He said that he had apologized many times before, but it had not worked. That was interesting to me because I did not know what "it had not worked" meant. I asked him what that meant. He said that regardless of how often or how he apologized, she would not forgive him and take him back. We discussed that for some time.

Then, we agreed that he might try to apologize simply for hurting her by his affair and for his great part in the breakdown of his marriage. We discussed some language and that he should remain silent at the end and not expect anything from her, not even words and not even any acknowledgement. He understood that if he really wanted to apologize, then it was her prerogative to accept the apology or not. He also understood that this might be his last opportunity to have a meaningful conversation with his soon-to-be ex-wife.

Then, I brought the wife into the room. I said, "Before we resume, Husband has something he would like to say." He called her by her name and said, "I know that I have failed you in every way that a man can fail a woman. I know that this divorce is my fault. I also know that no matter how I try, I can never make it up to you. I just want you to know that not a day goes by that I don't regret the hurt that I have caused. I also want you to know that if I could take it back, I would, but there is no way to change the past. I am sorry for the pain that I have caused you and I know that I don't know how much you are suffering. I realize that today I will not have it, but one day I hope that you can forgive me."

I did not know what to expect from her. She was silent. I mean, amazingly silent, which was a different thing than before when she could not stop commenting or being sarcastic. She said, "Thank you."

It was not a moment of reconciliation. I wish I could say that this marriage reconciled. It did not. But, in that moment, there was a little peace that the wife finally got. In that small moment, I saw a change to her. When it was over, the husband exited first. With the wife, I asked her, "How do you feel?" She looked at me and said, "Free." Submitted by Beatriz Pelayo-Garcia.

If the alleged perpetrator will not apologize, the mediator familiar with apology may try to help the victim on the forgiveness journey by explaining why some people find it difficult to apologize. The mediator might even tell the victim that the perpetrator has never said it, but the mediator believes the perpetrator realizes he made mistakes or should have handled the situation better.

Technically, only the perpetrator has "standing to apologize." While it is flawed, I sometimes apologize for what happened to a person when the perpetrator will not. This "mediator as surrogate apologizer" is subject to scrutiny but has been helpful to some victims. This limited recognition by an objective person may assure the victim that they are not crazy in his or her desire for an apology. The mediator can remind the victim that the therapeutic approach is a unilateral model of forgiveness designed to relieve the victim when the perpetrator is unwilling to apologize.

But what about when the perpetrator offers a full and complete apology and the victim is not ready to accept the apology or forgive? Should a mediator offer a form of surrogate forgiveness? Only the victim has standing to forgive! Should a mediator at least confirm to the perpetrator that they have done what they can (tell the truth and take responsibility, including offering reparations), but remind the perpetrator that forgiveness is process and the victim may need time or may never be ready to forgive? Should a mediator fluent in the dynamics of apology and forgiveness at least offer comfort and support to the perpetrator whose full and complete apology has been rejected? Is this comfort and support a form of surrogate forgiveness?

Two students reacted to the concept of a mediator providing surrogate forgiveness.

> ... [W}e discussed the debated issue of the mediator as the surrogate of forgiveness. The main question is, "Who has the standing to offer forgiveness?" Most people would say that the mediator does not have the standing to offer forgiveness on behalf of another person. Instead, it is the victim who has the power and standing to offer forgiveness. One way to approach this as a mediator is to offer counsel, rather than grant forgiveness.
>
> Using Professor Robinson's example of the separating husband and wife, the mediator could say, "I've been clear that this is not what God is asking you to do, but I do want to say that I don't think this is an unforgiveable sin. I don't think this is a shining moment for you, but God is a God of grace and forgiveness. I hope that you will continue to seek his face and his grace. Cling to that and turn towards God and not away from him." In this situation, the husband had already moved on, but the wife wanted to reconcile and restore the marriage. The mediator as the surrogate forgiver is a complicated topic. ...
>
> As a mediator, I do not think I would feel comfortable being the surrogate of forgiveness, but I do see myself doing something like Professor Robinson did in the Christian reconciliation program. Although I would not grant forgiveness on behalf of another party, I would encourage both parties to forgive, emphasizing the freedom that would come along with this.
>
> Especially in a faith setting, the Redemptive motive of forgiveness could be emphasized. Just as God has forgiven us, sinners who do not even deserve forgiveness, we should feel a responsibility to forgive others, especially considering the fact that God loves them just as much as He loves us. As the mediator, I would use different descriptors of forgiveness to appeal to parties who have different motives. Submitted by Beverly Cawyer, emphasis added.

I like and accepted the idea of the mediator being able to provide surrogate forgiveness. In a situation where the victim is hanging on to anger and flourishing in the victim narrative even though the perpetrator has done everything they can to make the situation right, I think the mediator can offer closure for the perpetrator. If it is clear that the perpetrator has offered a full and authentic apology and made or attempted to make reparations, I would feel comfortable having a conversation with the perpetrator that let him/her know that as a person who mediates, I recognize their efforts and they should feel some sort of vindication and closure surrounding the dispute. Submitted by Lauren Wilkins, emphasis added.

10.7 Full Disclosure- Limited Success in Encouraging Forgiveness in Mediation

For this chapter to be complete, I need to disclose my personal experience in which few of the participants in my mediations have forgiven during the mediation. Maybe my desire to teach this course and write this book is driven from my own frustration and disappointment about how infrequently forgiveness was fully embraced in my mediations. This disclosure is necessary, so readers do not have unrealistic expectations.

The rarity of forgiveness in my mediations is more surprising because I started with the Christian Conciliation Service where forgiveness is a core value. My interest in assisting people to heal from their conflicts extends to clients of all religious beliefs. In many of my mediations in faith communities where forgiveness and reconciliation are core values, I have self-selected a constituency that should increase my forgiveness frequency.

My limited success is significantly caused by my approach. I invite people but let them decide. In a faith setting, I often ask each party what their religious beliefs expect from them in the area of forgiveness. The response I often get is appreciation for reminding them of their beliefs or recognition that they need to forgive, quickly followed by the declaration, "but I'm not ready today!" They explain that they are still in deep pain. Reaching an agreement/settling the complaint has been very helpful because it took the burr out from under the saddle, but the wound needs to heal before they are ready to forgive. (Decision or feeling … Process or Event?) Sometimes they accentuate where they are on the issue of forgiveness by concluding, "if I said I forgave him today, it would be a lie!"

My response when offered this reaction is to accept their assessment and empathize. Sometimes they assure me that they will get to forgiveness, just not today, and it can't be rushed. Even before I committed myself to studying forgiveness, I had enough sense to listen to others on how they needed to navigate this sensitive topic.

So, my hope is that mediators will be forgiveness conversant, and respectful of participants' approaches. Mediators should know how to encourage forgiveness without being pushy. Mediators will make the participants aware of the possibilities of individual healing and interpersonal reconciliation while understanding that forgiveness is rarely effectuated as part of the mediation. Mediators will be content with planting seeds of forgiveness and allowing parties to decide what to do with those seeds.

10.8 Stewing Siblings –Forgiveness Mediation Simulation

Mediator's Role

You are a mediator who has been paid to mediate between four siblings between the ages of 70 and 78. The oldest, a male, and his two sisters accuse the youngest, also a male, of mismanaging their parents' trust. The accused became the Trustee of about $12,000,000 of assets when their father died fifteen years ago. They noticed that their brother's lifestyle became much more extravagant soon after he became Trustee and were suspicious that he was being over paid and using Trust assets for his personal benefit.

The attorneys and accountants for the trust advised the Trustee that his mother was the beneficiary until she died and that he should not give any information about the trust to his siblings. The Trustee complied with these instructions. The siblings complained to their mother, who totally supported the Trustee and threatened to disinherit the siblings if they ever complained again and even made them sign a legally enforceable release of liability for the Trustee.

When the mother died, the Trustee inappropriately hid and benefited from a comparatively minor asset in the distribution of the trust. (Each sibling inherited about $3,000,000.) When the siblings learned about the hidden asset a few years later, they hired an attorney and filed a lawsuit. Each member of the family is a committed Christian, and they have hired you because you have a reputation for mediating in a way to encourage forgiveness and reconciliation. At your suggestion, two days have been reserved for the mediation, but you will only charge them for the time used. All parties are capably represented by counsel at the mediation.

After seven hours of discussion and negotiations over the Trust's finances (about 75% of which has consisted of shuttle diplomacy in caucus at the parties' request), the parties have agreed to settle the lawsuit with the Trustee paying $135,000 to resolve all legal claims arising out of his administration of the Trust.

After a written agreement has been executed, you ask the Trustee if he would like to continue the mediation with a focus on reconciliation of the relationship with his siblings. He responded that he would like that and would be willing to either continue the meeting into the early evening or return the following day. Your task in this assignment is to handle the conversation to explore this possibility with the three siblings, who are all together in another room with their attorney. `

The oldest brother seems to have been the ring leader and most determined to make his youngest sibling give an accounting and pay them for the minor shortage in the distribution. He retired from a successful healthcare executive position and seems mainly concerned about his own happiness.

The second oldest sibling is a sister who seems mainly interested in the family. She is concerned that both her brothers are over seventy years old and have had heart attacks in the last two years. The four siblings live in different cities within a 1000-mile radius, but she is concerned they may never be in the same room again.

The last sister decided not to marry or have a family so she can more available to serve God. She was very hurt by the Trustee/younger brother's apparent opportunism. She trusted him completely and was devastated when her oldest brother convinced her that her younger brother misspent their money.

Stewing Siblings------Forgiveness Mediation Exercise

Role for Oldest Brother

You are the oldest, a male, of four siblings between the ages of 70 and 78. You accuse the youngest, also a male, of mismanaging their parents' trust. The accused became the Trustee of about $12,000,000 of assets when your father died fifteen years ago. You and your sisters noticed that your brother's lifestyle became much more extravagant soon after he became Trustee and were suspicious that he was being overpaid and using Trust assets for his personal benefit.

The attorneys and accountants for the trust advised the Trustee that his mother was the beneficiary until she died and that he should not give any information about the trust to his siblings. The Trustee complied with these instructions. You and your sisters complained to your mother, who totally supported the Trustee and threatened to disinherit any of you if you ever complained again. Your mother even made you sign a legally enforceable release of liability for the Trustee.

When your mother died, the Trustee inappropriately hid and benefited from a comparatively minor asset in the distribution of the trust. (Each sibling inherited about $3,000,000.) When the siblings learned about the hidden asset a few years later, they hired an attorney and filed a lawsuit. The family members are all committed Christians, and they have agreed to go to mediation with a mediator who has a reputation for encouraging forgiveness and reconciliation. At the mediator's suggestion, two days have been reserved for the mediation, but you will only be charged for the time used. All parties are capably represented by counsel at the mediation.

After seven hours of discussion and negotiations over the Trust's finances (about 75% of which has consisted of shuttle diplomacy in caucus- at the parties' request), the parties have agreed to settle the lawsuit with the Trustee paying $135,000 to resolve all legal claims arising out of his administration of the Trust.

After a written agreement has been executed, the mediator has come into the room with you, your sisters and your attorney and stated that the Trustee would like to continue the mediation with a focus on reconciliation of the relationship with his siblings. He is willing to either continue the meeting into the early evening or return the following day. You, your sisters, and attorney are now talking with the mediator about this request by your brother.

You are the one who first noticed that things didn't seem right, and you served as the spokesperson for your sisters in most of this matter. You are angry that your brother hid behind the lawyers and your mother and didn't share the details about the trust management for most of the last 15 years. You didn't find out until today the amount of his monthly salary (which your attorney has confirmed was reasonable) and he didn't bring any substantiating documents. You are 78 years old and enjoying retirement from a successful healthcare executive position. You are glad your brother had to admit that he messed up on the last aspect of the trust and that he had to pay some money to acknowledge that he was wrong. You just want to go home and not get into any touchy /feely group hugs.

Stewing Siblings ----Forgiveness Mediation Simulation

Role for Older Sister

You are the older sister of four siblings between the ages of 70 and 78 who accuse the youngest, a male, of mismanaging your parents' trust. The accused became the Trustee of about $12,000,000 of assets when your father died fifteen years ago. You, your younger sister, and older brother noticed that your younger brother's lifestyle became much more extravagant soon after he became Trustee and were suspicious that he was being overpaid and using Trust assets for his personal benefit.

The attorneys and accountants for the trust advised the Trustee that his mother was the beneficiary until she died and that he should not give any information about the trust to his siblings. The Trustee complied with these instructions. You and your siblings complained to your mother, who totally supported the Trustee and threatened to disinherit any of you if you ever complained again. Your mother even made you sign a legally enforceable release of liability for the Trustee.

When your mother died, the Trustee inappropriately hid and benefited from a comparatively minor asset in the distribution of the trust. (Each sibling inherited about $3,000,000.) When the siblings learned about the hidden asset a few years later, they hired an attorney and filed a lawsuit. The family members are all committed Christians, and they have agreed to go to mediation with a mediator who has a reputation for encouraging forgiveness and reconciliation. At the mediator's suggestion, two days have been reserved for the mediation, but you will only be charged for the time used. All parties are capably represented by counsel at the mediation.

After seven hours of discussion and negotiations over the Trust's finances (about 75% of which has consisted of shuttle diplomacy in caucus- at the parties' request), the parties have agreed to settle the lawsuit with the Trustee paying $135,000 to resolve all legal claims arising out of his administration of the Trust.

After a written agreement has been executed, the mediator has come into the room with you, your older brother and younger sister and your attorney and stated that the Trustee would like to continue the mediation with a focus on reconciliation of the relationship with his siblings. He is willing to either continue the meeting into the early evening or return the following day. You, your older brother, younger sister, and attorney are now talking with the mediator about this request by your younger brother.

You were angry that your brother hid behind the lawyers and your mother and didn't share the details about the trust management for most of the last 15 years. Now that your brother has had to pay for how he handled the final distribution of the trust your main concern is the family. You are concerned that both your brothers are over seventy years old and have had heart attacks in the last two years. The four siblings live in different cities within a 1000-mile radius, but you are concerned you may all never be in the same room again. You know that your parents would have wanted a family reconciliation before any of you dies. For the sake of the family, you are willing to continue discussing things with your younger brother, but you aren't going to push your older brother or sister to it, if they are resistant.

Stewing Siblings----Forgiveness Mediation Simulation

Role for Younger Sister

You are the younger sister of four siblings between the ages of 70 and 78 who accuse the youngest, a male, of mismanaging their parents' trust. The accused became the Trustee of about $12,000,000 of assets when your father died fifteen years ago. You and your older sister and older brother noticed that your younger brother's lifestyle became much more extravagant soon after he became Trustee and were suspicious that he was being over paid and using Trust assets for his personal benefit.

The attorneys and accountants for the trust advised the Trustee that his mother was the beneficiary until she died and that he should not give any information about the trust to his siblings. The Trustee complied with these instructions. You and your siblings complained to your mother, who totally supported the Trustee and threatened to disinherit any of you if you ever complained again. Your mother even made you sign a legally enforceable release of liability for the Trustee.

When your mother died, the Trustee inappropriately hid and benefited from a comparatively minor asset in the distribution of the trust. (Each sibling inherited about $3,000,000.) When the siblings learned about the hidden asset a few years later, they hired an attorney and filed a lawsuit. The family members are all committed Christians, and they have agreed to go to mediation with a mediator who has a reputation for encouraging forgiveness and reconciliation. At the mediator's suggestion, two days have been reserved for the mediation, but you will only be charged for the time used. All parties are capably represented by counsel at the mediation.

After seven hours of discussion and negotiations over the Trust's finances (about 75% of which has consisted of shuttle diplomacy in caucus- at the parties' request), the parties have agreed to settle the lawsuit with the Trustee paying $135,000 to resolve all legal claims arising out of his administration of the Trust.

After a written agreement has been executed, the mediator has come into the room with you, your older brother, older sister, and your attorney and stated that the Trustee would like to continue the mediation with a focus on reconciliation of the relationship with his siblings. He is willing to either continue the meeting into the early evening or return the following day. You, your older brother, older sister, and attorney are now talking with the mediator about this request by your younger brother.

You never married or had a family because you were so involved in international mission trips for your denomination. You were very hurt by the Trustee/younger brother's apparent opportunism. As the sibling closest to him, you completely trusted him were devastated when your oldest brother convinced you that your younger brother misspent their money. You were also angry that your brother hid behind the lawyers and your mother and didn't share the details about the trust management for most of the last 15 years. You feel like most of the bad things you believe he did as Trustee were not discussed in the mediation because of the legally enforceable release. You don't want to explore reconciliation until he accepts more responsibility for the things he did, even if he has a legally enforceable waiver. You are a deeply religious person and believe that people need to accept responsibility for their errors as part of the reconciliation process. Otherwise, we end up with "cheap grace."

A student's experience in this simulation is instructive.

> In the role play, I acted as the older sister who wanted to heal and reunite the family. My agenda was clear, and I helped the mediator a lot. At some point, I felt a little bit of animosity not toward my younger brother who was the original offender, but my eldest brother. He kept talking about how he didn't care and how we were not his close family anymore, so he'd rather go golfing. That hurt me when he said that, and I ended up getting upset with him until he finally gave in just so all of us would get off his back.

> That role play is designed for forgiveness and our mediator really pushed forgiveness. I felt a little uncomfortable and I think in a real mediation I would have thought as the older brother that it was inappropriate. <u>There is a hazy line that is hard to know if you crossed between offering forgiveness as an option and pushing it onto clients.</u>

> Your story helped address that dilemma. It was helpful to end class with a mediation story that did not end with a picture-perfect story of forgiveness. It is a skill that can work, backfire, or plant seeds. I wish there was a way that we could follow up on the parties you mediated with to see if they recovered better because of your offering of forgiveness. I am sure that it helped more parties than you know. I like this idea because it fulfills my own needs as a mediator, connecting back to a passion for peacemaking. Submitted by Emily Tanaka, emphasis added.

Endnotes

1.   Mnookin, Robert H., and Lewis Kornhauser. "Bargaining in the Shadow of the Law: The Case of Divorce." The Yale Law Journal, vol. 88, no. 5, 1979, pp. 950-997.

2. Roger Fisher & William Ury, *Getting to Yes* 40-45, (1981).

3. Kenneth Cloke, *Mediating Dangerously: The Frontiers of Conflict Resolution* 73, (2007).

4. *See id.*

5. *See id.*

6. Aristotle, "Thoughts On The Business Of Life," Forbesquotes (last visited October 1, 2018) hhttps://www.forbes.com/quotes/642/.

7. *See* Rita Milios, "Let's Talk About Diffusing Defensive Communication," Recovery.org (Oct. 16,2017)   https://www.recovery.org/pro/articles/lets-talk-about-diffusing-defensive-communication/.

8. Robert A. Baruch Bush, Joseph P. Folger, *The Promise of Mediation: The Transformative Approach to Conflict* 71-75, (2004).

9. *Id.* at 34.

10. *Id.* at 55.

11. Carrie Menkel-Meadow, *Mediation: Theory, Policy, and Practice,* (2001).

12. *See* Karyn Hall Ph.D., "Revenge: Will You Feel Better?" PSYCHOLOGYTODAY (Sep. 15, 2013) https://www.psychologytoday.com/us/blog/pieces-mind/201309/revenge-will-you-feel-better. (Finding that "[r]evenge can be a strong urge, but you may not feel better if you act on it.")

13. Tian Dayton, *The Magic of Forgiveness* 84, (2003).

14. Fred Luskin, *Forgive for Good* 111-120, (2002).

15. Cloke, *Mediating Dangerously* at 73-75.

16. *Id.* at 75.

17. *See id.*

18. *See id.*at 82, 98.

Part III

Reconciliation

Chapter 11

Defining Reconciliation

"If you start granting amnesty to people for following their conscience, pretty soon _everyone_ will be following his conscience."

CartoonStock.com

11.1   Introduction

Reconciliation is the glue that allows people to be in integrated caring communities. The context could be personal and familial, or it could be political and national. The opposite is partition and isolation which at times appears appealing. The concern is that the partition within a family or country may be an illusory solution. People who cannot learn how to live with others different from them in the first group and use partition as a solution are likely to not be able to live with the members of the new group.

This is demonstrated in recent history in Sudan. A very simplistic view is that the non-Muslims in southern Sudan did not want to be subject to the Muslim dominated government in northern Sudan. A civil war was resolved in 2005 with an agreement for a plebiscite in southern Sudan in 2011. When the time came, 98% of the citizens in southern Sudan voted to split with Sudan and create a new country of South Sudan. The new country was created in July 2011. In 2013 another civil war erupted between the two dominant tribes in South Sudan, which is unresolved as of the time of this writing, 2019.

Partition need not be a physical divide. It could be emotional boundaries or social isolation. An article by Andrew Higgins in New York Times International Edition on November 21, 2018 describes a community with invisible but clearly understood boundaries. The city of Mostar, Bosnia was the front line of the war between Muslims and Catholic Croats from 1992 until 1994. The 1995 peace agreement, reached in Dayton, Ohio, created a mixed Muslim-Croat Federation. According to Mr. Higgins, "Rupert Smith, a British general who commanded United Nations forces in Bosnia at the time of the Dayton agreement, said the American-brokered deal was never meant to be a long-term settlement but simply 'a cease-fire agreement' that mirrored and inadvertently reinforced the ethnic divisions on the ground at the time."

The result is that there is one city government for Mostar but many municipal services are duplicated and assigned to serve either the Muslim section or the Croat section of the city. Mostar has two garbage collection companies, two fire-fighting brigades, two electricity companies, two hospitals, two bus stations, and two soccer teams. These normally unified municipal services are divided so that each section of the city is served by a sub-division of that department with employees of the same identity group. For example, the fire dispatcher determines whether the call for assistance is in the Muslim or Croat section of the city and only notifies the fire brigade staffed by members of the same identity group.

While there are no visible barriers between the two communities, everyone knows where their neighborhood ends and rarely intermix. Mr. Higgins reported that some Mostar citizens worry that wartime divisions are hardening because most people know only members of their own group and do not have any shared experiences with members of the other group. For example, high school students study in the same building, but the Muslims attend at 7:30 a.m. and the Croats attend at 2 p.m.

Defining reconciliation is personal. People have different understanding of the meaning of reconciliation. This chapter will create a conceptual roadmap and language so the reader can understand a variety of definitions of reconciliation. The goal of "understanding a variety of approaches" contrasts with proposing a correct approach. While understanding a topic can be weaponized to evaluate and critique a particular execution of reconciliation, those valuations will be left to the reader.

Reconciliation describes relationships. The three aspects of relationship we will use to assess reconciliation are animus, trust/vulnerability, and future contact. These measures are like those used for forgiveness, but the reparations category is replaced by dividing future relationship into trust and contact. Animus refers to whether I wish them well or wish them harm. Trust/vulnerability asks the extent that trust has been restored and how willing I am to be vulnerable. Future contact measures my interest in connecting with the other person. The variety of combinations of these three relationship descriptors allows us to construct multiple meanings of reconciliation.

The comments of three students provide different perspectives and experiences with reconciliation.

> Reconciliation, as the final step in the overall process of apology and forgiveness is the most interesting element to me. As some people may easily be able to carry through with the apology and forgiveness process on the surface, but many will not be able to fully reconcile or move on in a relationship with the person that they feel has wronged them. This is what I have seen as a common theme in my personal experiences, with friends and family. Many are willing to apologize and "forgive" as an idea in general but are not usually as easy to reconcile with that person. …

> Differently, in my personal experiences, regarding smaller scale issues and apologies, I have noticed that many people pretend to forgive others, for whatever reason, while still holding on to their feelings of anger and disdain. <u>The reconciliation step of this process I find is the most difficult to move forward with in general for these reasons. It takes an extreme amount of grace and mercy for someone to forgive and move on, an amount in which I can honestly say that I may not have. It would take me a great deal of time and emotional strength to fully forgive and reconcile with someone who had wronged me.</u> Submitted by Kaleigh Du Vernet, emphasis added.

> I was struck by how much harder it was in this instance to be confronted than the previous week when I was able to come in to a confrontational situation. It was with a student leader in my program. We are very different in our work styles and leadership needs, and different in personality and outlook. There is also a power differential at play since I am her employer, and the staff-student dynamic.

I had decided the week before to make extra effort to get to know her better and not get hung up on things about my interactions with her that I was not pleased by. She was working, and I greeted her. I made a point to continue the conversation because of our strange dynamic. At that point I felt she became very critical and pointed in a public place in front of other students. I could sense the other students paying attention to what was happening and seeing how the interaction would go.

I was aware that I was being tested both by my student and potentially by the observing students. In the moment I decided to listen, answer without defensiveness, and ignore, for the short-term, the inappropriate nature of her conversation given the circumstance. But I also decided long-term I needed to address with her our situation more directly.

These types of scenarios can be mentally tricky for me to navigate because sometimes it's hard to tell when apology, forgiveness, and reconciliation should be in play and when they should not. I completely believe A, F, and R are not just important for moral reasons, but also because they are foundational for real relationship and for practical purposes.

People who can hold their own and others' pride and dignity with import but lightly, while still holding a healthy sense of self and boundaries seem to swim more easily in these waters than those who do not have a good sense of what is and isn't theirs to control and how seriously to take themselves and others. I can get caught up in the import without a light touch sometimes. However, I struggle with which human moments need this overt treatment and when to let time handle it. Submitted by an anonymous student, emphasis added.

The first class about reconciliation made me think about the possibility of classifying this process in terms of internal and external. I mean, sometimes the perpetrator needs first to reconcile with herself or himself before thinking about building the reconciliation process with the victim. Perhaps it is the case to think in terms of therapeutic and relational reconciliation.

I experienced an incident at the beginning of this year marked by plenty of offenses and wrongdoings during a vacation trip with friends. In the first moment, a couple of friends offended my wife and me, even after we warned them at least three times about displeasure with their bad and inadequate behavior in a card game. After the fourth or fifth misbehaving I blew out and told them some ugly truths about a few points we disapproved of in their competitive personalities.

Then I left the table, expecting that my wife would follow me, but she did not. She stayed at the table. It started a two-against-one game. I was listening to it from the bedroom, but I was so physically and emotionally devastated that I could not return. I was weak and wrong, and my wife made me see how insensitive I was in leaving her during the discussion, but it took some time for me to assimilate.

I needed some time to understand what I did and why I did that to her. I had my point because it seemed that walking away was the better choice at that moment. Later I realized that I was right in leaving because I did not want to damage the relationship even more, but I was wrong in not returning. I should have come back and supported my wife against two people that I did not recognize anymore as my oldest friends. Hours later, my friend wrote me an apology letter and apologized to my wife, but I barely could read it.

I apologized to my wife the next day when we were traveling back home, but she needed time for processing the grief.

However, I could not contact or forgive my friends for three days, because I was not ready for reconciliation. I wanted to reconcile with them, but first I needed to reconcile with myself. Part of me did not understand or accept what I did. Only after I rebuilt the facts and talked about them with my wife, could I think of an explanation – not a justification – for my acts. After I reconciled with myself, I forgave him.

One does not need an apology offer to forgive. True. However, in reconciliation, there will be sometimes when you will need to be at peace with yourself before starting a reconciliation process with either the victim or the perpetrator. Therefore, with all the respect, I suggest an approach to the types of reconciliation we could have. I learned different types of apology and forgiveness, and I wonder if there is only one type of reconciliation. Submitted by Fernando Hoffman, emphasis added.

11.2   Gradations of Relationship

Some people use a binary approach to reconciliation. If you have reconciled then you wish the other person well, trust/vulnerability have been restored, and you are interested in spending time with the other person. If any of those measures are lacking, you have not reconciled. Reconciliation is either accomplished or not, like a light bulb being either on or off. The contrast is to construct a continuum of meanings for reconciliation that measures various dimensions of relationship. It is like installing a dimmer switch for the light bulb so that the light can provide various degrees of brightness.

I experienced these competing approaches to reconciliation as the Director of the Christian Conciliation Service (CCS) of Los Angeles, a faith-based mediation program. The leaders of about thirty CCS chapters met annually to discuss policy and technique. Each chapter had an independent board of directors and could establish the policies for that chapter. One of the contentious issues we wrestled with was whether we should mediate between Christians seeking a divorce.

Because the Christian sacred text instructs Christians to not divorce, some CCS chapters had policies that allowed them to mediate only if both parties were seeking reconciliation, meaning the continuation of the marriage. Some of the chapters had policies that allowed them to mediate if one of the parties was seeking to continue the marriage and the mediation services would only address that issue. (Many of the programs with the above policies had exceptions that offered assistance in situations of domestic abuse.) The construct was that the parties' shared religious beliefs called them to reconciliation and obedience required them to continue the marriage.

The program I directed took a different approach. My board and I viewed reconciliation as a measure of love and kindness in a relationship. At full strength, the marriage would continue. But we believed we were advancing reconciliation when we assisted people who were hurt, angry, and hostile by encouraging them to move toward love and kindness. We were satisfied with assisting people to disengage with kindness. We informed our clients that our approach to mediation would encourage reconciliation, but that did not necessitate that the marriage would need to continue. They would be free to decide the extent of their future relationship, and we would be encouraging them to be kind and loving to each other in and after the process if they decide to separate.

As we attempt to assess the quality of relationships, can we imagine a situation where a relationship will continue, but one or both parties feel the need to be cautious. A party may conclude that they want to restore the relationship, but on qualified terms. They may decide that it is unwise for them to be fully trusting and vulnerable in one or more areas like money, time, honesty, or confidences. They want to resume the relationship, but with some boundaries. These types of qualifications will not meet a purist's definition of reconciliation, but our discussion will treat it as a type of reconciliation.

The continuum of the combination of relationship markers (animus, trust/vulnerability, and future contact) from closest to most estranged is:

1. <u>I wish you well</u>

   Trust and vulnerability are restored
   I am eager for future contact

2. <u>I wish you well</u>

   Trust and vulnerability are restored
   I am NOT interested in future contact

3. <u>I wish you well</u>

   Trust and vulnerability are NOT restored
   I am interested in future contact, but will be cautious and have some boundaries

4. <u>I wish you well</u>

   Trust and vulnerability are NOT restored
   I am NOT interested in future contact

5. <u>I DON'T wish you well, but DON'T wish you harm</u>

   Trust and vulnerability are NOT restored
   I am NOT interested in future contact

6. <u>I wish you harm</u>

An illustration will help clarify the differences. Imagine an employer who has confronted an employee who lied on expense reimbursement statements. Depending on the employee's response and the personality of the employer the possible outcomes of the confrontation related to the descriptions numbers one to six above are:

1. <u>The employer has no hard feelings against the employee.</u>

   The employer trusts and is vulnerable to the employee again.
   The employer retains the employee without any limitations regarding future expense statements.

2. <u>Same as 1 above, but the employer decides it is best for the employee to find work elsewhere and will give a good reference.</u>

   (A legitimate question is why the employer doesn't want to have a future relationship if they have restored trust and vulnerability. I agree with the question but also have observed this approach to reconciliation. I believe it is possible to trust again, but not feel the need to be connected.)

3. <u>The employer has no hard feelings against the employee.</u>

   The employer does not trust and will not be vulnerable to the employee.
   The employer retains the employee with limitations regarding future expense statements and other financial dealings with the company.

4. <u>The employer has no hard feelings against the employee.</u>

   Trust is NOT restored, and the employee will NOT work for the company.

5. <u>The employer has neither hard nor good feelings about the employee.</u>

   Trust is NOT restored, and the employee will NOT work for the company.

6. <u>The employer wishes the employee harm.</u>

   Trust is NOT restored, and the employee will NOT work for the company.

Two students shared their perspectives in journals.

> I had a misunderstanding with a friend that led us to not speak to each other for four years. Applying the ideas of apology, forgiveness, and reconciliation, there was no apology from either side. In my part, I forgave within the idea of therapeutic forgiveness since we have not spoken since. However, I cannot honestly say that we have reconciled. … I believe that to reach reconciliation there must be a reconnection.
>
> From my point of view, my friend and I would reach reconciliation if we started to talk again and started reestablishing a connection. Nevertheless, <u>I don't wish him harm and do which him well. But for me, this is forgiveness. … There can only be reconciliation with connection or reconnection.</u> Submitted by Fabio Franco, emphasis added.

> It seems impossible this can happen when I feel wronged. It feels impossible when I have wronged others. So how can it be possible for people from war-torn countries ever to reconcile with their violent pasts? Perhaps reconciliation is the piece of hope that God gives humanity when pain and suffering occurs. Reconciliation, in theory sounds beautiful and in reality, also displays such magnificent beauty. One human soul asks for repentance … another soul gives forgiveness and overcomes unimaginable pain by healing.

Reconciliation is the marriage of the apology and forgiveness material we have covered in class. I am excited to see the synthesis of these two topics and learn the nuances of reconciliation. <u>I do not believe that reconciliation happens, or it doesn't. There seems to be a considerable factor of where trust comes into the picture of reconciliation. Trust takes time to rebuild.</u> For some cases it can take an entire lifetime to restore trust. When the perpetrator issues a remorse apology and the victims heal through relational forgiveness, an intimate reconciliation occurs. Submitted by Nina Sprenger, emphasis added.

This spectrum describes the levels of commitment to the relationship by one person. Reconciliation involves two parties, so it may be helpful to consider how this relationship continuum applies to both parties in a matrix format.

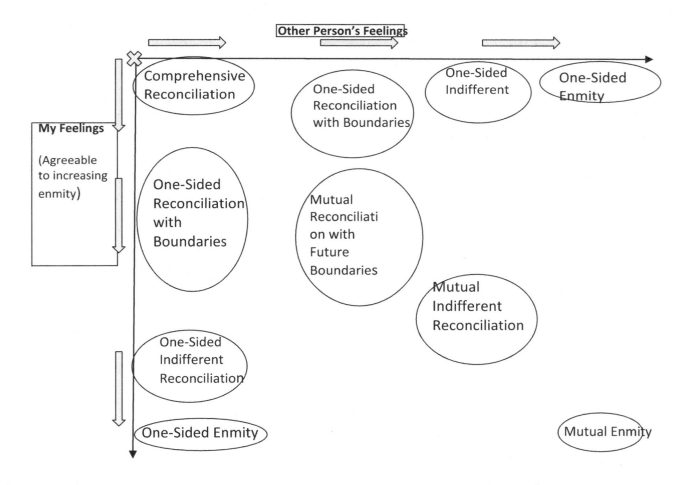

The chart provides a picture of the various combinations of both parties' feelings. Many would argue that reconciliation has not been accomplished if one or both parties are guarded or indifferent towards the other. I suggest that whatever state the parties' relationship is in, if it is an improvement from prior states, they have accomplished a measure of reconciliation.

Also note that this model could suggest that a measure of reconciliation is accomplished when one of the parties abandons enmity and move towards love. The other party may not be ready, but when one side adopts a posture of wishing the other well, restoring trust in the other, and desiring future relationship, a type of reconciliation has been accomplished. I understand the scrutiny about this "one-sided reconciliation," but remember that this person is reconciled in his heart regardless of the other party's feelings.

This one-sided reconciliation is when a person is at peace with herself and the other, regardless of whether this is communicated or reciprocated. One-sided reconciliation could be viewed as another name for forgiveness. If so, the chart's middle corridor from enmity to reconciliation could be viewed as the reconciliation continuum. A student shared experiences that illustrate some of these dynamics.

> For my final journal, I thought It would be appropriate to reflect upon the impact that this class has had on me. First, at the beginning of the semester when we were learning about apology, it prompted me to seek forgiveness and reconciliation from a couple of people to whom I had not been a very good friend. I believe that the Lord had been nudging me for a while to contact these people, but it wasn't until I started studying for this class that I followed through on re-connecting with them.
>
> Unfortunately, the former friends who I contacted and with whom I hoped friendships would be renewed did not reciprocate my feelings. One had no interest in re-connecting and would not tell me if/what I had done to offend her, thus robbing me of an opportunity to genuinely apologize. The other person wrote to me telling me that he forgave me, but everything about his short, terse email indicated to me that there was not true forgiveness behind those words. I gathered that his response of "forgiveness" may have come from a sense of obligation, not of true forgiveness.
>
> <u>I was surprised and discouraged by these interactions because I had assumed that my attempt to apologize for my inadequacies as a friend and reconcile our relationships would be welcomed. I learned that reconciliation is a two-way street, requiring that *both* people *want* to reconcile.</u> I also learned that when forgiveness is seemingly withheld from me after I offend someone and seek their forgiveness, I must in turn forgive that person for refusing to extend the same grace and forgiveness that I believe I would offer to her if the table was turned. Submitted by Alyssa Ayotte, emphasis added.

11.3   Apology and Forgiveness as Building Blocks

A different approach to reconciliation is to view apology and forgiveness as the building blocks of reconciliation. This book has largely presented apology and forgiveness as unilateral acts, meaning that they can be exercised independent of another person. They are not reconciliation because a perpetrator's apology may not be accepted. Some approaches to forgiveness can be practiced by the victim without any involvement of the perpetrator. This model defines reconciliation as when the stars align so that the perpetrator apologizes, and the victim forgives.

The deconstruction of this simple model provides a way to understand the variety of outcomes.

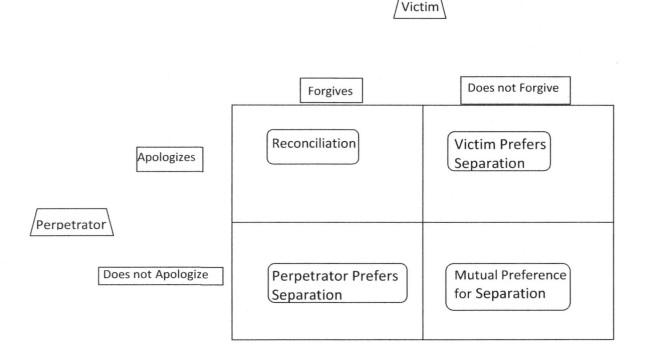

The observations of two students reveal their views about these concepts.

In my opinion, <u>reconciliation is the next step of forgiveness, but reconciliation cannot happen without forgiveness. Reconciliation is something not easy and not everyone can do it because you need to make yourself able to forgive and to live with this person without hating him or her.</u> My religion, Islam, always encourages people to reconcile and Quran mentioned that people cannot live together without reconciliation because they are like a body and if the body has a problem, all the body will suffer for it.

Also, reconciliation is important in my country. There are many stories about reconciliation because all the society back home (Saudi Arabia) are taking care of it because tribes is the first thing. Without reconciliation we will lose everything. Submitted by Abduallah Sulaiman Alluhaydan, emphasis added.

When we started to talk about reconciliation, I realized that the class has come full circle. Reconciliation seems to build upon concepts from apology and forgiveness. I liked the section from the book that described apology and forgiveness as building blocks to reconciliation. Reconciliation is ultimately what happens at the crossroads of forgiveness and apology: when there is an apology and forgiveness, you get reconciliation.

To me, reconciliation also seems to be another step in the healing process. Additionally, when forgiving, you are now moving into an area where you repair a relationship. Essentially, instead of healing yourself, you are now in the process of healing that relationship with another person. This type of healing is important because typically in these cases you reconcile with people that you care about ….

Last class we talked about partition in the world on a national and international scale. It was interesting to discuss separation in the world, how that affects people, and brainstorm on how to fix the world's problems. The we shifted to a more personal note: partition in your own life. Separation between family, friends, and the people you care about. It got me to think about the partitions in my life and how they have been removed or if they stay standing. It reminded me of a time back in high school when I first decided to reconcile with someone.

One of my best friends had said some unkind words to me one day, which completely upset me. After that incident, I made up my mind that I would not forgive her or be friends with her anymore. For two weeks I avoided her and did not speak with her. We shared the same friend-group, and everyone knew we were not talking. We would be at the same places together with the same people and I would not speak to her at all.

Looking back as a 23-year-old this is ridiculous, but for 14-year-old me, it made perfect sense. One day after a group project meeting, Christina came up to me and asked if we could talk and I obliged. She was upset that we were no longer talking and wanted to be friends again; she issued what I can now describe as a remorse apology and I accepted.

Even though I readily accepted her apology, it took a few more days for me to truly forgive her and an additional week for us to actually reconcile. We did not reconcile until we went to compete with our fellow teammates at a science bowl competition. On the ride to the competition we sat together and talked. I was reminded why we became friends in the first place and how nice it was to spend time together again. After that we were friends again and I no longer held on to the pain of the incident or thoughts of revenge.

I did not know it at the time, but that was an introduction to reconciliation for me. I knew how to forgive others because of my upbringing, religion, and moral code, but I had never considered the reconciliation part or the importance of reconciliation until that incident. Now that I am older, I understand the importance of reconciliating with others if they are truly important to you. While the incident that caused the partition and the pain you have towards the perpetrator is valid, life is too short and precious not to make amends with people who are meaningful in your life. I have learned that again and again since that day in high school. Reconciliation is hard, but I think it is important. Submitted by Jenieva Abner, emphasis added.

Using the apology and forgiveness building blocks allows an analysis of how various approaches to apology and forgiveness impact the resulting reconciliation. The reconciliation will be different if the perpetrator delivers a remorse apology compared to a social harmony apology. Likewise, the reconciliation will be different if the victim's approach to forgiveness is therapeutic compared to relational.

The matrix for various kinds of reconciliation is:

Victim

Perpetrator		Relational Forgiveness	Therapeutic Forgiveness	Redemptive Forgiveness
	Remorse/Regret Apology	Intimate Reconciliation	Perp Initiated Partial Reconciliation	Perp Initiated Pragmatic Reconciliation
	Social Harmony Apology	Vic Initiated Partial Reconciliation	Mutually Convenient Reconciliation	Relationally Superficial Reconciliation
	Externally Motivated Apology	Vic Initiated Pragmatic Reconciliation	Mutually Self-Serving Reconciliation	Mutual Ulterior Motives Reconciliation

I grouped the remorse and regret apologies together because the conversation about why the perpetrator does not condemn his own behavior can lead to an improved relationship where both parties are more honest about who they are and their beliefs. The victim knows what to expect in the future due to the open communication. A student's journal reminds us about a perpetrator's potential resistance to apologizing and reconciliation.

> I was especially interested in the discussion on being estranged from family. It was nice to hear about a personal story from the professor where he may have acted questionably. It's always an eye opener when something big happens in your life … an event that marks you for some reason or another …. When you take a step back and look on it… it all seems so insignificant. I just think it's crazy that you wouldn't apologize to your aunt!

It kind of reminds me of what I do sometimes though. Sometimes, I get so stuck in the "I'm right" mode that I refuse to think in any other way. I usually rationalize it to myself and blame it on the other person as well. Making them seem like the bad person for trying to make ME apologize when I didn't do anything wrong. I've learned that sometimes when you think you didn't do anything wrong … no matter how strongly you feel about that … other people might not agree.

When they don't agree, you have to make a decision. If you feel that you're right, and they feel that you owe them an apology, you either need to try to find some empathy and see if you can step into their shoes for a minute or if you're so stubborn that you can't do that-you'll need to give up the relationship. …

I don't think you have to be reconciled with everyone on the planet, but I do think some relationships are worth saving. If it's something you are reminded of often (like a relationship with a relative), you should probably consider reconciling. Or at least expressing that you did not mean to hurt anyone's feelings. I had to do that recently … and it was not easy. … So, I apologized. But now that I think about that, I'm still pretty bitter over that interaction. Maybe it wasn't the right thing to do. Submitted by Monica Ryan, emphasis added.

Scott Peck's description of the evolution of relationships helps explain why I view the regret apology as possibly resulting in an intimate reconciliation.[1] Scott describes how relationships start out superficial, with participants conforming to expectations.[2] People correctly assess what others expect and behave accordingly. For example, early in dating relationships, parties are considerate, kind, and sensitive. The relational dynamics are wonderful, but unrealistic.

Peck says that the second stage is chaos.[3] Chaos occurs when one person is more honest about who they really are, including the ways they do not conform to expectations. The other person in the relationship objects and tries to get the first person to conform to the original expectations. The second person likes the relationship better when the first person tries to please, even when that means he is not his true self. In dating relationships this is when one or both people makes less of an effort to please. Always putting your best foot forward is a lot of work and can be exhausting. Either person begins to relax and not make as much of an effort. Chaos describes the conflict that occurs when one person confronts another about not conforming to expectations.[4]

Peck uses the label of emptiness to describe the third stage of relationship when people give up their demands that others live up to their expectations.[5] The participants are free to be who they really are, not who they need to pretend to be to gain acceptance. The other(s) in the relationship accept them for who they really are without trying to change them. Peck says that when relationships are in this state, the fourth stage of relationship has been accomplished, authentic community.[6] Participants are honest about who they are and what they believe and are accepted. The regret apology can lead to this kind of relationship because it provides an opportunity for dialogue about each party's needs, values, and beliefs.

A student's journal illustrates many of these concepts.

> Your book showed that forgiveness and apology can be unilateral acts, "meaning that they can be exercised independent of another person." On the other hand, the reconciliation between the offender and the victim will not be possible without the participation of both. In that sense, I understand that the reconciliation will depend on the intention of the parties to have a close relationship in the future. Without this motivation or even necessity of having a future coexistence between the parties, the reconciliation will be superficial, and the relationship may disappear naturally over time.
>
> Therefore, I understand that when the remorse apology matches a relational forgiveness, the relationship will be healed, and this overcoming can make the connection between the parties stronger and healthier than it was before. The parties might have a chance to test, voluntarily or not, the limits and barriers of each other and the respect between them can increase later if the reconciliation is reached. This is a tremendous incentive to seek reconciliation in my life or recommend a client to seek reconciliation. Nevertheless, I believe that most of the people, including myself, do not realize the possible outcomes from the reconciliation and prefer to stay in a conflict cycle for years.
>
> I have to confess that my relationship with my father was STUCK in this kind of cycle for more than twenty years. Finally, I realized that I was suffering much more than I should because of his lack of interest. I realized that my father could not offer me or my family more than what he had done. On the other hand, it would be easier for me to overcome this barrier and have a respectable relationship in the following years.
>
> It was a kind of therapeutic forgiveness, I must confess, in a superficial reconciliation. At least, it brings me peace and mitigates any guilt that used to come to my mind when I felt some regret about this cold and distant relationship. In that sense, this kind of reconciliation could be considered more than superficial. It could be considered a therapeutic reconciliation because, in my case, it reconciled my internal conflicts and improved the interaction with my father. To sum up, it reconciled my thoughts and feelings in favor of having a healthy relationship with him and, indirectly, CATCH his empathy about me or about our relationship (I believe!).
>
> The matrix in your book showed this kind of interconnection between apology and forgiveness that is totally linked with the possibility or necessity of having a future relationship. How important is the perpetrator in my life? Can I live without the presence of this person for the rest of my life or not? In my personal example, it was ABSOLUTELY necessary to find a better way to deal with my fears and resentments against my father. It makes me feel better. But there are situations where the coexistence is not a matter of choice but something almost mandatory.

In a divorce, the parents will remain connected to resolve questions related to the children's lives. Thus, I was wondering if it could be possible to build another kind of reconciliation. I mean a reconciliation for a common purpose like a reconciliation between former spouses that may want to remain divorced forever. Then, considering the concepts in your book, I realized that this kind of reconciliation is possible because it could be a combination of an externally motivated apology and therapeutic forgiveness. In that sense, the parents will be healing their relationship with the mutual interest of making the kids' lives better. Submitted by an anonymous student, emphasis added.

11.4   Donald Shriver's "Mutual Remembering" Model

Donald Shriver describes an approach to reconciliation titled and based on "Mutual Remembering."[7] The context of his work is the reconstruction of post genocidal communities.[8] The reader will need to assess the extent his principles are instructive for interpersonal reconciliation. One of his maxims is that people must do something with a painful past to have/create a new future.[9] He breaks down steps and missteps towards reconciliation and how they affect the perpetrator and the victim.[10]

Shriver's first observation is that perpetrators sometimes suggest that we forget the past and move forward; perpetrators refuse to remember or acknowledge the injury because it is too hard for them to accept that they committed offensive behavior.[11] While this is more comfortable for the perpetrator, it leaves the victim to "stew in their memories."[12] The victim remembers and the unwillingness of the perpetrator to recognize and remember their offense is a second injury. This scenario is the basis for his theme that "mutual remembering" is integral to reconciliation.

Mutual remembering requires both parties to abandon something.[13] Perpetrators must abandon "professions of innocence" and victims must abandon the desire for revenge.[14] These are difficult for each of them to do because victims are entitled to pay back the wrong and it is difficult for the perpetrator to include their bad behavior in their self-image. These abandonments may occur independent of the other, or they may be interrelated.[15]

While Shriver first describes a dynamic of mutual relinquishing things (professions of innocence and revenge), he follows with a description of a mutual positive exchange: apology for forgiveness.[16] The perpetrator gives the victim an acknowledgement of the wrong in exchange for the victim's promise of forgiveness.[17]

The apology-forgiveness exchange is based on the principle Shriver describes as, "The truth about the past can be more important than punishment for the past."[18] This principle may not be universal but may be often true in Shriver's context of the healing of post genocidal communities. It is the basis for the more than 250 Truth and Reconciliation Commissions around the world that have advanced healing after community wide offenses.[19]

A student's journal applies this concept to interpersonal relationships.

> We had an interesting conversation in class this week about the value of telling the truth. Sometimes telling the truth is a substitute for an apology. When I was a child my parents always emphasized the importance of telling the truth. To teach me that my dad would always tell me that he would not be mad at me if I had done something wrong if I just told the truth about it. In contrast, if I did not tell the truth and he later found out about it, the punishment would be worse than had I told the truth. I was taught that forgiveness came easier when I was honest, and the punishment was less severe.
>
> I was thinking about why hearing our perpetrators admit the truth is so important, sometimes more so than wanting to hear them apologize. I think it is because hearing the truth gives us validation and closure. It allows the victim to feel a sense of relief and move on.
>
> <u>I know that my parents proposed a trade of amnesty for telling the truth because they wanted to teach me right from wrong. But why do people in non-parent-child relationships propose this trade? I think that some people might just place a higher value on hearing the truth. Maybe they do not even want to hear an apology.</u>
>
> When you have been lied to or deceived, some people experience a sense of feeling stupid or naïve. When the victim hears the truth, this helps eliminate any of these feelings because you feel like you are now fully aware of the situation and not being misled. Maybe the victim is not able to give them complete amnesty in exchange for the truth, but the victim will at the very least appreciate that the perpetrator had the decency to give them the truth. Submitted by Caitlyn Peskind, emphasis added.

The most common approach for Truth and Reconciliation Commissions is truth for amnesty.[20] The point is that simply documenting the truth can be very meaningful for victims whose story has been omitted by historians; some victims are willing to forgo punishment to establish the truth. But the thoughtful student of apology should be concerned because an offer of reparations is usually an important component of an apology. Truth for amnesty violates the offer of reparations aspect of apology.

Another concern is whether confessing the truth is an apology? Is the admission of bad behavior accompanied by remorse, regret, or is it a social harmony or externally motivated type of apology? Shriver's description of a "mutual exchange" of apology for forgiveness should cause concern about the external rewards (forgiveness or amnesty) for the apology.

The goal of Shriver's approach is to generate mutual empathy between the parties.[21] The easier aspect is that mutual remembering will cause the perpetrator to have empathy for the victim.[22] The harder aspect is that mutual remembering will create empathy in the victim for the perpetrator. For the victim to have empathy for the perpetrator is such a significant dimension of reconciliation that it will be a primary focus in the next chapter.

Shriver's goal for mutual empathy is to restore both party's humanity.[23] The perpetrator sees the victim as human and realizes he has treated another person as less than a human. The victim sees the perpetrator as human despite her bad behavior and resists the temptation to retaliate in such a way that treats her as less than human.

My summary of the key points to Shriver's Mutual Remembering Model is provided in the following chart.

Action	Perpetrator	Victim
Forget or ignore the harm	More comfortable	Left to stew in their memories
Refuse to remember/ acknowledge	Too Hard.	A 2nd injury

The parties must do something with a painful past in order to have/create a new future

Abandon	Professions of innocence (An impulse to ignore the moral truth about the past)	Revenge.
Why Hard.	**Must include the dark side in their self-image.**	**Entitled to Revenge**
Mutual Exchange	Apology- Acknowledge the wrong.	Forgiveness Reconstruct memory of the other people.

Sometimes this takes the form of Truth and Reconciliation Process where truth is given in exchange for amnesty.
- **The truth about the past is more important than punishment.**
- **In war (conflict) we tend to denigrate the humanity of the other, making it easy to harm them.**

Result Empathy restores both sides' humanity.	Empathy for victims	Empathy for perpetrator -Accept evildoers as normal humans/ not monsters. We are all capable of evil.

Endnotes

1. *See* Scott Peck, *The Different Drum* 172, (1987).

2. *See id.* at 25.

3. *See id.* at 90-102.

4. *See id.* at 97-102.

5. *Id.* at 94-102.

6. *See id.*

7. Raymond G. Helmick, Rodney Petersen, *Forgiveness & Reconciliation: Public Policy & Conflict Transformation* 154, (2001).

8. *See id.* at 220.

9. *Id.* at 313.

10. *See generally* Raymond G. Helmick, Rodney Petersen, *Forgiveness & Reconciliation: Public Policy & Conflict Transformation.*

11. *See id.* at 155.

12. *Id.* at 154.

13. *See id.* at 153-54.

14. *Id.* at 156.

15. *See id.* at 154-65.

16. *See id.* at 178-79.

17. See *id.*

18. *Id.* at 159.

19. Bishnu Pathak, "A Comparative Study of World's Truth Commissions—From Madness to Hope," PCDNETWORK.ORG (June 29, 2017) https://pcdnetwork.org/wp-content/uploads/2017/06/Worlds-Truth-Commissions-published-on-June-29-2017.pdf.

20. *See id.* at 195.

21. *See* Raymond G. Helmick, Rodney Petersen, *Forgiveness & Reconciliation: Public Policy & Conflict Transformation*, 163, 218.

22. *See id.* at 313.

23. *See id.* at 163, 218.

Chapter Twelve

How to Reconcile

12.1 Introduction

Shriver's challenge for victims to have empathy for their perpetrators is radical.[1] The challenge to "love your enemies" is usually reserved for a theological context and recognized as an extraordinary (extra-human) response.[2] It is critical to carefully explore this aspect of reconciliation.

It is imperative to be clear that having empathy for the perpetrator does not mean to condone the bad behavior or excuse the bad actor. The authorities in the field agree that healthy forgiveness and reconciliation are honest about what occurred, that it was a violation of appropriate conduct, and that the perpetrator needs to take responsibility for his actions.[3]

Therefore, the suggestion that the victim have empathy for the perpetrator asks the victim to condemn the bad behavior and expect consequences for the bad actor while also resisting the temptation to villainize the perpetrator. Villainizing the perpetrator consists of seeing her as less than human, as a monster, antisocial, having no conscience, or as evil. Dehumanizing the perpetrator as a villain allows us to distance ourselves from them as opposed to moving towards them to reconcile. We don't want or need to reconcile with a monster. It is the recognition of his humanity, despite his wrongdoing, that compels us to value him and maybe reconcile.

The maxim "hate the sin, love the sinner" applies, but is it too simple? It is helpful because it separates the person from his actions allowing us to condemn one and embrace the other. Is there a more complicated paradigm that allows us to also condemn the person for acting badly *from a place of caring and wanting* the best for that person?

This is what parents do when they seek to rebuke and discipline children with a goal of character development. Some parents train a child to take responsibility for the bad act and assist the child in understanding that they acted selfishly because their heart is selfish. Some parenting programs encourage parents to focus on the heart of the child and not the symptomatic behavior. [4] Otherwise, the child might construct an understanding that he is not responsible for his behavior. The challenge is how to condemn the bad behavior and person who committed it, while assuring the perpetrator that they are loved and accepted in this relationship.

This chapter explores the foundational concepts supporting victims having empathy for perpetrators. A student's thoughts at this point in the class set the stage.

> In class we discussed reconciliation, the beginning of our final section for the class! The section of the chapter I found most interesting was the Donald Shriver's "Mutual Remembering" Model. When I first read this section and discussed it in class, I thought it was a great idea. Through emphasis on the truth, one can show a perpetrator's humanity and the victim can receive long-awaited answers/explanations. However, <u>the concerns present deep issues with this model that must be addressed in order for it to be a workable solution. It undermines an apology if it is extracted with the promise of amnesty. However, truth without apology could reopen or cut wounds deeper. …</u>

If the concerns were addressed, I think Shriver's model could be a good method of mediation on the ground in Cyprus. Both sides are victims and perpetrators. Thus, each side understanding their own wrongdoings and abandoning revenge would create a much more unified body. Turkish and Greek Cypriots would hopefully see their own identity change, as they are both victims and perpetrators in one body. ...

The film brought me back to a theme in forgiveness and reconciliation: seeing the humanity in the perpetrator. We are all perpetrators in some sense, by the sin of omission or commission. The film brings to light many issues inherent in the human psyche. Just as we are all capable of committing crimes or ignoring them, we are capable of forgiving them. We are capable of understanding the situation and perspective of others, thus we can consciously reconcile. Submitted by Emily Tanaka, emphasis added.

12.2   Complicating Identity

In *Difficult Conversations: How to Discuss what Matters Most* by Douglas Stone, Sheila Heen, and Bruce Patton, one of the levels of meaning in a conflict conversation is the message about a person's identity.[5] Am I being accused of being inconsiderate, insensitive, a thief, a liar, a poor leader, or worst? This triggers a defense mechanism for most people who deny the accusation, which escalates the conflict.

Difficult Conversations suggests complicating your identity.[6] Instead of seeing yourself as completely honest, capable, and sensitive, adjust your view of yourself to include some deficits. You can continue to believe that you are usually virtuous but allow that sometimes you do not live up to those standards. Now when someone launches an attack at you, you don't need to circle the wagons and offer a defense. You can acknowledge that sometimes you act that way as well, and a more productive conversation can follow.

This concept was described in the apology section of the book to enable a perpetrator to admit to himself that he has acted badly.[7] I resurface this concept here because it may assist the victim to the have empathy for the perpetrator if the victim accepts that everyone is complex. Nobody is virtuous all the time, and it may help the victim to have empathy for the perpetrator whose deficits were exposed. The perpetrator may be embarrassed and ashamed because his reputation has taken a hit by those who know about the violation.

Seeing the perpetrator as a complex person who is sometimes virtuous and sometimes offensive allows the victim to condemn the bad behavior and character failing of the perpetrator. He is not always offensive. He is like the victim with good and bad moments and characteristics. The victim can empathize with the shared humanity that we all have including moments our mothers would be proud of and other moments which would cause our mothers to be ashamed. Villainizing the perpetrator allows me to believe I am not like her. Complicating both of our identities confronts me with a fuller picture of both myself and the other person.

A student's journal describes the internal resistance to empathizing with some perpetrators.

> Almost every class I go to kind of wrecks me. The content of this course is really heavy for me, and it is opening a lot of doors for deeper philosophical thought. I know I have a tendency to really read into things, and maybe this is just another one of those times, but our first class on reconciliation was really thought provoking. It made me question a lot of things I had previously been so secure about.
>
> I used to be confident in my beliefs in the power of reconciliation, and that everyone deserved the chance for forgiveness and reconciliation. From an ideological standpoint, based on my religious perspective, I still find this to be a theoretical truth, but now I am questioning the realistic possibility beyond divine intervention. There are some people in the world, that beyond divine power, may never find reconciliation. Honestly, there is a large part of me that doesn't want some of the people we discussed in this class to be reconciled. It makes forgiveness and reconciliation seem really cheap to me. No matter what you have done, or whom you have hurt, God has the power to reconcile you.
>
> Specifically, the people we watched in the movie are the most challenging areas to think about. The serial killer who harmed and murdered young boys was seeking reconciliation and forgiveness. I know God has the power to forgive him, but it seems so unfair. We discussed in class today that to work in reconciliation you have to look at the face of evil and then decide how everyone is going to move past it. ...
>
> To reconcile, we have to humanize the victim and the offender. When it comes to some of the really deep pain caused by violent actions, I want to dehumanize the offender, so I am not associated with their actions. If I can label what they are doing as not human, then I can try and convince myself that people I love, and my own humanity does not have the capability to do such horrible things.
>
> The human race is insatiably selfish, and of course when reconciling another person's pain, I somehow connect it back to myself. However, given that anecdote, I do not want my humanity ever associated with such horrible pain. I would rather write them off as unhuman animals, than try to accept that this could be a facet of human nature. Submitted by an anonymous student, emphasis added.

12.3   Complicating the Narrative

In the relational forgiveness section of the book, we discussed how telling a more complicated story enables a victim to avoid one-up or one-way forgiveness.[8] Telling a more complicated story may also help a victim have empathy for the perpetrator.

The simplistic story conveniently focuses on the ways the perpetrator harmed the victim without consideration of mitigating circumstances. Mitigating circumstances include: expanding the timeline of the incident to better understand the context; explaining the objective the perpetrator was trying to accomplish when he was offensive; considering the perpetrator's background, history, and how he learned the offensive behavior; and whether he has been a victim of the offensive behavior earlier in his life.

A student's journal provides a personal experience with this concept.

> ...Then lastly, we need to have empathy for the other side. Whether we are the "perpetrator" or the "victim" we need to look at the situation from their perspective and empathize with them. These strategies will do wonders for beginning and facilitating the process of reconciliation.
>
> I have seen the power of these processes help to heal relationships in my family. My mother's father divorced my grandmother when my mom was very young, and he sort of abandoned my mom and her siblings (from what I have been told.) As the oldest sibling, my mother pretty much had to raise her brother and sister. When she met my dad around 18 years old, she took the first chance to move out and start her own life.
>
> My mom's relationship with my grandpa was very strained because she felt abandoned by him and left to take care of her fatherless siblings. My aunt and uncle felt abandoned by my mom when she moved out at 18. There was a whole chain of messy events that played into the broken relationships of my family. But as they aged more and more, they began to start having conversations toward reconciliation. There were a lot of questions asked through tears and frustrations over the phone. The relationships are still far from perfect, but they are much better than before.
>
> <u>My mom still sees her father as selfish, but she has more empathy for him because his father was the same way.</u> My mom has spoken to siblings to explain her behavior and try to heal those relationships. It's still an ongoing process. But they always keep their love for each other at the center of each of those conversations and throughout this long process toward restoration. Submitted by an anonymous student, emphasis added.

Another category of mitigating circumstance inquires whether and how the victim contributed to or could have de-escalated the situation. This is dangerous because there are times when someone is a pure victim and should not accept any responsibility for the perpetrator's offense; thus, acceptance of any of the blame would be unjust. But this danger should not prevent us from considering many situations where both parties are both perpetrators and victims in an escalating conflict cycle.

Consideration of mitigating circumstances should not be used to condone or excuse the offensive behavior or the perpetrator's responsibility for his actions. Both must be condemned, but the mitigating factors help the victim to understand reasons behind the bad behavior. This enhanced understanding might cause the victim to have compassion for the perpetrator while condemning the act and expecting the actor to take responsibility for his actions.

12.4 Situational Evil

Another intertwined concept that might help victims have empathy for perpetrators is called situational evil. The concept is that people are affected by their environment, the roles they are expected to fill, and how they have been conditioned to behave certain ways. The punch line is that all of us are capable of evil given the right circumstances.[9]

A well-known documentation of this phenomenon is the Stanford Prison Project conducted by Stanford psychology professor Philip G. Zimbardo.[10] He advertised in the local newspaper for volunteers to receive a stipend to participate in a two week study of prison life.[11] He screened the volunteers to make sure they did not have any criminal history and were psychologically well adjusted and assigned some of the volunteers to serve as guards in a makeshift prison in the basement of building on Stanford's campus.[12] The other students were assigned to serve as prisoners.

Here is a summary of the rest of the experiment in the words of Professor Zimbardo:

> Our study of prison life began, then, with an average group of healthy, intelligent, middle-class males. These boys were arbitrarily divided into two groups by a flip of the coin. Half were randomly assigned to be guards, the other to be prisoners. It is important to remember that at the beginning of our experiment there were no differences between boys assigned to be a prisoner and boys assigned to be a guard.

> To help us closely simulate a prison environment, we called upon the services of experienced consultants. An intercom system allowed us to secretly bug the cells to monitor what the prisoners discussed, and also to make public announcements to the prisoners.

> Blindfolded and in a state of mild shock over their surprise arrest by the city police, our prisoners were put into a car and driven to the "Stanford County Jail" for further processing.

> Each prisoner was systematically searched and stripped naked. He was then deloused with a spray, to convey our belief that he may have germs or lice.

> A degradation procedure was designed in part to humiliate prisoners and in part to be sure they weren't bringing in any germs to contaminate our jail.

The prisoner was then issued a uniform. The main part of this uniform was a dress, or smock, which each prisoner wore at all times with no underclothes. On the smock, in front and in back, was his prison ID number. On each prisoner's right ankle was a heavy chain, bolted on and worn at all times. Rubber sandals were the footwear, and each prisoner covered his hair with a stocking cap made from a woman's nylon stocking.

The use of ID numbers was a way to make prisoners feel anonymous. Each prisoner had to be called only by his ID number and could only refer to himself and the other prisoners by number.

The guards were given no specific training on how to be guards. Instead they were free, within limits, to do whatever they thought was necessary to maintain law and order in the prison and to command the respect of the prisoners. The guards made up their own set of rules, which they then carried into effect under the supervision of Warden David Jaffe, an undergraduate from Stanford University.

As with real prisoners, our prisoners expected some harassment, to have their privacy and some of their other civil rights violated while they were in prison, and to get a minimally adequate diet – all part of their informed consent agreement when they volunteered.

All guards were dressed in identical uniforms of khaki, and they carried a whistle around their neck and a billy-club borrowed from the police. Guards also wore special sunglasses, an idea I borrowed from the movie Cool Hand Luke. Mirror sunglasses prevented anyone from seeing their eyes or reading their emotions, and thus helped to further promote their anonymity.

Push-ups were a common form of physical punishment imposed by the guards to punish infractions of the rules or displays of improper attitudes toward the guards or institution.

Because the first day passed without incident, we were surprised and totally unprepared for the rebellion which broke out on the morning of the second day. The prisoners removed their stocking caps, ripped off their numbers, and barricaded themselves inside the cells by putting their beds against the door. The guards met and decided to treat force with force. They got a fire extinguisher which shot a stream of skin-chilling carbon dioxide, and they forced the prisoners away from the doors.

One of the three cells was designated as a "privilege cell." The three prisoners least involved in the rebellion were given special privileges. Every aspect of the prisoners' behavior fell under the total and arbitrary control of the guards. Less than 36 hours into the experiment, Prisoner #8612 began suffering from acute emotional disturbance, disorganized thinking, uncontrollable crying, and rage.

There was a visitation by family members allowed, so to prep the prisoners and the prison everything was cleaned, the prisoners groomed, fed, and even allowed to listen to music. Some parents were surprised by the state of their sons, but nevertheless let it continue.[13]

To summarize the rest of the experiment: the next day there was a rumored escape plan that 8612 would storm the prison with friends to help the rest escape. The warden and guards spent the whole day formulating a plan on moving the prisoners to different areas. It was at this time that professor Zimbardo found himself emotionally involved as a warden of the prison. There was no escape attempt, and afterwards, the guards increased the harassment, especially at night when they believed they were not being monitored. A colleague of Zimbardo visited the prison and found that the project must be stopped because the guards' treatment of the prisoners was morally wrong. The guards had allowed themselves to abuse the power they had over the prisoners, even though they knew this was just a pretend experiment and that the prisoners were the same as them at the start of the experiment. The study was terminated on August 20, 1971.[14]

A student's reaction summarizes the hoped-for reaction to the Stanford Prison Experiment.

> We also watched a creepy and powerful documentary in class. For me it was a reminder of our malleable humanity. We are social creatures, subject to both biological and environmental factors. The idea that someone is inherently evil and chooses to be that way is very naïve. The movie boldly showed that all people are capable of horrific acts, even the most moral and upstanding, if put into the right situation.
>
> I was surprised that a few people in class did not agree that we are all capable of evil. I am a pretty morally upstanding person (or so I like to think), but I am also in a Christian graduate school in Malibu, California. I was raised by two educated parents with a stable education and household. I understand that my environment formed me into a moral or "good" human. But what if I was in a war-torn country? What if I lived in poverty with minimal social structure to guide me? What if I was put into the Sanford Prison test? Submitted by Emily Tanaka, emphasis added.

12.5   Defining Empathy

If we are encouraging the victim to have empathy for the perpetrator, we need to define empathy. The Greek root of empathy is the word pathos, which literally means suffering.[15] In Greek, the prefix of em means "with." This construct gives a picture of recognizing that the perpetrator is suffering, and the victim suffers with the perpetrator. The key is that the victim can suffer with the perpetrator without discounting their own suffering. Ideally, the apology, forgiveness, and reconciliation journey will include the perpetrator having empathy for the victim, but the value of the victim having empathy for the perpetrator is present in any event. So long as the victim's suffering is not diminished.

Empathy is a powerful force for good in the world. In *Empathy: Why It Matters, and How to Get It* By Roman Krznaric, describes that empathy is "an ideal that has the power both to transform our lives and to bring about fundamental social change" because it is already happening around the world from radio soap operas in Rwanda delivering messages of empathy to both Hutus and Tutsis to Roots of Empathy teaching school children in Canada and around the world empathy skills.[16]

A student's experience provides a personal example.

Can we think of reconciliation and peace synonymously? Two years ago, I spent the summer in Northern Ireland. There I learned about the Northern Ireland conflict since the 1500's. To write the history of Northern Ireland in a one-page journal would be doing it an injustice. However, I mention the 1500's to showcase how long and deep the conflicts within Northern Ireland between the Catholics and Protestants are. I jump to modern day Belfast by the Peace Wall. At the "peace wall," I met my two guides, Mark, a Protestant, and Liam, a Catholic. However, I did not meet them at the same location as they reside on two different sides of the wall.

The conflict of Northern Ireland as I mentioned is deep, and for centuries there has been bloodshed, abuse, and fear from both parties. Yet, today they are in their peacetime. Both Mark and Liam saw evil acts happen to their loved ones and community members. They even were the ones who engaged in such fighting and war. Liam was, in fact, an ex-IRA member and Mark was an ex-parliamentary. One was seen as a terrorist and the other a soldier for the war. Was either of them that different in their titles? Not really. Both were fighting to survive. Today both are fighting even harder to keep the peace. Mark and Liam extend an olive branch through their peace wall by leading tours to tourists who come to learn about their dark history. They also take children from the Catholic side of the wall and children from the Protestant side of the wall to camps away from Belfast where they can get to know each other.

So, it appears that there has been some reconciliation between the two parties, yet how can there still be a wall dividing them? The gates to the wall close every night. Neither side can get to the other. The children always stay on their side of the wall for school. The only time they meet is at the camps away from Belfast, and they cry when they get home knowing that they likely will not be seeing their friends again who came from the other side of the wall. Mark puts his passion into proposed legislation and tries to get them to take down the wall. There is pushback from both sides of community members. The elders who lived during the Troubles remember the atrocities. These wounded memories lead them to believe that the wall is a necessary evil...

Both men meet in the middle and shake hands and speak as with candor as colleagues do as Liam finishes the Catholic part of the tour and passes us to Mark to learn about the Protestant view. I sat there on the bus thinking how remarkable it was to see such a relationship after so many difficult, horrific, bloodshed, uneasy years between their two communities. Thirty years ago, such a relationship was hard to come by. The men to me revealed a level of remorse for their actions. Relationships are so important in the Irish culture, so it appears to me that a relational form of forgiveness was central. Submitted by Nina Sprenger, emphasis added.

12.6 Inspirational Historic Case Studies

In *The Language of Peace: Communicating to Create Harmony* by Rebecca L. Oxford, Oxford describes peaceful versus destructive ways we use words, body language, and the language of visual images.[17] While exploring the many dimensions of peace such as: inner, interpersonal, intergroup, international, intercultural, and ecological, Oxford uses historical voices from the past such as Gandhi and Martin Luther King Jr who embodied empathy. Such an embodiment of empathy and peace is a map that helps us resolve conflicts, avoid violence, and reduce bullying, misogyny, war, terrorism, genocide, circus journalism, political deception, cultural misunderstanding, and social and ecological injustice.[18]

Both Gandhi and King used nonviolent means to protest injustices in their times, injustices that continue to this day. Non-violent protest made sense to them because they implemented empathy, love, forgiveness, non-judgmentalism, and moral strength in their approach to protesting the injustice they were experiencing.[19] Both Gandhi and King strongly promoted empathy because it allowed those suffering to better understand and perhaps forgive their oppressors.

In "Empathy with the Enemy," Roman Krznaric explores the extremely important role that empathy played in the life of Mahatma Gandhi. Krznaric explains that:

> Mahatma Gandhi was one of the great empathetic adventurers of the twentieth century, a master in the art of looking at the world from another's perspective. His philosophy was embodied in what is known as 'Gandhi's talisman', a moral code which calls on us to consider the viewpoint of those living on the social margins when making ethical decisions, and to ensure that our actions benefit them in some way. The challenge he raises is to imagine ourselves into the lives of people whose everyday existence might be vastly different from our own, symbolized by 'the poorest and weakest man whom you may have seen'.[20]

Gandhi's ability to expand his perception to focus on the everyday existence of individuals from all walks of life explains how Gandhi found it possible to protest against the injustices in his time without resorting to violence.

Gandhi also said, "Three-fourths of the miseries and misunderstandings in the world will disappear if we step into the shoes of our adversaries and understand their standpoint."[21]

Gandhi's nonviolent philosophy was built on the "idea of satyagraha, literally meaning 'grasping onto the truth' and freely translated as 'truth force.'"[22] Satyagraha means that "both sides in a conflict could learn from each other in seeking truth and that truth could not be reached by physical force."[23] For peace to exist, Gandhi believed that there must be peace between different groups' positions or views.[24]

Martin Luther King Jr. put it this way:

> Here is the true meaning and value of compassion and nonviolence, when it helps us to see the enemy's point of view, to hear his questions, to know his assessment of ourselves. For from his view we may indeed see the basic weaknesses of our own condition, and if we are mature, we may learn and grow and profit from the wisdom of the brothers who are called the opposition.[25]

As you can see, this perspective is revolutionary because if it is put into practice by both victims and perpetrators, each side would recognize and feel the suffering of the other and attempt to stop and alleviate that suffering rather than continuing that hurt and the hate.

Taking it a step further MLK, Jr. stated: "Was not Jesus an extremist for love: 'Love your enemies, bless them that curse you, do good to them that hate you, and pray for them which despitefully use you, and persecute you.'"[26]

Martin Luther King, Jr. knew how important it was to walk in the shoes of those that he represented and worked for as well as those who opposed him. Walking in their shoes included understanding precisely their needs, challenges, circumstances, and having a finger on the pulse of their spirit.[27]

He often spent time with those he represented. "Sometimes that happened formally through town hall meetings, and in other instances, it occurred informally with impromptu conversations as he went about his work."[28]

A partial understanding of MLK's teachings can be glimpsed by the following collage of quotes from his speeches and writings.[29]

> Returning hate for hate multiplies hate, adding deeper darkness to a night already devoid of stars. Darkness cannot drive out darkness; only light can do that. Hate cannot drive out hate; only love can do that. Hate multiplies hate, violence multiplies violence, and toughness multiplies toughness in a descending spiral of destruction. So, when Jesus says, "Love your enemies," he is setting forth a profound and ultimately inescapable admonition. Have we not come to such an impasse in the modern world that we must love our enemies– or else? The chain reaction of evil–hate begetting hate, wars producing wars–must be broken, or we shall be plunged into the dark abyss of annihilation.

> Non-violence means avoiding not only external physical violence but also internal violence of spirit. You not only refuse to shoot a man, but you refuse to hate him.

May I say just a word to those of you who are struggling against this evil. Always be sure that you struggle with Christian methods and Christian weapons. Never succumb to the temptation to become bitter. As you press on for justice, be sure to move with dignity and discipline using only the weapon of love. Let no man pull you so low as to hate him.

We must develop and maintain the capacity to forgive. He who is devoid of the power to forgive is devoid of the power to love. There is some good in the worst of us and some evil in the best of us. When we discover this, we are less prone to hate our enemies.

But I am also concerned about our moral uprightness and the health of our souls. Therefor I must oppose any attempt to gain our freedom by methods of malice, hate, and violence that characterized our oppressors. Hate is just as injurious to the hater as to the hated. Like an unchecked cancer, hate corrodes the personality and eats away its vital unity. Many of our inner conflicts are rooted in hate. This is why psychiatrists say, "Love or perish." Hate is too great a burden to bear.

Gandhi and MLK, Jr. did not become famous around the world for simply preaching a message of empathy, but rather because they put their words into practice even though they suffered to do so. No one says practicing empathy or loving your enemy is easy, but sometimes doing the right thing is difficult.

Two students observed ways people are divided in the US.

While it seemed that conflicts that Northern Islanders face are unlike any that Americans face, the more time I spent thinking about it, the more connections I began to identify. We may not see as much violence as was seen in Ireland, but our society as a whole is just as divided. There are Trump supporters and Trump haters. There are pro-lifers and pro-choicers. There are Republicans and there are Democrats. There are whites and there are ethnics. There are men and there are women. There are gays, straights, transgenders and queers. Each group digs their heels in and focuses all of their efforts to make change in their own favor and the more each party becomes ingrained in their own belief, the greater the divide becomes.

Perhaps something as simple as an athletic game comprised of integrated teams would do Americans some good as it has for the Catholic and Protestant populations in Northern Ireland. But there's an uneasy feeling in my gut that tells me that Americans, who pride themselves on being educated, high-brow innovators, will not have the wisdom and humility to take the first small steps needed to bridge the gap between communities who simply cannot recognize the shared values and goals they each have that can help unite the country. Submitted by an anonymous student, emphasis added.

When it comes to race relations in the United States, I don't think that "white-black" reconciliation is complete. Since the 1960's, <u>outside of the major metropolitan areas of Los Angeles, San Francisco, and New York, I believe that for the most part that black and white Americans have not been part of the same community but have peacefully co-existed in separate communities.</u>

For example, two years ago I was travelling in St. Louis, Missouri with my wife during 4th of July weekend. It was an oppressively humid Midwest summer day when we came upon a beautiful park with fountains in which children were cooling themselves. All the children in that particular park were white. We continued walking for another three blocks when we discovered another park. Yet this time, the park was run down with dead grass and rusty playground equipment, and the children were wetting their heads in a drinking fountain. The children in that park were black. My wife, who had never been to the Midwest before asked, "Why don't these kids just go back three blocks and play in the fountains?" Having spent many summers in the Midwest and understanding the racial dynamics that exist, my response was, "This isn't Los Angeles, Honey."

I am part of a mixed-race marriage. Traveling to major cities such as Boston and Chicago have been eye-opening for me. My wife and I get strange looks from people, and once in Chicago, we were told by a couple from Indiana that "in their hometown that after dark, people who don't look like them end up hanging from trees." And this was in 1998! Unfortunately, I think these attitudes are more prevalent that we think, and because we reside in the melting pot of Los Angeles, we are often blind to what is occurring in the rest of our nation. It is only when incidents such as Travon Martin's arise that we realize that there is still much work to be done. Submitted by an anonymous student, emphasis added.

12.7 Mediators Encouraging Reconciliation

This section explains a progression of dynamics that can create a serious psychological obstacle to reconciliation. Awareness of this obstacle can help the peacemaker to have empathy and compassion for a person resisting reconciliation. Frustration with a self-righteous and rigid person can be transformed into understanding how the challenge to reconcile can create a threat of psychological disintegration. Psychological disintegration occurs if a person is asked to process new information that is too threatening to his belief system too quickly; this causes him to refuse to acknowledge the new information and cling to his existing world views. The reconciliation advisor or advocate should be aware of this obstacle.

12.7.1 Attribution Error

The attribution error explains the phenomenon of most people assuming the best possible motives and intentions for their own behaviors compared to assuming the worst possible motives and intentions for others' behaviors.[30] In conflicts this can result in both parties viewing themselves as the victim.

Each party interprets her own behavior as innocuous compared to the other party's intentionally hurtful behavior. A conversation seeking to establish shared memories about the incident quickly becomes an impasse where each sees himself or herself as the victim and the other as the perpetrator. A mediator or reconciliation advocate may try to address this issue with one or both parties to encourage reduction of the judgement of the other and mutual understanding.

12.7.2 Identity Development

Donna Hicks presents a robust explanation of how identity formation dynamics can sometimes affect efforts at reconciliation.[31] She relies on Piaget's theories of development and learning. The pertinent abbreviated version of the progression of principles follows:

a. Every person has a collection of beliefs about himself, others, and the world. These collections of beliefs contribute to his identity and are a source of comfort and stability.

b. People learn by interacting with their environment. As they have new experiences that are not consistent with their existing beliefs, their beliefs are adjusted to integrate the data from the new experience. For example, a child believes fire is not dangerous until he puts his hand in the fire and learns otherwise. The child's evolved beliefs include that fire can be dangerous.

c. People navigate a balance between their need for stability that comes from their current beliefs and their need for growth that comes from new experiences. Sometimes the pendulum swings so that they need more stability and sometimes it swings to welcome more new experiences.

d. People have limits on how severely their belief system can be challenged in a given period of time. If a person is asked to process new information that is too threatening to his belief system to quickly, it can cause him to refuse to acknowledge the new information and cling to his existing world views. He responds to the psychological stress by refusing to change and finding safety and comfort in the stability of his existing beliefs. Too much change too fast can create "psychological disintegration."[32]

A student's journal explains this with a chart showing a neuroscience perspective.

Learning

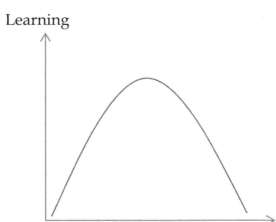

Amygdala Activation

This chart displays the basic, evolutionary human response when experiencing uncertainty, fear, anxiety, or anger. Up to a certain point, some amygdala stimulation is healthy. It promotes learning. It makes us aware of dangers. But when activated too much it can trigger an individual to take on survival instincts. According to Dr. Louis Cozolino, a clinical psychologist who has written extensively on this topic, this response to stress is called the general adaptation syndrome and results in a range of physiological changes designed to prepare the individual for fight or flight.

The implications of this syndrome are vast for those mediating conflict, specifically as it relates to identity reconstruction and reconciliation. Learning about oneself and the other requires a certain level of amygdala activation or stimulation, but if confronted too forcibly it can become detrimental to mediation and reconciliation. This is where Hicks speaks of the conditions of conflict, most notably what takes place when the interaction between victim and perpetrator is excessively threatening. Self-preservation takes place, and the individual or group withdraws. Information ceases to flow, and isolation sets in. It then becomes once again an 'us versus them' mentality, and the cycle will continue. Submitted by Dr. M. Hunter Stanfield, emphasis added.

Two other students describe how this applied to them personally.

In today's class we learned about how learning new information that challenges our understanding of the world can cause instability within. It is too much too fast and can create psychological disintegration. This causes us to revert to our own world views and refuse to listen anymore to the new information. Too much pressure will cause people to cling to their world view. I had never heard this concept spelled out before. It is something that makes so much sense because I know I do it all the time and I see others do it all the time. Now that I have seen it spelled out, I will probably notice it even more.

It happens a lot to me when my family and I have dinner together and we start to discuss politics or what crazy things are going on in the world. This is something I prefer not to do during dinner, but my father cannot help but bring it up anyway. Sometimes the information is too much and too upsetting that it makes me cling fiercely to my own world view and I completely shut off listening to any other world view. I do that because I feel so attacked or I feel so much fear and anger that my mind cannot possibly process this new information. All I know is that I want to get away from it.

This information is valuable to know because it will help me in how I address other people in the future, especially when I want them to see my world view or if I conduct a mediation. Now I know that when I discuss something with someone and I want them to hear me out and understand my world view, that it is important that I do not bombard them and make them feel pressured and attacked. This is something that seems intuitive, but I think is less obvious during real human interactions. Submitted by an anonymous student, emphasis added.

Hicks does not address how individuals, rather than communities, can or should respond in such situations, but I would like to give a brief example from my personal life. I was recently offended by a close friend, and although I knew at the time that the offense was likely an inadvertent one and was not malicious, I felt myself quickly assuming the worst of her and emotionally distancing myself from her. She had hurt me more deeply than most people can because she is a very close friend, and in my emotional state I reasoned that I could prevent her from hurting me again by distancing her from me.

Thankfully, though, I was convicted of my behavior, and instead of assuming and believing the worst of her, I looked for her side of the story, which enabled me to have a more reasoned, rational response to the situation rather than one based purely on emotions. I reminded myself of how much I value her friendship and that distancing myself from her emotionally would only damage our relationship in the long run. I finally decided to value our friendship more than my feelings or my "side." This required emotional reengaging with her rather than pulling away.

Once I had made the commitment to do that, I was ready and willing to have a difficult conversation with her for the sake, and with the hope, of reconciling. Going into the conversation with an open mind and heart, my negative assumptions about her and her behavior (which could have become my "frozen beliefs") were finally dispelled, and I could see that choosing to engage her in relationship rather than cease interaction was the better choice by far. I recognize that this example of reconciliation is perhaps too simplistic to use for communities and general people groups, but I believe it has value for non-traumatic individual conflict and reconciliation. Submitted by Alyssa Ayotte, emphasis added.

12.7.3 Reconciliation Application

In situations of moderate conflict, the identity development dynamics explain the amazing opportunity of a conversation about a conflict. If the conflicting parties engage each other directly or in a more structured mediation process, they can hear and understand the other party's perspective. This new perspective is new information that is inconsistent with the party's current world view. The party has an opportunity to integrate this new information into his world view and have a different understanding of his world and the conflict.

The conflict can be a catalyst for change, growth, and learning. The conflict conversation might lead to a new understanding that the party has been a perpetrator, despite his attribution bias; he may be willing to tell the truth to himself and others and take responsibility for his mistakes with an apology. The new understanding may give him greater insights into the humanity of the other party, even though he has been a perpetrator, and create empathy for perpetrator; this might empower forgiveness.

The descriptions of both the ability to apologize and forgive have been in the context of the identity formation paradigm that people learn and change by being exposed to new information. This assumes both parties are safe and stable enough to absorb the information they are exposed to in the conflict conversation. The parties can accept other viewpoints because they have learned that their beliefs are not always the full story or because the new information from the conflict conversation is not dramatically threatening to their current belief system. The parties' belief systems can evolve to include the building blocks of apology and forgiveness, making reconciliation possible if all parties embrace the opportunity to reconfigure how they see themselves and the conflict. A student journal provides an illustration.

> There is a healthy way to learn new information, which is maintaining an inner balance while integrating new information. However, if people do experience "too much, too fast," they start to shut down their learning processes and become defensive, locking into their set identity. This is something to keep in mind when looking at identity-based conflicts.

> I really enjoyed the material from this week and found a number of ways it applies to my personal life. One of these is within my relationship with my boyfriend: Before my boyfriend and I officially started dating, but were exclusive (from my perspective), he went to a party and (from his perspective), was taken advantage of by a girl when he was almost blacked out drunk. The next day he asked me to be his girlfriend. I did not learn of this incident until about eight months later, and it has been somewhat of a pink elephant in our relationship.

> A few nights ago, we were in an argument and he brought up something I had done from the past. So, I retaliated by bringing up the incident. He seemed very upset because he has already apologized for what happened in the past, and he said, "When are you going to let that go?" I was somewhat embarrassed because I have been talking about apology and forgiveness for the past couple months, and I honestly could not answer as to when I would let the incident go. Then I read the Donna Hicks article about identity reconstruction.

> I realized that although my boyfriend has done all the right things since that incident and proved himself time and time again, I was locked into a victim identity. When I learned about the incident, I took hold of it as a power tool and shut down my learning processes. I was unable to hear that men can be raped, too, and I was very insensitive to the issue. I was also unable to hear any reason that he would go to a party without me, and I was unable to hear any of his sorrow. I simply put him into the box of a cheating boy, because those experiences have been all too familiar to me.

Two and a half years later, I am trying to open myself up to the idea of letting go of my victim identity although it gives me an odd sense of security. I am trying to allow myself to move towards a shared future where we have a safe space to address the tough issues in our relationship. I know that to have that I need to let go of the power I have. Although I am not there, I am trying to move in that direction. Submitted by an anonymous student, emphasis added.

But either of these factors could sabotage the attempt to reconcile. What if the conflict is about a topic that one or both parties is not mature enough to acknowledge other perspectives? Or what if the accusation in the conflict is dramatically threatening to the accused belief system? Asking a party with attribution bias to accept that they have perpetrated a harm might be asking him to change his understanding of the situation and himself too much, especially if we envision this transformation in a single conversation or even a single day mediation. Likewise, asking a victim who has suffered serious injury to embrace the humanity of the perpetrator and have empathy might be another form of attempting too much change too fast. A student journal shares how she approaches these topics.

I have realized that there are certain things that I am somewhat resistant to, things that I do not want to face changing. One of these is my faith. I am a Christian and I had grown up Christian, so it is very much a part of my identity. I have learned about many different religions but almost every time that I am exposed to a new idea that is contrary to what I believe, I either try to find a piece of evidence contrary to the new idea presented, and congruent with what I believe so that I can subconsciously write off what I have recently been exposed to.

If intelligence means being open-minded, that involves taking in other ideas contrary to your own. Does that mean that if I am not willing to consider different ideas regarding religion, I am closed-minded? I have realized that often I will write people off as judgmental if they will not consider my perspective on faith, but maybe I am the judgmental one for classifying them as judgmental.

I have found that it is very important to understand where other people have come from that helped form their belief systems, or the circumstances that they were raised in, which contributed to who they are. I have also found, though, that it is equally important to realize how we, ourselves, have come to adopt our way of thinking. If we simply believe that we are correct solely because what we believe makes sense, we are basically saying that anyone who believes something contrary either is unable to comprehend life at the same level we are or has not thought about their beliefs as much as we have ours. But are we not all seeking purpose and trying to figure out what this short crazy life means?

> I think that it would be very difficult to reconcile with someone who has a very different belief system than you if the relationship is hostile or adverse. <u>But if that person is willing to listen to your perspective with an open mind, and you are willing to do the same, both parties can grow tremendously. I do not believe that reconciliation requires both parties to believe the same thing, but simply that both parties are able to listen to each other and respect each other's opinions.</u> Submitted by Shelby Warwar, emphasis added.

The identity development paradigm explains why one or both parties to a conflict conversation might not be psychologically able to adjust their beliefs to enable reconciliation. Instead one or both parties cling to their well-rehearsed professions of innocence and victim stories. Understanding that they need to do this to avoid psychological disintegration helps those encouraging reconciliation to have compassion and empathy for participants who stubbornly refuse to tell the truth and take responsibility or to have empathy for the other.

It is interesting that the final thought is to appeal to those of us who encourage reconciliation to be patient and supportive of our family, friends, and clients who are not ready. We need to accept that presenting how the other party views them as a perpetrator may need to be done over time and gently. Likewise, when we are encouraging a person who has suffered to acknowledge the humanity of their perpetrator, we peacemakers need to accept that when we encourage reconciliation, we are asking people to reconstruct their understanding of themselves, the world, and this conflict.

The experiences of two students about how this concept helps mediators is useful.

> I was very intrigued by the notion of psychological disintegration and how it is a very real phenomenon that should caution any mediator or attorney in their attempts to get people to reconsider their perspective. … I had a mediation where the plaintiff had brought a small claims court case against a cruise line following a nightmare honeymoon. The wife expected special treatment where she only mentioned it once that it was their honeymoon; on top of it all, this cruise line is known for being a budget cruise line. She wanted a full refund plus compensation for emotional damages.
>
> <u>I know that she would have had a complete and total breakdown --a psychological disintegration-- if I had brought up the possibility or presented the reality that she may have had a part in the cruise not meeting her expectation.</u> It was obvious what she should have done —called and explicitly asked for (and likely paid for) the special treatment that she assumed would be there when they first got to the ship. It was hard to imagine a constructive conversation. <u>However, what I could do is make subtle gestures that might get her to possibly question her position. Mediators do this all the time when they let the parties know the concerns that they have for their case.</u>

I asked her how long she wants to stay chained to this story and this cruise line that she obviously does not like. Mediators too can use the techniques of "these are questions that the judge is likely going to ask you." This does well in objectifying the exercise (less likely to be perceived as an attack on the person) as the party might see it as assessing the merits of the case.

Additionally, if the mediator draws off his gravitas of having experience with the judge, this can keep the party in check and reduce the possibility that they are going to have a breakdown. "If you don't settle, this is likely what you are going to have to do if you go before a judge" is a mantra which can see your actions as preparation, not as an attack on something that has come to mean a great deal to them – their position on the issue. Submitted by Benjamin Reccius, emphasis added.

One of our classmates brought up an interesting way to bring reconciliation into more personal disputes that we might witness in a professional setting in the US. There were two co-workers who were upset with each other, and we advised ways that a third person could mitigate the issue and work toward reconciliation. I suggested that she tell the parties, "You can listen to the other person's truth without compromising your own." This allows people to be more open to listening and take a second before getting defensive.

I think this might be a way we can find reconciliation. Help people to listen to other's perceptions, experiences, and stories so that we can feel their humanity align with our own. In order to open the door, we can tell them plainly that there can be two truths. In mediation, we are not in the business of discovering the truth and laying out the perfect fact background. If we did that, there would be no end. Instead, we open lines of communication which in turn can lead to apologies, forgiveness, and hopefully reconciliation. Submitted by Emily Tanaka, emphasis added.

I summarized a simplified version of Donna Hick's identity formation material in the following chart.

Identity Reconstruction and Reconciliation

1. Learning/Developmental Mode

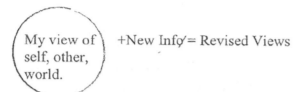

+New Info = Revised Views

- More complex
- More able to tolerate challenges
- More ambivalence about our views
- Tolerance for uncertainty & ambivalence is a measure of egocentrism

2. Limits to new info, that contradict our world view

Too much change, too fast – Psychological Disintegrate – fear, anxiety, anger, exhausted

Self preservation process shuts down learning mode
- World view becomes rigid
- Regain balance

3. Moderate Conflict

My view of self, other, world.

New info flows both ways. Both views evolve to adapt new info. My understanding is affected by the other.

Your view of self, other, world.

4. Extreme Conflict

My view of self, other, world.

Conflict is one form of too much change too fast. Parties retreat to regain psychological stability.
- Hold my view rigidly
- Isolated – not in relationships to receive new data.
- Resent the source of destabilization (other person) – form a negative image of them.
- Isolation means the other doesn't have the opportunity to challenge the negative images...their perspective/new info isn't available.
  Result is cognitive distortions

Your view of self, other world.

12.8 Kenya Case Study

The Los Angeles Times presented an example of a reconciliation initiative after widespread violence. [33]

> RUMURUTI, KENYA — In a sun-drenched valley of central Kenya, a few dozen villagers gather each Saturday to sit under the trees and conduct the painstaking work of reconciliation that their government leaders seem happy to avoid.
>
> These traumatized victims of Kenya's post-election clashes meet to talk, pray, sing and -- they hope -- heal. More than half a dozen tribes are represented, including some that attacked one another in the weeks after the disputed December 2007 presidential voting ignited long-simmering ethnic tensions. More than 1,000 Kenyans died in the clashes.[34]

This article goes on to explain how Kenyans from all different ethnic groups, some seeking to forgive and others seeking forgiveness, gathered under the largest tree in the village.[35] At the start, the groups would be segregated by tribe, "[b]ut singing, dancing and a touch of pragmatism have helped break the ice."[36]

One of these reconciliation seekers was Paskwaloena Wanjiru, 70, whose son and grandson were killed by a mob from a rival tribe. She was reluctant to meet with members of the other tribe, but she was conflicted because two of her other sons participated in the killing and house-burning of another tribe. She said she decided to participate in the reconciliation group because, "we are all here for the right reasons: to forgive and to be forgiven."[37]

The article explains the challenge of reconciliation after such a horrific incident.

> "'You can't just tell people to go home,' said human rights activist Maximilla Winfred Okello, who started the grass-roots reconciliation meetings in the Rift Valley town of Rumuruti during the fall. 'It won't work if people are still afraid of their neighbors.' She said that unless Kenyans were encouraged to express their anger and learn to trust one another again the nation was destined to repeat the violence. 'It's the circle of conflict,' she said. 'The government is still in denial.'
>
> Peter Lolino, 28, a flower farm worker who has been attending the sessions since the fall, said the group helped him deal with the anger he felt after he was struck in the face by an arrow. As he recovered in a hospital, he plotted his revenge against those who assaulted him. But talks with his pastor and the weekly (reconciliation) meetings persuaded him to work instead toward forgiveness. Recently, he confronted the neighbors who attacked him, told them he forgave them and moved his family back to his land.... 'I realized the best thing for me is just to forgive,' said Lolino, whose gaunt face bears two round scars where the arrow penetrated. 'Even if the government gave us something, that's not going to matter if we haven't forgiven.'

Some of the participants view the reconciliation meetings like their church or an Alcoholics Anonymous support group. [38]

12.9 City of Balad Assignment

On November 7, 2006 the LA Times article published an article by Borzou Daragahi titled, "The day the hatred boiled over in Balad.[i]" The article describes a massacre in Balad on October 13th, 2006. As you read the following summary of the situation, assume your dispute resolution consulting firm has been invited by the U.S. Government, Iraqi Government, The League of Arab Nations, and United Nations to propose a plan to encourage reconciliation among the citizens of the Balad region. You have been informed that money is no object and the timeline can last ten years if your firm can devise a plan that will work.

The Context

120,000 people live in the city of Balad, located up the Tigris River from Baghdad. Daragahi describes,

> "For decades this farming region north of Baghdad has been a caldron of mistrust between the Shiite Muslim tribes living in town and the Sunni Arab tribes spread out in the surrounding farmlands. In the 1970s, the city became a stronghold of Shiite activist of the then-outlawed Islamic Dawa Party, which had strong ties to neighboring Iran. After the Iran-Iraq war erupted in 1980, President Saddam Hussein and his Baath Party supporters cracked down, executing Dawa members, uprooting orchards and seizing the property of well-to-do Shiites to hand over to Sunnis. The U.S.-led invasion in 2003 upended the balance of power. Shiites began asserting their muscle, angering Sunnis. In 2004, a group loyal to radical cleric Muqtada Sadr took over a Sunni mosque in downtown Balad, declaring it its own."

While the Shiite and Sunni rivalry in the Balad region created a steady stream of abductions and shootings, the two groups are economically interdependent. Sunnis grow produce in the countryside around the city, which serves as a marketplace for their products. Only 200 or so Sunni families lived in Balad in early October 2006, but many Sunnis regularly commuted into the city to buy and sell goods, use the hospital, and buy and sell cars.

The Cycle of Revenge and Massacre

U.S. troops handed over control of the Balad region to Iraq's Shiite-dominated police force on September 13th with a commitment to let Iraqis take the lead and only intervene at the request of the local authorities. In early October a Sunni man visiting the Balad hospital was found dead. A few days later a group of Sunnis attacked a unit of the Shiite-dominated Iraqi army. Early on October 12th, Iraq's Shiite-dominated army killed an alleged Sunni insurgent. That afternoon fourteen Shiite laborers were shot at close range and bore signs of torture after working on the home of a respected Sunni in the countryside.

When the news of the murder of the fourteen Shiite laborers circulated through Balad the next day, the Shiite community planned its revenge, despite the pleas for calm by Friday prayer leaders in mosques. Retaliations against Sunnis men started Friday afternoon. Groups of Shiite gunmen from Balad killed any Sunni men they could find. At the hospital, employees went room to room identifying Sunni patients, who were then abducted and killed. Gunmen killed the Sunni car salesmen at car lots and burned their vehicles. A few hours after refusing the U.S. Army's offer of assistance to restore order, the local authorities declared a curfew at 5:00 p.m., about nine hours after the discovery of the murdered Shiite laborers. When it was over, 36 to 70 Sunnis had been killed.

Balad's Shiite residents and the U.S. forces believe the killings were perpetrated by local Shiites, many of which were thought to be family members of the murdered laborers, on their neighbors. Daragahi's article concluded, "The hatred that day was homegrown." And quoted an anonymous U.S. officer's assessment, "They hate each other. How are you going to get rid of that? You're not going to give these guys sensitivity classes."

After the massacre

A reconciliation conference was held in the nearby provincial capital for the civic, military, and religious leaders of Balad, but it failed to diminish the tension between the Sunnis and Shiites. Most nights Sunnis fire mortar shells into Balad and Shiite police and soldiers battle Sunnis for control of a checkpoint on the edge of the city. Most of the Sunni families who had lived in Balad before the massacre have moved to the surrounding Sunni villages in the countryside. Some Shiites deny that Sunnis were targeted in Balad on October 13 and assert that the Sunni families who moved out of the city did so because they wanted to.

Your assignment is to propose a long-term plan to encourage reconciliation between the Shiites and Sunnis in the Balad region.

12.10 Closing Reflections

Two students provided poignant closing comments about the topics of Apology, Forgiveness, and Reconciliation.

> Given that this is the last journal, I feel that I should take a moment to reflect on the class and what I feel I now know walking away from the class.

You were right --this class ruined me. I can never look at the concept of apology, forgiveness, and reconciliation the same; specifically, I feel that this is especially true of apology. For instance, I have tried to do my best to never say "I'm sorry" except where I am expressing empathy or remorse to the person. Additionally, when I hear a person begin to make an apology, I can feel myself getting out my mental checklist and evaluating it against all the criteria we discussed in class. It is sad and encouraging at the same time. I am, in this sense, no longer innocent.

I can no longer stand by when I hear a person giving a poor apology. I find that not properly acknowledging the offense is often the biggest offense – or second injury – that an offender can perpetrate on the victim. What stands out to me too is the lack of humility that is often present in many of the apologies that I see. Simply put, apology is an act of humility and its message cannot be communicated with full force where the apologizer is holding on to some piece of the conflict that he believes that he is not responsible for. This is completely at odds with the spirit and intent of the act.

I think the notion of forgiveness is perhaps most important. I believe this because it is the conciliatory gesture over which the parties have the greatest control. That it is a remedy for the victim too points to the import of this act. Unilateral forgiveness is perhaps the most interesting. Not only does it act to possibly get that offender to apologize, but it is a real concrete step that can be taken by the victim to help themselves start to feel differently about the problem. It represents a dramatic shift in the climate that has in large part defined the scope and nature of the conflict.

This is indeed starting to sound more like therapeutic forgiveness – the band of forgiveness in which the victim does his part to let go of the hurt so that they go on to live their life to the full extent. I have seen not just how valuable this can be for others, but also what it can do for me. If there was anyone who had a habit of renting out space in my head to people who had no business being in there, it was me. This made me realize just how much time I used to spend thinking about this other person and what they did to me; more importantly, I saw just how pointless this is. Indeed, if there is one point to what I was doing, it is that I was allowing this person to drive me even more crazy than they already have.

Finally, there is the notion of reconciliation. This is the path forward for persons who have been involved in a conflict and it is the terms of how these people agree to live their lives. It is the playing field created by the apology and forgiveness processes. In this sense it can be an incredibly powerful tool not only for personal issues where people are looking for a way to live together, but in the legal context too where clients often want to know what, in moving forward, is the exact nature of the plan. In this sense it gives the party a sense of control over the issues that they would not otherwise have. And where there is a sense of control there is peace. And where there is peace there are improved human relations – the exact goal of the apology, forgiveness, and reconciliation processes. Submitted by Benjamin Reccius, emphasis added.

The discussion during the close of our last class about "stepping out of the comfort zone" was extremely important. I think most of the time, people don't vary from their everyday routines, and because they don't, hatred and misunderstanding, particularly in a racial sense, continue to exist in this world.

I have spent the better part of the last eighteen years living out of my comfort zone. It began when I was a freshman at UCLA. Having taken two quarters of history at what is deemed by many to be a "liberal" university, I was surprised that my courses focused primarily on the "white male" version of history I had become accustomed to in high school.

During the spring quarter, to broaden my horizons, I decided to enroll in an "African American Humanities Cluster," comprised of three courses in English and History focusing on African American history and literature from the 1990's. Not only was I the only white male in the cluster of courses, I was the only non-African American. At first my classmates looked at me with skepticism and I was treated like an outsider. After several weeks of course study and discussion, however, I was accepted by my fellow students and I think we began to realize that at the core, we are truly not very different from each other.

Following that experience, there have been countless situations in which I am the only white person in the room, including at family gatherings, where I could tell in the beginning, that many of my wife's extended family members, without even knowing me, were not fond of me. <u>Every time, the experience began and ended the same way – funny looks and distrust, a cautioned greeting from the new people I am meeting, followed by growing acceptance, and concluding with the comment, "You're not too bad for a white guy – are you sure you are white?"</u>

I don't know why people come in different color shades. Whether it was adaptation or God simply wanted it that way, I think it is one of the biggest man-made impediments to peace and harmony in this world. We have seen race wars, miscegenation laws, hate groups and segregation, among other awful race centered things in this world. Yet, when people get together and actually learn about each other, we see that while we do have some differences, at the core, we are all pretty much the same. We all generally share in the desire to love and be loved, and to be accepted into a group.

Racial reconciliation can only truly take place if everyone takes time to step out of their comfort zones so that they can see that people throughout the world generally share the same needs and desires even though we may look different. Donna Hicks is correct that humans need to gain new information to revise their views of a situation or of a people and to reach a point of reconciliation. The only way that we will be able to do that is by making ourselves uncomfortable and engaging others visibly different from us in conversations which will ultimately reveal that at the core, we are all very much the same. Submitted by an anonymous student, emphasis added.

Endnotes

1. *See* Raymond G. Helmick, Rodney Petersen, *Forgiveness & Reconciliation: Public Policy & Conflict Transformation*, 163, 218.

2. See Matthew 5:44.

3. *See* Fred Luskin, *Forgive For Good*, (2002); Tian Dayton, *The Magic of Forgiveness*, (2003); David Augsburger, *The New Freedom of Forgiveness* 36, (2000); Lewis B. Smedes, *Forgive and Forget*, (1984).

4. *See* ABC NEWS, "Book Excerpt: It Takes a Parent," ABCNEWS.GO.COM (Aug. 18, 2005) https://abcnews.go.com/GMA/story?id=1004250&page=1; *See also* Gary Ezzo, Anne Marie Ezzo, *Growing Kids God's Way: Biblical Ethics for Parenting*, (2002).

5. Douglas Stone, Sheila Heen, Bruce Patton, *Difficult Conversations: How to Discuss what Matters Most* 109-28, (2000).

6. *See id.*

7. *See* Part I.

8. *See* Part II.

9. *See* Ira Hyman Ph.D., "Good People, Evil Actions: What leads good people to do horrible things?" PSYCHOLOGYTODAY.COM (Feb. 27, 2017) https://www.psychologytoday.com/us/blog/mental-mishaps/201702/good-people-evil-actions.

10. *See* "The Stanford Prison Experiment: A Simulation Study on the Psychology of Imprisonment," STANFORD PRISON EXPERIMENT (1971) http://www.prisonexp.org/.

11. *Id.*

12. *Id.*

13. *Id.*

14. *See id.*

15. "Pathos." MERRIAM-WEBSTER.COM (Oct. 16, 2018) https://www.merriam-webster.com/dictionary/pathos.

16. Roman Krznaric, *Empathy: Why It Matters, and How to Get It* ix, (2014).

17. Rebecca L. Oxford, *The Language of Peace: Communicating to Create Harmony* 45-46 (2013).

18. *Id.*

19. *See id.*

20. Roman Krznari, "Empathy with the Enemy," THE PEDESTRIAN No. 1 (Nov. 2013) https://www.romankrznaric.com/wp-content/uploads/2013/11/Krznaric-Pedestrian-Essay-print-version-020810.pdf.

21. Oxford,*The Language of Peace: Communicating to Create Harmony* at 45.

22. *Id.* at 45.

23. *Id.*

24. *See id.*

25. Martin Luther King, Jr., "Martin Luther King, Jr. on the True Meaning of Compassion," BERKLEY CENTER FOR RELIGION, PEACE & WORLD AFFAIRS (April 4, 1967) https://berkleycenter.georgetown.edu/quotes/martin-luther-king-jr-on-the-true-meaning-of-compassion.

26. Martin Luther King, Jr., "Letter from Birmingham Jail." 16 Apr. 1963.

27. Sonia Thompson, "3 Skills Martin Luther King Jr. Mastered to Become a Transformational Leader," Inc.com (Jan. 12, 2018) https://www.inc.com/sonia-thompson/3-essential-martin-luther-king-jr-leadership-skills-all-good-leaders-should-master.html.
28. *Id.*
29. Martin Luther King Jr. Quotes, https://www.goodreads.com/author/quotes/23924.Martin_Luther_King_Jr._.
30. *See* Manuela Heberle, "Fundamental Attribution Error: Definition & Overview," Study.com (Oct. 23, 2018) https://study.com/academy/lesson/fundamental-attribution-error-definition-lesson-quiz.html.
31. Donna Hicks, "Identity Reconstruction in Reconciliation." In *Forgiveness and Reconciliation*, by S.J. and Rodney L. Petersen Raymond G Helmich, 129-149. Pennsylvania: Templeton Foundation Press, 2001.
32. *Id.*
33. Edmund Sanders, "Members of Kenya tribes work toward reconciliation," Los Angeles Times (Jan. 4, 2009) http://articles.latimes.com/2009/jan/04/world/fg-kenya-peace4.
34. *Id.*
35. *See id.*
36. *Id.*
37. *See id.*
38. *Id.*
39. Borzou Daragahi, "The day the hatred boiled over in Balad," Los Angeles Times (Nov. 7, 2006) http://articles.latimes.com/2006/nov/07/world/fg-balad7.

Made in the USA
Middletown, DE
13 June 2023

32535499R00190